Telling Tales

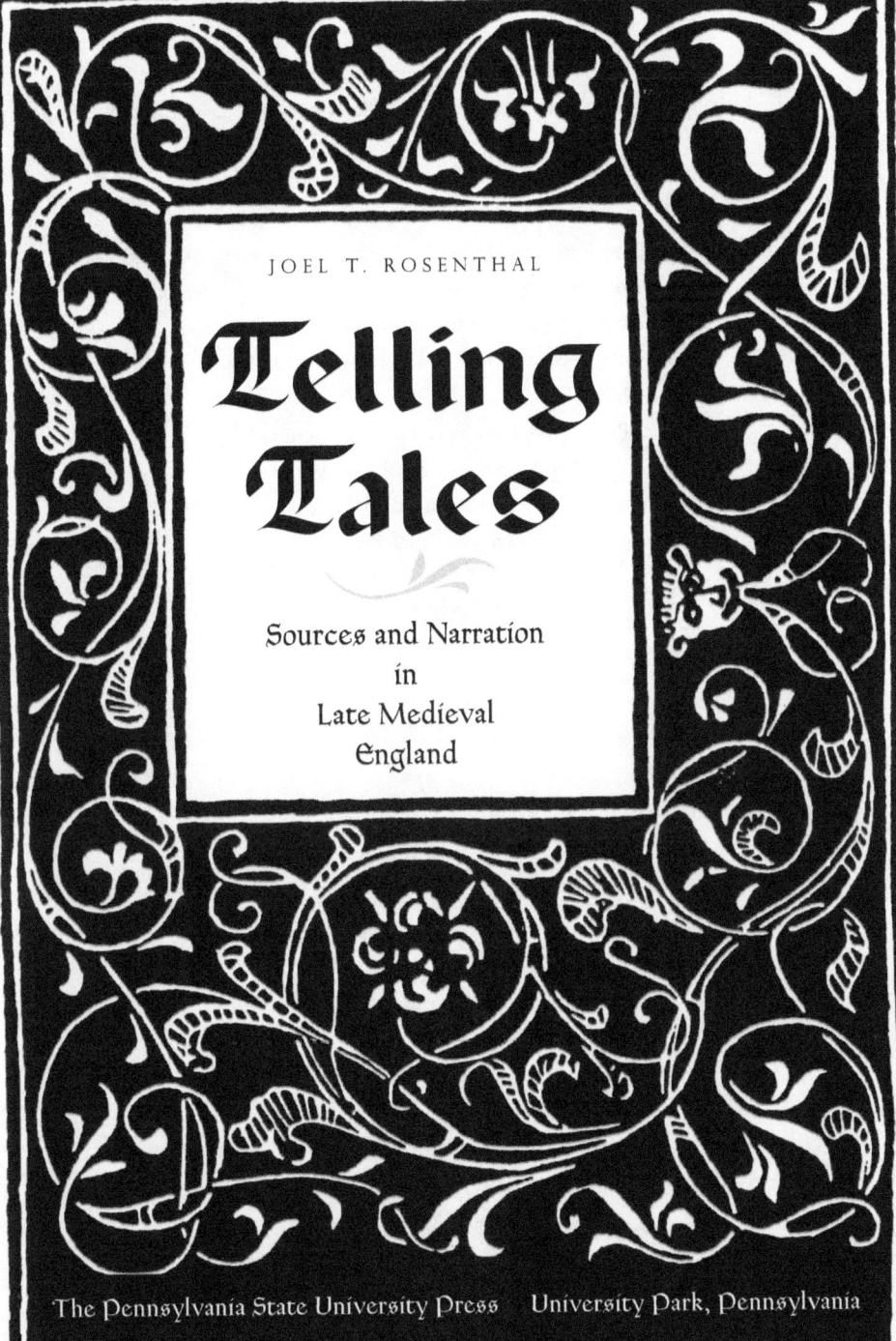

JOEL T. ROSENTHAL

Telling Tales

Sources and Narration
in
Late Medieval
England

The Pennsylvania State University Press   University Park, Pennsylvania

Library of Congress Cataloging-in-Publication Data

Rosenthal, Joel Thomas, 1934–
Telling tales : sources and narration in late medieval England / Joel T. Rosenthal.
p.   cm.
Includes bibliographical references and index.
ISBN 978-0-271-05848-1 (pbk : alk. paper)
1. Great Britain—History—Medieval period, 1066–1485—Historiography.
2. Great Britain—History—Medieval period, 1066–1485—Sources.
3. Heraldry—Great Britain—History—To 1500—Sources.
4. Family—Great Britain—History—To 1500—Sources.
5. Jury—Great Britain—History—To 1500—Sources.
6. Paston, Margaret, 1423–1484—Correspondence.
7. Great Britain—Genealogy—Sources.
8. Narration (Rhetoric)
9. Paston family.
10. Scrope family.
I. Title.

DA170 .R67 2003
942.04'07'2—dc21
2003010255

Copyright © 2003 The Pennsylvania State University
All rights reserved
Printed in the United States of America
Published by The Pennsylvania State University Press,
University Park, PA 16802-1003

The Pennsylvania State University Press is a member of the
Association of American University Presses.

It is the policy of The Pennsylvania State University Press
to use acid-free paper. Publications on uncoated stock satisfy the
minimum requirements of American National Standard for
Information Sciences—Permanence of Paper for
Printed Library Material, ANSI Z39.48–1992.

Now concerning genus *and* species, *whether they have real existence or are merely and solely creations of the mind, and, if they exist, whether they are material or immaterial, and whether they are separate from things we see or are contained within them—on all this I make no pronouncement.*

—BOETHIUS, TRANSLATING PORPHYRY

CONTENTS

List of Figures and Tables   ix
Preface   xi
Introduction: Telling Tales in a Social Context   xiii

1 Proofs of Age: A Rich Fabric of Thin Threads   1

    The World of Jurors and Testimony   1
    The Mechanics of Recollection   9
    Jurors' Life Cycles and Life-Cycle Memories   15
    Ecclesiastical Memories   25
    Memories of the Secular World   38
    Communities Large and Small   52
    The Construction of Memory in the Proofs   57

2 Sir Richard Scrope and the Scrope and Grosvenor Depositions   63

    Recollection Re-creates Fellowship   63
    Cognition and Recollection   66
    Tales of the Scropes: Battles and Banners   79

3 Margaret Paston: The Lady and the Letters   95

    Letters as Artifacts   95
    Constructing the Letters: How to Tell It Like It Is   114
    First Stuck at Home and Then Mostly Alone   133

Conclusion: Some Final Reflections   149
Notes   155
Bibliography   197
Index   213

FIGURES AND TABLES

FIGURES

1. The Scrope Genealogy   81
2. The Paston Genealogy   97

TABLES

1. Jurors' Ages, by Decades, on Juries for Male and Female Heirs   6
2. Average Age of All Juries by Five-Year Age Groupings   7
3. Age Spread, by Decades, Between Oldest and Youngest Jurors on a Jury   8
4. Jurors, by Age, Using Their Own Marriages as Mnemonic References   17
5. Jurors, by Age, Using a Child's Birth as a Mnemonic Reference   20
6. Categories of Deaths Used as Mnemonic References by Jurors   23
7. A Fourteenth-Century Time Line: The Scropes and the Kingdom   82–83
8. Margaret's Letters in the Context of "Current Events" and Family Matters   98–99
9. The Pastons as Letter Writers   101
10. The Pastons as Recipients of Letters   103
11. Margaret's Letters, Year by Year   105
12. Margaret's Scribes, as Identified by Davis   106
13. Margaret's Letters, by Length, as Printed in Davis's Edition   116
14. The Dating Styles of Margaret's Letters in 1465   127

PREFACE

Three books moved me to try my hand at coupling together the disparate essays that comprise this volume. I absolve their authors from all faults, shortcomings, and errors found below. They do, however, have to take some responsibility for furnishing inspiration as well as intellectual and methodological guidance. Natalie Zemon Davis, for her *Fiction and the Archives: Pardon Tales and Their Tellers in Sixteenth-Century France* (1987), Michael Clanchy for his *From Memory to Written Record: England, 1066–1307* (1979, and then in a second edition, 1993), and Barbara Hanawalt for her *The Ties That Bound: Peasant Families in Medieval England* (1986) are the scholars and works referred to. Despite or because of my deep debt to these books and their authors, I have deliberately avoided combing these works for specific points, let alone for apt and pithy quotations. Some distance is good for scholarship, even it if comes late in the day and, no doubt, at the price of even more guidance and insights.

Over the years I seem to have developed a personal and professional support group—as many of us do—and a preface is the place for due acknowledgment. Whether these colleagues really think my work worth encouraging or they are just being friendly, I want to attest to the help and the confidence I have derived from conversations—especially about the Paston family and their letters—with Caroline Barron, Carole Rawcliffe, Barrie Dobson, and Ralph Griffiths. Many others have listened to my ideas in the years it took to put this book together, amidst other commitments (including those to my students). I owe particular debts to Lorraine Attreed and the New England Medieval Studies Association, and to Lister Mathisen, Barbara Gusick, and Susan Ridyard for inviting me to participate in conferences and panels (the first two at the International Medieval Congress at Western Michigan University, the last at the University of the South). In addition, I pay tribute to Colin Richmond's vast knowledge of the world of the Pastons. His work has spurred me on, sometimes in agreement with his views, sometimes to offer an alternative interpretation. Finally, there is Roger Virgoe, with whom I discussed some of this work in its early stages. Though he can no longer respond, I still wish to say thanks—fully conscious of the likelihood that he would have taken me to task over various points I make about East Anglian gentry society. The Pennsylvania State University Press has been encouraging and forthcoming with much useful advice; Peter Potter, Laura Reed-Morrisson, and a number of anonymous readers have done their (much appreciated if not always heeded) best. One, in particular, helpfully warned me against an overly casual approach toward the age differences among heirs' and heiresses' jurors. Nor can I conclude without a tribute to the role of the Institute of Historical Research of the University of London. A "home away from home" is a bit fulsome, but days and weeks of work there are hard to match for efficiency of research and collegiality of environment.

Academic authors frequently conclude prefaces by thanking their immediate families—supposedly slighted for years on end as they kept their scholarly noses to the grindstone. In my case, my children are long out of the house, and when they come back to visit, they frequently suggest—in concert with my wife, who has been reworking my skill at drawing tables for more than thirty years—that perhaps I would like to go into the other room and work on some manuscript or other. Sometimes, as shown below, I take their advice.

INTRODUCTION: TELLING TALES IN A SOCIAL CONTEXT

These essays spring from two convictions. The first is that a close reading of familiar historical texts from late medieval England can illuminate aspects of a society that we take for granted. The second conviction, which grew from the first as this analysis took on a life of its own, is that a close reading of these sources raises questions about some basic presuppositions on which our efforts to explore late medieval society rest. The issues I take up here concern the nature of the sources, the concept of community, and the role and construction of collective or social memory, especially as we track it in its transition (or meandering peregrination) from orality to fixed written form.

A close reading of various kinds of testimony, memory, and narrative enables us to reconstruct, by way of eavesdropping, a synthetic tale of the relationships and interactions of daily life. The three bodies of sources that I dissect—Proofs of Age from the reigns of Richard II and Henry IV, the depositions on behalf of Sir Richard Scrope in the Scrope and Grosvenor controversy, and Margaret Paston's letters as they stand amid the totality of the Paston family letters[1]—are familiar sources, often used by historians, unlikely to contain many secrets or surprises. As sources go, they are jejune and, to a large extent, formulaic. The Proofs of Age are aggregations of short statements; even when jurors' testimonies are combined, the entire record rarely takes up more than half of a printed page. The Scrope and Grosvenor depositions mostly run to a single paragraph, and even some of that was boilerplate, enunciating a deponent's identity and age before moving on to his memory/testimony. And Margaret Paston's letters, while mostly of greater length, were never intended as coherent overviews of her world. They were separate pieces, each created for the occasion—beads on the loop of ongoing and circular (or two-way) communication.

Given the nature and inherent problems of these sources, it is important to be explicit about the task I have set. It is, in effect, to impose narrativity—to synthesize the scraps of information, the scores or hundreds of throwaway vignettes about fourteenth- and fifteenth-century life—in order to illuminate the social context whence these snippets of memory and communication emanated. While working to turn these micro-tales into an overarching mosaic, I also keep in mind a subtext that addresses modes of cognition and types of memory—as well as *what* our speakers knew and said, how they came to know it, *how* they told of it, and *how* memory became a text.

The historian is usually on safe ground by opening with a discussion of the sources from which his or her tale is extracted and constructed. The three bodies of sources I use are obviously quite distinct. All three, however, can be considered documents created for or of an occasion. They mirror innumerable familiar twists and turns of lived experience, achieving credibility and inviting us to weave them together, to "enchronicle" them into a larger whole. That this synthesis had not been envisioned by those involved in their original telling and writing—those whose interests and needs they were created to serve—makes this, of course, an exercise of the historian's license.

Written sources are to the historian what the periodic table is to the chemist, leather to the shoemaker. And yet, for all the great diversity of source materials on which we can draw in our effort to depict contemporary perceptions of lived experience, the ancient (or old-fashioned) paradigm of the synthetic narrative as *the* historical source par excellence still looms over us. It may seem perverse to offer these views of medieval society that I provide as a mosaic, constructed as it is of so many disparate tiles and fragments. We are worlds removed from the grand pageant of the prototypical chronicler, one whose tale revels in the luxury of a beginning, a middle, and an end. The view of behavior and causation found in Bede or Matthew Paris is going have an impact hard to rival in a presentation based on hundreds of memories and testimonies produced for the needs of the occasion (and no more than that).

The distinction, however, between narrative overview and the tale I offer— history as (re)constructed from a medley of recollections and reminiscences— may be more significant in theory than it often turned out to be in terms of reader reception. It is easy to laud a medieval chronicle for its literary breadth and synthetic overview. But when we actually survey the fate of many such chronicles and the saga of manuscript migration, acknowledging the power of the scissors and the whimsical, eclectic tastes of scribes and patrons, the gap between the world according to the synthetic chronicle and the world of orchestrated snippets of records and family papers can narrow a good bit. The intellectual and explanatory virtues of the chronicle as master narrative were often lost because the text available to a given reader might be but some fraction of the whole, some segment now copied into a codex as part of an odd miscellany. Gone, or well hidden, was the unity of composition and explanation that had been the author's pride and joy and, to the modern reader, the compelling voice that speaks of cause and effect, of God's ways and man's world.

This is a deconstructive view of the chronicle as narrative. For a case study of such fragmentation, we can consider the magisterial edition of Henry of

Huntington's *Historia Anglorum* that Diana Greenway published in 1996.² As Greenway indicates in her exhaustive introduction, Henry's vast work was more likely to have been read in some fraction—one author among a jumble of works bound within a single cover—than as a complete and unified text. He might have among his codicological bedfellows Nicholas Trivet, or the *Anglo-Saxon Chronicle*, or John of Worcester, or William of Jumiege, or Gerald of Wales, or Gildas. Greenway's search for manuscripts took her (in person or via microfilm) to London, Oxford, Edinburgh, Glasgow, and Rouen, among other stops, and her search turned up no fewer than forty manuscripts, all with varying portions of "the real" *Historia Anglorum*. So while we may posit a unified text—one author, one work, one history—Henry's authorial unity and worldview were likely victims of scribal practice and consumer demand. His grand narrative, the one to which we can now turn with little difficulty, was more apt to be accessible as an excerpt, copied into a miscellany such as John Paston's *Great Book*, than as a total text.³

This belabored discussion of sources, as written and read, is offered in defense of a methodology that will seek to impose social or sociological (if not literary) unity upon a world re-created by weaving together jurors' testimonies, depositions from the Court of Chivalry, and a string of letters from a diligent wife and mother who wrote them over the better part of four decades. Each source, as a species within the genus "primary sources," comes with its own tale, its own administrative and bureaucratic genealogy, its own diplomatic. The background story to each body of sources is not wildly engaging, to be sure. Proofs of Age, Scrope and Grosvenor depositions before the Court of Chivalry, and private family letters were legal and documentary instruments that were shaped to meet specific needs. Form facilitated function, though in reality, the action or process under scrutiny and the record created to preserve it had a reciprocal or symbiotic relationship.

Though these matters will be touched on at greater length below, for the sake of clarity we can turn to the emergence of the Proof of Age proceeding and record—a case study about form and function that will introduce one of our basic data sets. Whose proof of whose age? By the mid-thirteenth century, the process whereby an underage heir could claim his or her land (when it was held in feudal tenure or "in chief") had become a peculiar and distinctive one. The recovery was launched when the heir, or a representative thereof, obtained a special writ—a writ *de aetate probando*—to trigger the proceeding. This writ instructed the sheriff to empower the escheator of the county to empanel a jury of twelve free men to determine whether the claimant was indeed of age: twenty-one years for a man, sixteen for an unmarried woman, fourteen for a married woman. Thus the findings of a Proof of Age rested upon the aggregation of jurors' memories regarding the date of the heir's birth (or baptism) and upon their sworn testimony that that event had taken place sufficiently long ago so that the jury's collective memory would indeed be a convincing "proof of age." Because almost all the fourteenth- and fifteenth-century Proof proceedings came to a successful conclusion, from the heir's perspective, we can say that it had all become fairly routinized. Real doubts about age must have been dealt with off the record, before escheator and jurors went through their motions in public. But of that there is little record; the official version was that the jury's work had sewn up the issue.[4]

If this tale of the evolution of writs and hearings is a bit arcane, another aspect of the Proofs has attracted considerable attention: their branding as infectious carriers of misinformation. Some allege that they give us fabricated, prearranged, and even false tales![5] One scholar notes the Proofs' reliance on "an element of common form" in jurors' memories, bespeaking a degree of sameness suggesting that "the particulars sworn to were fictitious."[6] Another critic calls attention to the fact that in Proofs from 22 Henry VI, some witnesses were "a few years younger" in 1446 than they had been in 1444.[7] Nor does the virtual replication of memories from noncontiguous counties do much to bolster the Proofs as solid bedrock on which to build our edifice of historical inquiry.[8] Indeed, they were let off lightly when a critic as astringent as John Horace Round was content to call attention to "their amazing coincidences."[9]

These flaws are certainly awkward ones to sweep under the rug, even the vast and floppy rug of social history. A reasonable surmise regarding duplications of memory, the limited repertoire of stock tales, and perhaps some outright errors (or fabrications) was offered by T. A. M. Bishop, who wrote that "correspondence between the recollection of different jurors suggests that jurors were furnished with a set of answers prepared in advance."[10] There is little doubt that somewhere along the line the formulaic nature of the proceeding, plus the unlikelihood of any serious challenge regarding the heir's age, made it all surprisingly casual, given the seriousness of the issues at stake. The process of transcription (as Proofs bridged the gulf between oral and written) also worked in favor of their standardization as a form of record. The desire to reduce them to a terse written form perhaps served to make the final records more alike than they had been at the time of their origin as oral testimony. Or, conversely, the knowledge that they would ultimately be standardized may have served, from the start, to eliminate many eccentricities of individual recollections and narrations from the written record. Much of my brief on behalf of the Proofs, however, rests on the idea that a juror, speaking in concert with his peers, was recounting a *probable* memory—one not out of harmony with the aggregate pattern of recollection being established by the twelve combined voices.

The Proofs, along with Inquisitions Post Mortem, constitute our largest body of contemporary data to focus explicitly on age and demography. As such, they were examined in detail by Josiah Cox Russell, who applied a battery of statistical and demographic tests to their findings. He came down firmly in their favor, arguing that critics made much of slips and replicated memories while overlooking the riches at hand. Russell's work on age and longevity, where he cross-referenced Proofs and IPMs, argued for a degree of accuracy well within a margin of error we are happy to accept for medieval data.[11] Though his validation of the Proofs is more in reference to heirs' ages (about which we have but a slight interest) than to the self-stated ages of the jurors, a general aura of numerical credibility supports them. More recently, Lawrence R. Poos has subjected the Proofs to more complex questions and statistical tests than those applied in the 1940s. He, too, working from a demographer's agenda, has argued for their basic reliability.[12] And approaching them from a legal rather than a demographic perspective, Sue Sheridan Walker has likewise argued that they can bear a good deal of weight. When she has been able to track cases regarding age and wardship by way of the Plea Rolls, where the material may be considerably expanded from the one-liners of the escheator's inquisition, the evidence generally argues in favor of the Proofs' reliability.[13] Furthermore, as our historical interests move beyond the genealogical agenda of Round and students of his era, scholarly appreciation for the Proofs as windows upon the common exchanges of daily life has grown as well.[14]

Occasionally, a false Proof was presented in an effort to claim property for an heir not yet of legal age. In such instances of serious and deliberate fraud, royal wrath could be unleashed, though it was directed against the claimant, not the jurors, whether they were actually complicitous or mere gulls. The turnover of real property was a serious matter—and for it to hinge on the public performance of a Proof proceeding, with its possible reliance on memories that might incorporate inconsistencies, argues that the "real" question about age was probably beyond dispute. Common and collective memory came fairly close to the heir's probable age; assertions about his or her majority that were out of line were not likely to be offered, let alone accepted.[15] The voice of the people may have been routinized, but it was articulating the collective consciousness of the marketplace and, as such, was taken seriously, at least as a social convention.

Moving from Proofs of Age to the Scrope and Grosvenor depositions is to go from a tale constructed by assembling hundreds of brief memories, similar in form and function, to one built by pooling separate testimonies intended, *ab origine*, to be read as a collective gloss on a core theme or text. The issue at stake, judged by the Court of Chivalry when the depositions had been assembled, had to do with two claims to the same coat of arms. Sir Richard Scrope of Yorkshire and Sir Robert Grosvenor of Cheshire each asserted that he, and he alone, had the right to display the arms in question (Azure, a bend or).[16]

Sir Richard Scrope was a peer of the realm, an important administrative and military figure, a power in the North, and an old servant and companion of John of Gaunt as well as Edward III and Richard II. Sir Robert Grosvenor was the head of a knightly family from Cheshire, a much lesser figure in terms of wealth, political contacts, and reputation. When Grosvenor displayed his coat of arms on King Richard's Scottish expedition of 1385, he provoked Scrope into challenging his right to their use; the two men, or their heralds or secretaries, had hit upon an identical design. We can judge how seriously such matters were taken by those atop the social pyramid by noting the length and gravity of the controversy—not to mention the amount of paper and parchment its records consumed. In 1385, when the affair erupted, disputes over coats of arms fell within the jurisdiction of the Court of Chivalry, under the command of the constable (Thomas of Woodstock, duke of Gloucester, Richard II's uncle). The Court had emerged in the middle years of the fourteenth century to serve as a peripatetic and martially oriented tribunal that could adjudicate matters arising from disputes on or near the battlefield, such as coats of arms, prisoners, divisions and distributions of ransoms, and the chain of command. Though its proceedings were under the eye of the constable, a complex and celebrated case of this sort meant collecting depositions at a variety of sites, by a host of officials, over the course of several months.[17] Just as the Proofs were the product and record of a specific legal and administrative procedure, with a special writ designated to launch and define their business, so the Court of Chivalry had its own procedures and course of action.

In the late fourteenth and early fifteenth centuries, a number of celebrated and protracted cases came before the Court, and inquiries into lineages and inheritances, sometimes highlighted by an investigation of a coat of arms, were central to its workings.[18] We are (in 1386) in an age and a social milieu where old men could offer memories running back to the creation of the Order of the Garter in the 1340s, one that continued to regard the formal challenge and the judicial duel as the ultimate tests in chivalric matters.[19] Accordingly, the martial court's prestige and authority was of considerable import, its findings adjudged to be definitive. In the Scrope and Grosvenor controversy Richard II himself presided over the formal decision, thereby putting his imprimatur on the proceedings and demonstrating the royal privilege of expounding on matters heraldic.[20] Though the decision in this elaborate dispute was in favor of Scrope, as was always likely to have been the case, Richard II showed compassion for Grosvenor.[21] A mere knight, Sir Robert was excused the punitive damages and costs that could befall the loser, and his new coat of arms was allowed to be very similar to the one he had hitherto borne.[22]

As testimony and memory, the depositions taken on behalf of each claimant were formulaic. If the set questions that launched a Proof of Age focused on "how do you know the heir is now of age," those put to these deponents were not so different. Each man was to address a simple agenda. How do you know the arms under dispute are those of Sir Richard Scrope (or of Sir Robert Grosvenor)?

Do you know of any gaps in the Scrope (or Grosvenor) use and display of the arms? Did you know of Grosvenor's claim to the arms before Scrope's recent challenge (or vice versa)? Deponents' testimonies fell back on fairly standard memories—the battlefield, the camp, and the chevauchée, with appropriate variations for the clerical and monastic deponents who came forward. The statements are variations on a common theme, and as such, my intention of melding them into a single narrative of memory and family history does not seem at great variance from nor a distortion of their original purpose.

In contrast to the sources developed by the king's servants in response to new sociopolitical and administrative needs, letters and letter writing have a long and honorable history. But for our purposes, the critical moment comes at the turn of the fifteenth century, when letters begin to cut a new byway as family-cum-personal communication—a significant departure from an epistolary high road that ran from Cicero through such literary giants as Alcuin, Bernard of Clairvaux, and Peter the Venerable.[23] Modern scholars have traced the course of medieval epistolography as practiced and inculcated by the literary lights and humanists (including some women) of the Church and the schools. We can follow the way in which "how to" advice became incorporated into the *ars dictaminis* and exemplars whereby masters instructed students and imitators.[24] By the twelfth century, the semipublic or open letter had such a high profile as a literary, moral, and educational endeavor that men like Peter of Blois spent years refining their texts to achieve the form in which their letters were to circulate after their deaths.[25] But this was a very different world from that of the Pastons, whose style of letters and letter writing really only appears among serious historical sources at the end of the fourteenth century.[26] The new medium of private letters took root and quickly flowered, giving us the four sets of family letters—from the Pastons, the Celys, the Plumptons, and the Stonors—that have become part of the historian's stock-in-trade.[27] All four of these collections have received attention from recent editors, and to fill our cup even further we can now add the Armburgh correspondence, though it is a tad different in substance and style.[28]

Because my interest is in the letters of Margaret Paston, I hope to separate her from the general context of Paston family business, as far as this can be done without losing the thread of her narrative or obscuring the setting within which she wrote. I will not make any effort to seek out the innumerable—and often striking and quote-worthy—parallels and analogues to what she says, or to how she says it, in other Paston letters or the other collections. Indeed, much of what I offer regarding Margaret could be matched by material from the letters of John I, John II, or John III. (We find additional rich pickings if we turn to the Stonors or the Plumptons for parallels and similarities; the Celys and the Armburghs add still more.) My focus on Margaret is not a claim for unique style or singularity of expression, perception, or emotional timbre. It simply recognizes that one focal point is enough, given the vast volume of available material. Margaret, with 104 extant letters to her credit, suffices in both quantitative and qualitative terms.

A major factor separating Margaret from most of the other family letter writers—Paston and non-Paston—is her sex, or, if we prefer, her gender. Not that female letter writers were a novelty. Many a medieval woman who left a powerful record of her ideas and influence is known to us, as to her contemporaries, from her epistolary output. Hildegard of Bingen and Catherine of Siena wrote letters with a zealous and ready hand on how to reform Christendom, how to heal the schism, and how to lead a good life, seeking advice from holy men who were (ostensibly) role models and teachers, and more. These women wrote to the high and mighty as well as to those of lesser station, and they wrote letters that, in number, compare well with those of many of their famous male counterparts.[29]

But such letter writing is a mainstream literary activity and spiritual expression, in marked contrast—in learning, tone, and recipients—to the family letters of fifteenth-century England. And in those family collections women are second-class, at best, in terms of the number of letters written and received, their epistolary representation being perhaps a guide to their overall social and family standing. The letters they did write were generally as lengthy and as well phrased as those of the men, and sometimes it was a woman's voice that conveyed news of great importance. In quantitative terms, though—insofar as that is a marker by which to judge importance and centrality—only Margaret Paston really stands out. Of 970 Paston letters, 170 were by women, 92 addressed to them. This level of activity (covering 27 percent of the collection) far surpasses the other collections. For the Stonors, women wrote 31 and received 15 letters out of 358 (for 13 percent of the total); for the Plumptons, the respective numbers are 16 and 17 of 504 (or 7 percent), and for the Celys it was but 2 written, 1 received, of 247 (or 1.2 percent).[30]

We need not cover here the intriguing story of the survival, publication, and eventual canonization of the Paston letters, though some of the lessons of the historiographic survey do provide grist for our mills.[31] What we can observe, going from the expansion of the original edition of the 1770s through modern studies, is the way in which the social and familial material in the letters more or less took over from the political—less Wars of the Roses and more husband-wife, mother-sons communication as the material became thoroughly assimilated among the sources for the fifteenth century.[32] This interpretive approach, from John Fenn's first volumes and almost ever since, was also marked by a serious appreciation of Margaret Paston.[33] Among a rather unlovely crowd, she quickly and easily stepped forward as one of the more attractive and stalwart of the *dramatis personae*. Subsequent students of the letters have tended to endorse this positive assessment, though just for an evening of good conversation her eldest son (John II) might be our best bet.

No amount of persuasion here is going to convert the one-line memories of jurors, the depositions on behalf of Richard Scrope, or Margaret's letters into narratives that hold their own against Henry of Huntington and his fellows. But I do hope to show how the gulf between kinds of sources can be narrowed, if not closed, depending on who is doing the synthesizing, and when—then or now, Henry or this author. The three bodies of sources are far from traditional narrative history and differ from one another. But they can be linked, or at least lined up in a row, in keeping with a certain self-explanatory logic; their degree of similarity and compatibility allows me to fold them into a meta-narrative. I deal with them in an order that moves us forward in time, though there are backward loops because of the circular power of recollection. The earliest Proofs we look at go back, in memory's embrace, to the 1350s, and some Scrope and Grosvenor depositions rest on memories that antedate the accession of Edward III in 1327. At the other end, we conclude with Margaret's letters of the 1470s.

This current, from older to more recent, also carries us from a trilingual England that used French, Latin, and English to one in which, by the late fifteenth century, the literate laity mostly used English. English had "triumphed" in speech and in most private or family record-keepings. Nor is this linguistic narrowing the only cognitive and communicative transition (or revolution). We will also deal with the tortuous movement from the oral to the written, though here too the transition happened by way of loops and simultaneous reliance on multiple modes of communication rather than by an evolutionary development. The Proofs rest upon and are a record of oral testimony offered in English and transcribed into terse and formulaic Latin, with an occasional touch of English preserved or quoted for its memorable bite. The Scrope and Grosvenor depositions are preserved in French. They catch the essence of oral testimony that was probably in English, for the most part (perhaps with some French), but the written account, at least, was recorded in French, still the proper language of chivalric discourse.[34] And when we come to Margaret Paston's letters, we find almost nothing other than English. (None of the Latin documents found among the Paston Papers were hers.) We can say that in 1350 England's trilingual upper-class culture reflected an ambivalence about identity: English essentialism, still at odds with political-administrative and chivalric cosmopolitanism, was expressed in both Latin and French. By the days of the Paston letters, the laity generally wrote and spoke English, regardless of what chancery clerks and scribes were doing.[35]

Furthermore, as we move through the sources we also move in the direction of narrativity in terms of prose and loquacity, even if our journey ends well short of a promised land of full-fledged, freestanding discourse. We approach the three bodies of sources in an order of ascending effusiveness. The memories in the Proofs are virtually a string of one-liners. The depositions run, in published form, to a paragraph or two. Given their common style and rhetoric (whether pro-Scrope or pro-Grosvenor), they were offered with little need for individualized formatting. And when we come to Margaret Paston's letters we find many of considerable length, with a multifaceted agenda and space for personal and domestic matters. There was room for the apt phrase, or for a complaint about one of the sons (or brother-in-law William), or for a shopping request, or for a sharp comment on the interval since the last letter. If she never gave us all the gossip or news, neither was she wholly confined by a pre-scripted agenda or questionnaire. All of our records are those of recollection (and retelling), though the business covered might range from a Paston letter about yesterday's events to an old soldier's reminiscences about seeing Edward II in arms.

Finally, we must look at the idea of community and the nature of memory as we consider how the historian converts records of memory and pragmatic discourse into a reconstruction of the society that gave them birth. Community, as a term or concept, has recently come under scholarly fire. Some critics doubt the value or accuracy of using "community" as the centerpiece of sociopolitical analysis. Into this debate I have little wish to enter; it largely centers on county and gentry studies and is often expressed in a language and with a zeal beyond my scope and comprehension. Scholars debate whether the county—the community of the shire—offers a realistic, accurate, or useful way of approaching political configurations, the networks of gentry and aristocracy, parliamentary selection, bastard feudalism, the ebb and flow of clientage and cooperation, family ties and marital patterns, and so forth.[36]

Given its terse and formulaic nature, the testimony found in each body of sources discussed below makes sense precisely because it can be heard, and read, as a representative voice of the community whence the speaker comes and about which she or he proceeds to speak, with little need to elaborate on the recollections. My concern is not with the political community, whether imposed by the boundaries and dictates of royal government or created and nourished from below by an organic social and economic affinity of those working around common goals and with common means. It is rather an exploration of the shared world—and shared modes of recalling and talking about that world—represented by men and women who could communicate so fluently and so briefly because of their common socialization and long-term familiarity with the public culture, if not with each other in a face-to-face relationship. (Such social bonding or networking also operated in the political community, but that is only a minor concern in these discussions.[37])

INTRODUCTION

Social bonding is found and expressed in multitudinous ways. It can exist, potentially, between those who have not hitherto met, provided they share sufficient commonality of background and experience, outlook, and expression. Bonding among those in frequent contact does exist in practice and can be quantified.[38] Nor do we doubt its power among those who may now be in infrequent but empathetic contact as time and distance move them beyond the reach of daily intercourse; such ties may be in shared memory as well as (or rather than) in clasped hands. A Proof only came into existence, so to speak, when and because twelve men acted harmoniously as socio-legal midwives, cooperating through collective discourse to deliver a babe born of consensual memory. The Scrope and Grosvenor depositions reflect community at a distance, one now re-created by the recitation of memories of long-ago shared activity and values. Margaret Paston's letters were neither from, nor to, nor about strangers. Rather, as we have suggested, each letter is a bead on a necklace of sustained in-group interaction; it carries meaning within the context of continued communication and familiarity.

In this soft but ubiquitous sense, community is presented as the composite of those with sufficient links of culture, regional identity, and interaction. It is a strong thread, yoking memories and communications that constitute the written record of past life, a life whose very records are but the talk-into-writing aspect of old speech and current recollection. Community towers over our sources and enables us to interpret the social and personal context of what was said and why it was expressed in a form that ultimately found safe haven in the fixed annals of written record. The details and case studies of interaction at a distance, as well as of interaction in concert, are explored below. But commonality of culture and cognition bridged a gap between humble jurors and the king's escheator. Social and experiential *esprit de corps* opened their mouths and assured our jurors that their homey and prosaic memories were indeed just what the royal official wanted to hear. We may think of the Proofs as dubious and minor records, and they are if we stack them up against the statutes of the realm or the proceedings of the privy council. But it was a very different matter for those asserting legal majority and those testifying in the proceeding.

In comparable fashion, a summons to depose before the Court of Chivalry regarding a contested coat of arms served to re-create an old community in arms—in both its heraldic and its martial sense.[39] Old soldiers were only too eager to talk of the days when they had been young soldiers. Though they were now scattered across the kingdom, necessitating hearings in many venues, this community—the veterans of foreign wars—was reconstituted through speech acts.

Memory, recollection, and the process whereby such speech acts become written records constitute the last general topics to touch. Memory and cognition—in all their many manifestations—are now, rightly, of considerable interest to historians. The Proofs and the depositions are the written end products of oral testimony. As such, they rest on "knowledge" that was drawn from memory, and if we accept my argument for the primacy of community, then these recollections in the aggregate qualify as social or collective memories.[40] They are individualized variations on the common narrative: how the village knew and *remembered* the birth of the heir, or how old soldiers knew about Scrope's coat of arms. In her letters it was also *how* Margaret Paston learned what she was now passing along to John Paston.

Compared to the complex mental process that created and drew upon memory as explicated in serious intellectual pursuits—in the building of memory palaces, in debates about whether recollection was inherent to humanity, and the expositions of Augustine or Thomas Aquinas about how the mind worked—the kinds and styles of memories we deal with here are fairly lowbrow.[41] This is true for those who remembered and for us as we analyze their recollections. And yet these seemingly superficial recollections of things done, seen, and heard, rather than reflections on how ideas were implanted and linked, are the stuff of daily discourse if not of deep cerebration.[42] The bald circularity of memory offered in the Proofs—"I know it was twenty-one years ago because that was the year in which I was married and that was twenty-one years ago," and hundreds of comparable accounts—are the pragmatic memories of daily life, expressed in a familiar idiom and meant for closure rather than for further reflection. If the memories of jurors and deponents (and of various Pastons and their informants) were not wholly shared, we can assume a good deal of overlap in recall and expression. We have husbands and wives, brothers, fellows in trade, companions in village life, men in a common enterprise, men linked by marriage, those gathered in a church on a given Sunday, and so forth. Pastons of the same household and facing the common foe, or soldiers who had stood beside the Black Prince in a massed rank, had comparable bonding—first at the time of the shared experience and then in their overlapping memories of the experience. They likely relished the opportunity to dredge up the memories and thereby freshen (and no doubt embellish) them.

We know that being told to focus on a specific point in past time, being asked "where were you on this day twenty-one years ago," resurrects and clarifies much that may have seemed lost and forgotten. Memory is recaptured and sharpened by concentration and repetition, and it is likewise affected by the very act of retrieval. We say something akin to what we have heard others say, and there is a momentum toward convergence when the memories are expressed through a form of public performance, the questions and their answers being much the same for all. Moreover, in the setting of administrative and legal routines, public recollection and public recitation become a form of drama, enacted from a partially determined script and choreographed to emphasize the harmony of the words and actions of the cast. As readers of the records, we are fortunate to be situated so that we can watch this process unfold as hundreds of men and one woman tell their stories.

How much does our interest in recovering and analyzing memory and testimony alter the essence of the recollections? Certainly, the need to compress memory into channels of scribal usage—whether in a Proof or a deposition or a letter—did militate in favor of a common way of telling the why, the how, and perhaps even the *what* of what one remembered. We are sensitive to the role played by selective memory in the shaping of our written sources. We are social animals, as The Philosopher reminds us, and speech and recollection are both inescapable and desirable elements in the structure and function, the meaning and operation, of social relations. Let us now turn to the threads that memory spun on the great social and cognitive wheel of recollection and recitation.

Proofs of Age: A Rich Fabric of Thin Threads

THE WORLD OF JURORS AND TESTIMONY

Among the great battalions of narrative sources, Proofs of Age can be thought of as offering us rank upon rank of enlisted men. They dash forward, release their fire, and quickly and quietly move back into the shadows, their power spent. But like the footmen-archers who made English armies so successful in the great set pieces of fourteenth- and early-fifteenth-century warfare, their collective impact is both effective and memorable. The high drama of narration and orality-into-memory may be reserved for those of ancient lineage and famous coats of arms—as we shall see in the Scrope and Grosvenor depositions—but the fleeting tales of "mortal men, mortal men" serve their purpose. They offer a striking lesson in the value of so-called lesser sources.[1]

The Proofs of Age, despite their laconic nature and dodgy reliability—problems that seem to diminish as we move from considering them as a genre to an analysis and synthesis of their contents—enable us to uncover intriguing aspects of the localized society that produced and "consumed" them. That they are written documents is a vulgar truism; were they not, we would have no records, no reach into or memory of the proceedings whence they come. But that they stand as the written record of what had originated as an oral proceeding is still worth pointing out. They offer a wealth of opportunities for the study of the process behind their creation, as well as a glimpse at the short- and long-term interactions of those whose common efforts are recorded therein. They reflect a re-created past and are evocative regarding that process of re-creation.

A Proof of Age proceeding began when the heir or heiress, or an agent acting on his or her behalf, petitioned for a writ *de aetate probando* to instruct the escheator to hold a judicial (and oral) proceeding to determine if there was indeed, in literal terms, a proof of the heir's age. As typically stated: "writ to the escheator to take proof of age of the said William son of Robert, kinsman and one of the heirs of William de Felton, tenant in chief" (xv, 76).[2] The interval between the petition and the escheator's action was usually brief, mostly measured in days or weeks. This may have been a sign of urgency, but it may also simply indicate that the hearing was merely part of the ordinary business of countryside and town, to be dispatched without elaborate preparation.[3] The proceeding or inquiry brought the escheator into direct contact with men unlikely in any other way to figure prominently or frequently in the records of government, men with whom royal officials were not apt to have business. Though there are men of higher status in our universe of impaneled jurors, the overwhelming majority of the almost two thousand men called to serve were of minor consequence. They are best thought of as village spokesmen and elders, figures of little weight beyond the boundaries of their own community: free tenants, peasants of the middling range.[4] There are no signs that it was hard to find an adequate number of such jurors, nor is there any indication that they were considered deficient in the performance of their duties.

In this localized and parochial world of village and community, the escheator—hardly very high in the hierarchy of royal servants—was perhaps a towering figure, an extension of the king's arm, and he was now about to sit down and do business with our honorable but humble plebeians.[5] By the same token, these undistinguished peasants and artisans were, at least for the moment, elevated and dignified by virtue of their moment in the sun. The ephemeral mantle of status and credibility fell upon those summoned to participate in the king's affairs—and they were both seen and heard to be so involved. The ritualized and performative nature of the Proof of Age proceeding, along with the fact that its results were *written* into the official record, affects the testimony and its meaning within the community that generated it.

There is a link between the ritual of creating the record and the significance of the data it preserves. In reading jurors' narratives and reconstructing their brief tales of memorable events and daily social routines, the special place on center stage that each man fleetingly held should be factored into our assessment of his testimony's social context. We accept that standardized questions were apt to produce standardized responses. Moreover, standardized answers, drawing upon a familiar body of experience and articulation, helped elicit and frame the standardized questions.

The top-down nature of the inquiry was balanced by the two-way thoroughfare of local discourse. Related to the temporary elevation of the twelve jurors, privileged by their moment of participation in government, is the fact that they functioned as an officially empowered micro-universe, a small but linked community. Common testimony bound them together; the diplomatics of each document express this. Their names, ages, and perhaps some simple identifying tag are enrolled atop the record, often reflecting existing patterns of community activity and even defining and clarifying them. Shared moments of interaction, engraved in memory, might well take on a subsequent life of their own long after the escheator had rolled up his records and moved on.

The actual dynamics of a jury are not easy to determine, though we will tug at what loose strings we can find. We have an occasional indication of a *modus operandi*, though these glimpses are not so common as to make them a sure guide to a standardized procedure. Sometimes we are told that the jurors were characterized as twelve good men, who perhaps had been carefully examined as to how they remembered the date.[6] Sometimes it looks as though the first juror—as per the order of statements—served as a sort of foreman, and while not necessarily the eldest of the twelve, he is rarely the youngest. Furthermore, in some Proofs he offers the normative memory; the other jurors merely indicate their assent or, by way of variation, offer a tale as a confirmation of or a complement to his. In one instance the first juror's memory rested on the fact that he had been the heir's godfather, though this coupling of a past and a current role was unusual (xix, 105). But whatever the case regarding the first juror's role, the memories that followed were sometimes arranged in some logical sequence or contingent order. Subsequent jurors might indicate agreement with the first statement or with some other that had preceded theirs. Each in turn then added his own brick to the wall of credibility. In xv, 159, 660, and 891, for example, each juror agreed with the basic statement of age and then offered his own supplementary memory as an additional confirmation.

There are virtually no indications in these Proofs that heirs anticipated difficulties in claiming their property. Most of the heirs we encounter were accepted as proper heirs, of true age, and they usually came into their own without serious dispute.[7] How naturally did the jurors speak? And how far from their regular idiom were they led by the solemnity of it all? We can look in both directions. In Shakespeare's plays we have instances of respectable villagers—men not so different from our jurors—who become instant buffoons, sometimes garrulous and sometimes tongue-tied, when summoned before their betters. But against this we can invest the jurors with the comfort and support of their community: they recall common business, carried out in the familiar setting of peers and neighbors, many of whom were also related by blood, affinity, or spiritual links. It was this aspect of the juries—their bonding, for the day and often for the long haul, for many and varied purposes—that looms large as we assess their tales.

In a Proof, each juror stated his name and age before relating his memory regarding the heir's age and the reasons why he could fix the critical time, the requisite twenty-one (or fourteen, or sixteen) years ago. These self-stated jurors' ages are worth some attention, for they too speak of memory and community. It is easy to say that medieval numbers are uncertain, at best, and that jurors could (and often did) fabricate or exaggerate their own longevity. It is usually held that either jurors or scribes were inclined to push ages up or down to reach a round number and that they resorted to the stock formula of "N years and more." In one Proof, for instance, every juror stated his own age: 42, 40, 44, 43, 40, 46, 50, 46, 48, 50, 42, and 40 (XVII, 275). But in another, all the jurors were listed as being "N and more": 51 years and more, 49 years and more, and so on (XVII, 429). We should take a good look for ourselves, however.[8] Several considerations suggest that the numbers and ages are believable. One is that on this day in particular—as perhaps on few others—a degree of numerical accuracy was part of an official public agenda. As Dr. Johnson observed about hanging, if anything could concentrate one's thoughts, sworn testimony under the gaze of the escheator might do so. If this hardly argues for pinpoint accuracy, it runs counter to the view that the responses came out of thin air.[9]

Apart from what the Proofs offer by way of demographic data—to be enlarged on below—we have the fact that the jurors *chose* to give their ages as they did.[10] If their statements say more about the presentation of self than about years as such, what they lack in precision they gain in terms of social contextualization. A statement regarding age is offered within the constraining channels of common sense and, in one's own community, of shared experience. While age is expressed in years of life, it is also a moving point in the life cycle; years of life and age-linked activities are closely related. Age is socially framed and expressed, especially for lives spent in a village. It was calibrated to marriage and parenthood, to maturity and adulthood, and to other life-course milestones—moveable, perhaps, but in some fixed relation to each other. Age also publicly linked one to one's cohort, to siblings, and to parents.

The jurors as a community, whether for the day or in some form of long-standing unity, offer us scores of groups of twelve, usually composed of men of varying ages. These men did common business, and they never seem to disagree (in the final record, at least—what pruning was needed to coax their accord is beyond us) about the substance of the Proof. They stood united in voice, despite disparities in age, in status (though it was not so great on most juries), and in experience. We see a slice of community life wherein men in their fourth or fifth decade attested to a common purpose alongside men in their sixth or seventh decade. The years and age spreads that separated jurors were no barrier to their articulation of a common finding. Furthermore, many of the crucial memories rested on "deeds done" on *the* day, deeds and undertakings that had often involved several of the jurors in a common enterprise. We can see the age spread for groups of four or six who had come to church together, or who had jointly embarked for Santiago, or who were returning in tandem from market when they met an inebriated, effusive father or godfather on his way to or from the heir's baptism.

Men of property claimed estates at age 21, while married women needed to be but 14 (and 16 if unmarried, though most of our heiresses were already married). Were jurors who swore on behalf of male claimants noticeably older, as their memories had to run back an additional five to seven years? Table 1 gives the self-stated ages of jurors considering the cases of both male and female heirs. The contrast between the ages of the two groups is not very great, though it is sufficiently significant to be worth a passing comment. For both sets of jurors, we have a modal group of men in their 40s and 50s, at least as they reported themselves. Because one had to be of legal age to serve as a juror, the interval between the heir's birth and the time of the Proof would give us a universe of jurors now at least in their mid- to late 30s, at the lowest end of the chart, and considerably beyond that in most cases.[11] Of male heirs' jurors, 80 percent were at least in their 40s and 50s. For female heirs, the incidence of such jurors was nearly the same, though there were actually more over-60s for the heiresses (which seems counterintuitive, given the heiresses' younger age and the shorter interval between the birth and the Proof). We have a goodly number of jurors whose self-stated ages put them well into the ranks of the elderly and beyond: 405 jurors (combining those for male and female heirs) were in their 60s or more, representing 21 percent of the universe of 1952 jurors.[12] Of jurors from male heirs' Proofs, 20 percent (325 of 1627 men) were 60 and older, while from heiresses' Proofs, the number comes to 25 percent (or 80 men of 325).

All in all, this is common sense in statistical wrappings, and few—either then or now—would have reason to balk at accepting and recording such data. We might think of the prominent men of a village as being in what may have seemed advanced middle age, men in their 40s and 50s, seasoned and experienced, not quite over the hill. Medieval theories about aging and the stages of life do not interpret things in this way, looking rather at life-cycle stages and prepackaged categories of age. A preponderance of jurors in their 40s and 50s, however, is much in line with demographic analyses of members of Parliament and other comparable groups for whom we have hard information.[13] Virtually no one was only in his 30s. Given the nature of a Proof—with its resort to a remembrance of things past—the universe of jurors is obviously tilted toward life experience, even if the interval between the heir's birth and the Proof was the same for young jurors and old.[14] The tendency to impanel older men may have been reinforced by the fact that few jurors were men of note. Though a peer's heir might emerge

Table 1 Jurors' Ages, by Decades, on Juries for Male and Female Heirs

CIPM Volume	Jurors' Ages on Juries for Male Heirs					Jurors' Ages on Juries for Female Heirs				
	30–39	40–49	50–59	60+	Total	30–39	40–49	50–59	60+	Total
XV	3	140	128	36	307	3	20	18	7	48
XVI	–	47	97	27	171	–	32	30	17	79
XVII	–	65	98	53	216	–	16	12	8	36
XVIII	–	164	194	87	445	2	31	27	23	83
XIX	5	169	192	122	488	1	27	26	25	79
Total	8 (1%)	585 (36%)	709 (44%)	325 (20%)	1627	6 (2%)	126 (39%)	113 (35%)	80 (25%)	325

in the public sector while barely in his 20s, our yeomen did not rise in their neighbors' acclaim quite so easily or so rapidly.[15]

Like the jurors as individuals, the jury—an institution or a mini-community—also had an age profile. Each jury had a demographic and social fingerprint, and the age, social standing, degrees of relationship or friendship, and mnemonic experiences of the jury's members all figure into its moment of micro-history. Table 2 presents data on the age of juries as units, relying, for want of anything better, on the self-stated ages offered as part of the jurors' testimony. Though medieval computation did not reckon averages (the median) as I have done here, this seems a reasonable way for us to compare and frame these units as social entities. Even in the crudest assessment of the jury, based on the most casual of glances and wholly divorced from numerical appraisals, the graying factor for a jury with an average age of more than 60 would have been apparent. Though we only have six such juries (or 4 percent of the total), we take note of what such numbers tell us about survival and village culture. But these are extreme cases. Seventy percent of the juries came in with an average age that fell somewhere between 45 and 55.

Table 3 offers another approach to the self-reported ages and the demography of juries as social units. This time we consider the age spread between the youngest and the oldest members of the jury, though calculating by decades (e.g., men in their 40s, and so on) exaggerates the difference. If we are not exactly confronted by a mix of May and December when we treat each jury as an entity, we do see that it was common for juries to encompass a fairly wide spread of older and younger. Our ephemeral micro-communities were not thrown off their stride by combining same-purpose testimony from men of 40 and men of 60, or, on occasion, men of 70. At the same time, many a jury, perhaps reflecting a strategy of selection-by-convenience, reported all twelve men as being of the same age, usually somewhere in their 40s or 50s. About 7 percent of the juries were composed of men all in the same decade of life, and some Proofs give specific ages

Table 2 Average Age of All Juries by Five-Year Age Groupings

CIPM Volume	Number of Juries	Average Age of Jury				
		< 45	45–49	50–54	55–59	60+
XV	23	3	8	9	2	1
XVI	16	1	2	9	4	–
XVII	20	1	5	9	4	1
XVIII	36	1	9	14	11	1
XIX	45	1	9	23	9	3
Total	140	7 (5%)	33 (24%)	64 (46%)	0 (21%)	6 (4%)

NOTE: In XIX, six juries report ages only for eleven of the twelve jurors; they have been included in the calculations.

for such a jury, juror by juror. But at the other end of the spectrum, Table 3 shows most juries with an age spread of three decades, and a four-decade one within a single jury was not uncommon. In fact, 57 percent of the juries had a three-decade spread in jurors' ages, though the oldest man in his 40s and the youngest in his 60s might only be eleven or twelve years apart. Whatever secrets of village life are hidden, these data argue against a social dynamic that centered primarily on age, cohort, or generation as the main axis of structural or functional activity—whether it was youth or old age.

These numbers take on a bit more life if we look at some particular Proofs. One Proof might highlight individuality, documenting twelve separate ages and twelve separate and different reasons for remembering the heir's age. In another, the ages of the jurors appear separately: 60, 56, 50, 46, 58, 60, 64, 48, 62, 52, 60, and 47 (XV, 76). And at the other extreme are those Proofs with a single or common age for all twelve: "[twelve men] each aged 50 years and more" (XV, 654). Between these poles of individualization and commonality lie countless permutations and variations, though we cannot say whether age kept men apart or brought them together. We find juries with two men aged 44, four men aged 54 (and stated as two pairs of 54-year-olds), three aged 58, and three of 48.[16] Did the jurors themselves take control of the process and decide to say that six were of one age, the others scattered? Or did the escheator line them up and call them forward in such a pairing when it came time for their moment in history?

There is a dimension to this material easily missed in a straightforward numerical analysis—one critical for demographic probability and for the social psychology of the village. The jurors knew each other; they lived in the same community as young men, as mature men, and finally as old men. Their self-proclaimed ages, in years and in arrangement, had to be set upon a grid of social credibility, of community awareness and acceptance.[17] The jurors and their fellows presumably

Table 3 Age Spread, by Decades, Between Oldest and Youngest Jurors on a Jury

CIPM Volume	Number of Juries	Age Spread Between Oldest and Youngest Jurors			
		1 Decade	2 Decades	3 Decades	4 Decades
XV	23	3	9	7	4
XVI	16	2	6	8	–
XVII	20	1	5	11	3
XVIII	36	1	8	23	4
XIX	45	3	7	31	4
Total	140	10 (7%)	35 (25%)	80 (57%)	15 (11%)

NOTE: In XIX, six juries report ages only for eleven of the twelve jurors; they have been included in the calculations.

knew who were the oldest, who were of much the same age, and who were the youngsters of the twelve. In Proofs where sets of jurors attest to a common event or memory, groupings of same-age men are the most common but hardly the only pattern for shared or paired memories. In these, it was a common practice for the twelve to be divided into subgroups, members of which were identified as of the same age and the same memory. In one case we have three men each given as 42, then a group of five of 45, then four of 50 (XV, 452); in another, we have one man of 44, three of 43, three of 50, three of 44, and two of 42 (XV, 448); in still another, three different men and memories of 60, three together in age and memory at 50, three lumped at 43, and three more of 40 (XV, 447).

But variations exist here, too. A common memory might be shared by jurors well apart in age. This was not as frequent as the common-memory/common-age pattern, but it can be found. A group of four men, aged 63, 59, 44, and 60, might share the memory that the fourth juror had been married three days before the heir's birth, the others present at the wedding (XV, 891). In one Proof we have three groups, each sharing a common memory. The ages within each group were 52, 48, and 56; 64, 58, 54, and 61; and 54, 68, 62, and 60 (XVII, 186; one juror in the first group neglected to state his age or to have it recorded). At the far end is a Proof with six groups of jurors with six memories, and each pair was one of mixed ages: 44 and 50, 50 and 46, 48 and 50, 60 and 54, 45 and 41, and 40 and 50 (XVIII, 316).

Some of this material about jurors' ages might stand as solid demographic data, could we test it. Some reveals more about pairing off to offer social memory within a small community than about numerical precision. But when we take into account the solemnity of the day and its emphasis on precise information, we should not be too cavalier about the ages being entered on the king's record. Neither the jurors' nor the heirs' ages were being challenged, certainly not by the late fourteenth century. This credibility, or socio-administrative acceptance of what was being attested to, may not argue for the literal accuracy of memory or of testimony. But it does incline us against writing off the ages offered by the jurors on the great day being recorded for posterity in the Proof of Age.

THE MECHANICS OF RECOLLECTION

The world revealed by the Proofs (and re-created by our reading) can be divided into two parts, bifurcated or perhaps united by a time line. First, as we pick up and read the documents, we are at "now"—the time of the jurors' testimony, some twenty-one or sixteen or fourteen years after point zero. Then, in the body of the testimony, we are taken back to point zero, to the moment of the event now being recalled and from which the counting of years toward full age began. In the written record, the Proof, the event, and the recollection of the event that yokes them together have all been stitched into a single fabric.

Because the individual testimonies are brief and formulaic, it is easy to overlook the complex structure of recollection and collective social memory—some of it explicitly stated, much of it left to be inferred—on which the legal procedure (or fiction) rested. Though a richer fabric of memory and attestation emerges from the Scrope and Grosvenor depositions and from Margaret Paston's letters, the tough substructure of recollection is present here as well. The idea behind the hearing is that some event in which the juror had been a participant, spectator, or auditor, or about which he had learned in some fashion, or with which something else of note had coincided, had so marked the moment that he could still, despite the passing years, link it to the heir's birth or baptism—the point zero of the time line.

The statement or memory of each juror thus stands at a critical intersection of the event that was remembered and why it was remembered, the then and the now. The events themselves were apt to be recounted in a lapidary fashion, perhaps the most pedestrian of matters given a turn of phrase and wrapped in circumstantial packaging. In the testimonies, if not in daily life, dramatic vignettes and life crises were often near at hand. Or, if we wish, the unusual and the dramatic were superimposed upon the quotidian. Some categories of recollection, such as those associated with life-cycle milestones, appear in scores of testimonies. Others, such as a reference to Richard II's accession or an earthquake, are rare gems in the treasure chest of reminiscence.

The structure of testimony collecting was designed to produce a string of memories with some sort of guarantee that they really took us back the requisite twenty-one years (or fourteen, or sixteen). In this regard we find the Proofs relying on circular reasoning, though their assertions about the adequacy of the interval between "then" and "now" generally went unquestioned.[18] Matters were recalled in terms of recollection or narrative, mostly moving along a one-way line: ask a question, receive a satisfactory answer. In a typical Proof the first juror was "asked how he knows this," and without breaking stride he responded: "[he] says that he was then a household servant of John de Garton, the heir's father," and therefore he was in a position to know whereof he spoke (XVI, 948).[19] He knew *because* he remembered; memory reified history.

The process of presenting information to the escheator was not done without self-consciousness. Jurors might be "separately examined as to how they remembered the date" (XIX, 139). How did they interact through their interwoven attestations? How were they lined up to offer the appearance of a convincing case? Within the basic parameters of being chosen and sworn in, there seems to have been no single procedure or *modus operandi* that was followed, as long as the jurors all reached reasonable accord. Sometimes the Proof gives a collective summary before moving to the separate attestations: "The jurors say that Richard . . . is aged 24 years and more, having been born in London on 25 July 1380 and baptised in the church of All Hallows at the Hay in the Ropery. The jurors remember this for the reasons given," and then the Proof moves on to twelve separate attestations (XIX, 141). The men might be "separately examined as to how they remembered this date," or, as is sometimes stated, they had been "carefully examined" (XIX, 139, 105). Closer to the bone was the question, put occasionally to the first juror, that "asked how he remembers this after so long a lapse of time" (XVIII, 990; also XVI, 341). A variation on this was to establish the facts of time and memory in the first attestation, leaving subsequent jurors to talk in terms of "[he] agrees with the last written" and "[he] agrees in all respects" (XV, 663).

The vital "because" that links the recollection to the tally of the requisite years is, to us, the weak link on the chain. We look to the different kinds of memories for an indication that the medieval ear, or consciousness, was attuned to distinctions among forms and types of cognition. But this is *our* distinction; for the most part, we search in vain. There is little indication of contemporary efforts to distinguish memories culled from different levels and categories of experience. It sufficed to refer to a memory that rested on "because Robert his brother was born on that day" (XVIII, 315). One harked back to a tale of how "Edmund . . . sold a grey horse to Ralph her father on that 6 January and Ralph told him that his wife had borne a daughter, Thomasia, on that day" (XVIII, 692). We certainly understand why events of the Feast of St. Mark, 35 Edward III, were still vivid for Richard Beaupe and Peter le Cambray. They recounted that "as they went towards Shrewsbury, they were despoiled by Welsh robbers of two horses . . . and [they] went to the church of Le Pole to get help to take the robbers, and there found many magnates and other parishioners met together for the baptism [of Lord Cherleton's heir]" (XV, 659).

The responses were not fleshed out regarding the certainty that the event had taken place the proper number of years before. *How* do you remember, or *why* do you remember, was of central concern, and little attention was paid to determining how the interval itself was measured. The axiomatic presentation of linked events sufficed: "Richard Lust . . . had a son John baptised in the church on that day, and knows [that the heir is of age] by counting the years from that baptism" (XVI, 1053).[20] Indeed, this was a common formulation. One juror, John Colly, "aged 50 years and more, agrees and says that a certain John Barry, uncle of the said Richard, married Margery, his sister, and so by the offspring begotten between them he is sure of the age of the heir" (XVI, 106). Certainty of declaration provided adequate momentum: "on the day of the baptism Roger Naturcell his father was buried in the church of Turveye and that was 22 years ago" (XV, 297).[21] These were the legal equivalents of a Euclidean axiom. "The heir is the same age as my daughter; I know my daughter is 22; therefore the heir is 22: QED."

We saw that the notice to the guardian of the heir's estate offering an opportunity to rebut the claim to legal age either went unanswered or elicited little more than token response.[22] But this is not the issue here. It is rather the naked and undisguised reliance upon circular reasoning to fix a matter of fact: "William Brekenoke . . . agrees and says that at Easter next after the birth of the said Arnold he had a son called John born, who is now 21 years of age and more" (XV, 292). In some instances, the recollection was linked to an external event. These at least could have withstood a tougher evidentiary standard, had one been imposed: "William Hawe, aged 60 years, and John Lynge, aged 50 years, know this because John Pyel was mayor at that time" (XVII, 742). To us, this seems much stronger than the innumerable shifting buoys that often mark the channel of memory: they "know this because John Yonge, brother of the said Roger Yonge of Eppyng [the juror], died on that day" (XVII, 1110).[23] For the jurors, the internal or circular reasoning was as potent as an appeal to external or impersonal events. A memory was a memory.

But even though the testimony would be accepted at face value, the fabric of testimony and the mechanics of recollection touch on the ways jurors turned to their memories and on how and why they arranged and accessed them. As they step forward to tell their stories, they collectively present mix-and-match recollections. We wind up with accounts of personal participation, things seen, things heard, things seen *and* heard, and other forms of cognitive intake and mnemonic verification. Given the number of testimonies, we expect these variations and combinations. Some are bald assertions, while others point to complex acts of recollection and retrieval, to memories dependent on a string of other people's words and deeds in lieu of direct knowledge or participation.[24]

Personal involvement means having done something, oneself, as a part of the activity that fixed the memory. Often attestations of this sort are straightforward and circumstantial: "He carried fire to the church . . . at the time the said heir was baptised," or "he took water to the church in a silver basin for the godparents to wash their hands after the said Hugh's baptism" (XVII, 275, 955). In a Proof at Chelmsford, the first three jurors said that each had gone to fetch a godparent, and they could still recall what happened because of their direct and personal participation (XIX, 1005). Memories of such involvement were probable and prosaic, and in this vein two men in Dorset offered their version of a memory of common activity: "the witnesses remember because on that day the said Henry carried with him the sword of Nicholas Pointz [knight and godfather], and the said John held the holy candle before Henry, rector of the church" (XVI, 78).[25] Something tangible sufficed to peg the links between the celebratory and the personal: "this the deponent well remembers because on the same day he put together a house in the same town" (XV, 652).

If one had not been an active participant, testimony about seeing the key event would seem to be next best, the second of the concentric circles of recollection. The visualized memory could be fairly straightforward: "they saw him [the infant] carried to and from the church" (XVIII, 1179). Jurors might simply recall that they had been "in the church at Seterington [Settrington, Yorkshire] on that day and saw the said John baptised and John parson of Kyreham [Kirkham] baptise him" (XVII, 954). In one Proof, the twelve jurors offer a single, common memory: "this they know because the said church is dedicated in honour of St. Martin and they were [all] there in a company as pilgrims and [they] saw John de Brightwell, the heir's godfather, lift him from the sacred font" (XV, 654). In a Proof from Worcester, we have an instance of "the jurors collectively say . . ." as the opening, before we move to the individualized statements. These then give us four jurors who had seen the baptism (including two statements from men who had held torches), four jurors who had heard of the ceremony, and two who had seen the purification of the mother (XVI, 1057). Sometimes a more vivid slash of memory comes back: "they know this because they were present in the church at the baptism of the said William and saw him lift his right hand and take the said Philippa [his godmother] by her veil" (XVII, 1321). It might be the oft-told and ever popular tale of the man who "got on to a bench in order to see the child, and in getting down again he fell into the church and broke his shin," though this could be classified as personal involvement beyond what the accident victim had seen.[26] But memories could also be both personal and at second hand, as with the jurors who recalled that "on that day [they] rode towards Gloucester past the church and met Cecily [the infant] being carried from the church after baptism" (XVIII, 1179).

When we move from seen to heard we cross a line between direct or personal knowledge and what we now regard as its inferior, hearsay. How did one come to hear of events? What sort of things did one hear that, in recollection, assured the escheator of credible testimony? The basic thrust was usually fairly direct. One juror "remembered because his house burned and those who came to help him told him that Giles Henthill knight, had a son by Katherine his wife on that day" (XVIII, 529). In one instance the Proof brings us to the greener pastures of narration while still resting on oral transmission: the juror had been "in Pontefract on the day Edward was born and there saw a man unknown to him who had been arrested for casting the evil eye on the horse of his neighbor . . . and then he [the juror] heard that Anne de Hastynges had been delivered of a male child, whom he afterwards heard [had been] called Edward" (XVIII, 854).

News of births and baptisms was part of the stock-in-trade of local discourse and gossip: "Agnes formerly wife of John Taillour, foster-mother of the said Robert, met them and told them that the said Robert was baptised in the church of Cotes on that day" (XVII, 575).[27] Proud fathers announced their good news to dinner guests, and other jurors realized that the wheel of life had revolved when they learned of the heir's birth while at church for a funeral.[28] These statements, and their differing routes and pathways of communication, remind us of how people tell things to those they meet in the course of the day. Sometimes the news of birth or baptism was the centerpiece of an exchange; in other cases, it was almost buried amid circumstantial embellishments. And, of course, the Proof as a document gives an impression of direct communication that might belie a more tortuous discourse offered at the moment.[29]

Nor do these forms of cognition exhaust the possibilities for attestation and recollection. The continuum extends from doing and seeing and hearing to some form of written record. A juror might recall that he had seen the date of birth, or of baptism, or of some other memorable event written into a church's records or the father's missal. But we should pay attention to the way such a memory is presented; the juror is not reading the key line as it had been written. Rather, he is attesting that he saw someone write something, often at the request of a father or godparent who knew the mnemonic value of witnessing the act of scribal recording. In a few instances the juror had done the writing himself, or had read the writing, as when Geoffrey Deen and Thomas Mayhewe told their tale: after the baptism, "John Boson, uncle and godfather, asked Geoffrey to write the time of the birth in books of John Boson, Geoffrey Deen, Thomas Mayhewe, and others" (XIX, 777).[30]

But the bulk of our references keep us tilted toward the realm of oral and visual cognition. The juror had heard a request for the writing (that is, for a written record to be made). One man "knew this by inspection of a manual in the church in the calendar of which on the feast of St. Agatha it is written that Robert son of John atte Chirche was born in 49 Edward III" (XVII, 1110). But even here we encounter circular reasoning; four men were separately examined and they all said that they "came to church to make offerings before a picture of the Virgin Mary when the parson was baptising, and [they] saw him write the date in the missal in their presence, and that of several others, so they know the date" (XIX, 777). It is quite possible that we invest more in these references to literacy and the written record than the jurors did. But there are many references that link memories to scribes and the written record. Jurors said that they "know his age by inspection of a book of martyrs in the church in which his birth was noted," or that a death had been "recorded in a missal" and a note of a son's ordination was "recorded in the chapter book of the abbey."[31] While most juries' stories reveal a mix of cognitive routes, we have a few Proofs that really rely on this particular strand of verification. In one Proof there are four different contexts in which writing and written evidence are cited, contexts that include five of the twelve men. One juror saw the record of the baptism set down "in a great missal." Another, a bailiff at the time, referred to the dated acquittance of his accounts as the reason he still remembered. Another had bought land and had a written (and dated) charter; two others had witnessed a charter (XVIII, 886).[32]

Juries occasionally fell back on the allusive idea that they could have told much more but for the fact that they had already carried the day. One way of couching this aura of certainty about the heir's age was a lofty (albeit indeterminate) reference to common lore, that basin of communal knowledge. That "the age of the said William is generally recognized in the parish of his birth" summarized the wisdom of the unnamed many (XV, 888). This was elaborated in more pseudo-detail in a Northumberland Proof: "Moreover, his age is well known by common report in the whole parish . . . and he [the juror] has seen and heard it reckoned up in the parish and neighbouring places by known persons who are his kinsfolk and friends" (XV, 656).[33] Why pursue an issue further when "the jurors had other notable evidence if it were necessary to produce it" (XIX, 901)? An even vaguer variation was the casual resort to "moreover, it is well known throughout the parish that this heir is of that age"—and lest the circle of self-reinforcing testimony close in on itself too tightly, there was the assertion that "all the parishioners . . . as well as his godfather, neighbours, and friends have carefully reckoned his age" (XVI, 336). One trump card was "common talk." The resilience of this many-headed beast underlines the concept of community, perhaps not at the expense of "real" memory but at least as a shorthand for a string of circumstantial tales that can now remain untold.[34]

But such an imprecise foundation, placed beneath the usual structure of testimony and recollection, was not often called upon to carry the main weight. Rather, it was additional confirmation of the cumulative force of things seen and heard. We see the coupling of the evidentially rock-solid and the lore of the street in a Proof from Newbury, Berkshire. The jurors offered a common statement regarding birth and baptism. They had been at a small fair of St. Valentine on his feast day, and some of their number had gone into a nearby church of which he was the patron saint. While in church, "several [jurors] . . . saw John Hautlo and Thomas Baa, godfathers of the said John, lift him from the sacred font." And somehow the knowledge of an event that some had seen became infectious among the twelve: "all the other jurors believe and know it by testimony of their fellow-jurors and of very many trustworthy persons of the county who were present at the time" (XV, 658).[35]

There are Proofs in which a particular form of cognition swept the board.[36] It seems unlikely that the customary mix of cognitive routes was the result of a prearranged strategy between jurors and escheator or by the parties on their own. More likely, the mix of kinds of memories, like those of the incidents being recalled, was a natural (or at least a likely) result of assembling twelve neighbors who could be counted on to come up with something sufficiently convincing when they pooled their reminiscences. As lives and identities were a mixed bag of experience, interaction, and proximity, so testimonies can be read as credible reflections of this social reality. The kind of information offered by jurors in support of their recollections may seem weak in terms of precision. It is strong, however, in its reliance on the power of formulaic discourse and in its appeal to collective memory. After all, it was the community, now given shape through these attestations, that was the proper and trustworthy repository of knowledge about its own. Given the social and economic gulf between the young heir and the vast majority of the jurors who testified on his or her behalf, the tales of the Proof are a vivid witness to common knowledge, held by common people, about their betters, about events, and about a world of shared perception. That the jurors' knowledge served to reconsolidate the grip of their social superiors for still another generation was but to accept the order of life on this middle earth. A Proof of Age hearing was neither the time nor the place to question the transmission of wealth and power, status and hierarchy. It was, rather, the time and place for men to come together and, by the evocation of memories of things seen and heard, things done, and events and actions in which they had played a part, to reconstruct a small chapter of their communal lives.[37]

JURORS' LIFE CYCLES AND LIFE-CYCLE MEMORIES

Time for a transition. We move from a consideration of the jurors as a representative micro-community at the time of the Proof to the world they reconstruct through memory and reminiscence. For this reconstruction of lives within the setting of a community, I will group their tales into three main categories: memories related to the jurors' own life stages; memories that center on involvement with some aspect of the Church; and memories relating to secular events and activities, whether of the jurors themselves or of others—an external world as they knew and commented upon its people, places, and happenings. By life-cycle memories, I mean recollections that frame the heir's birth or baptism against an event or ceremony that had coincided with, or been connected in some memorable way, to a juror's own marriage or family birth or family death. All of these life-cycle events one recalled no matter how many years had passed—though numerical exactitude is, as always, open to question. Even today, in a world of literacy and ready access to the written and electronic record, these are the points around which we organize both personal and extra-familial memories. Such markers fix the course of our lives, siting the moments at which the dramas of the personal universe take over and govern the arrangement and memories of the external one.

Marriage

Marriage, as a major normative milestone, is a good beginning. While for most adults in late medieval England legal age may have preceded marriage by a few years, it was at marriage that full social maturity—the establishment of a new household and the articulated socio-sexual partnership of wife and husband—really began. And, like the other events and situations we will examine, the combination of the spiritual and the personal or familial, plus the ritualized communal and public roles of friends and neighbors, made the moment of marriage a memorable one for many beyond the bridal couple. Though a private promise or vow could create the indissoluble union, the Proofs focus on public events, public ceremonies. Marriage, as the jurors recall it, was an event for the community as well as for the couple.[38]

Though marriage is the first life-cycle event we consider, births and deaths also figure. In a procedure designed to focus on the dating of an heir's birth, comparable events and times in the jurors' own lives naturally come to mind. In a world wherein almost everyone married, most had children, and all could be assumed to have been closely familiar with death, the recollection of a life crisis or transition was likely to set the familiar pattern. We see more reliance upon the prosaic than upon the anomalous or the dramatic, though they too will occasionally have their time and place. But "ordinary" memories were the long threads in the tapestry of remembrance.

Tables 4, 5, and 6 show how often jurors resorted to such memories. For 72 jurors, their marriage was the mnemonic choice, while 115 used a birth or baptism and 97 recalled a death from somewhere within their circles of kinship. As well as the incidence of these kinds of recollections, we look at the jurors' self-reported ages when offering birth and marriage memories. The testimonies help establish a demographic grid for the age at which the jurors had married and fathered (some of their) children, though it can only bear so much weight. For deaths I do not offer this information, given the random nature of the milestone, but instead I offer material touching on the timing of the deaths of the jurors' parents.

Table 4 Jurors, by Age, Using Their Own Marriages as Mnemonic References

CIPM Volume	Jurors' Ages at the Time of the Proof						
	< 40	40–44	45–49	50–54	55–59	60–64	65+
XV	1	6	5	6	3	4	–
XVI	–	1	2	1	1	–	–
XVII	–	–	2	2	–	2	1
XVIII	1	5	3	2	1	–	1
XIX	–	2	6	8	1	2	3
Total (N = 72)	2 (3%)	14 (19%)	18 (25%)	19 (26%)	6 (8%)	8 (11%)	5 (7%)

Table 4 shows that a juror's age at marriage—at least as he chose to state it—is much in keeping with the "European marriage pattern" of the historical demographers, that is, marriage in the mid- or late 20s.[39] About half the jurors who referred back to their marriages were *now* between 45 and 54; thus they had been between 24 and 33 at the critical moment. Only about one man in five (22 percent) had been 23 or under at the time of the marriage he refers to, while slightly over one-fourth of the group (19 of 72, or 26 percent) had been 34 or more. As we said above, if the literal accuracy of dates and ages is shaky, we should also keep in mind that the jurors were making precise statements about personal-cum-historical events, memories that fellow jurors might easily confirm or deny. A common activity within an age cohort, such as a first marriage, was easily remembered, and collective memory was an effective check on any individual flight of fancy. Beyond this, there are references to joint or common activities: one juror had married another's sister, or had stood witness for another, or had been in church while the wedding was being celebrated. Our jurors were hardly meeting for the first time, as with the two men whose common memory was "they knew the date because on Thursday . . . they married sisters in the church and there were esquires and servants who reported the birth to them" (XV, 660).

The memory of having been married on that day, or that year, or the Michaelmas immediately before or subsequent to the baptism, was the gist of most relevant memories. The bald statements were good enough, though a few jurors tell a bit more about their own milestone moments. One man remembered that "on the same day [as the baptism] he engaged himself to Alice atte Mulle to take her to wife" (XV, 451). Another said he had married "Sibyl his wife, and the banns were asked on the day of the baptism" (XV, 659). We have a juror who told of how "on that day [he] contracted matrimony with Alice de Shetely whom he subsequently married," and another thought back to when he "came to the church on that day with Alice Goodman whose daughter Alice he married on the following Monday" (XIX, 102, 781). With marriage went the establishment of the new household: "he married a certain Felicia . . . and he took her home to Turveye [Turvey] the same day" (XV, 297). When a juror said that the union was still in place—"At Michaelmas in that year he married his wife who is still alive" (XIX, 785)—was he speaking with affection or actuarial wonder? Three jurors offered one of those common memories: "Joan, daughter of Thomas Ocle was married to Edmund Toby in the said church," and the three men had all been at the nuptial mass and had witnessed the heir's baptism (XVII, 578).

There were but few variations in these recollections, and the wording was fairly standard. One memory was from a juror who had been "with Robert Lambrook in the church and contracted marriage with Margery his daughter" while the baptism was being performed (XVIII, 858).[40] Another man, giving his age as 60 and referring to a marriage a mere fourteen years before (in an heiress's Proof), recalled that "he married his wife Margaret who is still living and on the day of the marriage they were jointly enfeoffed of lands in Rillington" (XVII, 954). A few memories offer the sort of precise information that might bolster his statement: "66 and more [and he remembers] because he married Margaret his wife on 6 January 1389" (XVIII, 1181).[41] The time frame is less precise in a case where the juror and his wife, "after her marriage," had simply been at the baptism (XVII, 954). Another juror said he had married "a woman called Rose"—a touch of mystery, if not of romance (XV, 293). More details appear in William Henrison's recollection: he was now 60, and back then he had taken "to wife Elizabeth, daughter of the aforesaid John Thomasson," the said John being a fellow juror and giving his age as 63 years and more. One marriage had been celebrated on 31 March, "and on the third day after the marriage the said Robert [the heir] son of Thomas was born" (XV, 891). And there are the usual references to memories firmly anchored by an entry in a missal: "he married a certain Alice Laumprey, and their names and the date of the marriage are written in the missal of the said chapel" (XV, 888; also XV, 656). "The wedding is noted in the missal in the church of Grimston" was standard phrasing (XVII, 954). Perhaps all the weddings were actually registered, and the reference to the written record was seemingly no more significant to either jurors or the escheator than any of the other mnemonic tags.

A sibling's marriage could also be dredged up to fix the time. Such recollections rarely carried much more than the bare fact of marriage: "his sister Margaret married Richard Bayvill of Grantham, bailiff of the father, in that year" (XIX, 478). We have already looked at two men whose joint memory was of marriage to sisters and who, during the ceremony, had encountered the baptismal party (XV, 660). Some circumstantial strength comes when the parties are named; sister Alice, who married John Pegg, or sister Philippa, who married John Mot (XV, 160, 665). Neither man is otherwise mentioned in the Proof, so this is a reference to the village's pool of names and people, not one internal to the Proof record. But in these laconic records, the terse entry remains the most common: "Joan his sister was married that day" (XIX, 898). If a sister's wedding still stood in memory, that of a son or daughter comes as no surprise. One juror offered a statement that touched a number of themes: "in the week of Robert's birth he had a daughter Alice married to Richard Riche of Turvey and she has been married for 22 years and more" (XV, 297). This was more than the simple recollection of a man who recalled that he "gave his daughter . . . in marriage that day" (XIX, 791).

Sometimes jurors' ages do seem problematic when they refer, twenty-one years later, to children's marriages. It is hard to place blind faith in a Proof in which a juror claims to be 42 while he is offering a memory of his daughter's wedding "on that day" when the heir had been baptized twenty-one years before (XVIII, 672).[42] But the needle of age on life's compass can swing the other way, as well; one juror, identified as being 60, recalled that his daughter's wedding day had coincided with the heir's birth. It was especially memorable because on that day he "rode to Newcastle upon Tyne to buy 3 casks of wine" (XIX, 342).[43] Another juror recalled a marriage of twenty-one years before and the birth that had resulted from the marriage, a year later: wedding and child, in proper order and timing (XV, 891).

Birth

Memories of the births and baptisms of children were more frequent than those of marriage, whether one's own or that of another. This may conform to life experience; people generally have more children than marriages. In terms of parental age, we expect a distribution similar to that of age at marriage, with the addition of a year or two out of respect for social and sexual conventions. And yet, according to the data of Table 5, memories of parenthood went back to a slightly earlier age (though presumably not for the same people). The shift is a slight one, however, and where the stated age does not look out of line, we have a picture of medieval men marrying and fathering children at the expected ages. If half the men who offered memories of marriage went back to a time when they had been between 24 and 33, about 42 percent of those who referred to a child's birth were of comparable years. A shift of 9 percent is not of great significance, and we work on the premise that the marriages being referred to were first marriages unless we are told to the contrary, whereas we have no idea of which child's birth was being mentioned (except in the few instances when it was stated—usually for the firstborn).

Our interest in testimony on these matters, as given in the company of one's fellows, is likely to focus disproportionately on those well above or below the median age for such activity. It may have been a more striking memory for them,

Table 5 Jurors, by Age, Using a Child's Birth as a Mnemonic Reference

CIPM Volume	Jurors' Ages at the Time of the Proof						
	< 40	40–44	45–49	50–54	55–59	60–64	65+
XV	1	10	6	5	3	4	1
XVI	–	5	3	5	2	2	1
XVII	–	3	1	3	–	2	2
XVIII	–	8	3	5	2	5	1
XIX	–	5	4	13	1	6	3
Total (N = 115)	1 (1%)	31 (27%)	17 (15%)	31 (27%)	8 (7%)	19 (17%)	8 (7%)

perhaps, and doubtlessly a more risible one for their fellows, assuming the self-stated ages are realistic. Very young bridegrooms and young fathers are a common theme, but only in those instances where the juror said it had been the birth of his firstborn child can we argue for the clear start of parenthood at the age stated in the Proof. Of related interest, but beyond our range, is the age difference between husband and wife when he had been in his 40s at the time of the remembered birth. This aspect of women's lives is completely hidden in the world re-created through men's memories.

As with memories that revolved around marriage, a few evocations of parenthood add a bit more to the mere fact of birth. The selection of jurors—or their choice of memories—may really have fallen on men with a memory of a life-cycle experience that had fallen within days, weeks, or months of the heir's birth, as with the juror whose daughter Alice was "22 years of age and the heir was born on the following 30 September" (XVI, 948). The jurors invariably did indicate whether their child had been a son or daughter. Other aspects of new parenthood come in for mention now and then. A poignant touch is the comment that the child whose birth is being noted did not survive, or that he or she had died in the interval. It was tersely stated: one juror "had a son Robert born and baptised on that day, and he died the same day" (XIX, 996). Another juror "had a son Nicholas, born on 6 December next . . . [and] had he lived he would have been 21" (XVIII, 854).

Some jurors added that the child in question was indeed their first: one's "wife gave birth to his firstborn son" (XV, 451). Others paid at least a passing tribute to the wife who had contributed to parenthood. Our old friend, the confirmation provided by the written notice in the missal, shows up again: "immediately after the birth of a son named Philip, whose age is written in the missal of the chapel" (XV, 888).[44] Details make a case stronger, though further verification never seems to have been called for: "William Wortham, aged 70, knows that

Nicholas [the heir] is 21 years of age because he had a daughter Joan born 21 January 1387" (XIX, 392).[45] We also get allusions to child-care issues; a juror recalled the time in question because "on Michaelmas day before the birth [of the heir] he had twin sons born of Maud his wife" (XVI, 81).[46]

Though I am concerned with life transitions, rather than with the Proofs as documents, some aggregations of memories remind us of the overlap of common experience. The routine life-cycle memories of the men in a homogeneous community are apt to be similar and to stem from a limited reservoir of events and situations. A case in point: we can turn to a Proof taken at Market Overton, Rutland, on Monday the Feast of the Nativity of the Virgin, 6 Richard II. Of the twelve jurors' memories, three rest directly on a recollection of the birth of a juror's child. One man, now 63, had had a son born at Oakham on 15 March, 34 Edward III, shortly after the heir's birth, and the juror "saw him [the heir] at the breast immediately after." Another juror, now 60, said that after the heir's birth his own son had been born, "whose age is written in the missal." A third, now 52, said he had been married a month after the heir's birth, "and in the following year they had a son . . . who is now 20 years of age and more" (XV, 891).

One kind of memory about birth and age does offer a check to the circularity of logic so frequent in this world of testimony and recollection. We have men who spoke with certainty of their child's age (or the interval between birth and *now*) because the child had been ordained or had entered the Church. Because the spiritual *rite de passage* carried its own age requirements, such statements seem to be on firmer ground, though there is no indication that they were accorded any special status on the day of the Proof. One man who referred to birth and baptism said "this he knows because John his son, who was born in the same year as the heir, took priest's orders three years ago" (XVI, 107).[47] A variation was the recollection of a son born "on the same day that William was born" and "now ordained subdeacon" (XV, 888). But the circularity is still there when we turn to the juror who said "he had a brother of the same age" (XIX, 392). Of some note is the statement about "a brother called Diggory who was confirmed that day . . . by Richard, bishop of Coventry and Lichfield" (XIX, 1001).[48] At least one nephew came in for notice: "Guy his brother had a son born of Agnes his wife on that day" (XIX, 900). And we note that many jurors referred to baptism, rather than to birth itself, as the basis of recollection. Though birth was hardly private, attended as it was apt to be by midwives and other women of family and village, it was not a public event comparable to baptism. At the sacramental ceremony, the link between infant and community was enunciated: children being baptized around the same time were a birth cohort and a spiritual cohort as well, moving in parallel steps through the course of life.

TELLING TALES

Death

In human society, death is usually the occasion for ceremony and prescribed behavior, with attendant rituals designed to bridge the gulf between the spiritual and the secular, between continuity and closure. But even within the wide confines of this generalization, late medieval society is noted for its elaborate construction of death-related rituals.[49] The activities centering around and being spurred by death and mourning link what we might refer to as the world of high religion with local and community forms of expression that focus on reintegration and commemoration. Accordingly, it is no surprise to see that many men used a death in the family as their compass point for remembrance, and Table 6 analyzes ninety-seven such references—a number greater than the references to marriage, fewer than those to birth and baptism.

Because the age of the bereaved juror is not usefully fitted to any set demographic or life-cycle point when we look at memories of death (unlike those of marriage and birth), Table 6 considers the categories of the dead, not the juror's age. The death of a child led the list of memories; the most common event recalled, and perhaps still the most poignant, it reinforces the case of historians who argue for parental affection toward children in this period. The loss of a child, even twenty-one or so years later, still signified. In terms of frequency, after references to children's deaths come those of siblings and parents (well over wives).[50]

At what ages had jurors suffered the losses to which they were still pointing? Here the spread is so wide that no simple pattern—be it of crisis and catastrophe, or of longevity and survival—stands out with clarity. Of those who referred to the death of a child, we find men spaced up and down the ladder. Young fathers spoke of having children born and then die in childbed, while considerably older men spoke of deaths and burials somewhere in the interval between the heir's birth and the day of the Proof. Siblings and parents, of course, could go at any age, and their deaths had no relation to the juror's own position on the life line. But the range of ages, like the variety of relatives and kinsfolk recalled, is of interest, fleshing out the concept of life being in the midst of death.[51] Children's deaths were a common (if still memorable) experience, and they constitute one of those categories of the probable and even the ubiquitous that many would remember. The simplest tale was the straightforward memory: "his eldest son John died that day" (XVIII, 663). Some recollections give a fleeting glimpse of deeper memories and feelings: "the same day he buried John his first born son" (XVII, 1318). One compact view of domestic tragedy comes from the juror who still picked at an old wound: "on that day Reynold his son fell into a well in Muston and died, and lay there for three days" (XVIII, 672).

The ritual of the bedside deathwatch is conveyed by one recollection: "Roger . . . 60 and more, had a daughter Joan who died that night" (XIX, 339).[52] And

Table 6 Categories of Deaths Used as Mnemonic References by Jurors

CIPM Volume	Categories of Deaths				
	Child	Sibling	Spouse	Parent	Other
XV	3	7	4	9	–
XVI	4	2	1	2	2
XVII	7	2	3	–	–
XVIII	13	6	–	3	–
XIX	8	6	6	9	–
Total (N = 97)	35 (36%)	23 (24%)	14 (14%)	23 (24%)	2 (2%)

the one-liners again lend themselves to evocative recollection. It is hard to improve on "had he lived he would now have been 21" (XVIII, 854). Some of the deaths had been recorded in missals and martyrologies, those useful repositories of information. One juror referred to a son, "whose death was in the death-register [*martilogio*, as glossed by the *IPM*'s editor] of Holt"; a daughter's "death [was] recorded in the church" (XVI, 1053; XIX, 781). Much of life flashes before us: "This he remembers because he had then by his first wife an eldest son, William, who died on the same day, and his death is recorded" (XVIII, 311).[53] Nor is the memory of loss wholly eased by the balm of time. Death may have come anywhere in the interval, as with the juror who remembers "because his son Robert, now dead, was born on the preceding 20 October" and so coincided with the heir (XVIII, 1181).[54]

Table 6 shows that references to the death of a sibling or parent were also fairly common. Clearly some brothers and sisters kept in touch, as we might expect in a world of limited geographical mobility; their deaths were readily recalled. A juror spoke of his sister: the "day of her death is written in the missal of the said chapel" (XV, 888). As adults, siblings seem to have been at high risk from accidents, especially—as the Proofs unfold the world of danger and chance—from drowning. Or perhaps these were dramatic touches that stayed fresh. One man tied his memory to the recollection that "his brother was drowned in the river called Lyne and was buried in the church of Wyderyngton [Witherington] on the day of the heir's baptism" (XVII, 275).[55] Nor was drowning just a male privilege. John Drew was certain of an heir's age because "in the same year, 34 Edward III, Maud Drew, his sister, was drowned at Lyngfeld [Lingfield] in a tank [*cisterna*] called 'Mulpend'" (XV, 665).[56] Men probably were at greater risk from accidents and chance violence, though we have no clarifying details in the recollection of "his brother [who] was killed at Preston in Amoundernesse at Easter before the birth" (XVI, 81). A memory with several layers comes in a Proof from Derby. A juror says that "in that year his elder brother, who would have been his father William's heir if he had lived, went to Scotland and died there, and so he [the juror] had his father's inheritance" (XVIII, 315).

Parents' deaths were a natural phenomenon, and if we really are transported back some twenty-one years, many jurors would still have had a living parent, or even two. One juror recalled that "his mother . . . was buried that day; he knows from the date of the obit" (XIX, 188).[57] One of the few urban Proofs produces a juror who remembered that "his father died in that month and was buried in the church of St. Martin in Coney Street [York]" (xix, 139).[58] But just as death did not have to be selective in its gathering, so memories expanded to touch others within the circles of kinship. In-laws, of various sorts, get mentioned—a sign of cohesion and bonding befitting village life and local communities. A reference to a father-in-law's death indicates that he "died the same year and made him [the juror] his executor" (XV, 160). A London juror remembered that "at that time [he] buried his wife's mother at Camberwell," and a juror in Surrey recalled the date because he had just "buried John Lorchen, husband of his wife's sister," also at Camberwell (XIX, 344). A reference to the death and burial of "his father's wife" may be to a stepmother. In this case the death had been a year before the birth (October 31 for her death, October 28 in the next year for the birth), and it was her anniversary obit that brought the juror to the church where he happened to witness the baptism (XVIII, 1180).[59]

A few references to the death of a grandparent expand our familial universe to a third generation. One man had been "at the church . . . to bury a grandfather of John Yonge [a fellow juror] that day" (XIX, 1004).[60] A juror in Preston, speaking before the duke of Lancaster's escheator, said that "Aline de Mirescogh, his [paternal] grandmother, died on Sunday." An uncle might figure in as well; another juror spoke of remembering such a death on the feast of St. Laurence before the birth of the heir (XVI, 81). Wives, near and dear though they may have been, were not well covered in these statements. Either they were outliving the jurors, or their deaths were too painful, or too commonplace, to be the memory of the moment. But one such death was memorable: the parson had received (or had taken) a red cow by way of mortuary (XV, 449).[61] One woman might not have died; we only know that her husband recalled the time when "his wife was at the birth and caught a serious fever" (XVIII, 405–6). Sometimes the long-distant pain of memory can still be heard: a juror remembers because "on that day his wife died pregnant of a son Christopher, which Christopher is aged 22 years and more" (XVII, 955). (This presumably was death in childbed.)

The material I have been presenting is not going to open new vistas into behavior, life experience, or family relations. But the Proofs do give us a good deal of material that is easy to digest and that reinforces some basic ideas about life and death in late medieval society: marriage in the mid-20s, parenthood fairly soon afterward, the likely death of some children, and good odds for deaths within one's own generation as well as in the previous.

A few problems surface, though, perhaps in keeping with some law of compensation, offering a counter to the wealth of data and the glimpses we get of a world of feeling and evocative expression. The statements found in a number of Proofs indicate that a life transition—marriage of a child, in particular—had occurred at a time in the juror's life that hardly accords with his self-stated age (XVI, 947, and XV, 665, among others). Men in their early 40s were not likely to have been at their own children's marriages some two decades before. Because the fact of the marriage was less malleable than the self-stated age, we read the latter as being less convincing, the one more apt to have been "stroked" for the escheator.

But a nod toward skepticism is a long way from crossing the floor of disbelief. When Proofs are read for what they offer on how men referred to the episodes of birth, copulation, and death, they show that vivid memories still revolved around such matters. In addition, we have the fallback position of inherent social probability; the gaze and cohort-awareness of one's peers was not so different from the collective memory of the crowd. Ages, cohort membership, and life experience, along with oft-recollected odd events and situations, were hardly matters a juror might simply conjure up. Any given juror had to negotiate the ground between what he liked to hear himself say while he briefly strutted on the historical stage and what some world of historical reality—that elusive if not wholly chimerical cosmos of "what really happened"—expected to hear and put to use.

ECCLESIASTICAL MEMORIES

Memories that rested on ecclesiastical activities or revolved around the public and social role of the Church were common. In the aggregate, such reflections may not have come quite as often as those relating to demography and the turns of the life cycle, but they appear in virtually every set of Proofs and shed light on many different facets of the Church in the world.

Hundreds of attestations illuminate popular religion—the relations between the laity and the Church. They reinforce the view that the boundaries between the sacramental and the secularized Church were not sharply delineated, at least as the jurors told their tales. Their recollections indicate a broad if not necessarily deep grasp of the Mother Church's workings. Jurors' accounts embrace many sorts of interactions, from holding a towel at a baptism to repairing a belfry or balancing the church wardens' accounts. They help us understand how people perceived the Church's rituals and its calendar, the normative backdrop against which secular life was measured and tallied, its high points noted for future reference: festivals and saints' days, pilgrimages, exchanges of clerical livings, love-days, visits by the princes of Church or state as occasioned by a birth or baptism, and so forth. The jurors were participants in, spectators at, and lively gossips and newsmongers about such doings. As this world was reconstructed (or reinvented) by their tales, jurors emerge as active parties and participant-observers, not merely passive recipients of the sacraments or objects of clerical control of ritual, routine, and regulation.

Baptism

Baptism was the ceremony or activity most pertinent to fixing the memory of birth, and indeed, some aspect of baptism or baptism-centered events figures in the majority of ecclesiastical memories. Baptism was the familiar social-cum-sacramental event that marked the acceptance of the infant into the visible fellowship of Christ's Church.[62] It was also the festive occasion around which much socializing and celebrating was arranged—gifts, journeys, the generous provision of food and drink, feasting and hospitality, expansive statements about patriarchy and family continuity (and probably a lot of bawdy jokes, now gone with the wind).[63] To appreciate the full impact of a baptism on the community, we should think of the key moment—the infant at the font—as being but the midpoint of a drama embracing delivery and childbed, then the baptism, and lastly the post-baptismal celebrations. The church service was the main and the middle act that would not be fully concluded until the mother herself had been churched some weeks later. Preceding the baptism, as our reconstruction is guided by jurors' memories, we have such events as men of the village being dispatched to bear invitations and summonses for the ceremony. Several links in this chain of vicarious involvement are combined in a statement from one of our more expansive jurors: he had been "present when William Anketill came from his house at Leigh where Thomas was born and asked Katharine wife of Arnold Fauconcer to be godmother. Consenting, she asked him to accompany her to the church. . . . He went, was present at the baptism and returned with her to her house where she gave him bread, cheese and good red wine and thanked him" (XIX, 997).

Fetching godparents meant having the honor of bearing good news. It was a break from the ordinary, and perhaps a fleeting moment for playing a role of some importance—being first in the know, we might say. Many jurors had served as messengers. Others told, at second hand, of this task as performed by friends and kinsfolk. Nor were godparents the only ones to be summoned on short notice; an absent father might have to be fetched from whatever "men's business" had beckoned when his wife's confinement was imminent. Three jurors told of how they had gone "immediately . . . to Ifield in Sussex and told Richard de Ponynges the father of Robert [of the birth], and he gave them 20s. each" (XVIII, 990). If being the messenger was of minor importance compared with the role of parents or godparents, there could still be the windfall of gifts and rewards. As well as presents from godparents and others to whom our heralds had brought the good news, the heir's father might respond in openhanded fashion. The pleasure of having sired a child and of seeing a spouse through her confinement was apt to be expressed through the transfer of tangible objects. In a Proof for a hereditary peer, the exchange was in keeping with the infant's status: "John Laurence, soldier, 48 and more, was sent to England by Elizabeth the mother to enquire about the status of the baptism [of the future Earl Marshal] and was given a new suit costing £10 by her" (XIX, 336).[64] Two jurors offered a common statement on the birth of the Poynings heir: they "saw Robert born in the house of Robert Fitzpayn . . . and they immediately rode to Woodsford . . . and told Guy de Briene, senior, knight, kinsman of Isabel, mother of Robert, and he gave them each 40s." (XVIII, 990).[65]

Recollections based on hearsay and second-hand involvement appear as well: "Thomas Frere, 45 and more, was shown 100s. in gold by William Chamberlayne who had been given it by John the father for being the first to bring him the news" (XVIII, 997).[66] It was the sight of the coins given to another—not the juror's own receipt of them—that had fixed his memory. And no doubt the gift was intended, in part, to preserve the moment in memory; it was still easy for Thomas to recall that he "was sent to Beawrepayre to announce the birth to Elizabeth wife of William de Wyham, which day the said Elizabeth gave him a pair of shoes" (XVII, 955). The juror who carried news of this birth to the godmother received 10s. for his effort. When a juror says that he "was staying with the heir's father and brought him news of the birth," he is leaning toward the language of social equality. But his lesser status soon emerges, for he concludes by adding, "for which he [the juror] was given a tunic" (XV, 663).

Godparents played a key role in baptism and its trappings. Their identity and the details of their arrival, performance, and general demeanor were a well-remembered aspect of many a tale. They are usually named, along with any link they might have had with the jurors. Whether they had come from farther afield than the parish and whether they did anything of note beyond their prescribed role was often worth throwing in. Every now and then we can see how the invitation to stand as a godparent was, in itself, part of a social exchange—a two-way negotiation in which the parent might bestow status and honor by making the request, the godparent in turn lending his or her blessing by accepting the invitation and publicly playing a vital role.

In many Proofs, the godparents' names are included in the general information set out in the first juror's statement (the boilerplate), framing the basic facts of the case. He would name them and perhaps add that they had indeed performed their task. By the later Middle Ages, the convention was for a male child to have two godfathers, one godmother; for a female, the ratio was reversed, and the first juror's recollection extended to the enunciation of such details.[67] His basic narrative might be, "Robert Chayne, knight, John Chelesworth, late parson of the church of Bokton Malerbe, and Margery, wife of William Malerbe, were his [the heir's] godparents. He is 21 years of age and more" (XV, 292).

Because the godparents of our heirs were often people of some substance, their identities could be conjured up to add *gravitas* to the day's testimony. When the heir in question was the child of a great house, memories could run to the day on which men and women with some celebrity status had appeared on the scene. The village was not apt to forget an aristocratic visitation. Such memories (and their elaboration through retelling) were the centerpiece of many an evening's talk over ale or the spinning wheel. When the earl of Salisbury was the heir in question, a juror recalled that he had "held the stirrup of Thomas of Woodstock, earl of Gloucester, godfather, when he descended from his palfrey at the church door and held the palfrey while the duke was in the church" (XIX, 655).[68] Several men remembered seeing the earls of Arundel and of Salisbury and Elizabeth Despenser as godparents at Richard Lestraunge's baptism, though no one mentioned any noteworthy words, deeds, or gifts (XVIII, 944).[69]

The formal duty of the godparent was to name the child—to give the Christian name that the priest would bestow upon the infant. We can detect negotiations about the choice of names and the pecking order of the godparents; lines of stress became visible amid the ceremony of the occasion. John Sperton, juror for a Beaumont heir, had been in church and "was surprised that Henry [the infant] did not bear the same name as his godfather, Thomas la Warre" (XVIII, 998).[70] Sometimes not even the presumptive godfather knew what was going on, as in the case of Hugh Kynder of Glossop. The juror had been at Hugh's house to negotiate the purchase of an ox. But, as he told the tale, "now Hugh was starting for the parish church . . . to be the heir's godfather, and because he stayed too long a certain Robert Hyde became godfather" (XVI, 336).[71] A variation on this comes from a juror who said that he "asked Robert, abbot of Myddleton, to take a son of his from the baptismal font, but the abbot could not do so because on that day he was to be godfather to the said heir" (XV, 663).[72] Though some jurors had served as godparents themselves and looked back on their role with every indication of pride, one man had to admit that "he was godfather . . . but was so ill that he was unable to be present on that day" (XVIII, 999). Memories of ill health resurface in these recollections, and perhaps the awareness of the proximity of life to death heightened sensitivities. A memory that involved the abbot of Missenden as a godfather concluded, "he had an illness called 'le collyk' and could hardly act." The recollection of holding the towels so the godparents could wash their hands may have been a nod to hygiene as well as to ceremony

(XIX, 339).⁷³ One ceremony was particularly problematic, as there had been six rather than the customary three (or four) godparents. The day was recalled for the "multiplicity of promises" that resulted from the extra hands at the font (XVIII, 944).⁷⁴

As well as the jurors who told of fetching parents and godparents, we have men who recalled the birth because they encountered people on their way to church for the baptism. These travelers might be key players coming from afar, or they might just be neighbors, now wending their way down the high street. Such memories were usually a mix of things seen, heard, and done. One juror was more particular. It had been the grandfather "who told him that his family had been increased because Beatrice his daughter had given birth to Isabel" (XVIII, 999).⁷⁵ Another recounted—no doubt to the amusement of his fellows— a visit with the heir's father: "For joy at the heir's birth [the juror] became so drunk that he fell down and broke his leg in the hall of Wyderyngton [Witherington]" (XVII, 275). (The memorable accident was a common theme, as we shall see below.) Sometimes the news was disseminated in that odd and casual way in which people recall and transmit items of interest—things we might have expected them to tell from the first. Two jurors said they had settled a protracted charge of a "plea of debt" with the abbot of Stradmerghell (Strata Marcella?), and after they had made their peace, the abbot invited them to dinner. It was "during dinner [that] the abbot told them of the birth of the said heir because he was his godfather" (XV, 659).

Beyond the socializing and the showing off, baptism was a sacred if not always a solemn matter. The great day began with a procession from home to church, and many of the family and community joined in somewhere along the way. They carried unlit tapers, wine, and other paraphernalia, and—neither last nor least—the baby, perhaps swaddled in fancy blankets and special clothing. The parade was clearly of interest to bystanders. One juror learned of the birth because he "met the party of godparents in the highway by the church" (XVIII, 309).⁷⁶ Another had been more central: "John Hemergy, aged 60 years and more, agrees and knows this because he carried the said Edward to the church on the day of the baptism" (XVII, 1318). The recollections are an odd mix. One juror had been in church for a loveday. And yet eight of his fellow jurors offered memories that centered on having been in the same church, and none of them made any reference to the loveday—seemingly a more striking memory and a more notable event than just another baptism (XV, 76). In the Proof of Lord Botreaux, two jurors, in a common memory, told of having seen young William "in the arms of various women being carried from the chamber to the hall and hence to the church with unlit torches" (XIX, 999).⁷⁷

In church, the priest naturally held pride of place, and many jurors supplied his name and such details as whether he had been new to the parish or whether he was still alive and holding the living. But he did not operate in a vacuum, and memories of the ceremony radiated outward to include those who had stood beside him, who had helped with the objects used in the ceremony, and who had helped record it.[78] The picture we get is of a sacramental ritual enacted amid a bustling gathering of kin and onlookers, conducted at the font in full sight and sound of invited guests and many others who, for countless reasons (and recollections), also happened to be in church. It was a disordered but usually rejoicing community, and the extent to which ritual merged into spectator sport reminds us of the fluid boundaries between sacred and profane. The scene, as testimony slowly reveals it, brings to mind an image depicted by a Flemish master; the circumcision of Christ, perhaps, being conducted amid a throng of kinfolk, parents, village elders, well-wishers, and strangely shaped, oddly dressed itinerants who jostle each other to get a glimpse.

The distinction between observation and an active role does get noted. John Lynton had "held the book beside the chaplain at the baptism," whereas John Longe had simply been in church "reading the third morning lesson and heard William crying at the font" (XVIII, 673).[79] One godmother certainly played an active role: she "carried him in her hands to the high altar in the church and all the other altars there, in accordance with custom," or so one juror recounted (XV, 159).[80] And details abound. A juror spoke of having seen the vicar "wrap him [the infant] in a linen cloth called 'crisme' marked at the head with a cross of red and gold silk" (XVII, 1110). Another, the parson's servant, had "with a towel brought the chrism from the high altar to the font when the said Hugh was baptized" (XVII, 955). A juror in Leicester recalled that after church he had gone "to the rectory to fetch salt for the baptism" (XVIII, 672). In a Proof that centers around memories of the baptism, no fewer than seven men refer to "things seen" in church (XVIII, 855).[81] A couple of jurors at Bromesgrove added an air of reverence rarely found in our accounts: "they knew because each of them at the time of the heir's baptism held in his hand a lighted torch on account of the solemnity of the service" (XVI, 1057).

Nor did the festivities end with the christening. The return procession, from church to house or hall, could be a grand one, fondly remembered by those who had participated in it and even by some who had merely seen it. On the way to church, the tapers and torches were as yet unlit; on the way home, they were ablaze, held aloft for all to see. Much of this testimony is of the "what I saw" sort, and the procession of torches was a signal that all had gone well. John Stowe, now 60 and more, remembered "four men carrying torches without lights to the church . . . and afterwards the torches were carried lighted from the church to the castle" (XVIII, 998).[82] After the ceremony and the return procession came the banquet marking the child's entry into the body of social England. If poverty and the pressure of another mouth to feed diluted the joy of the occasion for the poor, at the social level of these heirs, we can assume sufficient resources to make it a moment of joy and festival. There is a baptism-at-Cana touch in many of the recollections. Richard Roke had been serving as "a serjeant of the earl's buttery," and he had "carried two silver-gilt jugs of 'Clary' and 'Malmsey' from the manor to the church for the godparents and other bystanders to drink" (XIX, 655). One proud father set the table with roast goose and red wine and then announced, as his guests ate, that he "thanked God for sending him an heir" (XIX, 997).[83] A good servant knew his duties; the parker of Folkingham "took rabbits from the warren of Quarrington in his bailiwick for the dinner of those who were at the baptism" (XVIII, 998).[84] Some jurors, perhaps of more humble stock, had not been invited to the house but had been invited to drink "white and red wine sent to the church by the father [before] . . . returning to their houses" (XIX, 784); on their way home they had seen "Henry Tailour's house on fire and went to put it out." Whether the juror who "later in the day had a meal with Roger de Wyderyngton, the heir's father," was at the banquet cannot be determined (XVII, 275).[85]

Memories also ran to presents for the infant, either handed over in the church or at the banquet. For children of wealthy families, these could be valuable and gaudy, leaving a long mark on jurors' memories. Young Maurice Bruyn had been given a white palfrey by the bishop of London (and the messenger, a gift of 6s. 8d. "for his trouble"), a "silver goblet with a gilt cover" from the parson of South Ockendon, and additional silver from a London goldsmith (XIX, 343). A juror who had been an esquire of the prior of Worcester told of his master sending "a silver goblet with 100s. for the baptism," a gift he himself had delivered (XVIII, 855).[86] An heir of lesser rank probably meant more pedestrian gifts. When Robert de Stodhowe's son was born, the jurors told of such gifts as a red cow from the vicar, "a godfather's present," and "a pike, three feet long and more," taken from the Tees ("that runs by the vill") and given "as a present to the boy's father" (XVIII, 953).

As we have seen, numerous jurors mentioned births or baptisms recorded in a missal. The priest or chaplain was literate, and the Church and its records were the obvious repository for such data—an appropriate conjunction, regardless of what the jurors themselves could make of the written record. "John Spencer agrees in all respects with John Hachard, and entered the day of the birth, to wit, 22 May, 35 Edward III, in the missal of the church of Deuelyssh," to put it efficiently and concisely (XV, 663).[87] Again, it was the act of writing—in this case by the juror, John Spencer—that was attested. He was not giving the escheator a public reading from the missal.

Baptism was remembered as a ritual involving parents, godparents, and community. But the mother herself—in contrast to the father and many, many others—rarely figured in her own right in these brief tales. Memories of her plight are found in attestations that focus on her health, on the difficulty and danger of confinement, on the search for a nurse, and then on her churching. The odd touch of drama is always welcome. One juror learned of the heir's birth when he saw a group of village women carrying the baby to the baptism, "amongst them Katherine his niece who told him that Isabel mother of William was in danger of dying" (XIX, 1003).[88] Thomas Bell had accompanied one godfather "to the house of John Clervaux the grandfather to see the child's mother, who was very ill" (XVIII, 953).[89] Once in a while the mother herself was deemed newsworthy without even having to be at death's door: "John Wattes, 51, heard on the Monday after Palm Sunday that Margaret was delivered of Ivo, and sent her a gallon of sweet wine" (XVIII, 310).[90]

The midwife's identity and role might also be mentioned; many jurors were of the social stripe whence these invaluable women usually came, and midwives were woven into their fabric of remembered experience.[91] Two jurors, in a common statement, said they had met "several people coming from the church, including Cecily Goodfellow, the common midwife in those parts, who was carrying a child in her arms wrapped in a fine cloth, and [she] told them he was the son of Robert and baptized John" (XVIII, 995; other testimony here names the wet nurse—another juror's wife—and tells of meeting a woman who "was with Margery the mother at the birth"). A Cambridge juror attested that "his wife was with the mother all through the night," which probably means that she had witnessed and assisted at the birth (XVIII, 673).[92] One juror had been the receiver of Ralph Cromwell, a man of importance and the heiress's grandfather. Cromwell had instructed the juror, now a man of 60, to "give the midwife 20s." (XIX, 666).[93]

If the midwife's part came first, that of the nurse followed close behind.[94] In some instances, jurors offer statements that blur the distinction between these feminine roles. Two men learned of the birth "because on that day they saw Ellen atte Gate, nurse of the said Robert, carrying him wrapped in linen and woollen cloths of divers colours, who said that she was with the said Robert's mother at the time of his birth" (XVII, 1110). Which role had Ms. atte Gate played, midwife or wet nurse? One juror remembered the baby having been placed with its nurse because the nurse's husband, a carpenter, had built a house for the juror that year, while another man had been sent to check on the baby—placed with the nurse two days after the baptism—and "for his trouble" received a gold ring (XIX, 343).[95] Sometimes the juror's role was more central: he "was present, saw her raised from the font, and found her a nurse who stayed with her until she was weaned" (XIX, 666).[96] In one peculiar memory, six men had a common recollection of two other men who brought the infant from Dinsdale on Tees to Silton in Yorkshire, "to be in care of a nurse there on the morrow of Trinity, when he was aged 6 weeks" (XVIII, 530).[97] Nor were men always excluded from the world of "women's business." John Ouseby "had a discussion with the midwife and other women, through which they found a good wet nurse" (XVIII, 998).⁹⁸ The close-knit quality of village life shows here: a juror's sister had been the nurse, and another spoke of having seen the infant "at her nurse's breast" (XV, 663, 656).⁹⁹

Like most aspects of birth that were mother-centered, her churching is but rarely mentioned.¹⁰⁰ The churching of Geoffrey Loterell's mother—wife of Andrew but never accorded the full dignity of a Christian name—figured significantly in her son's Proof. One juror remembered the event because he heard mass on the day she was churched; a second had sold meats to the father for the churching feast; a third had sold her the clothes she wore to church for the ceremony (XIX, 158).¹⁰¹ Two jurors remembered the heir's birth because "on Sunday a month after the said 20 November they saw Joyce the heir's mother purified of her said boy" (XVI, 1057). The language of pollution was the normal mode of expression or discourse on such matters; the jurors were but men of their time. The mother's churching was a convenient handle for male memory, though the recollection might have little to do with motherhood. We learn that "Thomas Male of Gedney . . . was then a rent collector of James the father and delivered money to the steward of his household for the churching of the mother" (XIX, 1000). There was little role for the men of the community in the actual service, and it remains uncertain whether the four jurors who recalled a dinner "in the hall of James Daudelee of Helee on the occasion of the getting-up [*resureccione*] of the said Fulk's mother" were simply noting the time or describing a common feast (XVI, 74).¹⁰²

Baptism and the memories that swirl around it, considered in their social context, take us into the workings of community at a moment when common activity, bound up in feast and celebration, was the focal point of life and of recollection. If baptism was the *rite de passage* that marked the entry point for the child, it was also the opportunity for a public show that renewed fellowship and stressed the bonds of community, kinship, and shared experience. Other memories linked to the Church have no comparable common element. They are more a random scattering of things done, seen, heard, and somehow remembered.

Because baptism was performed in the parish church (and the Proofs are invariably precise regarding place and date), we can move on to other church-related activities that revolved around this physical center of community life.¹⁰³ As we might expect, many jurors refer to the fact that parish churches and chapels were built, maintained, and repaired by lay hands. Of course, Richard Waldeyeve may have been more of a donor than a hard-hat construction worker: he "had a wooden cross made and raised in the church on that day in honour of the Trinity and for the health of his soul" (XVIII, 667). Another juror recalled that he had been "with a mason in the chapel making a new window" (XIX, 779). Bigger projects needed more hands, and several jurors had been part of a work crew ("they and others") for the foundations of the belfry (XV, 652).[104] One large job had been hampered by the obstacles that plague such projects: "there were sixteen carts that day at Santon Downham laden with stone for the repair of Stowlangtoft church. One fell by the way with a broken axle," as the juror now recalled (XIX, 782).

The ornaments and sacramental paraphernalia of the church were probably the most precious as well as the finest objects in the community; we need not wonder that memories about them might stick. Sometimes the juror had simply been an observer: "the patron of the church . . . gave a whole vestment of green silk for the souls of his late father and mother" (XIX, 341). In one instance it was conversation, not property, that fixed the date for four men in a common statement: "on that day [they] were together when they heard that John Harewell, then bishop of Bath and Wells, had a new bell made at Wells weighing eight thousand [?] pounds" (XVIII, 390).[105] A Proof from Derbyshire offers a number of recollections that center on lay contributions to the parish. In addition to a bond regarding work that would "well and faithfully enclose the churchyard," five men (now all in their 60s) recollected that "they were there on the same day and bought a missal from the parishioners of Sutton and gave it to the church of del Heth because the missal of that church had been stolen," and two others said that "they were present on that day, and the parishioners of Sutton began to make two altars in the body of the church" (XV, 892). As the repository of goods and money, the church might also be a magnet for human weakness, and assembling an inventory of its valuables helped ensure that prized objects did not wander off. One juror recalled "at that same time Master William . . . archdeacon of Norwich visited the church and caused to be enrolled there in his register all the ornaments of the church, which enrollment was noted in the processional . . . by inspection of which the deponent is sure of Margaret's age" (XVI, 1053).[106]

Men who served as church wardens found that rendering their accounts was an acceptable milestone for subsequent recollections. Three men testified that "they were in the church that day to account for the church goods which they had in their custody as church wardens" (XVI, 339).[107] By the late fourteenth century, this duty was routine: the jurors had assembled and "rendered their final account of their terms as warden of the goods . . . before Robert Malstank, auditor of the said account" (XV, 894). Two jurors left a statement that sounds as though they had been guardians of and keepers or recorders of the accounts: "they rendered account of goods etc. bequeathed to St. Mary . . . at divers times, as is enrolled in the missal there" (XV, 449).[108]

The parish church was the center of the community, and, accordingly, the appropriate place for the celebration of lovedays, on which feuds were resolved and the peace of Christ and of forgiving brothers (and sisters) triumphed over the forces of wrath and rancor. Sacred space was hardly immune from pollution, and the rededication of a church was likely to stand out in memory.[109] A juror talked of the reconsecration of the church after blood had been shed and of a visit by Alexander Neville, archbishop of York (XIX, 341). We trust that "the effusion of blood and pollution" within church walls was not so common as to fade beyond recall (XIX, 1002).[110] In a Berkshire Proof, three men offered a common memory: "in the year of the heir's birth there was a dispute between the parish chaplain there and one of his parishioners, and the chaplain was killed" (XVI, 345).[111] Five jurors in Hampshire told of a quarrel between the prior of Motesfunte (Mottisfont) and the vicar of Little Sumbourne "touching tithes of lambs." They had been with the prior at the loveday when "an agreement was made between the parties" and the heir was born (XV, 451).[112] References to events of interest might be mentioned in such a casual fashion that we can only guess at what had been happening: "John de Walyngton, aged 60 years, knows this because he was in the church at a loveday at the time of the baptism" (XV, 76).

Other Ecclesiastical Memories

Beyond the boundaries of church and churchyard are other recollections that touched on ecclesiastical matters and contacts. When we looked at memories of births, we found jurors who referred to a son, now ordained or admitted into religious life, as the fixed point for their timekeeping. The memories might cover their own children or near relatives, or they could extend to others in the village or the church. A number of local networks are subsumed in the statement of a 70-year-old man in a Hastings family Proof. He remembered that "John son of Joan Askern, now parish clerk of Campsall and aged 22 years and more, was born in the year preceding the birth of Edward, whose wet nurse Joan was, and John owing to his age expects this year to be ordained priest" (XVIII, 854). Another man's recollections were of a similar sort: "he remembers because on the same Monday a kinsman [*cognatus*] of his named Richard assumed the religious habit of the monks of the order of St. Benedict at Wenlock" (XVI, 947).[113] Even the ecclesiastical career path of a woman might figure in a juror's memory. One said that "in the same year his daughter Katharine became a nun in the house of Katesby [Catesby] and was professed there," and another told of "Agnes his sister [who] was elected prioress of the nuns of Arthington" on the same day as the baptism (XV, 159, 893).[114]

Some jurors indicated whether the baptismal priest had been newly installed, or was still holding the living, or had died in the interval. Given local interest in such matters, this seems reasonable information to impart. The laity kept an eye on ecclesiastical personnel, and the priest who had performed the baptism was often named in the first juror's statement. The heir had been "baptised in the parish church . . . by Richard de Sunderland, then parish chaplain of the said church, who is still living" (XVI, 81).¹¹⁵ Sometimes memories were even more precise, more informed and informative. In an unusual touch, two jurors for one Proof were clerics: the prior of Kirkham and the rector of Bulmer. The latter recalled that "he was inducted and instituted to the church of Bulmer at Easter before the said John's birth and it is noted in the missal," and the prior attested that he himself had performed the baptism, and that he "named him John on the said day, 49 Edward III" (XVII, 954). Lay memories could also supply these details. Three jurors remembered that "James son of John le Vynour, chaplain, celebrated his first mass in the said church and they were there and made an offering to him as his first mass" (XVII, 274).¹¹⁶ Another priest's first mass was marked by "offerings [made] because of friendship with him" (XVI, 78).

Pilgrimage seems to have been as popular in life as in poetry. Dozens of jurors had either set off on such journeys around the critical time, or they remembered others who had done so. Pilgrimage was a major communal activity that took people a long way from the village—both in terms of miles and of duration. And of the scores of men who went to Canterbury, or Rome, or Santiago, or the Holy Land, few seem to have gone off without companions. Even for those who had stayed at home, the journey of friends and relatives remained memorable, especially when some now being remembered had failed to make the journey home.¹¹⁷ Canterbury was a natural magnet in this world. Four jurors of Bedfordshire had gone off together "on 10 June 1381 . . . and when they returned to Houghton Conquest six days later they found all their houses and barns in Chapel End there accidently burnt down." Incendiary accidents in the summer of 1381 were not uncommon.¹¹⁸ Another attestation shows how a soon-to-be father arranged his priorities, though the men were only setting out from Cambridge: "Edward Brond, 62, was on a pilgrimage to Canterbury with Fulk's father when his [Fulk's] mother was pregnant and gave birth" (XVIII, 1180).¹¹⁹ News from home might catch up with them as well. Three jurors recalled that "they were journeying on pilgrimage to St. Thomas of Canterbury, and during their pilgrimage they were told in London of the birth of the said heir by Robert de Hoo, the heir's godfather" (XVII, 429).

Many pilgrims set their eyes on a more distant mecca; memories of a journey to Santiago figure in some tales. Two jurors, each listed as being 54, told how, "on Thursday before All Saints in the same year they set out together for Santiago in accordance with an oath which they jointly took when in peril of water" (XV, 449). And beyond the shrine of St. James lay Jerusalem, far away, the goal of an even more ambitious journey. One man recalled that "Robert Stock, his father, in the same year started on a pilgrimage to the Holy Land, where he died" (XV, 159).¹²⁰ Two milestones, associated as cause and effect, came to mind: "in that year William de Waltham, his father, set out for Jerusalem and died beyond the seas and in that year the said John entered into his inheritance"

(XVII, 576). William de Sutton said "that on the same day his brother William started on a pilgrimage to the Roman Court, and has not yet returned" (XV, 893).

Hundreds of memories like these can be strung together to offer us a "merry England" perspective on the Church and the world. Baptismal festivities sound as though they were choreographed for a documentary film on popular culture and folklife in pre-Reformation times—if not for a painting by Brueghel or even by Bosch.[121] Dashing about with the news of birth, flocking to the road on the great day, helping the priest at the ceremony, feasting and cheering and drinking all combine for a picturesque view of traditional society. Carnival raised its chaotic head. Whether the vision so presented is true to life, let alone representative, is less easy to judge, as it was shaped by a series of one-line recollections resting on moments or occasions of high socialization. Such memories had been warmed at the hearth of harmonious relations between sexes and classes (with a few exceptions). Moreover, relations between spiritual authorities and the laity were probably more cordial on such occasions than on many others.

We can also, in these concluding comments, enlarge upon aspects of the Church barely touched upon, let alone significantly illuminated by the recollections. We had but a single reference to last rites—an interesting comparison to the several hundred recollections of baptisms and deaths. Two men in Essex recalled that "as they were walking towards the church of Eppyng [Epping] they met the parish clerk running for the vicar to visit and confess John de Eppyng, then *in extremis*, who died the same day about the hour of vespers" (XVII, 1110).[122] Two men in Cambridge thought back to the critical day, a day on which they had accompanied the chancellor of Cambridge to the church and afterward had gone "to the house of the friars minor to hear the preaching of holy scripture" (XVIII, 310).[123] This is virtually the only memory concerning the liturgical side of the Church, beyond the ceremonies accompanying a *rite de passage*.

There was but a reference or two to sexual scandal touching the clergy, and from Chaucer's England this would seem to be a remarkable tribute either to clerical morality or to a disinclination to revive prurient gossip. A reference from London is more puzzling than enlightening: "the same day the vicar of the said church was arrested at the Compter and was delivered for the baptism" (XVII, 1321).[124] There were mentions of quarrels between clerics and villagers (and even with other clerics), and some quarrels turned bloody, even deadly. But from a body of almost two thousand statements, a few such memories argue neither for a dissolute and irreligious clergy nor for a striking lay focus on clerical shortcomings.[125]

Rather, a routinized Church and an informed laity make up most of the picture. The sources reveal but also shape the realities and recollections of ordinary life. The mini-narratives were created and transmitted within narrow boundaries of discourse. One-line evocations leave tales unresolved, experiences undigested.

Could we but follow the tales of baptismal drinking and feasting to their conclusion, or the tales of one-way pilgrimages or wardens' accounts through to the "bottom line," less sentimental considerations might tilt the balance of the memory as offered. But in fairness, jurors' testimonies were normally grouped around moments of resolved or suspended conflict. They were rich in the aura of fellowship and reunion. If adversarial and confrontational episodes of life were not that easy to forget, there seems to have been little community interest in dredging them up when it came time to tell *why* and *how* one still remembered the events of the Tuesday after Michaelmas twenty-one years before. Individual dignity and pride in recollection, rather, were dominant. As we look back upon the public performances that collectively produced the Proof of Age, the sun had shone brightly (unless bad weather was part of the memory), journeys had been happy and successful (unless one fell and broke an arm or was robbed by Welshmen), and life had generally been good and festive (unless one had gone to church to bury the dead).

MEMORIES OF THE SECULAR WORLD

Memories that hearkened back to the events and milestones of the secular world were spread all over the map. The diversity of these attestations—and the inherent interest of some of the more unusual among them—makes generalizing about these experiences and recollections more a choice of impressions and anecdotes than of statistical incidence. At the same time, some types of recollections were common to scores of jurors; just because a theme is recurrent is no reason to treat it dismissively. The interplay of the ordinary and the dramatic is in keeping with the experiences and memories of life.

We can begin with what was consequential but mundane. Many attested memories went back to transactions involving real property. Men who stepped forward as jurors, even for this minor form of public role, were apt to be well above the humble toilers of the fields, the marginal and dispossessed. Many jurors, in fact, seem to have been men of reasonable if modest substance. The property transactions to which they refer may not have been their only ventures in this area, and for some, we may be hearing a convenient but hardly unique memory. Some, no doubt, were seasoned players in the land market: buying, leasing, renting, farming, exchanging, enlarging holdings, cooperating with neighbors and in-laws in deals and the many other forms of related activity we know from customals, rentals, and the courts of the manorial lord and the king.

Certainly more jurors talk of acquiring bits of property, under varying terms and conditions, than they do of selling or leasing it. But these are matters of impression and degree, not of dogma, and whether we are getting a representative take on the lower levels of the economic scene is hard to determine.[126] When we surveyed life-cycle memories we dealt with events or milestones well-nigh universal to the human condition. We might now suggest that most freemen were apt to have been involved in transactions over land at some point in their adult lives—an experiential and social life cycle that went alongside the biological one. Did their memories, as jurors, single out such involvement as an adult male prerogative, one that set them above the landless and, usually, above most of the women of their world? They certainly spoke, years later, with a voice of conviction and recollection about such matters that compares well with what they said about marriages, births, and deaths. Perhaps two jurors had been partners in a bit of business just after witnessing the baptism, as their common testimony of the critical date attests: "Richard acquired a messuage . . . from John to hold to himself and his heirs. Geoffrey Deen made a charter of enfeoffment, which was witnessed by the parson" (XIX, 777). Another juror had come to the chapel "to acquire 6 acres for life from John Plecy the grandfather for a rent of 6s.8d., payable at Michaelmas."

In keeping with a transaction involving real property, references to the written record are especially common: "he sealed the deed . . . and knows [the date of the baptism] by the date of the deed" (XIX, 664). Or perhaps outright purchase: "afterwards [the juror] bought a messuage and 20 acres from Thomas Tamise, godfather, rendering 10s. by equal parts at Easter and Michaelmas. Walter Clerk wrote the indenture" (XIX, 786). Nor were all the transactions rural. A juror in York remembered when he "took at farm the house in which he now dwells in Castlegate . . . for 10 years from the Martinmas then next following," and a fellow juror spoke of the time when he had "bought a tenement in York . . . by charter of enfeoffment" (XIX, 139). We also have references to "things seen." One man had been a witness when the heir's father enfeoffed the rector, "in all his land in Houghton Conquest on certain conditions after seisin" (XVIII, 665), and another took, together with his wife, "certain lands for life by indenture" from the heir's father. Business and life-cycle milestones might run together: "he purchased for himself and his heirs 6 acres land . . . from Thomas Chamberlayn, chamberlain of the said John de Cherleton [the infant's father] and the said Thomas could not come to deliver seisin because of business arising out of the birth" (XV, 659). Some transactions were substantial. Three jurors said they had taken "at farm from the lord de Ferrers the manor of Coton by Blakemere for 30s., as appears in an indenture" (XV, 894).

All in all, the references to land transactions confirm the lively level of activity that studies of manorial courts and peasant mobility reveal to be business as usual. We can cite jurors who remembered a birth and baptism because it coincided with the acquisition of a holding, with being disseised, with acquiring land by indenture, with leasing pasture, with paying rent, with acquiring the farm of a house, with buying a wood, with selling a toft, with taking possession of demesne land, with coming into control of "husbandland," and with a purchase under the terms of a charter.[127] Nor does this long list exhaust the possibilities. It simply gives an idea of their scope.

Some memories tallied for life-cycle material touched on moments of inheritance and the transmission of real property, either between or within generations. Death in the family was the likely time for such a transfer, as we can imagine, and one did not have to be particularly callous to recall that "in the year of the birth . . . his father died, and his father's lands descended to him by hereditary right" (xv, 664). A juror in Derby told of his brother's death and his chance to move to the head of the queue: the brother "would have been his father William's heir if he had lived" (xviii, 315).[128] We have testimonies that hinge on the writing of wills and the naming of executors as well. The juror who recollected that "in the same year John Philip, his father-in-law, died, and appointed him his executor," was on firm ground for his certainty (xv, 664).[129] A man in Hereford said that after the baptism the chaplain came to his house to "make a will for Margaret, his mother, now deceased," and, as her executor, he remembers the date. A Wiltshire man had a comparable memory, except the dying woman had been Alice, his wife (xix, 778, 786).[130]

Disasters in the Proofs

One feature of the Proofs that has invited derision among their critics is their frequent resort to two particular kinds of memories: those recounting an injury (to self or another) and those relating to buildings that either burned down or were blown down. Though such events may have been frequent features of "real life," the convenient way they jumped up to coincide with the need for (and timing of) a pertinent recollection is intriguing, to pass no harsher judgment. But regardless of whether such memories were of things that had happened then, or that had happened but at some other time, or whether there was leeway concerning both reality and timing, such memories were common and frequently offered, replete with circumstantial touches that give them at least a sufficient veneer of verisimilitude. Tales of injury were presented in a fairly formulaic fashion. The injured party had been on a journey (perhaps going to or returning from the baptism), or working on a roof or in some comparable exposed setting, when he (or a friend, relative, or some other resident of the village) had fallen and suffered sore hurt. It was usually a broken bone: legs (shins), arms, and ribs were the common loci of suffering.[131] Broken necks were also reported, but they have been dealt with in the memories linked to mortality. Jurors in a Proof held at Louth tried to vary the fare: one talked of a man who "was seen by many people to be caught by a gust of the north wind" as he fell from the roof, while two other jurors, in a common memory, tell how the latter man's father "was blind and fell into a well at that time and was almost drowned" (XVIII, 326).[132]

Though we might wish to dismiss them, these accidents (or "memories" of accidents) left an impression that could be summoned as needed. One man recalled that "as he was crossing the ferry at Berlynges . . . the ferry-boat sank and he hardly escaped with his life," though this may be misadventure rather than accident (XVII, 430). Another man in this jury told of having a horse, worth 40s., fall and break its leg. Insult was added to injury when a man said he had brought horses to the church for the baptismal party's convenience and one horse "kicked him in the eye so that he lost it" (XVII, 955). The most elaborate of these recollections, in keeping with the universal desire to regale others with details of one's health, came from a juror at Werkworth (Warkworth), who said that "a beam fell and broke his head almost to the brain." Nor did it end there: "a fortnight later he came to the leech at Werkworth to have his head cured, and saw the said Mary at the door of the church prepared to undergo the sacrament of baptism" (XV, 656). (This is about the only accident tale that mentions the victim seeking medical help.) Many were eager to add their touches: "on the third day after the birth he was struck in the back with a knife by John Casteleyn," or "he fell from a horse and was ill for a quarter of a year and nearly died" (XV, 891, 447).[133]

Pedestrian injuries, the result of mischance or negligence, were familiar features of daily life, and jurors who chose this theme might add an occasional touch of drama.[134] Injuries to children lingered in memory: one man remembered when "his firstborn son cut his left arm with a knife so that his life was despaired of," and another said that "his daughter Joan broke her shin that day" (XV, 450; XIX, 339).[135] Maybe injuries were likely with so much construction and maintenance always needed: jurors spoke of falls from roofs, or from the ladder to a dovecote, or while building a house, or while "tiling a new house."[136] Nor were journeys, especially on rough horses on rough roads, a guaranteed safe passage. One juror recalled that on his way from York to Beverley, he had reached Barmby on the Moor when he "fell from his horse and broke his left arm, and was laid up for a long while" (XIX, 139).[137]

That people fell off horses and roofs, and into ditches and wells, is not hard to accept. Nor is it unlikely that such accidents would fix themselves in memory. To extend this logic, it is hardly improbable that houses burned down or blew down due to "acts of God" and/or human negligence and corner-cutting in both construction and maintenance. Presumably both the quality of work and the materials used allowed for such happenings, albeit not so frequently or so casually that they passed without notice. Jurors at one Proof had tales of a chaplain's house catching fire and of the chapel's bell tower coming down in "a high wind" (XVIII, 675).[138] Great windstorms were long remembered, or at least conjured up when needed: "a great house called 'le Halle Berne,' which stood next the church on the east side, was blown down by the wind the day after the birth," and three jurors, now in their 50s, "saw it" (XVI, 88). Towns were places of even greater risk. Two 60-year-olds from Gloucester recalled the day when "divers shops of theirs . . . were burnt" (XVII, 578). The building might go up, lock, stock, and barrel: "his house was burnt with nearly all his goods" (XVII, 953). Disasters are exciting, and the day the windmill burned or the cross blew off the belfry was memorable in the most literal sense (XVI, 89, 54). But when a juror recalled that "the house of Richard Munceux in Bescoby [Bescaby, Leicestershire] was totally destroyed by fire," we find that no other juror, of the remaining eleven who stood with him, made any reference to Munceux or his misfortunes (XVIII, 672).

In fairness to our jurors, if they had many tales of house burnings and wind razings, they also had a store of memories that hinged on more positive aspects of construction, repairs, and alterations. The human landscape of town and village was not being systematically destroyed. Goings-up more or less balanced the comings-down. In one recollection, "[he] raised a newly built chamber in Mollington on that day" (XVIII, 663). In another instance, some of the jurors had gathered "to put up a newly built house," and then they went to church to *hear* mass and in church they *saw* the godmother hold the infant at the font (XVII, 274). Once it was a juror, supported in recollection by two fellows, who "was beginning to new-build a barn at Pembrugg [Pembridge]" when all three men saw the infant carried to church (XVI, 339). The touch that added a final splash of credibility is the line, "he built for himself a house at Ifeld [Ifield] wherein he still dwells" (XV, 77). Others offered variations: the building of a horse mill, an extension to a stable, an additional chamber to a dwelling (XIX, 998, 349; XVIII, 664).[139] One man had struck it rich. He was a carpenter, and at the time of the heir's birth he had been engaged by the earl of Salisbury "to build a new house," for which the earl's steward had paid him 13s. 4d. (XIX, 655).[140]

Workaday Memories

Beyond construction and deconstruction, all sorts of odd memories are recorded to plunge us into the busy and helter-skelter world of economic activity. Relatively few recollections refer to agricultural routines and the cycles of fields and crops in contrast to life and work in village and town. What most people did most of the time was perhaps so matter-of-fact that it provided little background against which memories were readily placed—at least in contrast to those occasional dips into the world of real property and construction. On a jury where one man said that he had "covered with reeds a great house called 'shepe,'" others had dug a fishpond for the archbishop and built a kitchen at Camberwell. One juror recalled that he had carried corn in his cart (XIX, 344). Another, of higher status, spoke of the day "his servants took some oaks in Inglewood forest" (XIX, 791).[141] Compared to this, having mowed a meadow was not very impressive (XVIII, 994). While we can make little of what jurors *did not* talk about, the drab nature of work in the fields was obviously brightened by any unusual incidents that could be set against its nondescript hues.[142]

Animals and stock, as assets, occasionally figured in our tales (more often than field crops). Dramatic and unfortunate moments came to mind: "a greyhound of the abbot of Langley entered the fold . . . and killed 35 ewes the following night" (XIX, 783).[143] Another juror, in a variation of the "falling building" motif, recollected that "a building . . . called 'carthous' fell down and a sow with 11 piglets and 5 calves were crushed and killed by the lower door" (XIX, 782).[144] But animals, too, were acquired as well as lost, just as new buildings replaced those that had blown over. One juror had gone to the market at Dudley "to buy four oxen for his plough" (XVIII, 994).[145] It is in the nature of recollection that most stories had a problem at their core. Two jurors, in a common memory, said they had learned of the infant's birth as they walked the fields seeking animals that had strayed. The baby was well, but "their beasts had been impounded at the manor," as the bailiff rather smugly informed them (XVIII, 995).

Work was what people were engaged in, most of the time, and though odd events during baptisms are far more numerous and presumably more memorable, we do have memories that zero in on dominant life activities. A number of jurors looked back to their apprenticeships. One recalled that he had been "apprenticed carpenter with master Walter Asshele, carpenter of West Woodhay" at the time of the baptism. The date was fixed in his memory "by the indenture of apprenticeship" (XIX, 188). He was 50 now; certainly he had not just begun his training at 29 or 30. Another juror, now 40, recalled that "his father caused him to be apprenticed . . . in the trade of a saddler, by covenant contained in certain indentures" (XV, 291). One juror said he had been bound as an apprentice to a butcher, though seven years would seem a long time for this rough craft (XVI, 1053). Still another man spoke of an eight-year term but did not specify the mystery or craft (XVI, 77). At the other end of the spectrum was the juror, now 49, who simply remembered having been "retained as a carpenter . . . to build a new chamber in the manor," for which he had received 10s. (XIX, 343).

One basic village craftsman only gets recounted in one memory, and even that is in a supporting role. A juror said that he had run into the village smith's house "to heat an iron rod with which the water in the font was heated for the baptism" (XVIII, 310).[146] Some references were to craft work, such as weaving, while others went back to rougher labor in the fields: making a fishpond and building a sheepfold (XIX, 188); covering a house with reeds (XIX, 344); building a sheepfold of eight posts (XV, 893); measuring a field called "Pirifeld" (XVIII, 666).

Jurors engaged in these activities had seen the baptismal procession on its way to or from church. Such memories are those of the outsider and his gaze—of the one not invited to attend. A lot of miscellaneous activity comes in for mention. Men were involved in buying and selling raw and finished goods, and they could be pretty frank about acknowledging their wiles. One juror recalled that "on the morrow of the baptism [he] bought a black horse from William Ryngwode for 10 marks and sold it next day to Richard Rose for 20 marks" (XIX, 999).[147] Quite a few men learned of the heir's birth while at a market or fair, a reasonable occasion for news gathering. Four jurors had been together "at a fair at South Petherton" when they were asked to witness the notation of the birth (XVIII, 858; see also XVII, 1320). Markets and fairs were memorable occasions, and testimonies often hinge on the opportunity they provided for bumping into people and catching up on the news. A market was for local business, and a birth of which a juror learned while at Corby was another of those unexceptional memories (XIX, 158).[148] Two men, in a different Proof from Corby, pushed farther afield and spoke of the market at Grantham (XIX, 478). (One juror saw the baby while he was at Grantham, and the other had journeyed back to Bassingthorpe, where he was told the news.)

Fairs make bolder lines on the economic graph than markets, although jurors were at pains to say that at Lekehamstede (Leckhamstead), Berkshire, "there is a small fair" on the feast of St. Valentine, the day of the baptism (XV, 658). News of an heir born at Bergh (Burgh) and baptized at Lokynton (Lockington) reached jurors who had gone to a fair at Aldborough in Holderness, and a man who bought three horses at the fair at Fakenham, in Norfolk, seemed to have no trouble fixing the date (XVII, 1320; XIX, 783).[149] Of all the references to travel for business (in contrast to pilgrimage), perhaps the most interesting—and putting us in mind of Margaret Paston's many requests for goods from London—was the recollection of a juror in Derby. He had gone "to London to get various colours for his art on that day." The heir's father, hearing of the intended journey, "asked him to buy various fowl for him, if they were for sale there," and in the conversation the infant's father happened to mention to our juror "that his wife had a daughter Thomasia on that day" (XVIII, 315). The fowl, presumably, were for the feast. Other references to economic activity appear, few so evocative but all reminding us that the daily routine, when it touched upon the memorable or unusual, was a realistic way of marking the occasion.

A good deal of what we refer to as daily routine embraced business ventures of some sort. Three jurors, for instance, had "entered into a bond in 100 marks with Richard Toggeford for wool bought from him" (XV, 448).[150] This may have been a larger transaction than most of their fellow jurors were involved in, though selling crops or wool was not all that novel (XVI, 1053; XIX, 139). A quick glimpse of some proto-capitalists emerges in references to posting a bond to cover a debt or mortgage. One juror paid the handsome sum of 100s. for a horse; in the bond, he said he would pay this by Easter (XIX, 781; the baptism had been on 7 January 1395, and Easter in 1395 fell on 11 April).[151] Men engaged in larger enterprises were likely to travel, and memories could be wrapped around their journeys. (As we asked when we talked of pilgrimages, was it the novelty of the journey or a reference to the familiar that kept it a focus of memory?) One juror recalled that the heir's father and godfather had been "joint owners of a ship bringing coals from Newcastle upon Tyne [and they] lost her at sea near Whitby in a great storm" (XIX, 341). Voyages and visits touched on familiar places as well as exotic ones. A man in York recalled the baptism because "he took leave of his neighbours in the said church on his journey to the Isle of Man" that day (XV, 893).[152] A juror at Guildford recalled the year "he crossed the sea to Normandy," and another said "that in the same year he crossed to Burdeaux [*sic*] and bought wine there, and that was 21 [years] ago and more" (XV, 657). Travel to Calais ("beginning a journey to Calais and heard mass in the church") was probably fairly familiar, but a trip to Italy proved to be the final one for a York juror's elder brother, who "crossed the sea to parts of Lombardy and there died" (XVII, 1318, 954).

Government and the Larger World

Though we read these Proofs as the voice of the village, many jurors were clearly more interested in recounting experiences in and of the larger world,[153] and memories bespeak a leap from local routines to cosmopolitan adventures. If the jurors were men familiar with the ways and byways of the kingdom, we can read their statements as signs of some wider sophistication. Quite a few Proofs refer to an involvement in the machinery of government, the heavy wheels of justice. The involvement might have been personal and direct—a victim, or a cog in the administrative machinery—or it might have been that of a spectator who just happened to be at an interesting place at the right moment.

Involvement in the procedures of government did bestow a measure of status, or of drama, upon those so touched. Holding office was certainly memorable; men were not shy about referring to these adventures as the substance of their one-line tales. A former constable of Tattershall remembered that it was on that day that he "arrested John Hunter . . . for assaulting and wounding Roger Egire" (XVII, 430). Four jurors had been "before the justices of assize" at Gloucester when "news of the birth" came to them (XVI, 1054).[154] One Proof rested heavily on the recollections of public-spirited men; four jurors had been at Deerhurst "on an inquisition taken before the sheriff of Gloucester at his tourn there," while four others had been at Gloucester "for the taking of a special assize" (XVI, 55). They might speak of the time they had held the lord's court, or had served as jurors beyond the village, or had appeared before the king's justices.[155] One man had been involved in raising the hue and cry after a homicide, and he was still eager to tell the tale: "on that day John Storme was killed by Thomas Dykson at Winderwath. Dykson fled to the park of Whinfell and Bertram [the juror] pursued him for the felony and was told of the birth" (XVIII, 675).

More exciting than service within the system was a brush, perhaps at some remove, with criminal proceedings. Men told of the taking of thieves, of jail delivery, and of the swift and irreversible consequences that often were the final chapter in such matters. Others knew the darker side of the "criminal justice" system. One complicated memory touches on a number of these themes. The juror had bought twenty stone of wool for ten marks. The bailiffs then "arrested the wool, claiming the custom, because he was a tenant and burgess of John late duke of Lancaster of his town of Wimborne Minster . . . and no tenant or burgher could buy or sell in any market or fair in England. He showed letters patent of the duke and was discharged" (XIX, 997). If this man got away without a blot on his copybook, others were not beyond reproach. One juror, now only 42, recounted that he had hit the bailiff of the heir's father "on the head with a sword, for which transgression he paid the bailiff 100s." (XVIII, 1148). Two jurors recalled that "they fought each other and drew blood from each other with a sword, for which they were amerced at the great tourn of Bradeford [Bradford] . . . before Henry de Wotton, steward there" (XV, 449).[156] But while one juror said that "in the same year a certain Henry Matte beat him and wounded him almost to death," a fellow juror could only fall back on a civil matter: "he was distrained of 2 oxen by the ministers of John Berners [the father] for arrears of homage and other services" (XV, 657).[157]

Men of experience and substance were apt, then, to offer memories that went beyond village and neighborhood, though the dynamic could run in many directions. Sometimes it was a victim's tale: "despoiled of a horse by robbers," or, as told by three jurors, "despoiled by robbers of goods and chattels to the value of £20 at Erbury by Blakemere in a place called 'le Walshepas'" (XV, 450, 894). A number of jurors had been present at coroners' inquisitions, some as spectators, others to testify (XVIII, 530, 677).[158] Memories were mixed; a juror in York had a tale of having been arrested "immediately after the baptism . . . on a plea of trespass" (XIX, 341), while another reminisced about a theft of "about 60 large eels" by Robert Mostarde, who had married Joan, the juror's mother (XIX, 349).[159]

A number of jurors had played the good subject's role in criminal cases and they were now disposed to speak of it. Two jurors in Beverley remembered that they had viewed the body for the coroner when the chaplain had broken his neck on the day of the baptism (XIX, 781). A juror in Suffolk related that a thief "was taken that day with a grey horse . . . he was taken to the gaol at Bury St. Edmunds where he was hanged at the next delivery" (XIX, 782).[160] Six men had been with the sheriff "about the death of John Boukyn of Gateshead" when they heard the news of the birth, "and by the date of the inquisition in the custody of the coroner . . . they are sure of his age" (XVIII, 530). We have one instance where an incident, no doubt quite dramatic some years earlier, now was related in the usual laconic fashion. The juror had presumably been more excited on the occasion. On the night after he heard of the birth, robbers had stolen his horse. But "afterwards they were taken . . . tried before the justices of gaol delivery . . convicted and hanged, and by a copy of the record and process he is sure of her birth" (XVII, 953).[161] Quick justice was common, and these terse memories bind cause to effect with admirable economy. A Norfolk jury returned two such tales: "that day an unknown thief was arrested at Loddon with 10 sheep stolen at Norton Subcourse, and he was taken to Norwich castle," and "Alan Morel, a common thief was arrested for felon on that day, taken to Norwich castle and remained there until he was hanged" (XIX, 783).[162] Other aspects of government and of politics beyond the village intruded into lives and left a lasting impression. For the men of towns, the more structured political framework might mean different activities, different memories. Urban jurors could look back to the day on which they had become freemen of the town, while others dated recollections by naming that year's office holders.[163] A variation on this was a recollection of officials who did *not* hold office: "when Christina was born there was a great split (*cisma*) in connection with the election of a mayor of Southampton" (XV, 452).

Nor was the colorful side of urban life without its mark, and the ritual of the pillory left an impression worth noting. Perhaps recalling such an incident was amusing and popular with one's fellows. Three Londoners had a recollection of a cook being punished "for selling a stinking eel pie and other unwholesome victuals" (XVII, 577). Though bad eel pie was a favorite for such treatment, we find variations; one miscreant stood "in the pillory for selling a stinking rib of beef and other unwholesome victuals" (XVII, 957).[164] Other urban memories were not as droll: "in the same month he was himself put and sworn upon the livery of the city [of York]" (XIX, 139). One Londoner's memory was very much in the mainstream: "on the same day Nicholas Brembre, then being mayor of London, held a common council at the Guildhall, to which he was summoned but was not present so that he was amerced" (XVII, 1321; this had been in January, 1 Richard II).

The world beyond the village was intriguing—less familiar but not wholly remote. Some mobility, even for agricultural and domestic workers, was part of the routine and rhythm of life. How much this translated into a systematic interest in the larger polity is hard to estimate, but we readily accept that scraps of gossip—news, "disinformation," tales of wider wonders—were all in common currency. Some degree of interest in their betters and in current events does show through. Were these occasional references merely the tip of an iceberg of curiosity and reminiscence? Certainly, in a world where one could pick up and go to Canterbury or to the shrine of St. James or even to Jerusalem, men of status were presumably not without some knowledge of affairs in London or York.

A few jurors tied personal experience to matters of larger import. Some recollections, though, are in the "more fun to talk about later than to live through at the time" category. One juror remembered the baptism because he "was taken prisoner in Brittany in the following year and held to ransom," while two jurors in Penrith spoke of the burial of a fellow who had been "killed by the Scots" (XIX, 392, 663). A less fatal variation came from the juror who himself "on that day was captured by the Scots enemy and taken into Scotland."[165] One northern juror's memory of having been taken captive touched on domestic rather than external disorder: he had been "that day captured by Thomas Grey of Hetton and taken to Norham castle against his will" (XIX, 897). If few recollections were frivolous, not all were as dire as those of abduction and captivity. Robert Vavasour—whose surname may connote a loftier social status—"was retained that day by Sir Henry Percy to serve with Richard II in Scotland" (XIX, 341).[166] It seemed reasonable to date a baptism by its proximity to the day on which "the king's French enemies burnt Portsmouth . . . and the king's bailiff warned them to be ready to resist" (XIX, 1002). Such references to the larger realm are intriguing. We have enough of them to support the idea of local interest in larger matters, but not enough to give much feeling for the scope or accuracy of this public awareness. Because of the terse nature of the statements, we have only hints at whole worlds of subtext and of understated narrative. Though 1400 was a dangerous year in which to refer to such matters, in a Proof at Coventry (XVIII, 313), we have memories that go back to Richard II's early days. One man claimed that he had been in London "in the king's chancery, seeking a common pardon for himself, such as the king granted to all his lieges." Two men, former servants of the prior of Kenilworth, remembered that "Edward III died on 21 June following the birth." Two servants of the heir's father "were sent to London to their master, who was awaiting the coronation of the new king," and two others had been "servants of Edward III at the time of his death and long before." They came home to Kenilworth "after the [king's] burial" and so "heard of the birth and baptism."[167]

Other news of the kingdom occasionally seeps in. A Proof that went back to events of the spring of 1388 mentioned "rumors touching King Richard" (XIX, 655). As with references to courts and crime, we hear of personal events as well as news that had been gathered at the common well. One man at Newcastle pinpointed the day because he "rode into Scotland with Robert Umfravill, uncle of Gilbert [the heir now coming of age], with a great force" (XIX, 1005). Other tales in the same vein were told: when "Henry, now earl of Northumberland, warden of the marches, rode with a large force into Scotland," or when "Edward late prince of Wales crossed with his army to Aquitaine." Jurors in Southampton used local news, referring to when "the lady of the Isle of Wight was dead" and "the time . . . [when] the abbot of Beaulieu died" (XV, 452).[168]

One odd touch came from a juror who said that a godfather of Lord Deyncourt's son was "a certain Roger Beauford, brother of the pope [Gregory XI], a prisoner of John duke of Lancaster in the custody of John Deyncourt in the castle" (XVIII, 313). In an effort to gauge what these men knew and cared of the world, we should take note of the man who had gone to church "to hear news from Ireland" concerning Edmund, earl of March (XVIII, 677). But this yields place to the juror who set Edmund Hastynge's birth in "the year after the rebellion of the commons of England . . . which was in the summer 22 years ago" (XVIII, 854).[169] Not much can be done to flesh out a reference to an heir's father who "was summoned to be at Stowe St. Edward before the sheriff of Gloucester to transact business on behalf of the king" (XVII, 274). Personal reflections showed men who had their own brush with the unexpected; an elderly juror in Lincoln said that "on the day of the said Hugh's birth he took passage to St. James in a newly built ship called *Le Marie* and on the way home the ship was broken by the sea" (XVII, 955).[170]

Who can say what would leave an ineradicable impression and be accepted as credible? We know that village life carried its share of disagreements, some escalating to violence and bloodshed, and such excitement could vie with snippets culled from the outside world. If the parish church was the site of lovedays and concords, quarrels and contentions were going on elsewhere. Sometimes the recollection indicates a low-key conclusion to strident business: one juror had just written out "a release of all personal actions" from the other—perhaps relating to debts rather than violence (XIX, 786).[171] In a Dorset Proof, four jurors, now in their 60s and "separately questioned," told of being in church while four others (including the heir's father) were "put to the arbitration" to settle a "longstanding dispute" between two others, "now deceased." The decision was "that each should release to the other, and they [the jurors] know by the date of the releases" (XIX, 664).[172]

Lovedays, as formal events, were not unfamiliar. While we note those of great ceremony by or between prominent people, they had prosaic counterparts all over the realm. One loveday between two brothers was settled with an indenture, "which for certain causes is still in the custody" of the first juror; by this, six jurors of a common recollection "are well assured of the age of Agnes" (XVI, 649). We find references to quarrels between churchmen, formally resolved in a fashion that was still remembered: "a dispute between the rector of Estisted and the vicar of Aulton touching tithes of wool." At the loveday "they were all present," and afterward the vicar performed the baptism of the heir (XV, 158; also see XV, 451). For a quarrel between a man and a woman—an unusual instance of male-female relations—the result was "peace between them" as arranged by the very juror who called up this memory, or so he now claimed (XVII, 954).[173] Some jurors were sideline guests, not active parties in the concord. Four Londoners had been in church with Nicholas Exton, mayor in 1386, "as witnesses for divers matters in dispute between the prior of Merton and William Moore, then one of the sheriffs" (XIX, 476).[174]

Death, whether near at hand or a bit removed, was always of interest. It stayed fixed in memory—the marker around which other events were arranged. In addition to family deaths, dealt with above, jurors remembered those of other villagers and even of notable outsiders. There is little to build on with a memory that "on the same day Sir John, rector of the said church, died" (XV, 452). Some deaths, we note, were recalled with a touch that makes them vivid in their compressed recitation. In one Proof, jurors recalled the day in question because the baptism had coincided with the death of Thomas, brother of John: he had died "on that day after 9 and before 3 o'clock" (XVIII, 860; this is one of the very few recollections that talk of the hour of the day in precise or numerical terms). Two London jurors spoke of how, "on the day of her birth, Edmund Holdernesse, 'maryner' . . . died suddenly in the king's highway without Algate" (XVII, 957). We learn no more about "one John Horne . . . slaughtered on the said day," except that the memory of his death was still alive some twenty-one years later (XVII, 1319). On the jury that aired details of the Southampton mayoral election, one man's tale bridged the provincial and the national. In a Proof for the sister co-heiresses, he said that "at the time of the birth of Juliana [the elder sister] the lady of the Isle of Wight was dead, and at the time of the birth of Christina [the younger sister] the abbot of Beaulieu died" (XV, 452). This was precise as well as concise. We can contrast it with a recollection that is remarkable for its ability to give virtually no details: "a certain parson of the said church was entombed the same day in the churchyard of the said church on the south side" (XVI, 341). One grim memory raises questions but offers few answers: "on the same day John Rokeley killed a stranger at Tetterbury at the market there, and at the same time the birth . . . was reported" (XVI, 76).[175]

Leisure and Social Life

Not all jurors conjured up such dark tales. Just as the Proof was put together as part of a public occasion, embedded in the community's performative life, so recollections could recall play, unstructured leisure time, and social rituals to set against the tableaux of broken arms and the quick resort to the noose. In fact, many of the stories of injuries told of drunken men falling in church or at the baptismal feast, sure ways of raising a laugh. We have glimpses of rustic humor, and ludic activity probably played a larger part in the routines of village life than the extant sources indicate. Memories of archery seem to have triggered a routinized tale: six jurors, in a common memory, told of "practicing archery in a field by the churchyard" when they saw the midwife carrying the infant to her baptism (XIX, 900).[176] No tales of mishaps from arrows gone astray: the picture is rather of group activity conducted in the center of the village, "opposite the church" and "beside the churchyard" (XVIII, 662, 890). Whatever else men did to while away the hours, their memories were recorded with virtually no reference to what women did beyond keeping each other company. One juror, with the rueful humor of the passing years, said he had been at the baptism "and played with a player at buckler play (*parmam?*) there and broke his finger" (XIX, 1000).[177] There was more of this sort. One juror said he had come to the village "to see some cockfights, as is the custom of the country, and when the fights were finished" he had gone to the new heir's house where he saw the infant "at his mother's breast" (XVI, 336). Sacred space could be made to do for purposes of a lesser sort, as with the juror who recalled that he "was at the church for a cockfight between John de Sikes and Robert de Heth" (XVIII, 677).[178] There are references to wrestling, though it may have been impromptu activity arising from competitive masculinity, not organized sport. Some memories take us back to those tales of accidents: two jurors had been "wrestling together within the sight of the manor . . . and John broke Stephen's shin" (XVIII, 890).[179]

We have Proofs that make hunting and the delivery of game the focal point of collective recollections. The Proof for Edmund Holand, brother and heir of Thomas, earl of Kent, was tightly wrapped around such memories. Jurors spoke of bringing twelve partridges to the heir's father, of killing a deer, of delivering two swans to the mother, of a wild boar killed and offered as a gift, and of presenting twelve capons and twenty-four hens (XVIII, 979).[180] If few Proofs are this focused, statements that rest on hunting memories are not hard to find. In a Proof from Corbridge, jurors told of meeting "some huntsmen pursuing a fox from his own woods" and going with some neighbors to "hunt with a greyhound" (XIX, 1003).[181] Other tales refer to the work of those charged with providing for the table. Certainly the lord's parker, who "took rabbits for the [baptismal] dinner," was not getting meat by mere chance while walking in the fields (XVIII, 998). One juror claimed he had been with the infant's father when he "saw a sitting hare, shot it in the head with an arrow and sent it to Beatrice the mother." Another juror "took two pheasants," however obtained, to the celebration (XVIII, 999). Though there are no hunting accidents of the William Rufus variety, a number of men told of having fallen from horses while hunting—in contrast, perhaps, to the large number who fell while otherwise engaged. There may be a sardonic touch to the statement of three Cambridge jurors: they remembered "because John Londen, clerk, as he went hunting on the same day, fell from his black horse near the church and broke his left arm, and they saw it" (XVI, 89).[182]

It is easy to accept that in a world so tightly governed by the demands of the agricultural calendar and the contingencies of nature, unusual occurrences could be well remembered—perhaps with the same impulse to dramatize and exaggerate that is commonly part and parcel of reminiscences about extreme weather. We would certainly like more information, in a Proof of June 1403, about the "earthquake through all England" when the infant was born "in May 21 years ago" (XVIII, 854).[183] A torrential rainstorm might not seem so far out of the run of ordinary events, but memories still revolved around it: two men recalling their attempt to reach Lincoln for Michaelmas said that "it rained so heavily and the waters rose so much that they scarcely avoided being drowned" (XVIII, 886). We return, in these tales, to that underreported realm of crops and fields: "heavy rain on that day, the waters overran the banks of the Bain and covered all the grass so that the hay was full of sand" (XIX, 665).[184] One elderly juror of 70 talked of a storm "about midday . . . [that] knocked men and women to the ground" (XIX, 783). Another storm also left its imprint; a juror recalled that the mill had been destroyed by the flooding of the Eden, and a fellow juror recalled that "William his brother was drowned in the river Eden by the chapel" (XVIII, 675).[185] In a world where nature ruled, we have a reference to the time when, in a great tempest, "the sea broke over the shore at North Coates [in Lincolnshire] and a great part of the country was submerged" (XVIII, 316). Though strong winds were blamed for many falls from roofs and ladders, sometimes they just became part of a general reflection: "a mighty wind throughout England 24 years ago" (XVI, 107).

COMMUNITIES LARGE AND SMALL

The general picture of domestic life in the Proofs is mostly noteworthy for its decorum; we find few references to sexual scandal involving clerics, and none touching anyone else at all. Whatever waves of gossip broke over the village, the sea was invariably calm when the escheator took his formal statements. Furthermore, traditional morality was the norm, at least as the Proofs depict life. All the children whose births, marriages, deaths, ordinations, and miscellaneous labors are mentioned were born in wedlock. The whores and bastards, the instances of infanticide, the undeserving and threatening poor and jobless and homeless, and the seduced and abandoned maidservants were tucked well out of sight and mind. No unruly youth gangs made after-dark pursuits hazardous. Merry England was mostly confined to getting drunk and then falling while trying to get up on a chair to see the baptism, though an afternoon at the butts was acceptable as well.

In their recollections, then, the jurors unfurl brightly colored banners of community as they march across the stage. "Community" has been a popular term for so long among historians that by now some have come to think of it as a concept unlikely to guide us toward any new insights or analysis. Some of the current interest in how community has been treated in the literature has been referred to in the introduction to this book. But whether we choose to approach community as an institution, an abstraction, or a methodological beacon to guide us through choppy waters of conflict and change, it is hard to sum up this journey into the world of the Proofs without a little more discussion of the issue.

In the world I reconstruct from the Proofs, several definitions or conceptualizations of community beckon. If we wish, we can concentrate on the idea of community writ large, that is, English society in the fourteenth and fifteenth century as some sort of coherent and comprehensible entity, albeit one riddled with class struggle and all the many woes to which the body social was vulnerable. And within this larger setting we can visualize each jury as a case study—the community in miniature, a representative fragment of a firmament of interaction and structure. The world revealed by any given Proof stands as a cross section; sometimes typical, sometimes deviating from a mythical or hypothetical norm in its depiction of life. But regardless of its eccentricity or its typicality, each Proof is read as a microcosm of the whole.

The community of a given Proof can be thought of as a social unit, frozen in time. It became incarnate as a result of a summons to twelve jurors, joined for the moment and now given set form for their common business. There is an element of circularity in this, as it locks into a single embrace the events of "then" (the time of the heir's birth), the "now" of the Proof, and the written record that preserved it all into an indefinite future. That the Proofs can be read as case studies through which the fabric of English society is revealed has been our working premise. Though we are well aware of their limits and blind spots, much has been made here of what they tell us at face value, whether it illuminates "what really happened" or some formulaic and/or imaginative depiction. Many of their throwaway memories have a terse and evocative narrative power, thanks either to the juror or to his recording angel. We are well within the accepted conventions of historical methodology when we offer a background of common tales, such as those legions of memories about being in the church at the baptism, and a foreground of the more eccentric and dramatic, such as the godfathers' quarrel over the infant's name or the thief taken in the market and his ensuing short journey to quick justice.

So the idea of each Proof as a representative chip off the rough-hewn block of late medieval society is our key to this kind of presentation. But there are other aspects of the concept of community to consider. One of these relates to the frequent resort to common memory, by groups of jurors, touching joint action or group behavior on that long-ago but critical day. This banding of men, their activities, and (now) their memories is another of our bedrock themes. We have noted how frequently two or more jurors—usually even-numbered groups, occasionally reaching to all twelve—offered a common statement or a joint memory of a common experience on the day in question. The jurors, as typical men of the village, seem true to form. For reasons we cannot fathom, these particular twelve had been constituted as the jury, the chosen twelve. Whether they were twelve who really had a relevant memory, or whether it was all by lottery in some random fashion, escapes us. Neither the intervening years nor the nature of their common activity, however, rendered their statements improbable. The memories in a Proof had to be realistic, and both individual and collective ones—whether genuine or fabricated—had to reach the safe harbor of collective credibility.

The Proof of Age, as an aggregation of memories, is one approach to the issue of community. We can also turn to the jury and the jurors. A jury of twelve men is a small group, too small to be statistically significant. On the other hand, a group of twelve is larger than most sports teams, and it exceeds by two those needed for the prayer service that marks a Jewish community's identity. The twelve were deemed, over many centuries and for many purposes, to be "big enough." The jury as a social unit gains strength from the very element of randomness (and presumed typicality) that marked its composition. In theory, any group of twelve men would do as well as any other; a medieval jury was not impaneled to uncover "new" information but to convey to the supervising official what they already knew, to lend their attestation to undisputed "facts."[186]

What emerges from this focus on the jury? As a group of free peasants and townsmen, jurors represent the middling men of their community, the respectable and substantial figures in the minor league of village and neighborhood society. On those juries where the first juror assumed a role as spokesman, his tale stands as the defining one, the court of first resort. Was he the "alpha juror" by virtue of casual and ephemeral selection, or do we have the village headman in action? In some Proofs, his statement establishes the basic facts; subsequent jurors just indicate agreement with his recollection. But this was by no means a prevailing pattern, and in many Proofs, tales follow with no acknowledgment of those that had come before.

When we say that a jury comprised men of middling free status, we refer to economic and social rank.[187] We have innumerable memories of jurors as buyers and sellers, of their role in construction and building, of trips to markets and fairs, and of freedom to pick up and head for Canterbury or Jerusalem. Any man who spoke of the day when he had "been robbed of 20 marks on the Ridge

Way," or of when he had returned "from the fair at Fakenham with three horses bought there," or when, as "patron of the Church of Weaverthorpe," he had been moved to give "a whole vestment of green silk for the souls of his late father and mother," was not a man mired in the lower depths (XVIII, 994; XIX, 783, 341). Furthermore, there are indications that many jurors had gone up a bit in the world in the years between the baptism and the Proof. Their position now—as village elders in middle age or beyond—was apt to be more dignified and affluent than it had been two decades before.

If most jurors were of middling status, we find a few who came from a loftier socioeconomic plateau. When one among them was a man of more substance, it was he who would serve as first juror, the spokesman who offered the leading information. And when men of serious prominence were among the jurors, we can usually assume that we have before us the Proof of an heir of a great family. The Proof for John Mowbray, earl marshal, rested on recollections of well-placed jurors: an alderman of Calais who was a former mayor, ten men with a military identity, a burgess of Calais, an esquire, and a final juror who identified himself as a former servant of the earl's father (XIX, 336).[188] This Proof is at one pole of the social and political world. Few others could match such a gathering. A Proof for the Dacre heir had no jurors of substance, that for Fulk FitzWaryn but a single knight, and he the first juror (XIX, 663; XVI, 74).[189] Other juries were somewhere in between. The Proof of John de Wyderyngton, a Northumberland squire, began with a statement from the two knights, followed by the two godfathers, and then eight nondescripts of the village (XVII, 275).[190] Though it was expected that jurors would be laymen, a few identified themselves as (former) servants of clerics, and an occasional cleric or man in orders did slip through the screening.[191]

More jurors had gone to fetch godparents than served as godparents. This too is a guide to status; the jurors were active participants, but mostly in supporting roles. But exceptions are always near at hand. Some had been godfathers, and others talked of their wives as godmothers. Lest this appear as a claim to more than is warranted, the juror as godparent rarely figured for a Proof of an important heir, and we mostly have cases of neighbors of modest station who stood in for friends and social equals. Though there was a social strategy in choosing godparents, few jurors were of sufficient status to be deemed a prize catch when they served in this capacity.

While a few jurors were clerics, and we find a few knights among their ranks, a more common role for those who identified themselves as linked to the rich and powerful was as a servant in the employ of important people, perhaps a member of a large household staff.[192] These ranks included a (former) household usher of the earl marshal, a steward of the heir's father's household, or—on the same jury—the godfather's chamberlain, and one who had been chamberlain to the heir's mother.[193] One juror had been "farmer of the land of John Chalers [the father] in Meldreth, and took his rent to Whaddon," where he saw the baptism in question (XVIII, 1178). Another remembered the date because his wife had been "a servant of Margaret," the mother, and had carried the infant to the church (XVIII, 310). One Proof, rich in such material, brought together men who had served as Lord Cromwell's chamberlain, gardener, and servant of his steward (XVII, 430).

These positions, we might say, were at the top of the "downstairs" world in which so many had spent some of their early years.[194] But for many jurors, an identity as a servant meant something a step below this, domestic and menial service carried out for a social superior. In most recollections the servant role is pertinent because it was in this capacity that the juror had had his contact with the birth and baptism. Many of these men had worked for clerics: servant of the parson of Turleigh, who had been a godfather, or esquire to the abbot of Shrewsbury, who performed the baptism, or esquire to Henry Cockfeld, then bishop of Worcester, who had done the baptizing.[195] A one-time servant of John, abbot of St. Albans, was one of those with the good fortune to carry the good news and so receive 20s. (XIX, 655).[196] A juror who had been an esquire to "a certain bishop called 'Seint Nicholasbisschop'" knew the less affluent world of suffragan bishops; he only received 40d. for his errands at the time of the baptism (XV, 159).

Many jurors looked back with pride and self-importance on memories emanating from their one-time subordinate status. We can point to those who carried food and wine to the church, who had been sent to fetch godparents, and who accompanied their masters and mistresses to church (XVII, 955).[197] But it was not all gifts and rewards and an up-close look at the rich and famous. There was a darker side, a counter to the memories of rewards for bringing good news and then of being plied with food and drink. Servants were to serve. One juror from that team of Cromwell servants recalled the critical time because "he was servant and chamberlain . . . and because he was not present in the chamber on the arrival of Sir Ralph from the chase . . . Sir Ralph struck him on the neck and felled him to the ground" (XVII, 430).[198] Another had a close call: "In the same year William de Fyenles, then lord of Hurstmonceaux, came to his house and would have beaten him" (XV, 160). In one instance it was the juror who spoke of his own servant, a memory from the other side of the line. John de Sereby, the juror, said that on the day of the baptism, "William Hamond, his servant . . . taking two jars of wine to the church, fell and spilled the wine out of the jar, for which the said John beat him" (XVII, 576).

The jury as a society in microcosm has been a running theme of this analysis. We have a mix of social ranks, a range of memories that were the consequence of close contact with social superiors, and a medley of positions of service and subordination. That the subordinate role played at the time of the baptism was no longer a mark of one's position might be something to look back on with nostalgia. It is easy to award oneself ex post facto dignity, though this did not hide the hard fist of a class-driven society. On the other hand, without drifting toward images of a village democracy, jurors' tales do speak of an easy mingling across class lines—a community in which no umbrage was taken because the humble knew about the sexual, obstetric, and domestic patterns of those who towered above. Babes at the breast and mothers purified in church so they could receive Holy Communion and marital embraces were as much a part of community lore as the knowledge of the brother lost in the swollen river or in a fall from the roof.

THE CONSTRUCTION OF MEMORY IN THE PROOFS

The world of jurors' memories is not one of rich verbiage. Proofs, as they made the journey from oral testimony to written record, are too laconic to give us much entrée into the realm of text and dialogue. But we can extract material that enables us to see how jurors pegged their memories in time. There is no way of determining whether a phrase used to indicate the timing of events was that of the juror or the scribe who ultimately scripted the Proof. But regardless of where credit should go, some credit is due. A juror—and usually it was the first juror—said that he remembered the time of birth or baptism because it took place at a time proximate to something else he could pin down. But usually he began the Proof with a declaration of the specific time or date of birth or baptism; the circular and self-encompassing aspects of the process relate to how the juror remembered, rather than to the "when" as such. A typical opening statement runs: "Madoc de Madoc . . . says that the said John son of John was born at Le Pole and baptized in the church there on Sunday the feast of St. Mark, 35 Edward III, and was 21 years of age and more on Monday after the same feast, 5 Richard II" (xv, 659).

Jurors had various styles of reference to link events and memories to the calendar, and they were not necessarily mutually exclusive. One style was to set the juror's "own" event against the birth or baptism in terms of degrees of temporal proximity, expressed in gradations of coevality. The event that triggered his memory took place on the same *day,* or in the same *week,* or in the same *month,* or even, at the outside, in the same *year.* This was a wide but acceptable range of precision (or approximation). It offers a degree of variation that runs from virtual simultaneity to memories of events spread some six months on either side of point zero. With a year as the boundary-setting unit, in the calendar and in common memory, we have an elastic but limited stretch within which recollections could meander. More than a year was almost never offered.

Though a full year certainly gives us a good deal of latitude, most memories were triggered by events considerably closer to the critical moment, and they fell on both sides of the zero point, with about an even distribution of before and after. Some Proofs have a heavy concentration of memories from one set interval or distance from *the* event, as when all twelve memories are from the same day. A Proof from Northumberland illustrates this: six men were in the church, for various purposes, "on the same day"; several were there "at the time" of the baptism; three others participated in the baptism itself (XV, 76). In another Proof the memories go back to "on the same day" of the baptism, though the recollections were of various activities.[199] One Proof asserts that the heiress had been born "on Monday after SS. Philip and James, 49 Edward III," and all the memories are of that "same Monday" (XVI, 947).[200] True or not, it was detailed and precise.

Some Proofs encompass a variety of dating schemes that conform to our rule of thumb of six months on either side. A Proof from Camberwell had recollections going back to "on the day," "in the week," "that month," and, in a memory of a mother-in-law's burial, simply "at that time" (XIX, 344).[201] In a February 1406 Proof from Sudbury, supporting an heir who had been baptized on 28 December, we hear of "within 15 days," "on 2 February following," "Easter week following," and "at Michaelmas," as well as some same-day events and five memories that went back to "the week following" (XIX, 785). At the other extreme is a Proof in which all twelve statements are vaguely placed within "the same year" (XV, 664).[202]

The ecclesiastical calendar was familiar, and there is nothing strange about the inclination of jurors or scribes to date memories in terms of the annual cycle of Church dates and feasts. A Proof from 3 Richard II was all over the calendar: memories of the Sunday after St. Peter's Chains, the feast of St. Michael, the Invention of the Holy Cross, the feast of St. Margaret the Virgin, and the Sunday before Midsummer day (XV, 291).[203] A Proof from the Welsh marches showed a touch of English chauvinism; events were dated in relation to the Thursday after St. Dunstan and "Monday after the feast of St. Augustine, Apostle of the English," as well as St. Mark, "St. John before the Latin gate [*sic*]," and the Invention of the Holy Cross (XV, 659). The statement of the first juror included the regnal year, a moderately common datum.

Within the time covered by the "same day" usage, there was still room for more precision, though these extras crop up in unlikely places. Jurors in Kent "collectively say" that an heir is now "of the age of 21 years, 7 weeks and 3 days," though their separate testimonies are of the usual "same day" and "same month" variety (XVI, 1054).[204] A few Proofs even plug us into the time of day: a juror learned of the impending baptism while having breakfast, and another fellow, drawing on some reservoir of knowledge from which we are excluded, knew that "the said Robert was born on the above day at dawn" (XVI, 648).[205] In one Proof the first juror says the heir had "been born at Mollington on 13 January 1380, before 9 o'clock and baptized . . . on the same day" (XVIII, 663).[206] Along this line is a Proof where the juror learned the news at nine o'clock, along with recollections of the father telling the news "at dawn" and of a juror's wife who had been with the mother "all through the night" (XVIII, 673). Lastly, in a common memory by some Norfolk men, the tale was of remembering the day (and time) because Thomas Norman, brother of juror John Norman, "died on that day after 9 and before 3 o'clock" (XVIII, 860).[207]

Though the jurors constituted a micro-community assembled for a specific occasion or purpose, and the Proofs constitute a reasonable and handsome collection of case-study segments of their world, they have aspects that make us pause. Jurors' memories, as we have said, had to *sound* credible. They were enunciated before neighbors and relatives as well as under oath. Even if they were rote fabrications and prearranged statements, they had to pass a standard of social reality and probability. After all, men did not marry and father children at twelve or thirteen, and one could neither claim a wife who never existed nor journeys to Jerusalem that had never been undertaken.

Even if individual statements had been rehearsed or assigned on the spot, and if different sets of Proofs turn up with a similar menu of memories, within the context of a given Proof there is little indication of memories being coordinated so they would fall together like ducks in a row. A few Proofs do display a striking focus on one particular activity, however, and for this reason they stand out. We have already seen a Proof that revolved around variations of hunting and meat-eating memories: a juror brought twelve partridges to the father, another killed a deer with the help of two greyhounds, one presented two swans, one killed a wild boar "in the said [New] forest," and one presented twelve capons and twenty-four hens (XVIII, 979). But it was unusual for a thematic concentration to embrace as many as these five jurors, though attestations that all the jurors had been in the church—usually on separate errands—are not hard to find. But in these cases the point often is that some, if not most, had been in church for a purpose other than the baptism (XIX, 777).[208] One Proof had three jurors with weather-related memories: a tower blown down "by a high wind," a mill destroyed by a flood, and a brother drowned by the same flood (XVIII, 675). In a Proof for two sister heiresses (and thus embracing twenty-four memories rather than twelve, as each juror had a separate memory for each sister), five jurors told of contact with the maternal grandfather on one or both birthdays, though once again this was out of the ordinary.[209]

The most striking single memories, apart from some that are obviously personal and pertain to such milestones as family deaths, relate to events such as the earthquake of 1382, floods, hangings, and the accession and coronation of

Richard II. And yet, with few exceptions, the pattern in the Proofs in which these memories appear is that the striking event is only recounted in the memory of a single juror. Because we invest so much weight in social memory and the collective culture and myth-history of village and community, we read the Proofs as a negotiated discourse between folk memory and written record. The Proof that talks of the earthquake also contains one of the two references to the "rebellion of the commons of England," and it has—in a reference to a man who cast the evil eye—the sole reference to the non-Christian supernatural and to folk magic. Meanwhile, the other jurors stood their own ground. Some learned of the birth by meeting the godfather, one knew the date because a boy born at the time was now approaching ordination, a daughter had been born, and two ribs had been broken in a fall (XVIII, 854).

At least there was no collusive effort to produce a single memory for all twelve men. There is no way to determine if there was a logic, or a strategy, in the selection and arrangement of the memories. In some Proofs, as in those centering on hunting, either a prearranged script was laid out or one memory triggered others of the same sort, and men who had worked together twenty-one years ago were probably quite inclined to reminisce about shared activities. In a Proof of 1385, half the jurors offered memories relating to contacts with the infant's maternal grandfather. Though the ages involved hardly made such recollection improbable, in no other Proof is the three-generation tie within a family mentioned so often (XVIII, 999). And why, given the status and curiosity of our jurors, do we have only one reference to Bishop Despenser's crusade (XVIII, 953)?[210]

I pose these questions as a reminder of the shifting sands of our sources and the mnemonic space within which the social construction of experience and memory is carried out. That we might expect, or hope for, more than two or three references to outbreaks of plague within a single Proof is, perhaps, our problem rather than theirs. Jurors' recollections can be thought of as an experiment we cannot replicate. If we ask friends or students to cobble together recollections centering on a common time or event (such as John F. Kennedy's death), we worry lest we load the dice with our phrasing of the question. The best we can do, in looking at the Proofs, is to accept that what they reveal is the way in which men chose to situate memories within the social landscape—controlled by an obligation not to subvert the business and by a desire both to be taken seriously and to foreground themselves among their fellows in recalling how an external event, such as a birth or baptism, was linked with the internal or the personal.[211]

Some final comments about the world revealed by the Proofs. All the jurors were male, of course, and all their memories are inflected by that masculinity. So in one sense, the Proofs are documents of gender exclusion. If they do not reflect "bias," as we use the term, they certainly are united in that they see the world from one side of the gender-constructed fence, and only and always from that one side. And yet they also open a door into community, one that, in this context, incorporates the domestic unit (physical, sexual, and personal) and the social processes and interactions of domesticity. No dialogue that centered so much on birth was apt to stray far from the subtext of women and sexuality, from labor pains and breast-feeding. We get many glimpses of male-female exchanges—between husbands and wives, brides and grooms, fathers and daughters and sisters, jurors and midwives and nurses and godmothers (who often outranked them socially), men at work and yet with sufficient free time to chat with the female passersby.

In many ways these exchanges blur the formalized and legalistic boundaries of public and private space. Most of the economic activity was man-to-man, or perhaps men-to-men. But we have enough exceptions—instances of men and women acting in concert or as opposites in a transaction—to keep us from an unyielding commitment to rigid lines of demarcation. Jurors talk, often casually rather than deliberatively, about news of births and baptisms they got from or imparted to their wives. Part of the scene that emerges is of women exchanging "women's news" with each other and of men doing the same with men. Another part is of men and women crossing gender barriers to gossip within and even beyond the home. But against this, almost none of the experiences beyond the village or neighborhood—trips to markets, pilgrimages, assizes in the county town—crosses gender lines. In these forays into the wider world, the records reflect male activity, at least as men later told the story. We know that women did not sit at home. Their own excursions, however, never seem to have been woven into the memories of their menfolk. Also, because many of the memories reflect experiences of the working world, we are reminded of how much labor was collective, social, and communal.

Memory selectively winnows and chooses what to include and what to omit. All memories in the Proofs are of some years ago; the waters of time erode sensitivity, as we see in the casual accounts of birth and death, drastic property losses, or tales of injury and misfortune. Only in the occasional reference to death is the poignancy of an earlier day still recoverable. The whole dynamic of the recollections emphasizes the cooperative and harmonious aspects of village life. Quarrels had been resolved in long-ago lovedays, losses softened by the years and the healing graces of mourning ritual and prayer. When we looked at memories that emerged from jurors as servants, we suggested that the harsh realities of service, with its explicit and brutal subordination, had largely been muted.

By extension, this irenic effect extends to the class and social conflict inherent in and endemic to community. Proofs reflect the memories of men of middling status offered at the moment when those of higher status were about to come into their own, thereby asserting dominance over the jurors and their world for another generation. And yet a Proof of Age proceeding was clearly not seen as the occasion for venting hostility, whether it centered on a specific wrong or emerged from a general sense of social malaise. The silence also speaks, sometimes eloquently, and the memories are but the articulated and recorded hints of lost biography, words and thoughts of men (and women) otherwise consigned to the dustbins of history. We have the fleeting tales of those who had a hand in the making of their history, albeit with little control over the larger and more intractable forces that drove them along.

Sir Richard Scrope and the Scrope and Grosvenor Depositions

RECOLLECTION RE-CREATES FELLOWSHIP

The Proofs of Age were assembled to form a mosaic of everyday life. Each juror's piece of colored glass has been arranged so that—under our hand and for our eye—the multitudinous harmonies and dissonances of begetting and burying, of journeys and labors, of kisses of peace and buffets of anger, and all the rest, take on a patterned meaning, an ordered significance that illuminates the course of the life cycle and the wonted routines of experience and recollection. And though the reconstruction is a historicist exercise, our goal has been to arrange a scene or to present excerpts from a drama that would have been familiar to those jurors, could we summon them once more to resume their fellowship and turn their eyes (and ears) upon our synthesis of their tales.

The world we now move to reconstruct is less comprehensive, based as it is on a close reading of the depositions offered on behalf of Sir Richard Scrope in his suit against Sir Robert Grosvenor concerning their competing claims to a coat of arms. It is not as suitable for a larger, more general depiction of the wide panorama of lived experience. On the other hand, the depositions have a focus and directed purpose that enable us, in synthesizing their collective "message," to coax from them nuances of cognition and memory and to re-create the fellowship of common experience and bonding on which they rest—to shore up the dike of social memory against the waters of time. If this is a smaller world than the one emerging from our reading of the Proofs, it is one whose personnel and patterns of interaction are more clearly defined. It takes us further down the corridors of recollection. What we lose in breadth we regain in depth, and the fact that we are working with longer statements and wider memories, even if they are almost as formulaic as those of the Proofs, augurs well for this endeavor.

In talking about the nature of our sources, we have seen that an elaborate administrative machine was set in motion when Richard Scrope issued his challenge against Robert Grosvenor. The Court of Chivalry held a series of hearings to determine the rightful bearer of the disputed arms—Azure, a bend Or. Obviously, this was serious business, a high-priority crisis that came without warning, one for which other agendas had to be put aside. That 209 deponents were summoned just on behalf of Scrope, for hearings in thirteen different locations, certainly seems like overkill; a lot of people had nothing better to do, presumably, and were all eager to add their mostly similar voices to an elaborate oratorio as it unrolled with pomp and circumstance toward what was pretty surely a predetermined grand finale.[1] Each deponent's statement was shaped—in his oral testimony and/or in its final form in the written record—to cover a number of essential issues. The individualized depositions are but variations on a set theme.[2]

Serious business, indeed, as confirmed by the substance of the testimony and by the status of many of the deponents, especially those speaking on behalf of Sir Richard Scrope. When called upon, each deponent was asked, in essence, a series of fairly basic questions, as is usual in inquisitorial proceedings. How did he know that the arms in question were those of Sir Richard? Was he aware of any break or interruption in the transmission of the arms through the course of the Scrope family's history? Was he aware of any previous challenge to the arms, whether by Sir Robert Grosvenor or any other party? The answers offered by the overwhelming majority of Scrope partisans rested on a series of simple assertions, each much in line with those coming both before and behind in the queue. Moreover, they were invariably enunciated with an air of gravity. The deponent had indeed *seen* the arms in question, borne by Sir Richard and usually by other family members as well.[3] In addition, in most instances, he had *heard* from others—from men of fame and honor—that these arms were most assuredly those of Sir Richard and the Scrope family and of no one else. Sir Richard was known to have borne them by descent, or by hereditary right, or by virtue of a family claim that ran back to time out of mind, as variously stated. And, lastly, our deponent knew of no previous challenges to the Scropes and he (in most instances) knew nothing of Sir Robert Grosvenor and his claim until the challenge issued by Scrope during the course of the king's last (that is, most recent) expedition to Scotland, the great campaign of 1385–86.[4] There were variations and some qualifications, and a few references to an earlier dispute over these arms, but for the most part this was the common form, the standard agenda.

In this close reading of the Scrope material, my interest lies in details and small distinctions in memories and varieties of expression. The depositions' repetitiveness is striking.[5] Such a basic similarity bespeaks (and in good part results from) a formulaic judicial process as conducted by the functionaries of the court. When material is preserved and transmitted by way of a standardized administrative or legal process, it is likely to be encoded in presentations that sound much the same, just as common memories and forms of articulation help determine and shape the formalism through which we learn of these findings. Thus in our effort to extract the essence of recollection and narration from the Scrope deponents, we encounter a common base of remembered reality.

In subjecting this material to a close reading, I follow two lines of approach. The first deals with what light the depositions shed on memory, recollection, and cognition. In what fashion did the deponents support their claims to knowing what they knew? What blend of recall, rhetoric, and narrative made up each deponent's tale? They were speaking from memory—regardless of whether the memories rested upon a foundation of orality, literacy, aurality, imagination, or some combination thereof—and their statements can be thought of as the distilled essence of what they themselves had accepted and were now transmitting as credible and convincing.

The second line of approach is to use the depositions, in aggregate, as a narrative—a Scrope family chronicle or a well-glossed genealogy. The depositions are a synthesized text by means of which we reconstruct a fellowship of men in arms and recapture many of the shared (and masculine) experiences that had once drawn the deponents together, as their knowledge and memories of the Scropes now reemerge. No single deponent offers, in his brief tale, the full version of the story of the Scropes per se. And yet, by the time we come to the end and read these testimonials as a constructed and unified text—an aggregated literary construct—this is what we have.

The deponents were a group of men with common experiences, memories, and cognitive interpretations; from their brief tales—their slightly longer moments in the sun—we extract and close in on a common segment of their lives. By reviving these common elements through their testimony, Scrope's old friends and comrades in arms were re-creating the good old days, those well-remembered days of action and fellowship—only now it was action at a distance, as revealed and governed by the passage of time and memories of foreign fields and long-ago campaigns. In sum, their tales become a chronicle of the Scropes—of Sir Richard and his valiant kin—and they cover three or four generations of valorous deeds. Some recollections were narrow in focus: a memory of one camp, one battle, one incident. But for most, the shutter of memory was set at a wider angle, embracing many years, many venues, and a large cast of characters. In either case, everyone put his metaphorical finger to the switch: he remembered Sir Richard Scrope and the Scrope right to bear the Azure, a bend Or, and he was pleased to recite his recollections on behalf of his old companion and friend.

COGNITION AND RECOLLECTION

The men who spoke on behalf of Sir Richard Scrope—like virtually all witnesses and deponents and jurors everywhere—"knew" certain things because either they had *seen* them take place or they had seen physical testimonials in support of their claim. In addition, they mostly said that they had also been told certain things—things *heard,* in contrast and in addition to things seen. Such things (or events) reinforced or corroborated their visually based conviction of the correctness of their testimony. And from the combination and melding of the seen and the heard, they *knew* whereof they spoke.[6]

We will accept, in this discussion, the substance of each deponent's testimony as he offered it.[7] Its veracity, we suggest, was Sir Robert Grosvenor's problem, or perhaps the court's, but certainly not ours. In any case it is too late to correct the record, to right the errors—both deliberate and inadvertent—of the 1380s. Our interest, rather, lies in examining how, and with what circumstantial trappings, a belief, or a point of view, or a history now being proclaimed was enunciated and supported. What actually had been seen and heard? How had men come to be so certain that what they "knew" was correct? How did they articulate their recollections, and by dint of what cognitive process did old recollections become today's sworn statement? In most depositions the first category of documentation—that is, its order in the statement—was of things seen. If these direct and personal visual memories were not always the most important or the most elaborately stated, by the time the deponent had finished, they laid a foundation of credibility atop which more elaborate tales and picturesque details could be imbricated.

For virtually every deponent, testimony that rested on visual memory was key. Usually deponents recalled having seen Sir Richard and, more often than not, other Scropes as well, all bearing a version of the disputed coat of arms. But the fabric was enlivened and enriched by what elements of individualization did creep in. Aside from the critical sighting of Sir Richard and some assortment of his ancestors, collateral kin, and descendants, the depositions contained long and impressive lists of things seen other than or in addition to armed men of Scrope lineage standing before their tents. We have tales of heraldic banners, of coats of arms in church windows and on seals and tombs, of family burials with blazons and engravings, of heroic deaths in far-off corners of Christendom and beyond, and of signs and seals set down in a corroborative fashion in charters and the like. Some references were to visual materials, some to written documents.

This testimony, like references to written texts in the Proofs of Age, sometimes argues for the literacy of the deponent, though references to artifacts of the world of writing and recording—now recalled and explicated through visual memory but as objects and icons—are rarely offered as texts to read. We might think of the categories of things seen as falling into two groupings: that of people and events seen and that of signifying objects based on reading and writing and linked in some fashion to Sir Richard. We have testimony that asserts direct knowledge of our key man and testimony linked to the Scropes as a sociopolitical web, both present and historic.

The most critical single germ of testimony seems to come when the deponent described what he had absorbed visually: "as we have in our time seen the said Sir Richard publicly armed in the arms Azure, a bend Or, and also others of his name and lineage, with differences."[8] Such a statement was invariably forthcoming; no deposition was without it, or something very much along this line. The variations regarding visual memories of Sir Richard and his arms could revolve around how often the deponent had seen him, and where, and whether it had been in special and therefore memorable circumstances. A deponent could furnish information that ushers us into moments of great activity, not to say adventure: he "saw Sir Richard or others of his lineage so armed in divers places in Scotland, at the relief of Berwick, in France, at the siege of Tournay, on a banner at the battle of Crecy, on a banner at the siege of Calais, at the siege of Vannes, in the expedition of the late King Edward before Paris, and other places which he did not then remember" (*S&G*, 2:367). But no matter how much it was glossed and elaborated, the basic tale of things seen was fairly straightforward. More information may have been better, but it was not really different.

The memory of having seen Sir Richard bearing the arms—a memory now recalled before the court—certainly constitutes direct evidence. One person had seen another and the first now tells of the occasion. It was the most useful form of testimony, neither apt to be varnished by the deponent nor to be challenged by Grosvenor. Most deponents then went on to buttress their tale with a complementary account of having seen other family members—often those of a previous generation (or more), but sometimes Sir Richard's contemporaries, and in a few instances young men of the succeeding generation. And because there was but one Sir Richard, as against a large cast of other Scropes, the supporting testimony about the others amounted to more than the basic attestation about the central figure himself.

The category of material objects seen and now recited in support of Scrope's claim is more complex than the simple assertions about having seen him in arms. In tales that rest on a visual memory of material objects, there are variations and, from our perspective, more room for the construction and manipulation of the cognitive links between places, times, and people. Objects that proclaimed the antiquity, honor, and heraldic devices of Sir Richard's family were held up—in verbal testimony, and sometimes literally—as witnesses in support of the claim. The objects, as well as their strategic placing in churches or on tombs, mostly antedated Sir Richard, perhaps by centuries. We find references of this sort in a number of lay deponents' tales and in virtually all of those offered by his clerical deponents. While the sight of Sir Richard had perhaps been a fleeting memory, recoverable by hearsay and word of mouth, a reference to an object encoded with the Scrope arms was a reference to a fixed star, be it iconographic, monumental, or architectural.[9]

This idea seems to have been grasped, if not articulated, by the deponents and by those presiding over the proceedings. The memory of objects seen, or of texts or scripts read, was a strong plank in Sir Richard's case as the memories were recounted on his behalf by his partisans. An interested party was presumably being invited, in 1386, to "see for himself" if he doubted the tale of an engraved tomb or a glass window. Furthermore, we have specific if not convincing references to the age and antiquity of the objects: when Scrope arms had been carved into the wall or painted onto the glass; when family tombs had been set in the abbey church; the age of the charter and its seals. Objects had voice, whether emblazoned with the formulae of heraldry or the mysteries of the written text. And now it was the oral testimony of the deponent that coaxed the mute voice into speech. Memory made the message audible and/or visible.

But the boundary that separates cognition and recollection based on things seen from other forms of recollection and cognition is by no means impermeable. Many of the visible, tangible objects cited in support of Scrope's claim to arms and honor, as well as the antiquity and continuity of his line, had originally been called to the deponent's notice by word of mouth, by hearsay, in lieu of or in addition to visual memory. The deponent had been *told* that the arms in the church window were those of the Scropes and that they had been there for generations. To carry this to its logical extension, we should remember that the first time a deponent had met Sir Richard Scrope he presumably had been told—by Scrope or a third party—that Scrope was indeed the man in question. Subsequent recognition of Sir Richard then rested on the conjunction of the message of the eye, in seeing him, and of memory, regarding the original identification, and it was memory originally based on the spoken word, on things said about things seen. In the same fashion, one may have seen a coat of arms in the church but one either read or was told whose coat of arms it was. The associative link, with or without another's help, then became part of one's memory bank.

When we turn to the physical objects mentioned, we find a range of the fairly obvious, many introduced with tales of family and cognitive associations. The recollections covered coats of arms in the windows of monastic houses, painted on walls and carved into stone and wood, on tombs and sculpted effigies, on vestments and banners, and even on scraps of old cloth. In addition, there are the references to written proofs: charters, chronicles, miscellaneous documents, and the seals that went with such diplomatics. The more loquacious deponents combined the seen and the heard. Once a man began to refer to objects in support of Scrope's claim, he was apt to bring in a whole cluster of items: the abbot of Jervaulx was but typical in his references to windows and paintings, muniments and charters, seals on the documents, and the like. The arms were "in divers places in his Abbey, in glass windows and painting, entire and with differences, and he had muniments or charters of the Scropes, and [he] showed a release without date, with their seal."[10]

Coats of arms set into church glass were among the more memorable items in this inventory of physical evidence. The abbot of Selby told of how "in the chapel [of his house] . . . were the same arms in a glass window, between those of Lord Percy and Lord Moubray, and had been in the said window and porch ever since the building of the said infirmary" (*S&G*, 2:271). The themes yoked by this testimony cover the antiquity of the window, a widespread knowledge of whose arms they are, and what we might call honor and status (and therefore proof) by association: Scrope beside Percy and Moubray (Mowbray). The prior of Lanercost recounted how "at the west end of his church are the arms of Scrope within a bordure Or in a glass window; and the same arms are placed in the refectory between those of Vaux and Multon their founders . . . [and in] the west window . . . are the old arms of the king of England, the arms of France, the arms of Scotland, and the arms of Scrope, Azure, a bend Or, within bordure Or."[11]

Funeral monuments argued for a strong link between the deceased and his family and the burial church. They, too, when marked with the relevant arms, constituted evidence not to be dismissed casually. The abbot of Coverham told of "one Sir Geoffrey Scrope . . . interred in the body of his church before the high cross, in a lofty tomb, with the effigy of a knight armed in those arms" (*S&G*, 2:277). As well as Sir Geoffrey there was "his son, who lies below under a flat stone, with a shield of arms differenced . . . and another of his line and name on the other side below ground." Another cleric recalled that "at the head of the deceased there was a escocheon sculptured and embossed with stone, with the arms of Scrope . . . and at his feet a similar escocheon."[12] Perhaps the most informed heraldic touches came from the prior of Guisborough. He spoke of a glass window "Azure, a bend Or, with a small lioncel purpure in the canton of the shield at the top, on the bend, which lioncel was granted to one of the Scropes by the Earl of Lincoln" (*S&G*, 2:277–78). The prior had learned these were Scrope arms "from tradition, and the information of old friars then deceased." The walls of churches and regular houses carried depictions of coats of arms in a variety of engraved and sculpted versions. The prior of Newburgh said that "the whole arms had been there ever since the building of the church and refectory. . . . He knew they were painted in memory of the ancestors of Sir Richard le Scrope" (S&G, 2:280). At Jervaulx, the tablet "on which the said arms were depicted" was on the wall, and it had been put in place "eight score years ago, as fully appeared by the writing" (S&G, 2:274). At Byland the arms were "painted in the refectory of the abbey on the wall."[13]

The arms were also set into or upon cloth, insubstantial though this may seem from our distance. In addition to their message in stone, wood, and glass, "the said arms were on a corporas case of silk" in the house of St. Agatha at Richmond, as Abbot John de Esby told the court. All knew that "the arms belonged of right to Sir Richard's ancestors" (S&G, 2:275).[14] Another distinguished deponent told of "an amice embroidered on red velvet with leopards and griffons, Or, between which were sewn in silk, in three places, three escocheons with the entire arms of Sir Richard Scrope" (S&G, 2:278).[15] And the association of Scrope arms with those of other distinguished families—an argument for dignity and credibility by association—showed up on cloth as well as on durable objects. On a coat of arms embroidered with Neville arms, "the quarters [were] to be all filled up with small escocheons of the arms of his friends." We have the arms of Hastings, Aton, St. Quintyn, and Marmyn, and "amongst these were the arms of Sir Henry Scrope" (S&G, 2:345).[16]

Testimony about written materials is, in some ways, even more evocative than recollections resting on sight and hearsay. Rolls of arms were familiar objects by the 1380s, though the only explicit reference we have to such rolls in the depositions concerns a knight's father—old Laton—who seems to have written (and probably drawn) one for himself as a project for his old age.[17] They were not otherwise referred to in the depositions, solid evidence though such rolls and catalogues presumably would have been. Instead, we have numerous references to other kinds of documents, some illuminated with arms and crests but lacking whatever semiofficial cachet the compilations of heralds and family historians might bestow.[18] Most references to written materials rely on and are parts of the same universe of well-born memories as the things seen and heard. Almost no one, even among men of education and clerical training, offered unambiguous references to a written text (let alone what we would call a direct quotation) to clinch his argument. All was shrouded in the mists of time and memory.

This is not to slight the large number of depositions, as well as the variety of recollections and testimonies, that rest heavily on written material. John de Sherburne, abbot of Selby, told of either owning or knowing of an old book, "illuminated in colours, full of escocheons of the arms of kings, princes, earls, barons, bannerets, knights, and esquires . . . amongst which are found the arms of Scrope" (S&G, 2:271). "Muniments or charters of the Scropes" would seem to offer strong confirmation of Sir Richard's claim, even when in the form of "a release without date, with their seal."[19] One deposition provided a barrage of material; quantity and variety might cover a job lot of questions. We have reference to diverse charters, sealed with large "solemn seals," as well as to books of chronicles and charters of other nobles in which a Scrope was named.[20] "An ancient release under the seal of Sir Geoffrey Lescrope with the arms entire" certainly sounds like strong support, especially when put into the record by Thomas de Cotynghamn, prior of St. Mary, York (*S&G*, 2:344).

Scrope arms, tombs, tablets on walls, and windows with shields were all items we would expect to find—and hear referred to—in the churches and ecclesiastical houses that the Scropes had founded or had taken on as special benefactors. Both clerical and lay deponents referred to a tradition of Scrope benefaction when they named churches and regular houses as emblazoned with signs of the family. St. Agatha, Richmond, was a Scrope foundation; within its walls many of them lay buried. Therefore we expect the monuments of Sir Richard's father (Sir Henry, as he "was called in his lifetime"), Richard's brother William, "and many others of their lineage interred under flat stones" (*S&G*, 2:274).[21] The parish church of Wensley, "of which Sir Richard was patron," had family arms in "certain glass windows." Furthermore, by now this was a venerable story: "the setting up of which arms was beyond the memory of man." Wensley housed the mortal remains of Simon Scrope, two Henrys and a William, all resting in tombs with appropriate markings and symbols.[22] A deposition from a layman, Richard de Beaulieu, esquire, tells us that a Scrope was buried at Wetheral and that stained glass at Lanercost also testified to Scrope patronage. In fact, according to de Beaulieu, the Scropes were held "as founders" of Lanercost, and both glass and vestments could be seen there in support of their claim (*S&G*, 2:441–42). He had "heard from his ancestors" of such matters, and his confident local knowledge carried the usual tone of firm conviction.

Characteristic references to material objects mention their age and antiquity. If many of the windows and engravings were just old—sometimes in the "time out of mind" category or assumed to be coeval with the construction of the building—others were tagged with more precision. It could be quite specific: glass that went back for sixty years, or a tablet or engraving of family arms that went back some eightscore years (*S&G*, 2:168, 274). The abbey church at Guisborough had burned ninety-seven years ago (*S&G*, 2:278), and the old building had had Scrope arms emblazoned within—or so the aged prior claimed, though it is unclear whether Scrope arms had been in the old church or just in the rebuilt one. Another northern church had Scrope tombs that went back for at least a century.[23] Written materials presumably were dated. Indeed, it is hard to imagine a charter or chronicle that was not, whether genuine or spurious. One charter, with its requisite Scrope references and witnessing, dated back a very long way. The notice was of a certain Hugh de Scrope, supposedly an ancestor of Richard: "they showed by chronicle, that he [Hugh] lived in the fifth year of King Stephen." Or it might be a reference to "King Edward" and was assigned, by its teller, to the time of Edward I.[24]

Forms of Memory

Most deponents offered information derived from more than one form of cognitive recall. To say that one had seen Sir Richard in arms did not preclude going on to talk about having seen associated objects that offered their own mute but durable confirmation of what one had witnessed. Nor did the visual recollections preclude the inclusion of tales and assertions that rested on hearsay. Things heard opened up elaborate vistas, often more complex than those offered by things seen. But these are imprecise boundaries. Because they all "knew" the truth about Scrope's rightful claim, the routes by which they reached the promised land were of no great consequence—and perhaps, in the absence of cross-examination or verification, of no consequence at all. After an initial assertion resting on things seen, which usually meant seeing Sir Richard, a deponent could move quickly to an account that coupled seen with heard.[25] As one deponent asserted: "We have seen and known that Sir Richard hath borne his arms . . . [and] we have heard from many nobles and valiant men, since deceased, that the said arms were of right the arms of his ancestors."[26]

Every pro-Scrope statement also carried a negative message, though I will not devote much attention to its adversarial or confrontational face. Testimonials for Scrope sometimes ridiculed or belittled the Grosvenor claim, using rhetoric that was a mirror image of that exalting and supporting Scrope. A deponent might conclude by saying something along the lines of "he had never heard aught to the contrary until the last expedition in Scotland . . . the which Sir Robert he never saw, nor had knowledge of him or his arms."[27] Unseen, and literally unheard of. In addition, a number of deponents emphasized that when Scrope had at various times been in the company of knights from Cheshire—men who *might* have known of Grosvenor's ancestry and claim—no one had taken exception to Sir Richard's heraldry.[28] Though some Scrope partisans were willing to accept the Grosvenors as men of honor, the hierarchy of old knighthood over new knighthood was keenly felt and strongly defended.

Information reported as learned and known because it had been heard constituted the bulk of the testimony. Material found under this broad umbrella can be divided into a number of categories. At the simplest level, one heard (that is, one had been told) that the arms in question were those of Sir Richard. Such hearsay, perhaps at one remove or even further back along the chain of transmission, was the auditory confirmation of the visual evidence with which the deposition had begun: "He had often heard . . . that the said arms were descended by right line to the said Sir Richard" (*S&G*, 2:221). Sometimes the assertion was couched in strong phrases, brooking no equivocation: "he had *always* heard . . . [and] he had *never* heard" to the contrary (*S&G*, 2:306; emphasis added). Some of what they had heard had been from men of good repute—"old knights and esquires," among the variations on this formula—and often these old knights and esquires had also been kinsmen of the deponent. Some hearsay regarding the right of Scrope to bear his arms was based on Scrope family lore, on claims that went back to time out of mind. Some of the wisdom was known because it was, we are told, part of the common lore of men of knightly status. And with a wonderful touch of specificity, deponent after deponent said that he had heard that the Scropes (or their direct ancestors) had come over with the Conqueror.[29]

These variations of hearsay are, in a literal sense, devices used to achieve credibility without the precision of date and place that we will look for when we turn to a reconstruction of Scrope family exploits and their roles in the brotherhoods of arms and on the battlefields of their day. If such statements did not serve to clinch the case for Sir Richard, they were certainly not easy to refute. Hearsay forged a strong chain of continuity. Moreover, in the recitation of the tales, the deponent's family was often intertwined with the Scropes; their honor and his, their credentials and his, and so forth. The scores of micro-narratives about extended kin groups in arms, on fields of battle, and on the great marches were also reflections of and contributions to the common culture of chivalry and martial lore. The Scropes were worthy subjects of such tales, just as each deponent (even in his callow youth) had been a worthy hearer. Telling heroic tales about families and their deeds was as much a feature of upper-class culture in late medieval Europe as it had been in a world that had once listened to *The Iliad* or *Beowulf*.[30]

Much of the tales' credibility was supported by information that had been conveyed to the deponents by that vast and vague legion of "old knights and esquires." As with other kinds of assertions, this was pretty much beyond refutation; the old tellers of tales were no more. That the tales had been passed down by "noble lords, valiant knights, and good esquires, now deceased," sufficed. Such pronouncements showed deference to the social milieu within which these men moved and replicated themselves (*S&G*, 2:222). Variations on this tune were never more than minor: "he was told by his ancestors and old knights and esquires, and other valiant soldiers now deceased" (*S&G*, 2:306). Or perhaps it had come from "noble and valiant lords, knights, and esquires, now with God" (*S&G*, 2:174). To refer to and quote the honored dead is to offer a tale that cannot, in decency and without offense, be questioned. Another rhetorical device that set the deponent on a pedestal, beyond the reach of refutation, was an emphasis on his youth when he had first learned the lore he was now recounting. Henry Bolingbroke, then earl of Derby, led off in this style: "we are young and have been only a short time armed" (*S&G*, 2:166).³¹ Less exalted deponents were equally deferential about their secondhand expertise: one man said that "in his youth he *often* heard from his ancestors and valiant men of arms now no more" (*S&G*, 2:318; emphasis added). Others chimed in on this note: "he had heard it said by many noble and valiant lords, knights, and esquires, and as a matter of common fame and report," or perhaps by way of "eminent persons . . . [who] say that the same arms appertained, as common voice and fame testified" (*S&G*, 2:170, 171).³²

In addition to those generic old lords, knights, and esquires, referred to almost as natural features of the landscape, deponents offered that they had learned of Scrope family lore from their own kinsmen of previous generations. Leading with one's father was a good way to open: "he had heard from his late father, on whom God have mercy." The next step, then, was the generation before: "he had heard from his grandfather."³³ But the chain of transmission could lead even further back and be more binding, as with the deponent who "had heard his father state that his grandfather and Sir Geoffrey Scrope were companions in divers battles and journeys" (*S&G*, 2:168).³⁴ This was topped by a statement that paradoxically drew strength from its imprecision: "as he had heard his ancestors say; and his ancestors heard it from their ancestors."³⁵ Another general appeal was to the sensitivities of chivalric society. One deponent "had frequently heard very old people say that they [the Scropes] had continually used those arms" (*S&G*, 2:391).³⁶

Beyond these person-to-person accounts of how old lore had been transmitted is a reliance on stock conventions of narrative and recollection. Voices from the past—some attached to names and dates, others only in ellipses—had transmitted tales that virtually anyone of birth and honor had absorbed as part of his socialization. Not least among the standard phrases was the ever popular "time out of mind," now offered as being reliable because of the "common report" that had transmitted these narratives. To these locutions (and circumlocutions) we can add the weight derived from the widely proclaimed idea that the Scropes were known to have come over with the Conqueror. Like the reference to tales told by honorable old warriors, now deceased, such evidence was presumably worth whatever value one chose to give it.

Ancient memory, at least, was recognized in common law and enshrined in centuries of official testimony. The deponent who said that the Scropes had been "so armed from time of which memory runneth not" was setting himself within a formal tradition that stretched back to the accession of Richard I.³⁷ Patriarchal piety reinforced the basic formula that held sway in the king's courts: he "had heard his father say, and from time immemorial he could not state how long the ancestors of Sir Richard have borne the arms" (*S&G*, 2:400). The power of imprecise information is not to be underestimated: "he had never heard who was the first ancestor of Sir Richard that bore the arms in question, for the family was ancient, and of times beyond memory" (*S&G*, 2:403–4). Knowledge of the antiquity and unbroken descent of the claim was part of the common stock of the deponents' background and culture, especially for northern families who ran with the Yorkshire baronage. This assertion created or strengthened an "us versus them" mentality that was always close to the surface for both sets of partisans and deponents. Only an outsider—and a boorish one at that—would question such a claim. We saw instances in which jurors for a Proof fell back on a reference to the common knowledge of the community; more details could have been offered, had it been necessary to do so. To profess ignorance of Sir Richard's ancient rights was to announce that one was not privy to what any gentleman of the region had learned (or should have learned) in his youth.[38] A deponent who simply iterated what was known in "all Yorkshire and all Richmondshire," that is, that the Scropes were "gentlemen of ancient lineage," was not to be crossed casually.[39]

The standard way of opening this door was to offer specific and focused testimony on behalf of Sir Richard and then, toward the end of the statement, to allude to what "everyone" or "everyman" either knew or *should* know—like the string of reinforcing "moreovers" we found in some of the Proofs of Age. There were variations on this: "as common voice and fame testified" (*S&G*, 2:171), or "according to public report" (*S&G*, 2:197), or "as the public voice and common fame testified" (*S&G*, 2:217).[40] More bite went into these assertions when they were reinforced by local expertise—what we might see as regional patriotism, membership in the northern upper-class community. Deponents talked of how "the Scropes were reputed throughout the counties of York and Richmond to have descended from an ancient line of ancestors" (*S&G*, 2:296).[41] An outsider was clearly at a disadvantage when he had to confront references to "the common fame ... throughout his country" (*S&G*, 2:342). The arms were known to have "lineally descended" from ancient ancestors to Sir Richard.[42]

The desire to portray oneself as the possessor of inside information—an unclaimed area, there for the taking, between hard knowledge and mere gossip—is a strong motivating force in discourse. We find this in the clerical as well as the lay depositions. Some of the regular clerics who testified were from the ranks of men who, in their youth, had been confidants of those old lore-masters, elderly monks who had transmitted the tales (instead of or in addition to the knights and esquires who had so much free time for reminiscences in their post-military days). The abbot of Selby had learned of the Scropes when "he had heard old monks who were in the said abbey in the time of his youth" tell of the family and its exploits (*S&G*, 2:271). Other powerful figures of the northern monastic world fell back on similar experiences. The abbot of Rievaulx learned "from old monks when he was a monk in his youth" (*S&G*, 2:272), and the prior of Newburgh "had heard in his youth [from] old canons of his house, now dead" (*S&G*, 2:280). The abbot also referred to "common report through the country where he resides." The prior of Lanercost spun the religious equivalent of ancestors' ancestors: "he had heard the prior his predecessor who was an old man say that he had heard from ancient lords, knights, and esquires . . . the prior who preceded him said that they were cousin to one Gant . . . as was known by common report in all parts of the North."[43]

That the Scropes were held to have come with the Conqueror is an intriguing if hardly novel conceit. It was advanced, with variations in wording, by dozens of friendly deponents. The genealogy itself was a bit tangled. Sometimes it was the Scropes themselves. Sometimes a vague forebear who had been at Hastings was linked to them in some unspecified fashion, as with the "one Gant" we have come across. Lesser claims were perhaps safer ground, if anyone cared: "Sir Richard's ancestors, having always used the said arms as ancient lords and knights since the Conquest" (*S&G*, 2:309), was a minimal presentation.[44] The case seems more circumstantial when we hear of monks who "have in their house a chronicle from the time of the Conquest, with the names of the lords who came over . . . [and] amongst them is the name of one of the Scropes, but he [the deponent, William Holme, canon and celerer of Watton Priory] does not recollect his proper name" (*S&G*, 2:283). In keeping with our views about porous filters and the two-way exchange between written and oral, we are not surprised at how casually the dots were connected. Nor were written materials invariably dated. One seal on a charter showed knights with swords "like those used at the time of the Conquest," and by virtue of listing a Walter Scrope among the witnesses, it shed a presumptive legacy of with-William-at-Hastings upon the family.[45] The Norman claim was largely couched in words and style to make it similar to the "time out of mind" school of testimony.

In summary, support for the Scrope claim to the arms under dispute ranged, in terms of the cognitive channels through which memory ran, from the most direct to a checkered and zigzag course that rested heavily on the vague if powerful dynamics of tradition and transmitted lore. A lot of ground is covered if we begin with testimony about seeing Sir Richard Scrope bear his arms on many battlefields and then end with testimony offered in the context of general moral and cultural support for a noble soldier whose ancestors had come over with Duke William. With allowances for social standing and sophistication, we see that much of their material was strikingly similar to what we encountered in the Proofs, though our well-born deponents were a bit firmer, their circumstantial tales easier to check against the happenings of the external world (had anyone cared or presumed to do so).

Most deponents provided more than one sort of testimony. They spoke of what they had seen; they recounted what they had been told, directly and personally;

they delighted in being part of the web of common lore and tale-telling that went back to ancient knights and a "common voice" that could be heard all the way back to the Conquest. Though the distinctions between the various cognitive routes did not worry the deponents, we do find indications that they were aware, at least in some instances, of the lines we are drawing here. Some men said, in stating their ages and their years in arms, that they themselves were but young (or had been so). The implication is that they were speaking as part of a common enterprise, rather than as individuals who could draw on great personal experience; their testimony was but a link in a long chain, their role that of spear-carriers. Others went out of their way to tell of grizzled veterans—unnamed, more often than not, though a grandfather might figure—who had told them that which they now so cheerfully passed along at the deposition.

But if the testimony rested heavily on hearsay and the funneling of oral culture to the written record, deponents were hardly uncertain of or inclined to undervalue their own statements. Humility is not a key ingredient in sworn testimony, and given the social status of these men, they were apt to be less humble than many—certainly a good bit less than those villagers whom we picked up for a few minutes on their great day. Some Scrope deponents proclaimed their certainty in a voice of overwhelming authority, both on their own behalf and in support of the family for whose cause they were speaking. The confidence of their assertions jumps the centuries and rings out from the old records. Men of high birth and valiant feats of arms did not take kindly to being doubted, especially when speaking on behalf of one of their own.[46]

Insofar as detailed and status-conscious memories help explicate the story of the Scropes as a family, they are dealt with below. But insofar as such depositions reveal *how* men told their tales, how they yoked memory and hearsay to presentations of self and a narrated investment in ego, the statements fit in here. John Thirwalle, veteran of thirty-two years in arms, still chose to fall back on his father's wisdom. The old man, knighted by Edward I, had been bedridden "through old age," and he had waxed indignant at questions about the Scropes' dignity and birth. They were descended from "great and noble gentlemen." Old Thirwalle concluded by saying that "if I were young I would hold and maintain my saying to the death."[47]

A good deal of this quasi-historical bombast was inserted into the depositions to enhance the dignity of the speakers. In such testimony, narrator and subject became inextricably bound; to doubt one was to doubt the other, and conversely, to believe one was to believe the other. This formulaic testimony narrowed the locative and cognitive gaps of disassociation and disbelief. The tales, as we have them, were a socially embedded device, presented and transmitted to overcome the realities of separate identities, of different times, and of far-flung places. Recollection and tale-telling are ways of re-creating experience and of renewing, through reiteration, social and cultural inclusions that loomed large in the world of family honor and chivalric conceit.

Some of the clerical deponents, whose briefs rested on references to material objects, actually brought examples of their physical evidence to court, mustering the tangible in support of the ideological. The abbot of Rievaulx "exhibited" two old charters in which Scrope bequests to his abbey were spelled out: "the one of Sir Henry Scrope, who gave divers lands to the abbey . . . and of the said Sir Henry, sealed with their arms in white wax." The abbot also said that while none of Sir Richard's ancestors was buried in his house, he had still more charters, "dated seventy years ago," touching their benefactions and sealed with their arms (*S&G*, 2:272). The subprior of Warter likewise displayed his prize exhibit, an amice embroidered on red velvet. He supplemented his show-and-tell with a reference to Scrope burials in St. Martin by Mickelgate, York.[48] So in addition to memories of things seen and heard, we have hands-on verification as a powerful pedagogic and discursive technique.

I have elaborated, perhaps beyond useful length, on the ways in which cognition was packaged and made credible in a specific context, for a specific purpose. Each deponent's testimony was an individualized statement, despite all the overlapping and duplication. But when the depositions are read in the aggregate, what emerges is the history of a prominent family—or at least some significant and evocative segments of that history—now presented as a chapter in the common lore "of Yorkshire and Richmondshire." In the cultural framework of their proponents, *everyone* who was *anyone* could be expected to know *something* about the Scropes, as they presumably did about the Percys, the Nevilles, the Stricklands, the Umfravilles, the Multons, the Atons, and many others.[49]

The deponents knew of and believed in this kind of family history—based as it was on things seen, heard, and "known"—because they all shared a life of common service and joint activity, a common background of culture and community. They knew the lore and arms and ancestors of the Scropes (and of the others) because, in a very real sense, heraldry worked. That is, the incessant blazoning of family arms in windows and on banners and on funeral monuments and on seals really was read by the initiated eye of soldiers and incorporated into their perceptual world and cultural heritage. The images and icons of genealogy and heraldry simultaneously reflected and helped shape a chivalric mentality in which family, common experience, and male bonding merged in some murky but useable fashion. Men recognized the coats of arms; they had been trained to do this. Furthermore, they not only saw but also remembered what they had seen, and they recounted their detailed and solemn stories about the meaning of these powerful symbols when it was time to step forward and tell their tales.

TALES OF THE SCROPES: BATTLES AND BANNERS

Testimonies on behalf of Sir Richard's claim to arms can be thought of as constituting a body of disparate but complementary material from which we construct a history of the Scrope family—a fragmentary chronicle that is also a synthetic case study in aristocratic life. The depositions are shards and scraps of primary data. While they may tell a tale now accessible and familiar, thanks to what we find in the *Complete Peerage* and the (old) *DNB* in addition to more specialized studies, they came first. Much of our modern amalgam of the history of the Scropes (and of the Grosvenors, had we so chosen) has been assembled through an orchestration of these fourteenth-century micro-narratives.[50]

When we talked about cognition and forms of memory and recollection, we had a lot of comfortable material about Sir Richard and his family's history and background. But gradually the solid and well-charted ground—things known because they had been seen—gave way to shifting and less certain footing, to such mythic and amorphous forms of certainty as "known since time out of mind," or "accepted by the common voice," along with claims resting on feats of ancestors who were said by men of probity to have come over with Duke William. Now, as we filter the testimonies and depositions, we focus on *what* it was the deponents had actually seen and *which* Scropes they had seen. We move from the process of recollection to the social and historical substance of the testimony, the substance of what they actually remembered, rather than how or why they did so. The deponents' common pool of knowledge and experience—the shared data and the similar ways in which they explicated their experience and formulated their perceptions—now becomes the substance of our inquiry. Again, the formulaic and ritualized nature of the hearings reinforced and emphasized this degree of sameness of form and content. As with Proofs of Age, their ultimate accommodation to the standardized mold of the written record has a reductionist effect on the original varieties of expression and memory: many variations, adjusted to fit a single paradigm.

Sir Richard Scrope's friends and partisans knew something of the history and genealogy of his family, as they presumably did for others of martial valor and high birth. As a regular part of upper-class socialization, and perhaps as the fruit of a special rehearsal held before the deposition, their variations on common themes became a rhetorical device of reinforcement—credibility through repetition. Some of the lore being declaimed pertained directly to Sir Richard and his kin: their links to each other, ages and generational cohorts, instances of common activity and travel, military experience and battle, and the like. Some of the common cultural baggage served to set the Scrope family—Sir Richard and his extended kin network—into the larger rhythms of aristocratic behavior and chivalric culture. Kings, wars and treaties, expeditions and sieges; all provide instances and occasions for the kingdom's political and martial destiny to embrace or enfold the individual and separate fortunes of our heroes.

To emphasize how this case study of a family illuminates the fortunes of military and political England, we can turn to the family tree, showing the men mentioned in the depositions, then to a time line to set their years of military activity against the wider panorama of English military and political history. Most of Sir Richard's deponents probably could have re-created this material from memory, though their depositions come draped in the banners of myth-history and formulaic rhetoric about brotherhood and long-ago glories.

Three main themes regarding the reconstruction of family history—elucidated by living memory, focusing on real events rather than just resting on hearsay and tales of coats of arms in the windows of northern churches—emerge from our reading of the depositions. We see that many members of the Scrope clan were familiar figures to many, or even to most, of the deponents. While Sir Richard was the key figure in this controversy and the focal point of the depositions, and by now (*S&G*, 2:1386) a peer of the realm and the patriarch of the senior branch of the Scropes of Bolton, he was but *primes inter pares* in terms of old soldiers' stories. The deponents knew or knew of his brother and his cousins, about whom they frequently had much to say. Mostly, being Sir Richard's contemporaries or younger, their firsthand testimonies centered on Richard's own generation, primarily on Richard and his first cousin Henry. But for some deponents, especially the older ones, there were still firsthand memories of Richard's father and uncle, in addition to what scores of men had absorbed second-hand from the tales of those long-gone knights and esquires. And for some of the younger generations, the deeds of Sir Richard's son William (Richard II's earl of Wiltshire, x. 1399) also figured. Clearly, this multigenerational lore was part of the cultural baggage of the upper classes.

A second theme that emerges is the existence of a vast and shared reservoir of military experience based on firsthand knowledge and personal involvement. Because warfare was the main business of these men, we can imagine how the Hundred Years War served as a two-generation catalyst to their careers and martial worldview. Nevertheless, the long years of campaigning certainly honed this side of life in both identity and recollection. Where else but in the army in the field, especially on the eve of combat, were the coats of arms—on the shields, before the tents, and on the banners of the retinue, as the war horses began to move forward—apt to be so fixed in memory's eye? As one elderly deponent—Richard de la Zouche, brother of Lord Zouche, aged sixty-seven at the time of his deposition—said, he had been around for fifty-two years and he had seen the Scrope arms "in *all* the places where he had served and where a knowledge of arms could be gained" (*S&G*, 2:449; emphasis added). The battles at which Sir Richard and his relatives fought and at

Figure 1: The Scrope Genealogy

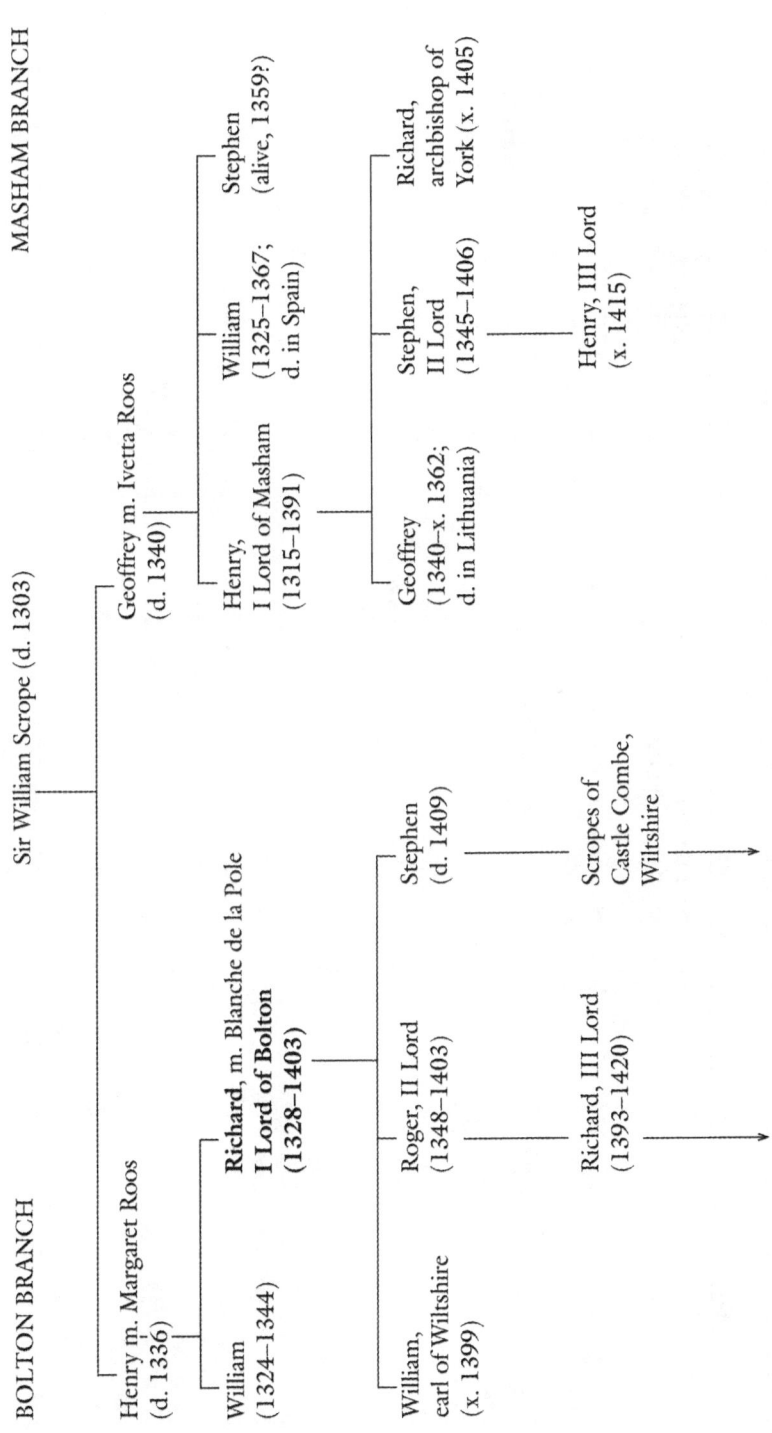

SOURCES: Nicholas Harris Nicolas, *The Controversy Between Sir Richard Scrope and Sir Robert Grosvenor*, 2 vols. (London, 1832); George E. Cokayne et al., eds., *The Complete Peerage*, 12 vols. in 13 (London, 1910-59).

Table 7 A Fourteenth-Century Time Line: The Scropes and the Kingdom

Year	Battles	Scrope Affairs	Other
1330			Edward III takes power; Black Prince born
1333	Berwick, Halidon Hill	Henry named chief justice, King's Bench Henry knighted and made chief baron of the Exchequer	
1334			
1336		Geoffrey becomes chief justice	
1337		Old Henry dies	Edward III claims French throne
1338			Flemish alliance with England against France
1340	Sluys	Geoffrey dies	John of Gaunt born; Chaucer born
1341	Scots take Roxburgh		
1342	Victory at Morlaix	Young Geoffrey born	
1344		William dies (wounded in 1342 at Morlaix)	
1345		Stephen born; William born (later earl of Wiltshire)	
1346	Crecy and Durham	Richard knighted	
1347	Calais falls to siege; naval victory at Le Croty		
1348			Black Plague; Edward III founds Order of the Garter
1349		Richard of age	More plague
1350	Espagnols-sur-Mer	Stephen born; Henry summoned as a peer	Philip VI dies; John II king of France
1352			Statute of Laborers
1355			Charles IV now Holy Roman Emperor
1356	Poitiers, Berwick recaptured		
1357			Scottish truce
1358			Jacquerie rebellion in France
1360		Geoffrey knighted	Bretigny truce
1361			Plague
1362		Geoffrey dies in Prussia	

Year	Event	Event
1363		Burgundy granted to Philip the Bold
1364		John II of France dies
1365	Richard serves as MP for York	
1366		Henry of Trastamare becomes king of Castile
1367	Najara	Death of Pedro of Castile
1368	Gaunt's great raid in France	
1369		Plague
1370		
1371	William dies in Spain	
1372	Naval defeat at La Rochelle	Gaunt claims throne of Castile
1373	Gaunt's chevauchée	
	Henry made warden of the west march	
	Richard becomes lord treasurer and a peer	
	Henry, III Lord Scrope of Masham, born (executed in 1415)	
1375		Treaty of Bruges
1376	Richard becomes warden of marches	Black Prince dies; Good Parliament
1377		Edward III dies; succeeded by Richard II
1378	Naval defeat at St. Malo	Great schism of the papacy
1379		Plague returns
1380	Edmund in Brittany	
	Richard becomes lord chancellor	
1381		Peasants' rebellion
1382	French victory at Roosebeke	Anne of Bohemia crowned queen of England
1383	Bishop Despenser's "crusade"	
	Richard becomes chancellor again	
1384	Gaunt in Scotland	
	William appointed seneschal of Aquitaine	
	Richard cooperating with John of Gaunt	
1385	Richard II invades Scotland	
	Roger knighted	
1386	Gaunt in Spain	
	Suffolk impeached; Scrope and Grosvenor controversy is born	

which they had proudly borne their arms were literally legion. Few major engagements since Edward III's early confrontations in France or along the Scottish borders had been fought without some representatives of the Scropes. They had stood beside the king himself, with his near kinsmen, and prominently among the ranks of his barons and his captains. By the 1380s their extended and collective experience not only ranged over France (enumerated by deponents as embracing Gascony, Normandy, Guienne, and Brittany), Scotland, and Spain but also included the occasional foray to Prussia, Lithuania, and the Near East.[51] The testimony representing four or five decades of pooled military experience and recollection, covering much of Europe and touching the fringes of Africa and Asia, was not without its own glories, even among men of the high estate comprising those whose fought. Sir Robert Clavering spoke for many of his fellows: "he had seen Sir Richard Scrope, and his cousins and other branches of his family, armed in the arms . . . at the siege of Calais, at Balyngham Hill, in the chivauchee in Caux, and before Paris . . . and also in both expeditions to Scotland."[52]

A third theme that emerges from the depositions is the weight and seriousness of all this family involvement and military glory—what we summarize as chivalry. In a sense it represents the combination of our first two themes, but it was more than that, too. Long and comprehensive family service, plus years of distinguished military activity, became the road to Fame and Honor.[53] The sum of accumulated family gentility and service and years in arms was greater than the separate parts. A self-reinforcing dynamic came into play as attestations touching dignity and birth and social order and military bearing came from deponent after deponent. It behooved these men, whose social and political status dominated their world, to create and promulgate an ideology about themselves that included family and martial career, one that rested heavily on the display of a coat of arms that, by itself and at a mere glance, signified descent from a string of valiant soldier-ancestors.

Related to this theme—or rather, one visible aspect of it—is the heraldic knowledge exhibited by the deponents. Because only Sir Richard (and his father and eldest son and heir, in turn) could wear the primary arms of the family, the other Scropes bore these arms "differenced," thereby indicating that they were representatives of cadet and collateral branches, not direct shoots off the main stem. Deponents were at pains to indicate that they understood, recognized, and remembered these critical distinctions. Whether they had been coached, as Denholm Young suggested, or whether this kind of visual acumen really did come back as they anticipated their testimony before the court, the niceties regarding rank and worth—reflected and proclaimed by the sign of Azure, a bend Or, and its variations—were duly offered and recorded.[54]

Remembering the Scropes

Virtually every deponent who spoke on behalf of Sir Richard said that he, personally, had seen Scrope use, wear, and display the arms in question. Only the clerical deponents offered no personal knowledge of battlefield appearances, and they usually compensated with tales of monuments, written records, and transmitted memories. In addition, virtually every deponent—lay or clerical—spoke of having seen *other* members of the family in addition to Sir Richard. While such broad-based testimony about the family reinforced his case, it also carried risks, though they were neatly dealt with. On the one hand, it was crucial that Sir Richard's own military activity and prowess be set within the context of the actions of his many kinsmen, both of his own and of other generations. He gained glory by association and by contributing to the aggregate weight of all those who constituted this impressive band of champions. On the other hand, it was imperative that Sir Richard not be outstripped by collateral kinsmen or by his dead brother; his exploits must not be seen as "second best" when set against other family heroics. Accordingly, the rhetoric of the depositions took the form of staccato statements about various men of the Scrope lineage and their battles and feats of arms. Individual Scropes were never compared directly against one another. No one tried to arrange Sir Richard in a pecking order of personal bravery or military responsibility. The exceptions to this, perhaps, are in the occasional accolades reserved for some of the dead. Their glory was reflective, and it could be reinvested in the living rather than presented as a competitive memory. All the Scropes mentioned were invariably heroes; all the brothers (and cousins) were (or had been) valiant.[55]

In 1386 Sir Richard, I Lord Scrope of Bolton, was a seasoned warrior, now well beyond the age of much frontline combat. He had been at the great battles of an earlier generation and could look back on a long and vigorous career, graced with military and civilian distinctions. As his deponents were wont to say, he "had been armed in these arms in many great expeditions, battles, and journeys, and achieved great honour in the same arms." One man had seen Sir Richard at Durham and at Espagnols-sur-Mer with the earl of Warwick, and "in the presence of the Prince, in the company of the lord of Lancaster" at Najara in 1367. Memory ran to having seen him when the Castle of Stirling was victualed by the earl of Warwick and at the great chevauchée "of the late king" before Paris, "when the truce was made and [then the] peace."[56] In the field, Scrope had invariably displayed the arms now in dispute. His partisans were explicit about this: he had been "so armed in coat armour, and with banner and pennon, in divers battles and journeys" (*S&G*, 2:170). Furthermore, it was indisputably the *right* arms, his—and only his—heraldic device: "his body armed Azure, a bend Or, his banner in battle publicly borne, and standards with these arms always placed outside his quarters [*herbergages*] and in full view of everyone" (*S&G*, 2:174).[57]

If the primary coat of arms was that of Sir Richard, the collective weight of the depositions comes from the way the tales of his presence and arms take root in the lush garden of endless family deeds and honors, the panoramic military saga of Edwardian (and Ricardian) England, and the lofty values of chivalry as enhanced and proclaimed by the trappings of heraldry. Accordingly, after the recollections of Sir Richard, we look at what was offered about others of his generation—personal recollections of the past. He had had an elder brother. Like the Kennedy brother who "didn't make it back," legends and long memories clustered around William, elder son of Justice Henry, when older deponents turned their thoughts—some forty and more years after his death—to his unfulfilled promise. Old memories were hallowed ones. One deponent recollected that he "also saw Sir William le Scrope, who was own brother to the said Sir Richard, and was wounded and died of his wound, which Sir William was armed Azure, a bend Or" (*S&G*, 2:170). Another deponent noted that Richard's "elder brother [had been] . . . so armed at the siege of Tournay" (*S&G*, 2:291). (As the eldest son, he would have borne arms undifferenced; Richard only gained this right after his brother died without legitimate male heirs of his body.) Sir William was remembered, a stalwart of the earl of Northampton's company at the siege of Vannes, "when the king was there," and finally at the siege of Morlaix. At that engagement he "was there wounded by a quarrel, of which wound he died a few years afterwards" (*S&G*, 2:326).[58]

Richard also had first cousins—men of his own cohort and age—who likewise had earned impressive military credentials. His father's brother Geoffrey had had three sons, only one of whom was still alive at the time of these proceedings. (William had died abroad in 1367, and Stephen probably around 1370 or shortly thereafter.) Henry Scrope, I Lord Scrope of Masham (1312–92) and Richard's first cousin, was a notable figure on his own and prompted many recollections and reminiscences. As they did for Richard, the deponents' memories of Henry ran to numerous campaigns and expeditions, plus a hearty brace of recollections touching how openly and regularly he had displayed his differenced version of the Scrope arms. A simple declaration suffices: "Sir Henry Scrope, son of Sir Geoffrey Scrope, used the said arms on his banners with great honour throughout his life." Another deponent went the hearsay route: "he had heard from his ancestors, in his youth, that Sir Henry Scrope was armed at the battle of Berwick in the same arms with a label, and in those arms received the order of knighthood in that battle." The heraldic variation was a sign of authentication. His banner "was constantly and publicly displayed during the whole expedition" at Balyngham Hill.[59]

Though Henry's brother William had now been dead for nineteen years, his ghost—like that of Richard's brother—was still a presence. A number of middle-aged deponents had campaigned with him. His death in distant Prussia lent additional mystique, as did references to still other Scropes who had fallen in the wars. We can throw a large net over various kinsmen, now deceased, whose feats of arms and peripatetic lives continued to evoke warm memories. There are references to Henry, seen before Paris "in a label argent"; to Geoffrey, buried in Prussia "under these arms with a difference," or to a recollection that he "died in these arms," and that he had been so armed "before the time that he went to Prussia"; to William, "own brother to Sir Richard, and [he] was wounded," "armed day and night at the same siege [of Calais]," and, being "so armed, was wounded" at Morlaix.[60]

The accomplishments of men from the generation prior to Richard's and Henry's had paved the route their families were to travel, from the ranks of service-gentry and the judicial bench to the lofty company of the military aristocracy. Richard's father, Henry, and his uncle Geoffrey (Henry's brother) had been the making of the Scropes. Both had had extremely successful careers as lawyers and king's judges, though their white-collar credentials could be used against them on occasion as a blot on their chivalric and military ones.[61] Henry had died in 1336, Geoffrey in 1340. Firsthand memories of them, with or without their proper coats of arms, were clearly a long stretch. But a number of deponents who claimed to be in their 60s and 70s spoke of them from personal knowledge.[62] For others, the references to the gentility and exalted status of Henry and Geoffrey were based on second- or third-hand information, drawn mainly from the dusty but many-chambered storehouse of hearsay, family lore, and stock tales of those old knights and esquires. There had been more than a few allegations about and disparagements of the family's pre-aristocratic past, and suspicions about the birth of men of law were not easily suppressed. Only a few deponents addressed this directly, however, and mostly it was to laud the older Scropes and to belittle those who dwelt on such reservations and qualifications.

Memories from an older generation are not hard to find. One deponent, John Thirwalle, told of having *heard* of Richard's father using the arms in question, and he had personally *seen* the occasion when Uncle Geoffrey had "used them with differences in the presence of the king" (*S&G*, 2:453). Geoffrey had been an active soldier, though he came to this career later in life. We have accounts of his leading retinues of ten and even of forty men in the field.[63] Before he had gone to the wars at Edward III's call, he had been knighted at a famous tournament at Northampton (*S&G*, 2:352).[64] Thomas Roos of Kendal, who now claimed to be eighty years old, remembered the older man, "the most noble tourneyer of his time that one could find in any country," and he told of seeing him perform feats at tourneys at Dunstable, Newmarket, and Guildford.[65] Nor was Geoffrey deficient on the field of battle. Sir Bertram Montboucher had learned from his ancestors of the time when Edward III, "who had good knowledge of all manner of right to arms," had told Sir Geoffrey, "then in his retinue, with forty men-at-arms," to raise his arms. This had been in those famous old campaigns, the expedition to Burenfos and the siege of Tournay.[66]

The generation of younger family men came in for some recollections as well. These centered on the activities of Richard's eldest son, William; there was little regarding William's brothers, Roger (who became II Lord Scrope of Bolton in 1403) and Stephen of the Scropes of Poulet and Castle Combe. A deponent told of having been retained by William in Gascony, where "he had been armed in the same arms with a label." Another man, with more esoteric adventures under his belt, had seen William when they had gone "beyond the Great Sea" in the company of the duke of Duras in Venice.[67] A deponent of William's generation (aged thirty-three, armed for thirteen years) had seen him, with his brother Stephen, in Lancaster's company on the "great chivauchee through France into Guienne," and their cousin John had also been in the expedition.[68] John was remembered as having been in Brittany, too, "armed in the same arms with difference" (S&G, 2:383). Distant journeys, vivid recollections: "when in Prussia he saw one Geoffrey Scrope buried under these arms with a difference" (S&G, 2:321). Nor was Geoffrey the only one to lie so far from home: "shortly afterwards the said Sir William passed the Great Sea in the company of his said Lord [the earl of Hereford] and there died" (S&G, 2:228). "Burial at Konisgberg in Prussia" was pretty strong stuff to throw in the face of a mere knight from Cheshire (S&G, 2:310).

Battles and Chivalry

Most of the recollections that touched these three generations, coming as they do primarily from old soldiers who had been companions in arms, relate to their presence in battle and on the attendant expeditions. This is what we would expect. The men chosen as deponents (except for the clerics), the kinds of memories relevant for a case before the Court of Chivalry, and the high points of martial life as seen in retrospect all make it likely that old soldiers' memories would set the tone. Nor are we disappointed. The male-bonded generalizations fall into place as social memory, and we think back to our comments about the deponents as a social group—a community dispersed as a physical entity but now reunited at a distance. The old fellowship was re-created through the individual articulations of a common narrative, with a strong generational preference for the bellicose days of the king's grandfather over the temperate foreign policy the young king now sought to implement.[69] Though old soldiers' memories are a reliable guide neither to past events nor to current policy, many of these men clearly thought Richard II an inferior chip off the Plantagenet block.

The tales of the battles engaged in by the Scropes carry us to the northern border, to the fields of France and Spain, and even to expeditions that took Englishmen to and beyond the outermost boundaries of Christendom. And because the tales run, in memory, from campaigns early in the reign of Edward III—as well as those of Edward's father or even his grandfather, in a few instances—to those of recent days, they lead us through the turnover of commanders and their principal engagements and expeditions during the long middle of the century.[70] For the older deponents, bragging rights went all the way back to the early days of Edward III. The great confrontations at Berwick and Halidon Hill (1333) and at Sluys (1340), along with memories of Crecy and the battle of Durham (Neville's Cross), both fought in 1346, rolled easily off the tongue. For the middle and younger generations, the high points had been Espagnols-sur-Mer (1350), Poitiers (1356), and Najara (1367). Even the more recent affairs were now covered with the rime of legend and nostalgia.[71]

In keeping with the relentless march of men and of reminiscences, we note the changing roll call of leadership. But in truth—as they all knew—the great days were over. The warrior-king who had ruled for fifty years was gone, as was his eldest son. If few of the old men could talk of Edward I or Edward II, the vigor of the young Edward III and the Black Prince gave luster to many of their tales. One memory goes much further back, as we hear of Sir Richard's grandfather having been knighted in Scotland "under the banner of the good king Edward with the Longshanks." The tale came from John Thirwalle, whose father had told him "and shewed him before his decease" (*S&G*, 2:426). Other men of years went back to the days of Edward II, referring to the Northampton tournament as well as to a grandfather who had been a companion of Edward of Carnarvon (*S&G*, 2:350, 210). Edward III was familiar to most, though it was the fellowship of his early days that had a particular élan. There are references to "the first expedition in Scotland with the grandsire of our Lord the King," to "the whole reign of Edward III," and even to the days "before the wars in France were commenced by the late king."[72] Mere references to Edward's "last campaign" were common, though such memories served as a convenient benchmark. One old-timer's trump card was to distinguish between "the new wars" and "the old wars" (*S&G*, 2:305, 285).

After the kings, in rank and order of memory, came the royal dukes. When we go back to the victory at Poitiers, it was Edward, prince of Wales (often just referred to as "the prince"), who still towered over memory—the charismatic and peerless first son. He figured in scores of statements from men of Sir Richard's generation. It might be a reference to having seen the Scropes when they were with Prince Edward at Poitiers, or "at Najara in Spain in presence of the Prince," or "when the Prince of Wales first went into Guyenne" (*S&G*, 2:243, 296, 307). After the prince in mythic affection (and strongly supporting the idea that the whole group now assembled on behalf of Sir Richard was pretty much the Lancastrian affinity), it was John of Gaunt around whom memories clustered. He and his inner circle, including Sir Richard, were figures to conjure with. Men had seen Scrope arms at the Battle of Spain, "in company with my Lord of Lancaster," or when he had marched through France. There were references to John as earl of Richmond, perhaps in deference to his northern identity and the loyalties elicited from men who knew the Scropes on their home ground.[73] Gaunt's military adventures (and his vast stable of annuitants and retainers) had shaped the lives and fortunes of many of the deponents, and memories of the "great expedition of that Lord through the kingdom of France to Bordeaux" were clearly memories worth taking off the shelf and passing around (*S&G*, 2:372).[74]

English armies that had gone to the Continent, as well as to Scotland, were large affairs, involving a good fraction of the peers and perhaps the bulk of the knights and esquires of the realm. Thus, in addition to the names and memories of kings and princes, Scrope's old companions had great barons to call to mind. Depositions referred to forces led by Henry, duke of Lancaster: "many great battles and expeditions" figured in these memories (*S&G*, 2:204). After Henry of Lancaster we have his grandson, Henry Bolingbroke (who also served as one of Scrope's deponents). The young Henry, a memorable fixture in the depositions, was the knight errant par excellence of fourteenth-century chivalry and latter-day crusades, if not yet (in 1386) a likely claimant for the throne. We hear of the time when William Scrope, in Henry's company, had "passed the great sea," and when Scrope arms had been displayed "at Satalia in Turkey, when a treaty was concluded between the king of Cyprus and the le Takka, Lord of Satalia."[75] The earl of Northampton, William Bohun, was a royal cousin, and the Scropes had fought under his command. Henry Scrope had displayed his variation of the family's arms on a banner when serving with Bohun's forces "when he chivaucheed by torchlight out of Longhaban [Longhaven] as far as Peebles" (*S&G*, 2:323).[76] Such links are not hard to find. When Sir Richard's arms had once been questioned at the siege of Calais, "his uncle, Robert earl of Suffolk, said that he marvelled at such a challenge of his crest" (*S&G*, 2:209).[77] The duke of Gloucester had also been a commander, and some of the veterans remembered him under his title of earl of Buckingham and commander of forces in Brittany (*S&G*, 2:462, 372). Both great northern houses figure; we have references to Nevilles and to Percys, as well as to the earl of Warwick.[78]

The collective reminiscences of the old soldiers—mixed as they were with those of the younger men—hardly constitute military memoirs in the classical sense. Our depositions are a long way short of Caesar's *Gallic War*, nor do they match the panegyric tone of the Chandos Herald's *Life of the Black Prince* or the *History* of William the Marshal.[79] They were not intended, tale by tale, as a synthetic presentation. Neither was any particular commander or any single battle their focal point, though these memories feature plenty of adulation and hero worship as well as repetition. They constitute rather a melded tale, a composite hymn to the sustained glory of English arms, to the joys of battle and the long campaigns—as in the now-savored recollection of the long march, or a great chevauchée, or the burning of Dumfries.[80] As firsthand testimony from a bellicose world that has left few such recollections, the depositions should not be undervalued. Like the Proofs, they can be readily dismissed as repetitious and formulaic chit-chat. But we should recognize that what was taken seriously then should be taken seriously now.[81] The memories of old battles and old companions were memories of the workplace, of what these men had done for a living. What came to mind when a peculiar proceeding asked them to recall the banners, the companions, and the confusion of the field as they had once formed their ranks at Crecy or Poitiers or Najara? This is not a rhetorical question. The depositions provide us a serious answer.[82]

A third line of exposition to reconstruct is that of chivalry, the military ethos and culture within which these men had lived, bonded, and now—toward what must have been later days for many of them—articulated their reminiscences. The summons to depose before the court was an invitation, an occasion for unlocking an old treasure chest. The experiences of the brotherhood in arms, of sworn and indentured retinues, and of weeks and months together in the field had implanted a still-bright set of memories to which the deponents now gave voice. The experiences of their military careers had provided these men with an on-the-field context within which to live out and enact the values and ideals they had absorbed from those "old knights and esquires, now deceased," who had long before discoursed on the antiquity of the Scropes and the validity of their claim to their arms and honor.[83]

Those who testified on behalf of Sir Richard adhered to the party line. The Scropes were valiant, they had long borne the arms, and they had served their king and his sons with honor in countless battles. Some deponents added a touch of personal pique because the Scrope claim to arms and honor had been impugned and because the deponent himself had been forced to devote some time and effort to refuting the jumped-up pretensions of mere Cheshire knights (though Grosvenor actually was the defendant, not the plaintiff, in the case). Some deponents were outspoken about the need to testify on behalf of an old comrade, driven by their sense of knightly honor. The young earl of Devon, aged about twenty-nine, backed up his words with a sort of oath: "on his chivalry, he is young" (*S&G*, 2:240).[84] Sir Brian Stapleton, an old companion in arms, was indignant that he had to dignify the proceedings. He "was ashamed to affirm 'upon his knighthood,' except to save his oath," that Scrope's arms had been challenged (*S&G*, 2:289). Sir Robert Laton's aged father had turned, in his later years, to writing down (or to drawing) the arms of the great families with whom he had served. His research supported Sir Richard's claim.[85] Another deponent was incensed. The hearings were but a charade; everyone, including Cheshire knights, knew that the Scrope claim had never been gainsaid (S&G, 2:327).[86]

Given the rich texture of these tales, it is no surprise that deponents' memories often ran back to the time when they themselves had been knighted and to how long and vigorously they had served in the wars. This aspect of memory—closer to the world of the Proofs of Age because it involves the active party, not just the object of the memory—approximates biography or autobiography more than those strings of "I saw" and "I was told" statements. Sir Ralph Hastings began by recalling the battle of Durham, when "he [Hastings] was first armed." It was "on the first day he was armed at the said battle" that he saw Sir Richard, "armed in the said arms entire, without a label" (S&G, 2:284). Sir Robert Grenacre worked back to his memory of Scrope in stages. He opened by saying that he had been "armed first in Gascony." This had come at the battle of Lymelenge, "when Sir Thomas Coke was Lieutenant." Then, having set himself in the picture, Grenacre spoke of William, Richard, and Henry—all Scropes of one generation—and then of the sons of Henry, Richard, and Henry's brother (S&G, 2:468–69).[87] A regnal milestone might be referred to: Guy Bryan had been "armed at Stanmow Park, soon after the coronation of the late king" (S&G, 2:254).[88] But if battlefield companionship and a deponent's honor were the wonted themes,[89] one (and only one) deponent admitted that his personal knowledge was limited because he had only seen Scrope in Scotland. When on the Continent, "he was in garrison," rather than in the heroic ranks of charging knights.[90]

One of the recurring themes is honor—the honor of the Scropes and, by extension, of their deponents. The honor of the deponent was implicitly upheld and demonstrated in the course of his tale. But for all the testimony, all the memory and reminiscence and knowledge gained through hearsay and supported by references to emblems and to arms in windows, tombs, and charters, there were peculiar problems about the Scropes. After all, they really were but one generation removed from lawyers. Their claim to knightly arms did raise some genuine doubts. Anything mentioned in the hearings that might have supported a counterclaim regarding their venerable status and knightly past was held up to ridicule. The family assertion of ancient gentility was trumpeted to overawe some nagging questions that clearly had a sort of underground life. Despite all the cover-up and assertiveness, we do learn of some stains and blemishes on the fabric that their partisans wished to present as nothing other than the pure linen of chivalric myth-history. One deponent told a tale of a proposed Scrope marriage, vetoed by the prospective father-in-law because he viewed the match as a mésalliance. But in our version, the good guys were eventually triumphant, and Sir Robert de Hilton, who had rejected Sir Richard's suit, lived to rue the day.

Hilton had originally said, "Now I am glad that he did not marry my daughter, for I have heard say that he is not a 'grand gentilhomme.'" The response, from Scrope's deponent Sir John Hasethorpe ("upwards of one hundred years old"), was, at best, a stand-off: "Oh Sir, say not so, for of certainty and upon my word, he is come of grands gentilhommes from the time of the Conquest" (*S&G*, 2:336–37).

Other references slip out now and then to indicate that the Grosvenor challenge was not the first with which the Scropes had been confronted. In an earlier dispute, a challenge from "one called Carminow of Cornwall" had been referred to the judicial wisdom of six knights, "now dead." They found that the Carminows had carried "Azure, a bend Or" since the time of King Arthur, as against a mere descent from the time of the Conqueror. The result—contrary to all we are usually told about the laws of heraldry—was that "both might bear the arms entire" (*S&G*, 2:165).[91] Smoke, in this instance, certainly suggests fire. Maybe the best response to such a challenge was to assert gentility and military valor and then to turn a blind eye on alternative readings. Friends were certainly happy to talk, some at length, about the undoubted gentility of the Scropes, and on occasion knightly tempers flared. John Thirwalle's aged father referred to their descent "from great and noble gentlemen," and, as we noted earlier, he affirmed that "if I were young I would hold and maintain my saying to the death."[92]

It would seem churlish to conclude this analysis of testimony without paying special attention to the deposition of the most famous (to us) of all those summoned on Scrope's behalf—Geoffrey Chaucer. Chaucer had known Scrope for some years as a consequence of his presence in Gaunt's circle. One recent Chaucer biographer has suggested that Chaucer's testimony was the high-water mark of his involvement with the upper classes and the court.[93] In any case, Chaucer's testimony does provide the only certain instance of his words as he spoke them. Here, as perhaps nowhere in his literary canon, we have the voice of the living man. He may leave us unsatisfied if we turn to him for enlightenment about the Peasants' Rebellion, or Wyclif and Lollardy, or the deposition of 1399. But never mind. He spoke out boldly when it really mattered—that is, on behalf of Sir Richard Scrope.

Nor is this the only striking feature of Chaucer's deposition. He alone, among the several hundred men who attested for one side or the other, offers what we can think of as a bourgeois reflection rather than a military and ancestral one. It was not the weight of northern lore, nor the sight of pennants before the tents and in battle, but rather a banner hanging from a rented room of a London inn that is the centerpiece of Chaucer's deposition. He said, in the usual fashion, that he had served in the wars ("del age de xl ans et plus armez par xxvii ans") and that he knew the Scrope arms from having seen them displayed on numerous fields abroad. But of Grosvenor he knew nothing until he was coming down Friday

Street ("Fridaystrete en Loundres") and saw the familiar arms, only now being openly displayed as those of Sir Robert Grosvenor. The son of the vintner had no doubt, we might say, about which side of his bread held the butter. He, like so many others, had little sympathy for the parvenu: "et ceo fuist le primer foitz qe unqes il oiast parler de Monsieur Robert Grovenour ou de cez auncestres ou de ascun autre portant le noun de Grovenour."[94] The man of letters spoke in the same voice, and the same words, as all the others—or so the reductionism of our text tells us. The Scrope team had been well trained (regardless of whether they were also well rehearsed), and now, on center stage, their most gifted creative thinker performed up to expectations.

And so, from our perspective—which is that of Sir Richard Scrope—the matter wound down. Though his opponents may have been valiant and credible, his case was eventually judged to be the winning one. The longer future, stretching some centuries beyond Richard II's decision of 1390, would give the more serious laurels to the Grosvenors—in the form of vast blocks of priceless West End property and the dukedom of Westminster. But that future lies beyond the tale that the court of the constable has shared with us.[95]

Margaret Paston: The Lady and the Letters

LETTERS AS ARTIFACTS

This is not biography. Such a project is beyond us. Only someone as relatively well documented as Margaret Beaufort or those fifteenth-century women, mostly queens, who lend themselves to a popularized "life and times" approach can be the subjects of a full life study.[1] About all we know about Margaret Paston (née Mautby) is that she was born of a good East Anglian family around 1420 or a bit later, married to John Paston around 1440 or a bit earlier—in a marriage that seems to have worked and that produced many children—and widowed in 1466. She helped hold the Paston reins until her death in 1484 (although she had moved back to her natal family's home at Mautby around 1473 or 1474). The closest she comes to a declaration of independence is her last will. Virtually everything that we know of her is from her letters, and these all emanate from and are redolent of her identity as a mother-widow-matriarch within and among the Pastons.

Despite these limitations in our sources, Margaret Paston is one of the most familiar women of late medieval England, perhaps eclipsed only in recent years by Margery Kempe and Julian of Norwich. She presents herself to us through the medium of her letters. To a lesser extent, we also know about her from the letters written to her, with a further smattering of material in other correspondence that mentions her, especially the letters between her eldest sons, Sir John (II) and John III. But for the most part what we know is what she tells us—what we can extract from her epistolary prose as she goes about her appointed rounds. Instructions from and assessments by her husband, in his eleven letters to her, offer a critical gauge by which we can evaluate her performance, though my tendency is to side with Margaret when his marking standards seem a bit harsh.[2]

The premise behind what I present in this chapter is that Margaret Paston, as an individual (and in many ways a representative woman of her class and culture), can be extracted from the encompassing and smothering context of the Paston family enterprise and pushed forward onto the stage in her own right.[3] As a strong matriarchal figure within the setting of family and family business, she has attracted both attention and admiration, as we saw in the introduction to this volume. To fit her activities into the pattern of the family and the kingdom, we can turn to Figure 2 for a Paston family genealogy and then to Table 8 for a chart that sets the dating and context of her letters against the flow of "current events" and the family's main concerns. But I also hope to lead her away from the family-embedded view of her role and persona that usually governs our interpretive interests. Instead, I will draw some personalized boundaries around the gender-defined problems that any woman of her class and status, married into a family on the make, would be expected to handle. That Margaret would be a good fit for the Paston agenda was accepted, by all parties, virtually from the start. She gave signs that she was up to their high standards of in-house loyalty and competence on that very first day when Agnes wrote to William I about her promise as a bride. Moreover, we should keep in mind that Agnes Paston's standards for a daughter-in-law were not likely to be casual or unworldly ones.[4]

In seeking to extract Margaret Paston from the onrushing current of Paston affairs and to give pause for her own voice as well as an examination of the mechanics of its articulation and the modes of cognition revealed in her letters, I will approach the world she creates in these letters in three stages. First, there is her life and world as explicated through the process of letter writing—the procedural setting within which or by means of which the letters were written. Then I turn to the way the letters, as texts and physical objects, were assembled. How did she move, as their author or overseer, to transmit the news and information she had collected? How had she come to know what she was transmitting? How did she funnel her information so that it fit within the framework of epistolary communication? Packaging the information meant embedding ideas into rhetorical devices and molds whereby credibility could be achieved. This covers a number of issues directly bound up with the process and procedures of letter writing: dating, expressing salutations and farewells, arranging the agenda, and taking steps to see that the letter would be delivered safely and quickly. These all had to be dealt with, step by step and letter by letter, on the road to the final product—a letter to John I or John II or the like. Finally, I will look at a number of topics that center more on Margaret herself: gender, domesticity,

Figure 2: The Paston Genealogy

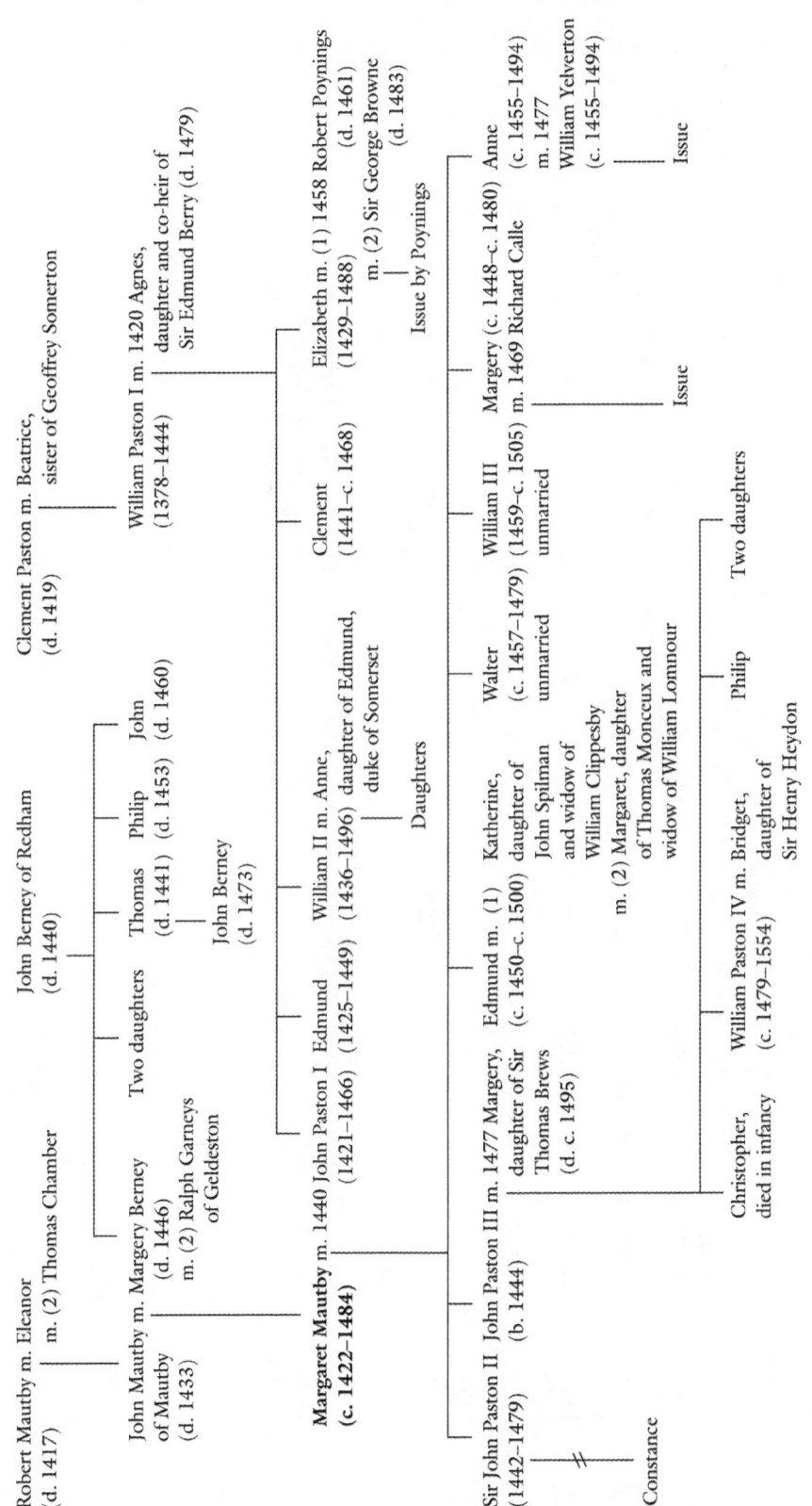

SOURCE: Adapted from Roger Virgoe, *Private Life in the Fifteenth Century: Illustrated Letters of the Paston Family* (London, 1989).

TELLING TALES

Table 8 Margaret's Letters in the Context of "Current Events" and Family Matters

Year	Paston Events	The Realm and Beyond
1440	John I and Margaret marry	
1442	John II born	
1444	John III born; William I dies	
1445		Henry VI marries Margaret of Anjou
1446	Margery Berney (Margaret's mother) dies	
1447		Deaths of Humphrey of Gloucester and Cardinal Beaufort
1448	Margery born; fight over Gresham (until 1451)	
1449	John's brother Edmund dies	
1450	Action against Tuddenham and Heydon	Loss of Normandy; murder of the duke of Suffolk; Cade's rebellion
1453		Loss of Aquitaine; birth of Prince Edward
1454		Duke of York protector; Henry insane
1455	Anne born (?)	First battle of St. Albans; York protector again
1457	Walter born	
1458	John's sister Elizabeth marries Robert Poynings	
1459	Sir John Fastolf dies; William III born	Battles of Blore Heath and Ludford
1460	John I MP for Norfolk	Battles of Northampton and Wakefield; York killed
1461	John I MP for Norfolk	Edward IV accedes: Battles of Mortimer's Cross, St. Albans, and Towton Earl of Oxford executed
1462		
1463	John II knighted	
1464		Edward IV marries Elizabeth Woodville
1465	Duke of Suffolk seizes Hellesdon and Drayton	
1466	John I dies	
1467	John II MP for Norfolk	
1468	Clement dies	
1469	John II betrothed to Anne Haute; Margery (secretly) marries Richard Calle; Caister taken	Battle of Edgecote: Edward IV captured

1470	Caister recovered	Readeption of Henry VI
1471	John II and John III at Battle of Barnet (on losing side)	Edward IV returns; Battle of Tewkesbury
1472	Caister lost to duke of Norfolk	
1473	John Berney dies	
1474	Margaret goes to live at Mautby	
1476		Duke of Norfolk dies
1477	John III marries Margery Brews; Anne marries William Yelverton	Charles of Burgundy killed at Nancy
1478		Duke of Clarence killed
1479	Deaths of Agnes, John II, Walter; William IV born	
1482	Margaret writes her will	
1483		Edward IV dies; Richard III becomes king
1484	Margaret dies in April	

and language. What of all this is peculiar to Margaret, and what is generally representative or typical of women of her status and background? Though much that she does and says can be matched by others, no other English woman of her century has left so many records in her own voice. She is a case study on her own and, simultaneously, a wonderful example of how men and women of the Pastons' world functioned and communicated.

Margaret's Output

Margaret and John I are the key figures of the second generation of Pastons who stand in the center of the letter-informed family saga. In the extant collection of family letters, we have 104 from Margaret—a figure we can set to her advantage against those of other women of her day and against other Pastons (see Table 9).[5] However we draw our comparisons, 104 letters are a lot for a fifteenth-century family collection. Such matters, of course, are relative. Margaret Paston's numbers look less impressive when compared to the 251 letters we have from Hildegard of Bingen or the 382 that Catherine of Siena wrote to 220 different recipients (plus her 25 to collective or multiple recipients).[6] But quantity is only part of the tale. Margaret's letters are beads on the string of family correspondence. There are no personal musings, no chats with girlhood friends, no spiritual exercises, autobiographical excursions, or personal indulgences. None was penned to reveal matters of heart or head—no spiritual counsel (wanted or not), no miniature sermons, no explications of revealed texts, no advice on a proposed crusade, the evils of a schism in the papacy, or the need to leave a husband's bed in pursuit of a chaste marriage and a personal relationship with the crucified Christ.[7] If Margaret is in the second rank when we focus on intellectual and spiritual concerns, we can counter by saying that in many ways she had a tougher agenda to cover than those saintly and learned women whose epistolary output overshadows hers. We should keep in mind that, whatever her many woes, not even the exalted Eloise had to contend with the duke of Norfolk breaking down the doors, and neither Hroswitha of Gandersheim nor Hildegard of Bingen was obliged to deal with wayward sons about cash-flow crises and whether it was time to crop the timber in Sporle Wood.

While Margaret Paston had no dealings with Christine de Pizan or St. Birgitta of Sweden—and there are few signs that their problems were her problems—she certainly did have extensive dealings with other members of the Paston family and with many others of their social and political circle. And in that league of writers and thinkers, at least, she more than held her own. Table 9 shows how members of the family rank in terms of (extant) letters and in terms of the interval between first and last letters. Margaret Paston not only wrote the largest number of letters but also is about on par with her mother-in-law, Agnes; William II,

Table 9 The Pastons as Letter Writers

Writer	Number of Extant Letters	Other Documents	Total	Span of Years
William I	8	4	12	1425–44
Agnes	13	9	22	1440–79
John I	26	17	43	1444–65
Edmund I	1	1	2	1447–49
William II	20	13	33	1452–96
Clement	7	–	7	1461–66
Elizabeth	2	2	4	1459–89
Margaret	**104**	**3**	**107**	**1441–82**
John II	70	16	86	1461–79
John III	70	8	78	1461–1503
Edmund II	6	2	8	1471–93
Walter	3	1	4	1479
William III	9	–	9	1478–92
Margery	6	–	6	1477–89
William IV	1	–	1	1493

SOURCE: Norman Davis, ed., *The Paston Letters and Papers of the Fifteenth Century* (Oxford, 1970–76), vol. I.
NOTE: The category of "other documents" is based upon Norman Davis's editorial conventions: it includes wills, inventories, indentures, memoranda, and so on.

her brother-in-law; and John III (her second son) in terms of the span over which the letters were written. Her numerical superiority over Agnes, her sister-in-law Elizabeth, and her daughter-in-law Margery merely underscores the picture we draw of her long-standing centrality for family concerns.

This depiction of centrality, writ large, helps explain why the Paston letters are the most interesting and familiar of the fifteenth-century family collections. They are reflexive or self-referential; that is, many members of the family and many letters refer to the same events, the same problems, the same cast of kin and other-than-kin. They are a soap opera of upper-class provincial life. New characters enter, though mostly to a slow cadence; old familiars often seem reluctant to leave the stage; shadowy figures hover at the edges over the decades. The plot line changes slowly, if at all, though we also have to be on the alert for the unexpected in the dramatic guise of violence, death, plague, and political reversal. If the Paston letters shed less light on the larger world than the Cely letters, they more than compensate by giving us a variety of readings on some sustained themes. And in so many of these readings it is Margaret—the stay-at-home, the most static of all the major figures—who stands in the center. It is not that she was a major decision maker. Our sympathy for her should not lead to an exaggeration of her independence or of the space allowed her for exercising much initiative concerning positions taken by her husband and sons.[8] She was the central clearinghouse, however—a role she played with honor and success for more than thirty years.

Among the families who have left letters, no other fifteenth-century woman has a role at all comparable (not even her mother-in-law, Agnes, who was too old and perhaps too quarrelsome by the time the tale becomes a rich one). Other letter collections from this world of fifteenth-century discourse give little scope to their women as agents, though they raise some interesting questions. In simple numbers, their returns are thin compared with the Pastons. Only one letter is directed to any of the Cely women, for instance, and that—to Agnes, Richard, and George Cely ensemble—is a news item about the duke of Burgundy's victory over the king of France.[9] The Plumptons and the Stonors give us better returns. Of the Plumpton letters, approximately fifteen are by a woman, seventeen are addressed to a woman, three are both written by and directed to a woman, and one additional document relates to a woman's business affairs.[10] The Stonor collection offers twenty-eight letters from, thirteen or fourteen to, and one by and also to a woman, with eight miscellaneous documents also falling within our circle of inquiry.[11]

There are other aspects to the issue of women as authors (and recipients), however, than a mere tally of their overall activity conveys. In both the Plumpton and Stonor collections, we have one or two women around whom a goodly cluster of letters can be fixed. In the seventeen months between 16 November 1502 and 26 April 1504, Agnes Plumpton wrote eight letters: six to Sir Robert Plumpton and one each to Thomas Everingham and Richard Plumpton. (She also received two letters in that span.[12]) For the Stonors, the comparable woman is Elizabeth Stonor, and her nova-like emergence—admittedly for a short period—is quite striking. Between 18 August 1476 and 26 March 1479, she wrote thirteen letters, and there is an account preserved from her household.[13] In this same period she also received seven letters. Her short-term prominence is apparent; between 18 August 1476 and 7 March 1477 she sent eight of the fifteen Stonor letters, and she received five of the fifteen that came in between 17 May 1478 and 1 August of that year. Bursts of real letter-writing activity not only left their mark but also reinforce the untestable but likely hypothesis that many more women's letters may have been written than have survived. This seems more likely than the idea of a meek and deferential Agnes Plumpton or Elizabeth Stonor just jumping up one day, fixing on the desirability of becoming an active correspondent, and then exhausting her interest after a year or two of intense activity.

The number of Margaret's letters, by itself, is but a limited guide to a woman's role. A count of letters received by all the Pastons highlights the gulf between the parts played by the leading men and the leading woman. Table 10 shows that John I received many times the letters he wrote. His views were sought, his favor petitioned, and he was kept informed—by others—far more often, and in more detail, and with more deference, than it fell to him to communicate on his own. That two-thirds of the letters he received were from other-than-kin indicates that

Table 10 The Pastons as Recipients of Letters

Recipient	Letters from Family Members	Letters from Non-Family Members	Total Letters Received
William I	–	12	12
Agnes	1	3	4
John I	109	265	374
Edmund I	1	1	2
William II	2	2	4
Margaret	55	29	84
John II	58	47	105
John III	62	70	132
Edmund II	–	1	1
William III	1	6	7
Margery	–	1	1
William IV	–	5	5

SOURCE: Davis, ed., *Paston Letters and Papers*.

he was the foreign secretary (as well as the prime minister) for Paston family matters—the one to whom others reported and with whom others sought to do their business. It behooved them to inform and beseech him as they sought his help, advice, and good lordship. John II and John III received many fewer letters than their father, but roughly half of those received by each son came from outside the family.

In this regard, Margaret's less-than-independent status shows clearly, and to her disadvantage, if we impose a quantitatively governed interpretation on these data. Most letters directed to her were from the men nearest her (eleven from John I, twenty from John II, and eighteen from John III, with another four from William II and one apiece from Edmund II and from Walter). It was expected that she would gather and transmit the news—mostly within the family—whereas she was usually bypassed by outsiders who knew that it was more useful to go straight to the men. Sometimes these outsiders sought her in her feminized role as intercessor, and sometimes they wrote because they knew how to contact Margaret, who was probably at home while the men were away or on the move. But rarely did outsiders expect her to be a decision maker, at least not for matters beyond the domestic sphere (though occasionally they consulted her on issues affecting local and manorial concerns when John I was out of reach or John II out of harmony).

Matters touching modes of cognition and news gathering, as well as those relating to the structure and content of the letters, will be treated below. But there are some further aspects of the mechanics of letter writing—the approach to the process whereby a letter was produced—that shed light on Margaret's roles and on how she perceived and executed them. One of her primary responsibilities was to assure the regular flow of news. She was diligent about dating her letters, though the year was often omitted. This omission of the year reminds us of the ephemeral nature and short-term purpose of the family letters; by that same point in the following year, a given letter would presumably have been covered over, buried by layers of subsequent ones. Though assigning years to the letters has plagued their editors, in my comments about the pace of Margaret's letters I accept Davis's judgments about their dating.[14] Table 11 shows the timing or spacing of her letters. It also shows the near monopoly John I enjoyed as the recipient of her letters, with a marked clustering in the years before his death in 1466. After John I, in frequency and importance, come John II and John III. Few other recipients were of much prominence. Her labors were almost exclusively directed to her husband, the two eldest boys, and but few others.

From her first recorded letter (1441) until the death of John I (1466), Margaret wrote 71 letters. All but one were to her husband. After his death she branched out a bit, and her change in tone from dutiful wife to matriarchal conscience (or nag) is a well-recognized characteristic of her long widowhood.[15] Writing almost exclusively to John I, she sent 12 letters in the 1440s, 18 in the 1450s, and 40 in the years of the 1460s in which he was alive. The 1460s were by far her most active decade: 10 letters to John I in 1461, 16 in 1465. After he died she wrote 12 more letters in that decade to a wider pool of recipients. In the 1470s she wrote 23 letters, mostly (but not exclusively) to her sons. And yet, when we look at Table 11, the whole pace—except perhaps for 1461 and 1465—is fairly casual. Her 104 letters in thirty-seven years is not exactly a literary landslide. If Margaret was the fifteenth-century champion, what can we say for the others?

The Scribal Role

In moving from quantitative considerations to questions of form and content, I turn to the process of constructing (and sending) a letter. In this discussion, Margaret's letters are de-narrativized. This endeavor runs contrary to current trends of historical and textual analysis—and in some ways runs contrary to what I did in the previous chapters with the Proofs and the Scrope depositions. The archaeology of the texts and the relationship between their form or structure and the way they "delivered" their substance now come under scrutiny. A letter is a text, one designed to impart cognitive substance of some sort, and it emerges as the end result of a process that involves the organization of content and the application of the social and physical techniques of letter writing.

Margaret Paston's use of scribes is a good place to launch this inquiry. The use of scribes for creating the letters as physical objects is, in part, a gender-defined characteristic of fifteenth-century family letters. Paston women, along with all other women of their social and educational ilk, did not pen their own

Table 12 Margaret's Letters, Year by Year

Year	Number of Letters and Recipients
1441	2 to John I
1443	1 "
1444	1 "
1448	3 "
1449	5 "
1450	1 "
1451	6 "
1452	2 "
1453	5 "
1454	2 "
1459	2 "
1460	4 "
1461	10 "
1462	4 "
1463	4 "
1464	2 "
1465	16 to John I; 1 each to John II and John III
1466	1 to John II
1467	1 "
1469	6 "
1470	3 to John II; 1 to John III
1471	1 to John II; 3 to John III
1472	2 to John II; 4 to John III
1475	3 to John II; 2 to John III
1477	1 to John II
1478	1 "

SOURCE: Davis, ed., *Paston Letters and Papers*.
NOTE: After 1478, there is just an indenture for a lease (1480) and a working copy of Margaret's will, dated 1482. Margaret wrote three letters to other recipients: one letter in 1466, one in 1473, and one in 1477.

letters. This stands in contrast to the Paston men, who often chose to play an active personal role in this physical part of the process. At one time, just as ornithologists hope for sightings of rare species, those who worked with family letter collections held out hope for signs of the women's hands. But the case for women's personal authorship and penmanship, alas, has pretty much gone the way of the dodo and the passenger pigeon. We seem to have little choice but to accept these letters as being in a (male) scribal hand, with perhaps a weak scribble here and there to argue for some minimal touch of female oversight.[16]

The analysis I offer here of Margaret's scribes—like that of the letters' dating—follows Davis. Accordingly, the material of Table 12 sheds some murky light on how Margaret went about "writing" a letter. It also serves as a further caveat about how much we do *not* know about the Paston household. That more than one-third of her letters was penned by one or another of the various "unknown

Table 12 Margaret's Scribes, as Identified by Davis

Scribe	Number of Letters	Duration of Scribal Activity	Notes
Main unknown hand	20	4/48–2/54	All to John I
Gresham	3	4/48–5/56	Postscript to 128; draft of 197
Gloys	20	3/52–11/72	208; 4 to John I, 3 to John II, 11 to John III
John III	11	9/59–3/62	169 (mix); all to John I
Daubeney	11	12/59–5/65	153 (mix); all to John I; postscript to 169
Calle	3	11/60–8/75	2 to John I; 1 to John III
Friar J. Mowthe	1	6/5/64	
John II	2	6/64–7/65	To John I
Pampyng	1	15/7/70	To John II
Wykes	10	5/65–10/66	
Edmund Paston	5	9/69–6/72	4 to John II; 1 to John III
Misc. unknown hands	15		

SOURCE: Davis, ed., *Paston Letters and Papers*.
NOTE: The references are to Davis's numbering of the letters in *The Paston Letters and Papers*, not to pages in his edition.

hands" is sobering, hinting perhaps at a whole host of secrets the Pastons have not yet been cajoled into divulging (and that the purposeful nature of the letters conspires to keep buried from our inquiries).

We can compare Margaret's total reliance on scribes with the practices of her husband and sons. The forty-three letters, memoranda, and petitions from John I reveal a distinct pattern regarding the process of writing. If Margaret—with no letters in her own hand at all—is positioned at one extreme, John stands on the independent or do-it-yourself side of the middle. Few of his letters or other written materials were wholly or only in a scribal hand, and few were wholly in his. Most were some kind of mix: John's hand and that of another, or of several other hands, or mostly but not completely by John, and so on. The picture that emerges is one of him doing business amid his familiar circle of servants and counselors, men like John Pampyng and James Gresham, men not too exalted to write the actual letter, the physical artifact.[17] John would naturally turn to one of them to dictate or perhaps to talk out the gist of the matter that was to be written. But in either case, John was wont to go over the document, quill in hand, before it was sealed. In some instances the letter's length and the time needed for its physical creation meant that a number of hands had been used as men, including John himself, would come and go. Rather than simple dictation here, we seem closer in John's texts to the epistolary counterpart of a modern speechwriter's relationship with a superior regarding what was to be covered, with room for the boss's personal touches toward the end of the process. If John I lacked time or interest to write his letters from scratch, neither, it would seem, was he apt to send them out without some personal editing, some additions from his own hand.

It is not surprising that many of John's identifiable scribes were men who played this same role for Margaret: Gloys, Calle, Gresham, and Pampyng (though with just one letter written for Margaret). Unknown hands abound for John, as for Margaret, especially for John's numerous legal documents and petitions (where his own personal touches might well have been counterproductive). Looking at his papers in full, the shared-hands style is the predominant pattern: John I and Gloys, an unknown hand with John's corrections,[18] John III with touches from John I, Pampyng's hand for the main text but the letter completed by John, Pampyng's hand but the address added by John, William of Worcester with John's additions, and so forth.[19] One letter, preserved as a draft, shows the work of five hands, whereas only three of his letters seem to be wholly in John's autograph.[20] All of this business was done openly within or shared with his trusted circle. The unknown hands, particularly for formal or formulaic documents, may have been those of hired scribes, local clerics, or men with legal training who passed through but who moved on with no long-standing connections or prominence elsewhere to reveal their identity.[21]

When we look at the letters of John II and John III, we can trace a path going from a heavy reliance on scribal hands toward increasing self-help. Of John II's eighty-six letters and documents, sixty-four were totally in his own hand. The other letters—whether the hand is known or not—were all a mix of John II and an amanuensis. Even some of his inventories and memoranda were in his own hand, whereas his father had been content to turn this sort of workaday stuff over to another.[22] And for John III—who had been called upon as a twelve-year-old to act as one of his mother's scribes—there was almost no reliance upon anyone else. Of his seventy-eight letters, all but seven were wholly in his hand. Only a few documents other than letters were given to a professional or scribal hand, and even here John III did the bulk of the work.[23]

Some of this distinction between the father and his sons may reflect a growing readiness by the gentry to take pen in hand because of increasing confidence in the tools and techniques of literacy. But it may also tell something of how the Pastons perceived their roles and images. We can posit that John I chased the goal of being seen as a serious squire in his community—a would-be John Fastolf or "good Sir Thomas Erpingham," to name some likely role models in the East Anglian establishment. Paston sons, though not without social clout and even with a knighthood, come across more as squires with an eye on the court and social climbing rather than as men aiming for a place within their own county and its provincial circle of attorneys and annuitants. They were another generation removed from the family's dubious roots, and perhaps their lack of status anxiety was reflected, paradoxically, in a willingness to write their own letters. This also meant that they could keep more of their own counsel, as we think of such matters, and it may offer an alternative reading to the picture of feckless character their parents were so eager to enlarge upon. This may be a great deal to infer from tracing the use of scribes over the years, but it does come to mind.

The Paston men, as letter writers, certainly had options regarding this key part of the whole process. They could, if they wished, do business pretty much on their own, or, alternatively, they could delegate some part of the task and then hand-finish it. The women of the family never had the freedom to decide. When Margaret was moved to write a letter, she had to turn to a scribe who was available; for her, the process always had to be a two-person affair (at the minimum). Table 12 shows her heavy reliance on a few hands: Gloys, John III, Daubeney, and the "main unknown hand." At the same time, the table indicates that she employed a large number of different hands during the course of her letter-writing career. (Davis estimates about twenty hands in all.) In contrast to the scribes who took her dictation ten or more times, five of the hands wrote three or fewer letters, as did a number of men lumped into the "miscellaneous unknown" category. While she clearly had her favorites—her "old reliables"—she used others as well, though whether from choice or necessity is beyond us. Some of her favorites were heavily utilized within a short span. Wykes wrote ten of her letters to John in that great flurry of activity in the mid-1460s. But others, such as Gresham (three letters over an eighteen-year interval) and Gloys (eighteen letters, spread over twenty-two years) were around for the long haul and may have been used as fallbacks, when needed, rather than as scribes of first resort.

This analysis of Paston scribes is as close as we come to opening a door into their household. Three of the sons were also employed—or press-ganged, if we wish—and Margaret first turned to John III when he was but twelve years old. (His hand in letters 152 and 154 reveals a pre-adolescent literacy.[24]) John III continued to be of service in this capacity for three years, or presumably until he was about ready to leave home and focus on making his own way in the world. His older brother, John II, was only tapped a couple of times when he was around the household in the mid-1460s; he was a more likely subject of his mother's letters than their scribe. Brother Edmund only appeared on the scene in 1469, when the older boys were long gone, and he too was called upon to shoulder a fair amount of scribal work in a short period.

That Margaret would use her sons as scribes seems quite reasonable; they were educated young men, being apprenticed into the family enterprise (and all the letters John II and John III wrote for her were to their father). But perhaps it was more than just convenience. In the mind games played within the family, it is possible that the son-as-scribe assignment may have been a way of co-opting him to his parents' view of the Paston world, in contrast to his brother(s), who constantly had to be brought up to the mark. Having a son act as scribe might open his eyes so that he would buy into the John I–Margaret definition of duty, sharing their diligent approach to business and thrift. Such a move was designed to play him against his brothers—the very sort of good son/bad son scenario that John I and Margaret (and certainly Agnes, even more so) would have found a congenial pattern of intra-familial relations. If we turn to the substance of the letters that her sons wrote as her scribes, presumably taking direct dictation from their mother, there is little in the text to distinguish these letters from those of other scribes, other hands. Whatever family dynamics were being played out when Margaret dictated a letter to John III for John I, or to Edmund for John II, the tone and message are unexceptionable. As with some of the other scribes, especially the main unknown hand, she made her most extensive use of John III and Edmund within a fairly short interval (ignoring John II's two letters dictated by his mother). John III was the hand for eleven of the nineteen letters between September 1459 and March 1462, a period of thirty months. Not quite up to this sustained level, Edmund did his duty five times out of a batch of fourteen letters, and he did all his secretarial work in a span of thirty-three months, from September 1469 to June 1472.

The letters the boys wrote contain many features of interest but no signs that the mother-son teamwork affected their content or style. Margaret's opening lines, as taken down by John III for his father's perusal, were those of conventional affection and deference: "Ryth worchepfull housbonde, I recommnde me on-to yow" (*PL*, I, 152). Political sensibilities in the autumn of 1460 argued for caution, but Margaret spoke as freely through her young son as she did through her other scribes: "Ther is gret talkyng in thys contré of the desyir of my lorde of York. The pepyll reporte full worchepfully of my lord of Warwyk" (*PL*, I, 154). She continues, "they haue no fer her but þat he and othyr scholde schewe to gret favor to hem þat haue be rewyllerys of thys contré be-for tyme." When she was a little waspish toward her husband—and this is about as close as she ever comes to open criticism—she lets her son write down the words, "I wot not whedyr ye had the lettyr or not, for I had non answer ther-of fro yow" (*PL*, I, 157). But sharp words to her husband were less common than those of solicitude, and she ended one letter in a son's hand by saying, "And the blyssyd Tryntyé haue yow in hys kepyng and send yow good sped in all yowyr materys, and send þe vyctory of all yowyr enemyis" (*PL*, I, 164). Nor were areas of family friction hidden from the boys, as a postscript to that November 1461 letter indicates: "My modyr wold ryth fayne know how þat ye and my brodyr Wylliam wer a-cordyd; sche wold ryth fayne þat all wer well be-twen yow."[25] And what affection Margaret did openly express toward John I might be in a letter taken down by her son: "for my hert schall nevyr be in ese tyll I haue tydyngys fro yow" (*PL*, I, 168).[26]

A similar tale can be offered regarding the content of the letters Edmund wrote at his mother's behest. The famous letter in which Margaret told John II of his sister's betrothal to Richard Calle was in young Edmund's hand.[27] But most of the letters followed the usual agenda, with no signs of reticence or circumlocution due to the scribe's identity. Margaret tells only the truth to her sons, or so she claims: she marvels they do not write, the brothers must help each other, there is general shame at John II's failure to build his father's tomb, and much more of this sort.[28] This reading of the mother-son team supports the view that the letters can be read as verbatim transcriptions of orality, with little scope in their final version (ignoring their orthography) for the identity of the scribe by whom they were transformed from speech into text.

Margaret's use of other favorites for scribal duties was presumably one of the conventional forms of service-cum-friendship expected within an upper-class household between a lady and her close circle of white-collar employees and servants. Some of the men she used also wrote letters for John I or their sons, which is hardly surprising; so did some of the unknown hands. Of those on whom Margaret relied a good deal, Gloys also had a hand in seven of John I's letters, Daubeney wrote one for John II, and Wykes penned three for John II. Richard Calle, the steward and therefore the highest ranking near-home servant, was active for Margaret but hardly for anyone else (at least not as a scribe).[29] We also have John Pampyng, who wrote fifteen letters for John I and one for William II, and James Gresham, who wrote three for John I. Margaret even had one letter in the hand of John Mowthe, prior of Holy Trinity, Norwich, the man to whom she and Agnes had taken their case on that exciting Sunday when Gloys had been assaulted in the street (*PL,* I, 129).

The unknown hands pose a number of questions, none of which we can answer. The main unknown hand was utilized for twenty letters, and all in Margaret's early days, between April 1448 and February 1454. Though Davis never speculated about the identity of this scribe, he traced his maturation (as revealed in his penmanship) and suggested a young Norfolk servant, perhaps one who eventually moved on to other things (or died).[30] That someone was so integral to the household as to be the scribe for twenty of his mistress's letters and yet leave no trace of his identity is, as I have noted, an indication of the mysteries of the Paston household. The miscellaneous unknown hands appear—or are resorted to—throughout Margaret's letter-writing years. From these scribes we have a letter here, a letter there, and no indication of whether they were clerical hands, hired for the moment, or men with legal training, or (more likely) literate figures who circled around the household, perhaps as dinner guests and traveling clerics.[31] Margaret's earliest letters are by unknown hands.[32] So are the letters at the far end of her long road and the draft of the will she wrote in 1482.[33] Shadowy figures always flitted at the edges of the main stage, more in shade than light; some of the various unknown hands also wrote letters, or parts of letters, for John I and others.[34]

There are a few more questions. Many of the letters from John I are in more than one hand; usually it was a scribe and John himself. For Margaret we also have a number of letters that bear the mark of more than a single hand, though the second one is never hers. Do these composite letters open any additional windows on her letter-writing operations? For Margaret it is a question of the mix of scribes rather than of "author" and scribe. In one letter to John of September 1443, the unknown hand of the text is succeeded by a second unidentified one for the postscript (*PL,* I, 126). This is the early letter in which Margaret worries about John's slow recovery from a serious illness. The postscript (by the second unknown hand) conveys regards from Agnes and concludes by telling John that, "Your sone faryth wel, blyssyd be God." The impression here is that additional family news came in at the last moment, perhaps after the first scribe had finished and gone off on another task.

Other multiple-hand letters give a similar impression. One man finished the original agenda (or perhaps he just ran out of time), and a second covered the later items. We see some of this in a very long letter, printed as 101 lines: Gloys wrote the first 25 lines and then Calle took over for 27 lines on the recto, plus 19 lines on verso (*PL,* I, 189). But Calle also made interlinear corrections and amendments in Gloys's text, indicating that an editorial hand or eye (whether of Calle or of Margaret) went over the first part of the text. Another multi-hand letter begins with an unknown scribe; Calle's hand enters to write out its second half; Pampyng provides marginal notes; and a "v" in John I's hand appears in the top left-hand corner (he being the letter's recipient). Furthermore, Calle picked up from the unknown scribe in mid-sentence: he inherited a line beginning, "Master John Salatt hathe," and he continued with "made a serge in the regestre this monethe" (*PL,* I, 193).[35]

The presence of a second hand in some of Margaret's letters stands in contrast to John I's working with his staff and seemingly turning to whomever was there and happened to be free to take down the gist of his letter. Does the presence of a second hand argue that a letter by/from Margaret can be read as a collective enterprise, a report from the entire household staff? While the letter was hers, it was also a newsletter from Paston headquarters, carrying information on many matters. That these were not personal letters—and that the business covered was of interest to the entire circle of Pastons—argues for this broader view of their scope and purpose. There is no indication that Margaret turned to any particular scribe for any given kind of business or for letters intended for any specific recipient. The "whoever is free and available" approach, when it came time to write, seems a likely method of operation. I think the data in Table 12 support this idea of a casual approach in the choice of the hand that actually did the writing, whether we can identify it or not.

Certainly, the dictated letter—not to mention the multi-hand letter—comes to us as an artifact from a world in which privacy was not much of a factor. Secrets were secrets for the Pastons and for their close circle, not personal messages.[36] Crowded and shared living quarters, the frank treatment of arranged marriages (and ages for consummation and signs of pregnancy), the familiar sight of the dead and the dying and the plague-stricken: who in a world of such common culture would be reticent simply because family business matters were aired before a servant, a retainer, or a son? We have tales of modern army life in which men of minimal literacy turn to comparative strangers for letters of personal and family intimacies. Why would Margaret hesitate to say that she longed for a daily letter, or that her pregnancy was now showing and everyone was teasing her about the present he had given her when he was home? Scribes were a fact and facet of upper-class life. For the women, they were but another piece of the paraphernalia and the process needed to get the missive on paper and then to its recipient.

Two scribal hands in a letter indicate a division of labor. They also reveal, at least in some cases, that the letter was kept open and unsealed until the last minute, the moment when it was handed over to the departing courier. It was held back against the chance of a postscript and finally for the address. The address—a non-contextual aspect of a letter—often was in a second scribe's hand (and this was sometimes the case for John I). It was part of the boilerplate, the conventional and standardized information that had no link with the letter's substance. Something along the lines of "to my ryght worschipfull husbond John Paston in haste" is usually about all we find (*PL*, 1, 193).[37] In printed editions of the letters, the heading or address appears atop the text, coming (in Davis's edition) before his editorial headnotes about dating, the hand, and scholarly citations. It is separated from the text by these insertions. In the manuscripts, however, the address is on the outside of the letter—on verso, with the letter on recto (or at least, having been begun on recto). As the paper was folded in preparation for the courier the address on the verso—and usually only the address (perhaps along with Margaret's seal)—could be read. The text was hidden by having been turned inward in the folding process, and it was confined to the inside of a sheet that may have been folded into twelve sections (three horizontal folds, four vertical, or some variation depending on size)—unless the message turned out to be too much for the first side of the sheet and had to be continued on what we see as the back or outside.

Some of Margaret's letters carry no address at all on the outside. If we are working with a draft, this poses no problems. But in some cases the letter was sent (and clearly reached its proper destination). Here the absence of an address might argue against the idea that the scribe, coming to the end of her dictation, immediately folded and helped seal the sheet, whereupon it was directly handed to a messenger, all primed and ready to hit the road. Or, alternatively, the messenger may have been a household servant or a familiar figure who did not have to be told that it was "to myn ryth worshipfull hosbond John Paston," let alone that it should be "delyveryd in hast" (*PL,* I, 238, 128).[38] Sometimes there is no address on letters penned by familiar hands: Gloys, Daubeney, John III, and Edmund, as well as those from the usual collection of unknown hands (see *PL,* I, 143, 173, 152, and 203, among others). And yet all the letters written by the main unknown hand are addressed, and in his hand. These date from early in the Margaret–John I correspondence. Perhaps in those early days messengers had to be sought and carefully directed, whereas in later years Margaret was more likely to hand the letter to a servant or a known courier with some confidence about delivery.

The process of collecting information, writing a letter, and seeing that it was safely delivered reminds us that we are in a world of little technology but many servants. Whether it was easy or difficult to write a letter can only be answered in relative terms, but an appreciation of the many steps and stages needed to produce what we now casually read on the printed page should be kept in mind as we think of how that which Margaret had learned was about to be packaged for delivery.[39]

A few more reflections on the need for and use of a scribe. In some ways this process or interaction implies dependence; a second party with the requisite skills (including discretion) always had to be found. *He* had to have free time as well as a supply of ink and paper or parchment.[40] Many of Margaret's letters were long ones by the standards of fifteenth-century family letters. And dependence upon someone else's technological skills—literacy and the requisite training to focus his literacy on an epistolary product—means a limit on one's personal freedom concerning when to write, what to say, how to phrase it, and so forth. And yet Norman Davis held that the wording of the women's letters was very much their own, with the scope for scribal variation largely confined to orthography, and I concur in this.[41] Whatever the collective discussions that went on before and even during the writing and dictating process, the linguistic and psychological arguments favor the reading of her letters as *her* words and thoughts.

To us, dependence and dictation carry connotations they did *not* carry for the Pastons, especially for the women. If dictation today emphasizes reliance on a scribe, it also connotes the unequal status inherent in hierarchical relationships: boss (typically male), secretary (typically female). The norm or stereotype is that he dictates, she transcribes. If he cannot proceed without her help, that assistance has been bought and paid for, whether at fair value or not. But this seems an anachronistic reading to impose upon a fifteenth-century process or interaction that did not noticeably hinder freedom of expression, a pithy turn of phrase, a temptation to backbite, or a need to talk of serious and private affairs.

For Margaret, the unvarying use of an intermediary between authorial intent and words on paper should not be read as a psychological impediment to frank and personal discourse. The use of an amanuensis was a standard part of the process—like the preparation of the paper or addressing and dating the letter—and it presumably was assimilated or subsumed within the larger rhetorical and cognitive process of organization and composition. We work from the premise that his presence hampered neither style nor substance. The scribe was the professional, and the convention of unburdening oneself in a letter while another took down the words was (and is) as acceptable as undressing before a doctor or telling all to a priest (or a stranger in a bar).

CONSTRUCTING THE LETTERS: HOW TO TELL IT LIKE IT IS

The letters between Margaret Paston and John Paston I were usually a matter of sticking to business. She supplied him with news and covered a fairly set agenda of local information, family affairs, and domestic needs. Here and there in the sixty-nine letters she sent to him and in the eleven we have from John I to Margaret, there are personal touches and exchanges between husband and wife that implicitly bespeak the sharing of bed, the begetting and raising of children, and the molding of a common outlook. Sometimes she filled him in on the way foreign affairs (e.g., French raids) touched upon East Anglia.[42] But if we are hoping to come upon a string of late medieval valentines, or of personal ruminations about the great chain of being, or of secular prose as affected by the romances and chivalric stories found in the libraries of the gentry, we have to look elsewhere.[43] The Pastons of Margaret's generation come across as serious people, and their letters—certainly Margaret's to John and vice versa—rarely include anything but serious business. And for what it is worth, Margaret's parents-in-law, William I and Agnes, seem even grimmer and more self-contained, judging from the small number of their letters that we have.[44]

By the fifteenth century, the family letter had taken firm root. Given that we have only the merest handful of such letters (especially from women) at or by the very end of the fourteenth century, the rapid flowering of and common resort to epistolary communication by the educated laity is a topic deserving of more attention than it is about to receive here.[45] Their personal circumstances certainly contributed to the Pastons' interest in writing and using letters. They must have had a family predilection for this form of self-contained, ongoing communication, as so many of them took to the medium.[46] Nowhere do we see any signs of reticence about letters as a form of communication. No apologies touching their fall from Ciceronian standards and Augustinian vision; no self-deprecation about either language or conceptualization. Business was business, and family letters were quickly and easily absorbed into the cultural and technical pool of skills known to and used by people such as the Pastons.[47]

None of the bourgeoisie from whom our letter collections emanate ever make any explicit references to those "how to do it" manuals we mentioned earlier, popular though such materials supposedly were. While this lacuna may reveal our limited knowledge of their libraries (or of their own reticence about their training and skills), it also suggests that the contents of those *ars dictaminis* had been so smoothly assimilated into the culture of literacy that men and women with some education could just sit down and "write" their letters. Moreover, a family letter was just a family letter; very few even hint at larger aspirations.[48] Nevertheless, the letters had both structure and purpose, opening with a salutation, then dealing with whatever contents or substance comprised the *raison d'être*, and then moving to completion with a closing formula, a date (sometimes), and some version of a signature. And from our perspective, their use and preservation offer insights into the lay voice on its meandering pilgrimage from orality to written record.

When Margaret Paston determined that it was now time to write to John, or to one of her other correspondents, both she and those who would actually write the letter (which probably means transcribe it) moved to block out the business before them. Given what we have said about her need to prepare for the task—scribe, writing materials, an agenda to cover, a courier to be lined up and instructed—we appreciate the effort and the seriousness of letter writing. Given this, it is interesting to see that most of Margaret's letters were of some significant length, as though once the effort was being made at all, it might as well be a serious and sustained effort.

Table 13 shows the length of Margaret's letters. (I use the lines given in Davis's edition; the manuscripts, though varying in width and density of penmanship, contain about two-thirds the number of lines of the printed version.[49]) Of course, a lengthy letter is a comparative or relative assessment, as is the question of how many letters it takes to become "many letters" when talking about Margaret's extant output. We see that about one-half of her letters run (as printed) to forty lines or more (51 of 104, or 49 percent). Of her 69 letters to John, 32 were forty lines or longer, as were 19 of her 35 letters to other recipients—the proportion of long to short being much the same, whether to John I or otherwise. Her sons, after their father's death, were her usual recipients, and her letters to them were comparable in length to what they had been to John I, despite the change in her tone. Of her 32 shorter letters (thirty lines or fewer, as printed), 22 were to John I. And of the longer letters, 13 percent of the letters to John I were between fifty and seventy-nine lines, and the same percentage ran to

Table 13 Margaret's Letters, by Length, as Printed in Davis's Edition

Writer and Recipient	Number of Lines							
	< 19	20–29	30–39	40–49	50–59	60–79	80–99	100+
Margaret to John I (N = 69)	7	15	15	14	5	4	5	4
Margaret to others (N = 35)	3	7	6	8	6	4	1	–
John I to Margaret (N = 11)	1	3	–	1	1	3	–	2
John I to others (N = 15)	2	6	3	1	–	3	–	–
John II to Margaret (N = 21)	1	4	4	7	2	3	–	–
John II to others (N = 49)	6	10	8	12	4	5	2	2

SOURCE: Davis, ed., *Paston Letters and Papers*.
NOTE: The four letters from Margaret more than 100 lines in length were 132 (15 February 1449), at 119 lines; 180 (10 May 1456), at 140 lines; 189 (7 August 1465), at 102 lines; and 192 (27 September 1465), at 129 lines.

eighty lines or more. Of letters to others, 29 percent (10 of 35) were between fifty and seventy-nine lines, and only one took up more than eighty lines. So we see that at least two of every three times Margaret wrote, she produced a letter of appreciable length: 72 of her 104 letters (or 69 percent of her extant correspondence) were thirty lines or more.

We can compare Margaret's practice with those of her husband and her eldest son. John I, writing far fewer letters (eleven to Margaret and fifteen to others, excluding the numerous petitions and memoranda), mostly wrote short letters *except* for two very long ones, penned with mountains of instructions for Margaret (and for Daubeney and Calle). John II followed no set pattern regarding length when writing to his mother, although he never went over seventy-nine lines and he was generally inclined to stay below fifty. When writing to others (mainly John III), he could be a little more expansive. His two long letters are to Walter Writtle in September 1469, during the siege of the Paston household at Caister, and to John III in February 1470. So Margaret Paston not only wrote a lot of letters but also tended to write letters of very considerable length, a further indication of how seriously she took her duties and of how diligently she worked to meet the expectations that befell her by virtue of her gender and her family-cum-domestic role.[50]

The address atop or outside the letter—that pointer that was literally external to its text—offers little material on which to expand. The absence of an address in so many letters, along with its occasional presence in a hand other than that of the main scribe, argues that addressing a letter was often separate from writing it, if we think in terms of the entire process as a series of discrete steps or stages. The fact that many of the extant letters are probably draft versions only complicates our considerations. Who would actually carry the letter might be a factor that affected whether it bore an external address (and, on occasion, what was said in the text), but the process of addressing was a terse and relatively unrevealing aspect of the correspondence.

Most—but by no means all—of Margaret's letters carried an external address. Usually this was simple and pragmatic, governed by the conventions of personal address and a need for clarity. Letters to John I set the tone: "To my ryth reuerent and worscheful husbond Jon Paston," or, for slight differentiation, "To my ryth worchepfull husbond John Paston be this delyuered in hast" (*PL*, 1, 216, 247).[51] And whatever dressing-down Margaret was about to deliver to young John II, a letter to him still had to be properly addressed: "To Ser John Paston in hast," or "Ser John Paston, knygt" (*PL*, 1, 205, 198).[52] John III was the baby of our familiar circle: "To John Paston þe youngere be þis deliuered in hast," perhaps a bit less dignified than the variant, "To John Paston, esquire, be thys delyuered in hast" (*PL*, 1, 206, 212). The only time an address gave much hint of the letter's tone was in Margaret's letter of 11 June 1477 to Elizabeth Brews, when John III and Elizabeth's daughter were courting: "To þe ryght wurchypful and my very good lady and cosyn Dame Elyzabeth Brews" (*PL*, 1, 226).

The address almost always closed with an "in haste" tag; it was virtually a standard prefix and/or a suffix in all the fifteenth-century family letter collections. Only a handful of Margaret's letters, among those that carry an address, fail to add this reflex instruction.[53] Obviously, given the near universal appearance of the tag, its presence bore little relation to the length of the letter or the conditions under which it had been written. She was as likely to talk about how rushed she had been when sending off a letter of some eighty lines as when she dashed off a mere twenty-five or thirty lines. None were mere postcards. Today, if we pay for priority mail, we like to think that we are paying for faster delivery. But once paid for, adding "please hurry" on the envelope seems unlikely to be of much avail. Did Margaret (and almost everyone else in all their letters) expect the messenger to dally along the way—*unless* explicitly told not to do so? And if the pleas for haste were to keep the messenger on the straight and quick path, does this mean that his literacy could be taken as a matter of course? Perhaps the "in haste" was to flatter the recipient, suggesting that those letters were especially important and would get written even when the author might not have managed to find time for anyone else.

In only a few instances is the address actually what we consider an address, that is, an indication of where the recipient is to be found. Margaret's first extant letter to John was so directed: "To my worshepfull husbon John Paston, abidyng at Petyrhouse in Cambrigg" (*PL,* I, 124).[54] A few letters to him in London were similarly marked: "John Paston, dwellyng in þe Innere Temple at London, in hast" (*PL,* I, 126; also, 133, 139). The only other address that rose above the perfunctory was on a letter sent via a ricochet: "To my ryth welbelouyd brodyr Clement Paston, for to delyuer to hys brodyr Jon jn hast" (*PL,* I, 155).[55] A letter to Cambridge, or to the Temple, suggests a messenger arriving at the gates of a Cambridge hall or an Inn of Court and then quizzing the porter for further directions. But for many others we imagine a London street-corner scenario— "hey, who around here knows where John Paston can be found?"—once the messenger arrived at his inn or at a market stall in the neighborhood. Margaret presumably had a good notion of where her husband (or sons) might be found, though in some cases the general "deliver to" was the best she could do. After that she had to rely on oral amplification when the messenger neared his destination, and we trust that her instructions about running John I or John II to earth were explicit and detailed, were the courier not yet versed in the art of Paston tracking.[56]

Salutation

If the address is for purely practical purposes, do the greetings and salutations that follow take us beyond the conventions of deference and formality? Though absent from a few of her letters, the salutation is the usual opening of the "real" body of the letter—the address being pre- or extra-contextual. Not much in the salutations hints at deeper feelings or personalized wording. The customary constraints upon epistolary discourse—and a feature of wife-husband letter writing to an extreme degree—kept them terse, formulaic, and standardized. This is the case with Margaret's letters (especially to John I, where she was more reserved than her children would be to her). She generally began with a deferential line or two, and in the most conventional of forms. Her regular short form was "Right wurchepfull husbond. I recommaund me to you." Once in a while she cut loose with a flourish: "Ryth reuerent and worsepful husbond, I recomawnde me to yow wyth alle myn sympyl herte."[57] But her own style in these matters seems to have been laconic, perhaps even beyond customary usage, and she rarely strayed far from the simpler polite forms. A letter to John II typically opened with, "I grytte you well, and send you God ys blessyng and myn." Even when she was at her absolute wit's end with his behavior and inaction, she managed to keep it from showing in her opening: "I grete you wele."[58]

Warmer maternal touches do come through from time to time: "Ryght wel-belouyd son, I gret yow well and send yow goddys blessyng and myn" (*PL,* I, 221).[59] We assume that her usage to others was in keeping with accepted forms as dictated by gender and status; never too warm and yet not so cool as to set obstacles for what was to follow. She was pretty straightforward with familiar figures, as when she opened to Gloys with "I recomaund me to you and thanek you hertyly of youre letteris," while to John Berney it was "Cosyn, I recommaunde me to yow" (*PL,* I, 220, 197). We saw the relatively fulsome address on the letter to Elizabeth Brews, and in that case the salutation was also in keeping with the formalities of two *grandes dames:* "Ryght wurchepful and my cheff lady and cosyn, as hertly as I can I recommaunde me to you" (*PL,* I, 226). But Margaret Paston's letters were basically business-oriented, whether to husband, sons, or others. To open with proper but conventional phrasing sufficed. Neither a crisis in family affairs (like a daughter's mésalliance) nor distress at her sons' behavior was likely to be hinted at in her opening line or two. Whether it was because of her gendered role or her personal style, she was unfailingly terse and erring on the side of formality, whereas letters addressed to her by her near and dear frequently were more effusive. Even John I mixed his usual "I recomaunde me to you" with one much stronger, more personal opening: "Myn owne dere souereyn lady, I recomaund me to yow and thank yow of the gret chere þat ye mad me" (*PL,* I, 55, 77).

Margaret's sons were respectful and even affectionate (as far as the letters reflect such sentiments). They also used careful language when they wrote to each other. John II to John III might open with "I comande me to yow," but he could grow warmer: "Weell belovyd brother, I recommaund me to yow" (*PL,* I, 264, 273).[60] Nor was John III to be outdone in these exchanges, for he used "Ryght worchepfull syr" and the more intimate "Ryght worchepfull syr and my specyll good brodyr" (*PL,* I, 334, 342).[61] John III to his mother could be quite expansive: in a letter of 8 July 1468, he writes, "Ryth reuerend and worchepfull modyr, I recommand me on-to you as humbylly as I can thynk" (*PL,* I, 330).[62] Nor were the younger Paston boys to be outdone in this competition, for we find Edmund opening a letter to Margaret with, "Ryght worchypfull and moste especialle good modyre, jn my moste vmble wyse wyth alle my duté and seruyse I recomawnd me to yow" (*PL,* I, 399). And the prize for this goes to young Walter, who in 1479 really let himself go: "Rytgh reverent and worchypfull moder, I recomavnd me on-to yowre good moderchypp besechyng yow to geve me yowre dayly benedyiccyon, desyeryng hartyly to heere of yowre prosperyté, whych god preserve to hys plesure and to yowre hartys desyyre, etc." (*PL,* I, 402).[63]

These last are closer to the rhetorical flights we would expect in the *ars dictaminis* than to exchanges between Pastons. But reading any larger meaning in a salutation is risky. We know from the Armburgh letters that an epistle full of reproach and dripping with hostility could open with honey-dipped phrases of kindly greeting and well-wishing.[64] Mostly it looks as though Margaret was just not inclined to say much beyond the dutiful and the proper when she began a letter. We shall see that she could be less close-mouthed (or repressed) when the business of the day had been taken care of and she moved to close. But first, the letter.

The Letter

The scribe was primed and ready, the letter launched with whatever version of the conventional salutation Margaret had chosen. Now, to business. We have seen that most of Margaret's letters were of goodly length; they were also letters with a multi-topic agenda. She almost never wrote to deal with just one issue. No matter how pressing her main items, how dire the news, how urgently an answer (in either direction) was called for, she usually managed to throw in a variety of topics. A typical letter of medium or full length was a catchall of news and information, regardless of where its opening salvos had been directed.

In writing a letter, Margaret Paston usually had a clear and fairly standard agenda to address regarding topics or categories of subjects. We can think of these as falling into three or four rough groupings, though the compartmentalization is hardly impermeable and the order listed is simply conventional. Usually coming first was what we can think of as the political and larger-world news—a mix of "foreign affairs" and home-front items. These touched the family's enterprises of aggrandizement, the political pendulum in the county as gauged by the presence and favor of various nobles, the choice and disposition of the sheriff and the county's members, the partisanship of the justices, and related issues. Then there were apt to be the domestic-economic issues: manorial problems, economic decisions, family finance, cash-flow crises, and the like. There might subsequently come items that combined the personal column with local news, usually presented with a slant that highlighted the Pastons as the center of power and favor: births, deaths, seekers of patronage, negotiations about marriage and other forms of partnership. This was the personalized window onto the East Anglian gentry, and the Pastons, as figures of good lordship and patronage, play a prominent role here. Lastly, the family and the domestic items: small children, shopping lists, household and servant problems, personal touches between husband and wife.

All this is familiar. It is not the substance of the letters, however, but their internal structure and the way they were assembled from building blocks of cognition and communication that concern us. How did Margaret "package" her news?

What did she tell her recipient about *how* she had learned what she knew? *How* did she link her method of cognition with the substantive information being transmitted? Firsthand, second-hand, hearsay, rumor, gossip, common knowledge, conjecture, eavesdropping, written communications—each had its moment on the stage.

Any and every route and pathway that brought in the news was to be tested and followed. Because Margaret herself did not usually cover very much ground in a literal sense, much of what came to her for transmission in a letter rested on information gathered and then passed along by the Paston staff and circle. The higher-echelon friends and retainers who often were her scribes were also sources of information: Gloys, Daubeney, Calle, and others. Her role, as the link between what was happening—or what they thought was about to happen—and what John I would be told about it was understood and fostered by everyone within the loop. Nor was Margaret just a passive receptacle for and a conduit of information. She too worked to learn as much as she could on her own—at church, while at the market supervising domestic purchases, on short journeys, at dinner parties, while entertaining guests, at social activities in Norwich, and in conversation with friends, relatives, and neighbors. What the household staff could pick up from other households' servants became grist for her mill, and we can assume that her minions were regularly "debriefed."[65] It seems reasonable to think of the Paston children as being taught to keep their eyes and ears open (and their mouths shut, though it is hard to be confident about John II) when visiting other homes and to pump their young friends when they came to play.

Margaret's standard style was to move quickly, after the letter's salutation, to business: "praying yow to wete," or "plesyt you to wete," and then she might tell him how (as well as what) she had come "to wete." That she thought, in so many instances, to include this information, and to do so in her opening delivery—re-creating the links of the chain of cognition and communication—shows her awareness of how such articulation bolstered her credibility. Naming the mode of cognition whereby she "wete" helped enclose the letter's recipient within her circle of discourse. Circumstantial references to who and whom, to when and where—often conveyed in quotations or running paraphrases—gave more weight to what she was now transmitting. As with the witnesses and deponents analyzed above, we can track a two-way interaction between *how* one knew and *what* one knew.

We might say that as a letter writer, Margaret Paston's working motto was, "How do I know this? Let me count the ways." The opening was rarely worded to build tension or drama: she cut to the chase, and virtually from the first whistle. "Praying youw to wete þat I haue spoke with Newman" or "Plesyt yow to wet þat I sent yow a letyr" were standard openings (*PL*, I, 147, 168). Then came the substance of the news and, in many cases, a reference to its source. It was useful to assess the source, even if it were left unnamed. When she was relying on a "good" source she might say so. On such occasions she was pleased that she could reassure John about the quality of the information: "On þat louyth yow ryth well told me how it was told hym so, and larnyd me þerof in secrete wyse," or "on sent me wurd here-of þat knowyth it for trewth" (*PL,* I, 138, 135).

The household books of Alice de Bryene reveal how a wealthy widow or matron ran her dinner table—a center of neighborhood social life, a place (or occasion) for rewarding servants and retainers and for them to report in with their news.[66] While we have neither itinerary nor household books for Margaret, we learn of the information garnered at dinner parties, both at home and away. Cousin Elizabeth Clere was probably closer to Margaret than anyone else beyond her nuclear family, and we are not surprised to learn that "my kosyn Clere dynyd wyth me þis day." In their exchange, Clere "told me þat Heydon was syth here qisterevyn late and he told her þat he had a letter . . . and scheuyd here þe same letter." This gives us a good idea of how the information loop was apt to be set: direct discourse between Margaret and Elizabeth, indirect information from Elizabeth, and finally a reference to a letter that Elizabeth had been shown. Presumably Elizabeth could have read it, though it is not clear whether it was actually offered to her (*PL,* I, 133). Nor did Margaret shut down her own antennae when she dined out: "I was at Toppys att dynere on Seynt Peterys Day. There my Lady Felbrygg and oþer jantyll women desyryd to have hadd yow there" (*PL,* I, 141).

Then there was the information Margaret picked up and passed on because—as deponents said in the Scrope and Grosvenor hearings—it was common knowledge in the county, though now we are in Norfolk, not Richmondshire. "It is noysed aboute Gresham and all that contré that the Lord Molyns shuld be there in hast," or "as it is reported the said son hath geue gret syluer" (*PL,* I, 139, 158). It was simultaneously vague and precise: "It is told me as for Gressam þe Lord Moleyn xuld not cleym it now" (*PL,* I, 132). This was good enough for John Paston, off in London and trying to time his movements and marshal what resources, human and economic, he could command.

Sometimes Margaret moved on to the next circle of certainty, moving outward—an imprecise reference to general hearsay. In a short account of news about tenants at Swainsthorpe, she does this no fewer than four times (*PL,* I, 164): "and also it is seyd in this towne þat"; "as it is seyd her"; "It is seyd þat he is scapyd all dangerys"; "as it is seyd." This is a distinct style of transmission, and it seems hard to gauge the strength of each link in the chain. She told John, when urging him to keep on good terms with Hugh of Fen, "it is reported here he may do muche wyth the knyg and þe lordes, and it is seid þat he may do myche wyth hem þat be yowr aduersaryes" (*PL,* I, 166). The letters are full of this sort of reportage: "it is tolde þat," "it is reportyd þat," "it is seyd her," "I hered sey," and more of this kind of imprecise information (*PL,* I, 177, and I, 143, with three such usages in five lines of the printed text). When Margaret was firing staccato bursts, she might throw in these phrases for credibility. Three times in a few lines, telling about a quarrel over paternity, she resorts to "I herde seyne" (*PL*, I, 127). An account of interaction with Lady Moleyns was much the same. Her "it ys told me þat . . ." is the opener for business that revolved around a letter she did not see: "qhat tydyngys þey hadde I wote nott," but soon she returns to the well-used "I here say."[67]

Margaret Paston had a distinct flair for narrative exposition. She could catch the dramatic side of events, both when she had been a participant and also on occasions when matters had been unfolded to her at second hand. By the same token, her reiterations of the "I herde seyne" theme conveyed a feeling of how the news might have come to her, bit by bit, rather than in one fell swoop. Even when it was being related orally it unfolded as the speaker controlled the narrative and as he (or she) parceled it out to Margaret. Some of her information was transmitted in straight narrative, as when she told John II about Norfolk's depredations at Heynford: "for thei haue felled all the wood and this weke thei wull carie it a-wey, and lete renne the wateres and take all the fyssh" (*PL*, I, 200). Certainly nothing second-hand or at a distance here; it was about as direct a call to action as possible. But we should beware of drawing too broad a line between what she passed on in the "it is seyd" fashion and what came directly from her own mouth and pen. Her news certainly did not seem to be from any safe remove when she told John I, "it was tolde me thys day that Master John Salatt hathe made a serge in the regestre this monethe . . . and be that hathe they founde suche evidence as schal be gret strenghthyny to the Dukys title, as it is seide" (*PL*, I, 193).[68]

When she went into high gear, as she did for moments of drama and episodes when direct quotation (whether genuine or subsequently fabricated) seemed appropriate, she could speak with considerable power. Perhaps the most arresting prose of all her letters is in the one that recounts Gloys's quarrel, in the street, with Wymondham and Norwode. Wymondham

> seid þus, "Couere thy heed!" And Gloys seid ageyn, "So I shall for the." And whanne Gloys was forther passed by, þe space of iij or iiij strede, Wymondham drew owt his dagger and seid, "Shalt þow so, knave?" And (th)-erwithy Gloys turned hym and drewe owt his dagger and defendet hym . . . and þanne Wymondham called Gloys thef and seid he shuld dye, and Gloys seid he lyed and called hym churl, and bad hym come hym-self . . . and thanne Wymondham called my moder and me strong hores, and seid þe Pastons and alle her kyn were . . . seid he lyed, knave and charl as he was. And he had meche large langage, as ye shall knowe her-after by mowthe. (*PL*, I, 129)[69]

If this episode of Gloys-in-the-street stands out as exceptionally well told, it is hardly a lonely eminence of quality reporting. Other conversations were dished out with a good ear for the conduction of heat, as when John learned, "Then Jenney answerd agayn, 'Be-cause he held a corte here we mad hym hold corte at London,'" and "'Ser,' quod Rysyng, 'I take þe ferme of my master and of Ser Thomas Howys.' Jeney seyd, 'And as for Ser Thomas . . .'" (*PL,* I, 173). Nor were some of the paraphrases that much weaker: "Purry felle in felaschepe wyth Wyllyam Hasard . . . and told hym þat he wold com and drynk wyth Partryche and wyth hym, and he seyd he xuld ben welcom" (*PL,* I, 130).[70] This move from the direct to the indirect and back again came easily and carried more punch than third-person narration. She told John of how "I spake wyth Maister John Salet . . . and how I haskyd hym she myght be demenyd. . . . He cownseld me þat she shuld get hyr a trosty frend . . . and so I told hyr" (*PL,* I, 160).

The Paston letters are frequently held up as secular documents that capture the flavor of spoken language—an observation that seems apt in the context of these readings.[71] One way Margaret achieved this was by the controlled and dramatic use of repetition—a device that emphasizes her material and that also, as we go from one "sche seyd" to the next, keeps us in mind of the forward or progressive dynamic of conversation, carrying us toward its climax or terminal point. We see this in a letter wherein Margaret tells John of her problems in placating Lady Moleyns: "Sche seyd sche had sett yw so many days to a-kord wyth here . . . and sche seyd sche was but a woman, sche must don be here cownseyl . . . and so sche seyd sche wyld do . . . and I seyd that I trostyd veryly . . . I seyd I wyst wel . . . and told her that yw had sergyd to a fownd wrytyng . . . and sche sayd sche wyst wele." This comes across as the verbal (and written) equivalent of watching a tennis match from mid-court (*PL,* I, 128).[72]

Nothing in this close reading of Margaret's prose is meant to argue for anything peculiar or idiosyncratic in the way she expressed herself and transmitted her information. Her power of expression was marked, but it certainly had parallels among her peers. Her references to methods of cognition and data gathering are matched by innumerable examples from other Pastons and in the other family letter collections. Furthermore, no matter what their length, letters were usually economical documents: not written without a serious commitment of time and resources, they were more likely to be to the point than to wander around. This constantly pushed them toward a terse, even lapidary style, best exemplified by their not infrequent resort to aphorisms and proverbial wisdom. Thus, apart from or in addition to Margaret's desire to give John reliable news and to "talk to him," her manner of dialogue and discourse must have seemed a natural way of carrying out her task.

Closing

The substance of the letter was finally finished, Margaret's multi-topic agenda covered. The next task was to bring the letter to closure. Her farewells, though rarely demonstrative, were more expansive than her salutations. They were longer and more varied, more likely to express some personal feeling, and even, on occasion, hinted at the sentiments we might hope to discover between wife and husband or mother and son. The closing portion of a letter can be seen as falling into three (short) sections: a benediction of sorts, the dating, and the signature.

The benediction or farewell clause was not requisite, but it was also not uncommon. Paston family business was often perilous: lawsuits, jailings, the sacking of manor houses, quarrels in the street, sons going to battle, worries about ambushes and muggings and poisonings. This could certainly add up, by the end of a letter, to an air of apprehension that might well trigger some expression of affection. The benediction served to narrow the distance and to diminish some of the uncertainties of lives in which absence, silence, and separation were commonplace. Letters often opened on a note of strained sentiment along the lines of "why haven't you written?" or "why didn't you send news?" or "why did you give me instructions I couldn't follow?" Now, at the end—business having been taken care of—there might be time for emotional amends. But Margaret was Margaret, and even here she fell back on short, standard phrases, phrases she used a good deal of the time: "the blyssed Trinyté haue you in his kepyng," or some variation thereon (*PL*, I, 150).[73] A few longer and more fulsome expressions give glimpses of her identification with John's enterprises, a verbal reminder that she was on his side and, vicariously, standing beside him: "the blyssid Trinyté have yow in his keping and send yow gode spede in all þat ye woll spede well inne," or "send þe vyctory of all yowyr enemyis" (*PL*, I, 140, 163).[74] In concluding a letter to John II, about whom she must have worried a good bit, she was moved to say: "And God have you in hys kepyng and make yow a good man, and gyf yow grace to do well as I wold ye shuld do" (*PL*, I, 175).[75]

The dating of the letter usually came next—after the benediction, before the signature. Though a large number of the family letters carry no date, Margaret was unusually reliable and conscientious in this regard (though we have noted that the year was apt to be omitted).[76] Furthermore, from the wide range of alternative methods of dating, she had several distinct favorites, chosen again and again through the years and in clear contrast to the methods of others. She used ecclesiastical points of reference far more frequently than simpler and less evocative secular ones. "On Sent Lukes evyn" appears many times for each "the x day of May." In addition, she was often at pains to add the day of the week: "on

Saterday," or—in combination with her ecclesiastical style—"þe Fryday next afore Michellmes."

To some extent the absence of a date on many letters stems from the fact that we have drafts and working memoranda mixed in with letters that were completed and sent. But it must likewise reflect poor letter-writing practice. In terms of days of the week, we find that she wrote on each separate day: eight letters dated on a Sunday, nine on a Monday, nine on a Tuesday, ten on a Wednesday, seven on a Thursday, fourteen on a Friday, and eight on a Saturday (as she sets it down, which is not a guarantee that the letter had been begun and/or completed, let alone sent, on that date).

Her preferences, from the options of the ecclesiastical calendar, were for saints' days, though she also was very alert to the church feasts that marked the seasons. About 50 of her 104 letters take note of a saint's day: a few days before, or right on the mark, or very shortly thereafter. The variations were familiar and obvious: "Trinity Sunday on St Leonard's even," or "Satudday nex after St Valentine's day," or "Friday next after Crowchmas day," or "Wedensday next after St Matthy." Many of the saints are those we might think of as universal residents of Christendom: St. Michael (St. Mehyllys), Saints Simon and Jude, St. Martin, St. Katherine, and so forth. Other saints were more likely to be invoked by an Englishwoman, and an East Anglian one at that. The martyred archbishop loomed large: "Seynt Thomas Day in Crystmas" (see *PL*, 1, 167, for his martyrdom) or, in a letter of 6 July, "The Fryday nextg be-fore Sent Thomas of Caunterbery" (*PL*, 1, 206).[77] St. George was riding a crest of popularity—"The Friday next a-fore Seynt George" (*PL*, 1, 143; also 146)—and for the local, East Anglian touch, "The Monday next be-for Seynt Edmunde the Kynge" (*PL*, 1, 164). Though Margaret herself never thought in these terms, we can see how a given month was staked out during the course of her letter-writing career. Her various letters, written over the years in the month of July, steer us to the feasts of St. Thomas, St. Peter, Saints Peter and Paul, the translation of St. Thomas, Relic Sunday, and the feast of St. Margaret. For November she noted, in different letters and from different Novembers, the feasts of St. Leonard, St. Martin, St. Katherine, Soulmas, St. Edmund the King, and St. Clement.

To follow her style under higher magnification, the precise dating of the sixteen letters she wrote to John I in 1465 is given in Table 14. With the exception of a letter to John III (number 186) and one to John II (number 187), all her letters from that busy year are to her husband—though there is no change in dating style when she wrote to others, either during John's life or in her widowhood. If reliable, pious, consistent, and conventional are the general characteristics of Margaret Mautby Paston, they are certainly borne out here.

In a few instances, Margaret has left some trace of what I refer to as exponential dating—dating expressed in relation to experience or behavior, rather than

Table 14 The Dating Styles of Margaret's Letters in 1465

Date of Letter	Margaret's Dating Style	Davis's Edition	
		Page Numbers	Letter Number
8 April	þe Monday next after Palme Sonday	292-3	178
3 May	on Holy Rode Day, etc	293-5	179
10 May	the x day of May	295-9	180
13 May	the xiij day of May	299-300	181
20 May	the xx day [of May]	301-2	182
27 May	the Monday next aftere Assencyon day	302-3	183
11 June	the Tewysday nex be-fore Corpus Cristi	304-6	184
24 June	on Mydsomer day	306-8	185
	(the Sonday next after your departyng)	308	186 (to John III)
	(in hast on Satyrday)	309	187 (to John II)
12 July	the Fryday next after Seynt Thomas	310-11	188
7 August	the Wednesday next aftre Lammes Daye	311-4	189
18 August	the Sonday next aftere the Assumpsyon of Oure Lady	314-16	190
August, probably	on Saterday	317	191
27 September	the Fryday next beyfore Michelmas day	318-22	192
27 August	þe Fryday next afore Michellmes	322	193
17 October	on Sent Lukes evyn	323-4	194
27 October	vppon the Seynt Symon and Jude ys Evyn	329-32	196

SOURCE: Davis, ed., *Paston Letters and Papers*.
NOTE: For letter 196, 27 October 1465, Davis observes that "Sonday" is canceled in the manuscript.

the calendar. There are only a few instances of such references: "Wretyn at Norwyche on þe Wedenys day nexst after þatt ye partyd hens." And for summing up in few words, "Wretyn þis day" was hard to beat, if a little vague from our perspective (*PL,* I, 128, 173). There are also references to the hours of the day (and night), a further gloss upon the saint's day or a fixed point in the religious calendar. She closes a letter to John I with a variation on the usual phrases—"Wretyn in hast the second Sunday of Lent by Candel light at euyn"—and in one to John II she signs off, "Wretyn on Sent Gyles evyn at ix of belle at nyght" (*PL,* I, 158, 202).[78] Another letter combines a number of the variations: "Wretyn in hast . . . at xj of the clok in þe nyth the same day I departyd fro yow" (*PL,* I, 170).[79] Virtually no other fifteenth-century correspondent, male or female, is as good as Margaret in framing the moment of creation.

Signature, Postscript, Crossing in the Mails

Written, dated, finished. Now to sign it and be done. Margaret's signature (although not in her own hand) comes to us in a few standardized variations. Because most of her scribes also wrote for other Pastons, and sometimes on their own to one Paston or another, we might ask if the recipient would know for certain that this was a Margaret letter, at least until the text (or signature) had been scrutinized—though an address such as "to my right wurchipfull hosbond" would be of considerable help. There are many remnants of Margaret's seal on the dorse of the sheets, though given the amount of leeway on most matters, it is hazardous to say that she could be counted on to use her seal as a regular part of the closing process.[80] When writing to John I, her signature was usually direct and to the point, which comes as no surprise: "Your M.P." or "Youres, M. Paston," or "Ywrys, Margarete Paston," or "Be yowyrs, M. Paston."[81] A few signatures strayed from the formulaic: "youre gronyng wyff M.P." (from a pregnant Margaret), or "by youre faynt houswyff at thys tyme, M.P."[82] Margaret to her sons was not very different: "Your moder, M. Paston," or "be your moder," or "be your modre, M.P." (*PL,* I, 175, 186, 200). In one letter to John III, she is just "M.P.," though she signs off with unusual feeling: "the Holy Gost kepe you bothyn and delluere you of your elmyse" (*PL,* I, 215). And to Dame Elizabeth Brews, in her only signed letter to someone outside the family, she closed with "By your Margaret Paston" (*PL,* I, 226).

So finally the letter had been written, dated, and signed. It only remained to line up a reliable courier and get it "into the mail." But no; not quite yet. In 20 of her 104 letters, Margaret added a postscript—a further message, inserted after she had gone through the conventions of closure. In most instances the postscript was short: a few scraps of information of varying importance touching matters that had been overlooked or perhaps that had just come in. Because the structure of the letters usually allocated the opening sections to secular or "foreign affairs," new items of this nature were perhaps better held for the postscript than tucked into later sections, where they might get swamped amid the domestic or local topics.

Of the twenty postscripts, eighteen are five lines or fewer (as printed). Some seem to reveal a last-minute thought: don't trust the sheriff (*PL,* I, 141), or "paper is deynty" (*PL,* I, 142), or cousin Crane says hello (*PL,* I, 145), or be nice to the courier (*PL,* I, 175).[83] This last seems to indicate that the courier, in this case the parson of Fylby, had been recruited at the tail of the letter writing, perhaps when it was learned that he was traveling in the right direction. Two postscripts indicate that mother-in-law Agnes, having learned that a letter was about to go its way, had something to add: once it was a general "hello," and once a more directed question about John I's troubled relations with his brother William (*PL,* I, 126, 164). In another case Margaret added that it had been too long since she had heard—a common complaint but usually one found toward the beginning of the letter, rather than at the end. Here she not only adds it as a postscript but puts it on the dorse of the sheet. (The recto side of the page had been filled, or perhaps the sheet had already been trimmed.[84])

Only two of the postscripts were of appreciable length. In a letter of May 1449 covering the Gloys-Wymondham street quarrel, a postscript of nineteen lines gives John I a final update on the affair. The letter (of fifty-one lines) was in Gresham's hand, while the postscript was set down by the main unknown hand so active in those early years. The postscript is so long that it virtually becomes a second letter; Margaret moves to a new benediction, topping her original "Almyghty God haue yow in his kepyng," with a more elaborate, "I prey yw hertyly here masse and oþer servys þat ye arn bwn to herr wyth a devwt hert, and I hope veryly þat ye xal spede ryth wele in all ywr materys, be the grase of God. Trust veryly in God and leve hym and serve hum, and he wyl not deseve yw." This was unusually long and pious. She was probably sobered by how close she and Agnes had been to violence in their own front yard (*PL,* I, 129).[85]

The other long postscript comes in a letter to John I of January 1462 (*PL,* I, 169). The letter's thirty-seven lines were written by the young John III, while Daubeney and Playter both had a role in the postscript. Daubeney began, getting his three lines onto the recto, giving news of Richard Calle. He then continued on the dorse for six additional lines, moving on to information about "Will Worcetre" (William of Worcester) and William's desire to seek Paston's good lordship. Playter then took over for the final three lines (printed by Davis as a new paragraph, but not so distinguished in the manuscript), and the text (from Margaret) opens with "Dawbeney and Playter avise me to lete Peers go at large," an interesting bit of self-referencing by Playter. These sound like items that had rolled in while the main letter was being written, though we may ask if young

John III was being let off duty for the postscript, or if some matters were perhaps thought unfit for his young ears.[86]

Now, we ask still once more, after the signatures and the postscripts, was there anything else to worry about? Can we finally turn to messengers and delivery? Not quite yet. There are a few further complications that Margaret had to take into account—and we, in turn, must as well. I have been talking of the construction of her letters and style of discourse, and of how she dealt with such matters as dating and signing, as if each letter were a freestanding, autonomous enterprise—a literary exercise with a set of internal components that governed its shape and form. In reality, of course, her letters were part of an ongoing (if mostly lost) correspondence. One of the problems any family letter writer had to face was the timing and sequence of his or her letters. Each letter in a business-oriented correspondence had a purpose. How quickly could Margaret write a letter when she was ready to send one? How soon could she respond to one received? Had the previous letter been received in good time? Did letters cross in carriage? Had letters from others arrived (or not arrived) that would put a different "spin" on her version of the news? Was there more than one letter in either direction in the mails at any given time?

A simple way of setting a given letter into its place on the chain—beyond what the dating clause tells us—was by positioning it against a known item or event, as John would survey them, back and forth: "Please it you to wyte that I recevyd letters from you on Wensday laste passyd the were wryten the Monday next be-fore" (*PL,* I, 184). If only we had an unbroken series of "prayng yow to wete that I haue receyvd your letter this day þat ye sent me be Yelvertonys man" (*PL,* I, 151). But it was rarely this smooth, and a more typical problem had to be explained at some length: "I recevyd a lettere from you send by Laurens Rede on Fryday laste past, whereby I understod that ye had no tythyngs from me at that tyme that youre lettre was wryten, whereof I mervayll, for I send yo a lettere by Chyttock ys son . . . whych was delyueryd to hym vppon the Thursday . . . he promysyd to ryde forward the same day and that ye shold haue it as hastely as he mygt aftere hys comyng to London" (*PL,* I, 128). The "reliable courier" problem had reared its head, and it too had several segments: finding the seemingly reliable man and then learning at some subsequent moment whether he had (or had not) lived up to his promises about delivery.

I offer a few more examples of these problems. They are interesting for what they reveal about the tangles of communicating across distance; they must have driven the parties in the correspondence to a distraction barely hinted at in those terse "I mervayll" bursts of exasperation. The next letter might have to carry assurances about the one before: "wet þat I sent yow a lettyr by Barneys man . . . wyche was wretyn on Seynt Thomas Day . . . and I had no tydyngs nor lettyr of yow sene the weke befor Chrystmas, wher-of I mervayle sore" (*PL,* I, 168). It was not reassuring that Margaret had to spell out how she had *already* taken care of business: "I receyvyd a lettyr from you on Sonday, the wyche I sent yow an answher in a letter . . . by Edmunde Clere of Stokysby" (*PL*, 1, 155).

If we think of the letters as beads on a necklace, we have to keep in mind that many of them, at least as we have them, carry inadequate instructions regarding their place in the final ring. Margaret sets out the attendant dilemmas in a letter of 29 October 1460: "so I sent you worde in a lettyr whiche was wretyn on the Tuesday next aftyr Seynt Lwke, and ther-in was an answer of all the fyrst lettry þat ye sent me. I sent it yow by yonge Thomas Elys, and I sent yow a-nothyr lettyr by Playter the whyche was wretyn on Saterday last past."[87] It was all so tangled: "Plesyt yow to wet that I receyvyde yowyr Lettyr þat ye sent me by John Holme on Wednysday last past. And also I receyvyd a-nother lettyr on Fryday at nyt þt ye sent me by Nycolas Newmanys man, of the whyche I thank yow" (*PL*, 1, 163).[88]

There are two letters from Margaret on which John entered small, lowercase roman numerals, indicating he was keeping his own record of their order (of arrival or receipt). Both letters were written on 27 September 1465; Davis comments that they were "evidently of a series the beginning of which is lost" (*PL*, 1, 192, 193).[89] Davis's marginal notes suggest that John kept the letters at hand for future reference, which would explain why their order was worth marking (beyond Margaret's own dating). The hand of the first letter is one of the many unidentified hands, and it is a hand that appears in two other letters of Margaret and in letters 66 and 67 of John. The marginal notes (entered after the letter had been received) are in Pampyng's hand, but a few of them, plus the tell-tale "iiij," are in John's. In the second letter, written on the same day, we have the main hand of the first letter for the first half. Calle then picked up, and the marginal notes—again written at John's end after delivery—were by Pampyng, with John again personally responsible for the "v" in the top left-hand corner.

Delivery

So—at long last—we have cleared all the hurdles. It is time to put the letter into the courier's hands and on its way to John I or John II or John III or whomever. Obviously, we have not escaped the realm of problems and difficulties. Who would deliver the letter? How reliable was he (or she)? How quickly would it arrive? Would there be a swift response? The texts of the letters indicate that sometimes the courier had been predetermined; he was either going that way anyway, or he had been specifically tapped for the job, as we learn when there is an internal reference to his identity. But in many instances this crucial final link in the chain was only forged when all else had been taken care of, the letter folded and closed, sealed, and addressed.

Many of the problems connected with the couriers and delivery have been dealt with in a series of papers by P. C. Pearsons.[90] He says that the Paston letters were delivered by three types of couriers: Paston servants or those of friends, or members of their own circle; professional couriers, who went back and forth for a fee; and "loderers and carteres" who carried heavier goods, with or without letters. Furthermore, all three sorts could be used for return-mail purposes. In his analysis of Davis's edition of the letters, Pearsons identifies 121 carriers, plus 29 additional "carriers of named persons" (such as "Richard, Playtourys man," or "man of St. Mychell paryche"). The information gleaned from Margaret's letters is pretty well covered by these general observations. But a close look at her comments takes us a bit deeper into the process. Was the convention that the messenger who had been charged with additional information would hold silent regarding his oral message until the letter itself had been read, or did he blurt it out upon arrival, before the text had been perused? Sometimes Margaret explicitly said that the messenger would tell more than she had written: "I trowe the bearer of this shall telle more by mouthe, as he shall be enfourmed, of the revell in this cuntré" (*PL,* I, 158). Sealed assurances regarding the courier's reliability were presumably a double safeguard, and we find them added, at the last minute, in a postscript: "Yf it plese yow to send aney thyng by the berer herof, he is trusty jnough" (*PL,* I, 193).[91] Margaret might indicate in her sealed text that the messenger should bring back the response: "I pray you send me word be þe bryn-ger of þis how qe wil þat I be demenyd" (*PL,* I, 132). Did the courier know from the start that he would be called upon for a round-trip errand?

With an eye on the dangers of travel and the usual Paston suspicions about a world of many enemies, it is no wonder that we find so much need for double signals and secret handshakes. Certainly, an indication that "I send you the now-che wyth the dyamaunth be the berere here-of" was a check, lest "the berere" showed up empty-handed (except perhaps for the letter, though if he absconded completely there might be no record at all of the undelivered letter).[92] The couriers were paid, and probably on a fairly standard scale, but we see that a higher-status intermediary was singled out for special notice: "I wold ye shuld make meche of þe parson of Fylby, þe berer her-of, and make hym good cher yf ye may" (*PL,* I, 175). That Margaret did not fall back on the return-mail service of the courier in at least one urgent instance must mean that not all her messengers were available for the return journey: "send me an answere there-of be þe next man þat comyth, etc." (*PL,* I, 199).[93] And as a last resort, a woman could be trusted with a letter's delivery. For a letter to John I from 15 February 1449, Margaret wrote, "I sent Kateryn on þis forseyd masage, for I koud geten no man to do it, and sent wyth here Jamys Holman and Henry Holt" (*PL,* I, 131).

We will look below at the requests in Margaret's letters—going in both directions—concerning domestic supplies and clothing, though such letters are usually silent on the problems of delivery. Some letters indicate that messengers could be forgetful or hard to find. Letters might lie around, written but unsent or undelivered, Paston business languishing—one more weak link in the long chain between the events about which she wished to speak and the safe, final delivery of the letter telling of those events. When Margaret fretted that she had not heard from her husband or her sons—or when John grew testy because he was awaiting news from her—the actual time needed for delivery does not seem to have been a serious factor in the delay. It was more "why haven't you written" than "you wrote but it takes so long for a letter to be delivered" that comes across. Various studies of the speed with which news and messages could cover the kingdom indicate that a regular missive sent along the heavily traveled London-Norwich route could go one way in about three days. Return mail, or round-trip delivery, could be expected in a week or less—at least as a best-case scenario—and we do note a few letters that moved in very good time indeed.[94] Of course, quick delivery assumes that the scribe, the paper, and the courier were on hand—ready to be employed, ready to go. If that were the case, then all Margaret needed was news and the time to arrange it—in her head and then, perhaps with scribal help—on the page. Still another Paston letter, off to London and ultimately destined, in some strange but fortuitous fashion, for the editorial hands of Fenn, Gairdner, and Davis.

FIRST STUCK AT HOME AND THEN MOSTLY ALONE

The survival of so many letters gives depth to our view of Margaret Paston. Beyond being wife and mother, and beyond being the long-lived feminine linchpin of the Paston household and domestic scene (especially during John I's frequent absences), she stands out as *the* correspondent par excellence. Given that we learn about the Pastons by means of their letters, her identity is easily fixed, at least for us, as the letter writer within the family circle. We cannot determine the extent to which this role defined her identity for herself or the way she was seen by her family and her inner network—though comments in other letters indicate that she was generally taken seriously. Was she primarily perceived as the stay-at-home wife, or the chiding mother of wayward sons and daughters, or the daughter-in-law or sister-in-law who was called upon to intercede, keeping family friction from reaching the point of conflagration? Or was she—to some significant degree—the lady of the letters? Or, we might ask, to what extent were these roles distinguishable?

Rather than run down every line of inquiry opened by Margaret's letters, I will look at some specific categories or areas of communication to see what they suggest regarding her outlook on her role(s) and identity. We will tiptoe past her relations with her sons, rich though this theme is when we consider how her chiding persona emerged or evolved (and with such freedom of expression) after the death of John I. The "two Margarets"—the married Margaret and the widowed Margaret, or the wife and then the dowager-mother—is a familiar topic. Nor will I worry about how she fretted over family finances, whether the crises touched overdue loans (often involving William, John I's brother), or the feckless John II, or the endless problems of cash flow, or the price of grain (too low when selling, too dear when buying), or whether Sporle Wood should be cut this year, or next, or never. And I pay little attention to what Margaret told John I (and then her sons, though to a lesser extent) about the larger politics of East Anglia: great nobles, shire elections, the king's friends, the ups and downs of overmighty subjects as they battered down their doors and assaulted their partisans, and more of this sort. Margaret Paston was *the* regional weekly newsletter for serious matters, we might say, even as we constrict the agenda.

Other subtopics invite attention. One concerns Margaret as household manager and her requests for purchases of household items, mainly either clothing and cloth or luxury foods and spices. H. S. Bennett talked about these requests, but I think we can elaborate on them beyond just tallying the burdens or demands dumped upon men in London by a provincial, household-bound woman.[95] I also turn to what Margaret says about vital statistics and the milestones of birth, death, sickness, and plague and how she situates and reports such material in her letters. The vector of her news was from country to city, in keeping with the current of the letters. (Was such news considered "women's business," defined by traditional gender divisions and confirmed as provincial news gathering worked its way from the point of origin to its London reception?) At the end, appropriately, is the familiar but intriguing issue of Margaret's will, about which a few closing comments seem almost *de rigueur*.

Margaret's Network

One more general consideration before we engage the texts. There is a gulf between the world according to the letters of Margaret Paston and Margaret Paston's own world. One aspect of Margaret's world to consider, as preserved through her letters, concerns the scope of the cast list she names in the course of her nearly four decades of letter writing. How many people did she mention, and at what levels of frequency and intimacy? The question of circles of reference—and of their spacing or arrangement in terms of intimacy and incidence—is a more likely topic for social psychology or network analysis than for historical inquiry. Obviously, hard data on this cannot be recovered—especially for a woman's world. To how many different people do we refer in various written forms and/or in our speech? And in trying to keep count of such references, do we get a better insight into social relations if we think in terms of contacts and references by the day, the week, the year, or some even longer span? And within the ranks of those referred to, how do we measure their turnover—those who quickly enter and quickly leave this universe, the regulars who stay, and so forth? This quantitative presentation will pay little attention to levels of exchange: polite words between semi-strangers and nodding acquaintances; serious and revealing conversation with familiar parties and old friends; in-house talk within the nuclear family, with its special touches and tensions of intimacy and secrecy.

The aggregate *dramatis personae* of Margaret Paston's letters comprise somewhere between two hundred and three hundred people, at least in terms of mere mention. In segregating them for rough analysis, we can begin in the most literal-minded fashion—that is, by counting those who wrote to her and the bare few to whom she wrote. Because her letters were all to her husband and sons (with but the three exceptions we noted), we are spinning a small and fairly intimate wheel. It is what we expect, given roles and opportunities, however. We find that John I's world of direct communication—letters to and letters from—was a great deal wider in terms of people named or addressed. The narrowness of Margaret's direct outreach is a striking characteristic of her world. So far as the "in-box" is a guide to direct contact, Margaret's circle was a small one.

How many people wrote *to* Margaret? Though there is some uncertainty in virtually any tally regarding the Paston letters, Davis identified twenty-four separate writers, a goodly number in comparison with recipients. But even in this regard, and with her extant total of 104 letters, Margaret lived in a much more confined world than her menfolk. John I received a great many letters; seventy-nine correspondents addressed him, and he in turn wrote to about twenty different parties.[96] His brother William, who wrote 20 letters (and 23 documents in all), had eleven different recipients. John II, with 70 letters (out of 86 documents), wrote to nine recipients. John III, with 68 letters (out of 77 documents), wrote to eleven. And against the twenty-four men and women who wrote to Margaret, thirty wrote to John II (46 letters received), thirty-six or more to John III (70 letters). So the stay-at-home wife and mother had far fewer direct contacts. Even so, if we see her as the critical funnel of family news gathering, she received material from many currents and subsequently directed it to a mere handful of channels.[97]

We are clearly not going to get anywhere near our universe of several hundred people just by counting those who sent or received letters. We must move on to the world of those about whom Margaret wrote. These folk—men and women, rich and famous or obscure and otherwise unknown, clerical or lay—were the flesh on the bare bones of her news. If we think in terms of concentric circles of reference, we can offer an inner core of frequent reference, then a middle circle of from-time-to-time, and finally an outer orbit occupied by those who just pass through, leaving but a footprint or two on the historical record. Nor is the cast list amenable to full clarification, given the vagaries of naming and identification. Many figures are so casually identified that not even Davis was willing to address the totality of the issue.[98]

Being mentioned by Margaret Paston may not be the fifteen minutes of fame we might have accorded our jurors, but it seems better than no mention at all. On the other hand, as we have indicated, a full analysis of all her men and women would be laborious and inconclusive. Hence some impressions, and a few names, will suffice. Margaret Paston's letters are family letters, and we expect the frequent references to members of the inner circle, such as the long-lived Agnes or a John other than the letter's recipient. Nor are we disappointed. But some of the close kin make only an occasional appearance, as the naming of names goes: the other children of Margaret and John I, John I's sister Elizabeth, sons- and daughters-in-law. John I's brother William figures in many letters, and the fact that he was often less-than-friendly to "our" perspective helps explain why he was so often a part of their waking worries. A more amiable William II might have been a less-mentioned William II.

The familiar figures of Paston household and faction are there, letter after letter. Richard Calle—ultimately Margaret's son-in-law but figuring here as their steward—is mentioned in more than two dozen letters.[99] John Damme, recorder of Norwich and executor for William I, is referred to in ten letters.[100] John Daubeney, a family servant of the higher sort or longtime retainer, is mentioned in eleven or so letters, mostly in the interval between letter 166 (3 December 1461) and letter 205 (September 1469).[101] James Gloys, Margaret's chaplain and confidant, was frequently mentioned, but as he also wrote on his own to John I and John II, his appearance in the innermost circle of reference is only to be expected. And this same pattern—mentioned by Margaret, serving her and others as an amanuensis or secretary, and being involved in the permutations of family communication—is found for the other members of the family's council or inner circle as well, including Thomas Howes, the parson of Blofield; John Heydon (along with his wife and son); Thomas Playter, family clerk and agent; John Wykes; and John Pampyng. Ties by blood, if hard to determine, brought a few more into this inner circle: the Berney cousins, John and Uncle Philip, and the Clere cousins.

Because Margaret was the newsletter as well as the personal link between absent men and home, she had occasion to talk of those atop the sociopolitical pyramid. In many cases she knew them, or at least had met them, as she had the royal family. She makes a curtsey or two to her own memories. Such references were more in the category of news than of personal or local information. John Fastolf straddled the larger political world and that of the Pastons; Margaret mentions him in eighteen letters, or almost one in five that she wrote. Edward IV figured, in some fashion or other, in a dozen letters, which is hardly surprising given that her sons were often at his court or in the royal circle. And of course, the duke and duchess of Norfolk, or perhaps several of that title over the years, emerge as regular figures, along with the duke and duchess of Suffolk. The archbishop of Canterbury appears in five letters, and Lord and Lady Moleyns figure some half-dozen times. The likelihood of a correlation between frequent mention and an anti-Paston stance can be taken for granted for most of these men and women of society's uppermost tier.

Many local people, men and women, also get invited in. Some of them did things, or said things, directly to Margaret; other things came to her ear. Her news was made more circumstantial by the inclusion of names: Thomas Daniel, steward of the duchy of Lancaster, or Thomas Hollers, father and son, or Thomas Shipping, or the priest Sir John Tattershall, and dozens more. They were hardly key figures, but their doings, like those of Moleyn's servant, John Partrich, were fuel for the engines that Margaret was constantly revving. Finally, in the outer circles of casual mention, we come to those who figure but once or twice (and so escape Davis's index). Sometimes they are a name and little more; two of the executors whom Margaret names in her own will only figure in that unique reference. Others are touched with the lightest possible stroke of the brush, as they—like jurors in the Proofs—come forward for their brief supporting role. We have the trio of "John Botillere, oþerwise callid John Palmere, and Davy Arnald your cook, and William Malthous of Ayulsham," all escorted under duress to Cossey without warrant one October day (*PL*, I, 194). There are numerous references to Brandeston as a place, but only one to the parson of the church, and he comes in because he passed some news along to Berney (*PL*, I, 197). These are typical of the ranks of spear-carriers at the edges, those who may have been of some familiarity and even importance but who rarely made the written page.[102]

Consumer Affairs

Margaret stayed home, collected news, represented John Paston to the best of her abilities, negotiated the tangles of family and East Anglian society, and presided over a large and expensive household. That she wrote to her menfolk in London for help with domestic purchases certainly seems reasonable, and presumably they accepted such impositions as part of the price to be paid for their urban lifestyle and their long absences. The requests for shopping fell into two main consumer categories: cloth and clothing as well as sugar and spices. Ready-made clothing was available in London in wider variety, or at better prices, or in higher fashion than at home, as were some kinds of cloth. By such a guideline, it is hardly to be wondered at that she included shopping instructions or requests in numerous letters. I suspect that she also was pleased, from time to time, to "let John take care of it" in terms of running a household from which he was so frequently absent.

The requests, or the shopping lists, were rarely very complicated, and it is likely that the Pastons had regular suppliers—clothiers, tailors, jewelers—to whom they turned. How else would John I or John II or John III know where to match a sample of lace or where to go for comparative shopping? Early in her marriage—probably during her first pregnancy—Margaret spoke in more personal terms than she usually did. John was to look for "govne cloth of mvstyrd-devyllere to make a govne for me." By this point in her pregnancy the tedium of the limited wardrobe that comes from months in maternity clothes was upon her. She was tired of her "blake and my grene" dress "þat is so comerus þat I ham wery to wer yt" (*PL*, 1, 125).[103] But she rarely went wild, and her requests seem modest: "I pray yow þat ye woll vowchesauf to remembre to purvey a thing for my nekke, and to do make my gyrdill" (*PL*, 1, 146).[104]

As the children came along, their needs also had to be taken care of, though there is little indication of why some items were on the London list while East Anglia sufficed for the rest. In 1451, when daughter Margery was not yet ten, John was told to "remember yowr fayre doughteris gyrdyl" (*PL*, 1, 140).[105] In a more complicated errand, he was instructed to buy lace like the samples enclosed in (or coming along with) the letter. In addition, he learned that the "cappys þat ye sent me for þe chylderyn, þey be to lytyl." But in this small regard life offered him a second chance, and this time it was to be "fynere cappys and larger þan þey were" (*PL*, 1, 127). (This letter is dated July 1444, so the children were very young.) Years later, when the father was dead and the instructions went from mother to son(s), there was still the matter of items for the sisters. In 1469 John II was instructed to buy "a kerchye of cremyll for you suster Anne" (*PL*, 1, 130). In a letter of the following month, Margaret explained this request in more detail, showing us the power of fashion and convention: "a nekkerchys . . . I am scheute of þe lady þat sche is wyth be-cause sche hathe non, and I can non gette in alle thys towne."[106]

Margaret might say that local stocks did not run to something she needed, as when her thoughts turned to a "murrey gown" that had "leyn in the kolere" but was short on the satin she wanted for the hood. Though Norwich was the second or third city of the realm, she still affirmed that "I kan gettyn non gode bokeram jn þis town to lyn it wyth."[107] A sizeable household must have needed constant supplies, and when specific items were required, a sample might be sent to London so it could be matched for price, quality, or style. For the black broadcloth that would make a hood ("hode") at "xliijj d. or iiij s. a yerd," it had to be from London, as "þer is nothere gode cloth nere god fryse in this town."[108] There must have been some back-and-forth regarding the buying, for in one letter Margaret indicates that the sample John has sent home will do the trick: "þe pris of a yerd þer-of is xiij d ob, and so me semyt it is wele worth" (*PL,* I, 132).

Though the Pastons raised sheep and had a hand in the wool trade that was just part of life for the landed gentry of East Anglia, they were a long remove from the world of trade or cloth making. And yet these activities on the landscape and in the political economy of the region were pervasive enough to make us wonder about Margaret's purported inability to find things closer to home. In paying attention to how she expressed herself, we note the power of a metaphor that centers on woolen clothing. When John I was still a recent bridegroom and languishing ill in London, she told him how highly she would rate a reunion: "yf it were your ese and your sor myth ben a wyl lokyth to here as it tys þer ye ben now, lever dan a new gounne, þow it were of scarlette" (*PL,* I, 126).

These requests from at-home mother to away-from-home father (and in later years to sons) are familiar ones. They come mostly in the early years, years in which Margaret was bearing and raising children. As they grew up, the Paston children either left home or their needs mostly fell out of their mother's epistolary agenda; her letters touched less frequently on this aspect of domestic life. In addition to what her requests add to our stock of information about gentry households, they can also be set into the context of communications between Margaret and John.[109] The requests for cloth, like those for luxury foods, almost always come toward the end of the letter. They are part of the intimate and domestic agenda—matters taken up after political and economic issues had been covered. Were they an indulgence permitted Margaret because she had done her assigned work so well?[110] Were the requests a muted way for her to assert the lesser but still significant importance of *her* domestic role, with its own share of responsibilities and obligations? There sometimes is a testy touch in the articulation of her requests, as though John had to be chided lest he forget or minimize their import. On the other hand, we should not read a wide gulf between the mother's requests and the father's compliance—at least, one no wider than their society's wonted definition of the sexual division of labor and of gender roles. That John had to be informed regarding what was suitable for young children, let alone what sizes they wore, is hardly by itself an indictment of his devotion. Fair or not, such knowledge tends to be women's-world knowledge, even today in circles where parenting is more evenly divided than in the Pastons' universe. A more positive reading is to see Margaret's requests, tantamount to instructions, as a way of binding John into a loop of domesticity—certainly to a greater degree than any other activities or interests he seems to have had regarding his numerous offspring, male or female.

As we noted, the requests for shopping come among the winding-up items, usually appearing after the serious news had been conveyed. But there are exceptions. Some of the requests are in short letters; a request's appearance toward the beginning suggests that it may have been among the reasons for the letter. It is possible to argue either way, as Margaret usually took a catchall approach to agendas and exercised her freedom to combine the major and the tragic with the ephemeral and the personal-cum-domestic as she chose. In one letter, with shopping instructions toward the end, she did signal a break as she went from the serious news to the requests, marking the segments with "I pray yow þat ye woll vowchesauf to remembre" (*PL,* I, 145). But in another letter to John I, she jumped right in at the beginning and spoke of the need for cloth for a gown ("iii yerdys and ij quarter") before she told him of a murder committed by one of Henry Inglose's men (*PL,* I, 149).[111]

Requests for sugar and spices, either alone or alongside those for cloth or clothing, are probably just what they claim to be—requests to replenish the supplies of fancy stuff in the family larders. There seems to be less room for interpersonal maneuvering here than with the clothing: children's sizes you should know, prices too high for our lifestyle, Norwich is too provincial and I'm stuck here, and more, implicit or between the lines as much of it was. When it came to luxury foods, the tone of the requests gives no hint that the items called for were unfamiliar, exotic beyond the customary tastes and purses of the gentry, or hard to find in the metropolis. It presumably was accepted that London was the place to shop. Harrod's food court had its fifteenth-century counterparts, though they were well east of the May fair and the knights' bridge.[112] Margaret's orders were straightforward: "I pray how þat ye woll vowchesaff to send me an þer sugowr loff, for my old is do" (*PL,* I, 142). A letter that talked of samples of cloth also carried a request for foodstuffs: "loff of gode sugowr and di. j. li. of holl synamum," along with the cloth (*PL,* I, 149).

Despite our interest in any signs of tension between Margaret and John as the unequal halves of their world fit together, we must posit a working partnership (though it was John who drew most of the boundaries). In Margaret's requests for London purchases, she might worry about the cost of cloth, clothing, or the decorative baubles and jewelry she asked for, but she did not have to discuss the actual method of payment. Presumably John—assuming that he was willing and able to carry out her request—would cover the costs as he did her bidding. Worries over prices were rather with an eye to domestic economy and the cash flow, not to separate pocketbooks or expense accounts between husband and wife. But when John I was no longer on the scene and Margaret bid her sons to do some shopping, she either sent money with the letter's courier or assured them that the accounts would be squared when they returned home. Though she could just tell John II to "remembyre þe spysys and þe malmesey," she might also think it best to reassure him about his out-of-pocket expenditures: "if ye pay more I shall pay it you ageys when ye come home" (*PL,* I, 231; she had already sent 10s. by the courier, "the berere here-of"). In what sounds like a serious re-stocking enterprise, she told John III to look into the price of pepper, cloves, "masis," ginger, cinnamon, almonds, rice, "ganyngell," saffron, raisins, and "grenys." But there was time for some back-and-forth on these purchases: "and yf it be better shepe at London than yt ys here I shal send yow mony to by wyth soch stwfe as I will haue" (*PL*, I, 209).[113]

Whatever the domestic arrangement between widowed mother and unmarried sons, they do not seem to have shared a common household in the sense of a common purse or a single set of accounts, even before Margaret went to live at Mautby around 1473 or 1474. We know this from the heavy thread of economic discontent that runs through the letters between them. The costs of stocking the larder are but another side of this tale. In the old days (that is, when John I had been alive), Margaret had instructed him to shop for the household's Christmas needs, *if* he could make it home for the holidays: "Also, if ye be at home this Cristmes it were wele do ye shuld do puruey a garnyssh or twyn of pewter vesshell, ij basones and ij heweres and xij candilstikes, for ye haue to few of any of thes to serue this place" (*PL*, I, 166).[114] In an earlier letter he had been instructed to get "iij dosseyn trenchers, for I can none gete in this town" (*PL*, I, 144).[115] Once, by way of variation, she indicated that she would take care of the winter shopping: "Please you to wet þat I was at Norwich this weke to purvey suche thyngys as nedythe me ageyns the wynter" (*PL*, I, 174).[116] This news let John know he was off the hook. It also served to remind him that the basic duties of laying in household supplies were being carried out locally and without his help.

Births, Deaths, and Other Local News

Another aspect of Margaret's news relaying is her coverage of the realm of vital statistics and life-cycle data (what I sum up as "hatched-matched-dispatched"). Births, deaths, marriages, sicknesses, and related personal crises and milestones were a regular part of her agenda. To some extent, this was simply local news gathered near to home and then sent to London (or wherever John I or John II or John III was to be found). But was such material simply data (and gossip) now being transferred from the domestic and provincial center to the metropolitan periphery, or was it also a gendered category of information? It is hard to be certain. We can argue that births and deaths in London rarely had much to do with Margaret's working world; John, therefore, would have felt little need to fill her in, at least not before he got home and they could speak in person.[117] In contrast, deaths in East Anglia might affect his plans, as could news of the plague, or illness, or the birth of an heir, or an heir or heiress now on (or off) the marriage market. Keeping him abreast of such matters had a practical side.

Even if we accept that such items were a regular part of Margaret's agenda, they are not that frequent. And because many of the death notices were in the context of a eulogy, some element of the personal enters in, at least for the letter writer if not necessarily for its recipient. Sometimes pertinent news was conveyed so as to remind us that the Pastons were Pastons, even if some had begun life as Mautbys. Margaret told John that "Ser Herry Inglose is passyd to God this nyght, hoys sowle God asayll." If John wanted any of his possessions, he should move with dispatch (*PL,* I, 141). When it was "Gerrars wyff," John was to recall the "fayre place of her to selle in Sent Gregoreys parysch," for which he might put in an offer (*PL,* I, 144). There is no reason to think that Margaret was not saddened by the news that "myn awnte is dissesid, whos sowle God assoyll," although this did not divert the family's gaze from the "lifflode that she had at Walcok" (*PL,* I, 166).[118]

Sometimes a death was just a death: "It is told me þat Rouse of Suffolk is ded." Sometimes it was a friend and old supporter, such as John Estgade, "whereof in gode fayth I am ryght sory, for I fond hym ryght faythfull to you."[119] And when the plague was ravaging the countryside, Margaret's news took on some urgency: "They dyy ryght sore in Norwich" (*PL,* I, 190). In one letter she reported the deaths of four people whom he knew or knew of: "ywre cosyn Barney of Wychshynggam . . . Veylys wyfe and Londonys wyfe and Pycard þe vacar of Twmland ben gon also" (*PL,* I, 209). She combined a shopping request—for treacle, presumably as prophylaxis against the plague—while noting that "on of þe tallest younge men of þis parysch lyth syke and hath a gretty myrre; how he shall do God knowyth" (*PL,* I, 141).

Margaret lived in a world where an infectious disease might well prove fatal. Beyond tidings of plague and infection, she offered one account of a man who perhaps suffered from psychological or psychosomatic problems. Roger Roke was sick with worry, as she saw the matter: "his drede makyth hym so seke þat but if he haue sokowr sone it is lyke to ben his deth" (*PL,* I, 136). Before her first lying-in, she told John that the midwife would cope with sciatica and come, if need be, in a wheelbarrow ("crod in a barwe") in order to attend the birth (*PL,* I, 125).[120] She once counseled her son not to bother their old friend James Gresham, who "hath ben passyng sekke, and ys yet." When cousin Berney fell ill, there was a request for "white wine or water," amplified in the next letter as "water of mynte or water of millefole."[121] Maybe the mint water would help, just as we put our faith in the unguent she requested when plague came to Norwich. And even Margaret could show gratitude. A letter to John II from 28 January 1475 says, "I thank yow for the flakons þat ye sent me; they be ryght good and plesyth me ryght well" (*PL,* I, 221). On one occasion she actually offered a testimonial on behalf of a doctor, uncharacteristic as this sounds: Uncle Philip ("Phelyppe") was very sick and he wanted to get to Suffolk, "for there is a good fesicion and he shal loke to hym" (*PL,* I, 144). But against this, and more typical of the family outlook, was her warning to John I: "fore goddys sake be ware what medesynys ye take of any fysissyanys of London. I schal neuer trust to hem be-cause of youre fadre and my onkyl, whoys sowlys god assoyle" (*PL*, I, 177).[122]

There is little more for the realm of vital statistics and life milestones. In the early days, when Margaret was carrying her first child, she did refer to her own condition: "ye haue leften me sweche a memraunse þat mekyth me to thynke uppe-on yow beothe day and nyth wanne I wold sclepe" (*PL*, I, 125). In a strange passage about knight service, she tells her husband his probable age: he, John Paston, as she reminds him, "shuld be now up-on the age of xxx wynter" (*PL*, I, 143).[123] That Heydon refused to accept his wife's child as his own offspring was hot local news. He threatened to kill the child, and as for the wife, "he xuld kyt of here nose to makyn here to be know wat she is" (*PL*, I, 127). We might like to think that when John did come home and found time to put his feet before the fire, his wife found him an eager listener; her store of gossip could be expanded, her lonely days and nights rewarded. But this is only speculation.

Even Margaret Paston finally wound down, though she left the scene with a rousing farewell address—her last will. Before we look at this final statement about the whole enterprise, a few words on behalf of and from the lady who was able to hold center stage for so long. In his commentary on the literary or rhetorical style of the Paston letters, Norman Davis remarked that their wording must have been strongly reminiscent of, and similar to, spoken English. Margaret Paston, while hardly standing alone in this respect, had a flair for the pithy phrase and the aphorism that could drive a point home with a flourish. We should not single her out unduly; she shared this knack for the shrewd summation with her mother-in-law, and John II was probably the cleverest and most interesting wordsmith of the bunch. But we should note Margaret's verbal dexterity.

A few well-chosen words could sum up—or put down—an object of her scorn. Their adversary Wymondham was "cursyd-hertyd and lwmysch" (*PL*, I, 129). Perhaps she was honing her sense of irony when she said, of Hugh of Fenne, that "he is callid right feythfull and trosty to his frendes þat trost hym" (*PL*, I, 166).[124] An early letter characterized John of Sparham as "schyttyl-wyt-tyd"—maybe not the way most of us wish to be remembered through the centuries (*PL*, I, 128). Numerous men who crossed the family's interests were put in place by being labeled as "fals schrew" (*PL*, I, 131; also, 134: "many fals shrewys and thevys"). Some with whom the Pastons could not deal would eventually get their deserts: "he ys a lewde felow and so he shalbe servyd here-after" (*PL*, I, 180). On occasion Margaret's words—presumably from her mouth and simply transcribed by her amanuensis—summed up a situation with a metaphor, or a simile, or a wider allusion. Of manorial tenants caught in the middle: "they had as leffe al-most be tenauntys to the Devell as to the Duke [of Norfolk]" (*PL*, I, 181). And in dismissing a fainthearted neighbor, she said, "Yf he do oght therein he doyth it closely, as he ys wont to doo, and washyth hys hondys therof as Pylate dyde" (*PL,* I, 185).¹²⁵ In debating the best disposition of family lands with her sons, she waxed poetic and said, "yf we lesse þat, we lesse þe fayere-este flowere of owr garland" (*PL,* I, 216). In this same letter she rued a lost opportunity: "We bette þe busschysse, and haue þe losse and þe dysworschuppe, and othere men haue þe byrdys." Comparisons often bring out the best in one's style. We saw that she would choose a visit from John over a new scarlet robe. In summing up the duchess of Suffolk's options, she reported that "the Duchesse of Suffolkes men say that she wull not departe from Heylesdon ner Drayton, she wuld rathere departe from money" (*PL,* I, 217). In praising her confidant James Gloys, in her days of widowhood, she told him: "Ye haue lyghtyd myne hert þerin by a pound" (*PL,* I, 220).¹²⁶

Both Margaret and her mother-in-law had a weakness for speaking in jeremiads. Though she was more restrained in writing to John I than she was to her sons, Margaret did let loose a bit in January 1462, when the duke of Suffolk was a looming presence: "God for hys holy mersy geue grace that ther may be set a good rewyll . . . for I herd nevyr sey of so myche robry and manslaut in thys contré as is now syth-in a lytyll tyme" (*PL,* I, 168). In taxing one or another of her sons—a frequent avocation of her later years—she hinted at a deep well of affliction: "all thes shuld haue holpe me wele þer-to, be-syde othere thynges þat I haue bore thys yeres þat I speke not of" (*PL,* I, 209).¹²⁷ In passing on grim news she took the usual relish in making much of evil times, evil men: "Trost not mych vp-on promyses of lordes now a days. . . . A mannes deth is litill set by now a days. Þerfore be ware of symulacion, for thei wull speke right fayr to you þat wuld ye ferd right evyll" (*PL,* I, 213). It would be hard to surpass her cheerful reflections on her world: "I wote not how we shall lyff but yff þe world a-mend. God a-mend it whan his wyll is" (*PL,* I, 224). And in a rare note of support to John II (in July 1470), she fell back on language reminiscent of our own clichés about "getting in touch with your feelings": "Ye haue assayed the world resonabilly; ye shall knowe your-self the bettir hereaftir" (*PL,* I, 207).

The Will

Finally, Margaret's will.¹²⁸ This long and unusually personal document holds our attention because it can be read as a late (or posthumous) monologue on Margaret's identity as a Paston. It is a thoughtful reassertion of her more prestigious original Mautby identity, though that is only part of its message. The will, dated 4 February 1482—more than two years before her death on 4 November 1484—can be thought of as consisting of three segments. I suggest we read them as thesis, antithesis, and synthesis. The reassertion or reinvention of a Mautby identity is Margaret's thesis: "I have stepped back and I am finally and once again myself, much as I was when it all began." Then she follows by casting the customary net of ecclesiastical benefaction over a goodly brace of churches and regular houses, influenced to some extent in her choices by family predilections, but mostly leaving money and goods to houses mentioned in no other extant Paston will and not known as recipients of any other Paston largesse. And finally, as though she had perhaps been too draconian about distancing herself from the role in which she had been cast for thirty or forty years, she drew back and left a generous spread of endowments to her children and grandchildren—the Pastons. *She* might be a Mautby, and she might help parish churches and poor folk all over Norfolk and Suffolk as she chose, but she was *also* the grandmother/matriarch of the family into which she had married so long ago. She had outlived her brother-in-law William and her mother-in-law, Agnes, as well as her husband and some of her children, and her eminence atop the family pyramid was worth claiming. She had earned it by fertility, by an impressive record of loyal service, and by longevity.

The reinvention—or the final assertion—of Margaret Mautby is perhaps the will's most striking characteristic. While this return to natal identity is not rare among upper-class widows in terms of bequests and choice of burial site—Agnes had done the same—Margaret offers an extreme example, especially as Mautby roots were hardly FitzAlan or de Vere or Beauchamp roots. At her death the Pastons could claim considerable status, even if the sons had been feckless and there had been many reversals along the way. But regardless of how she balanced her identities, she began by coming down firmly on the Mautby side of the line. She was to be buried "in the ele of the cherch of Mauteby . . . jn which ele reste the bodies of diuers of myn auncesteres." Then came a string of related instructions—fueled mostly by her assertion of Mautby identity, Mautby origins, Mautby relations, and Mautby relationships. The escutcheons on the tomb were to be consonant with this newly asserted (or rediscovered) priority, though the chantry priest was to offer prayers for her, her father and mother, and "the sowles of the seid John Paston, late my husbond, and for the sowlys of his aunceteres and myn."[129] Burial in Mautby church was for Margaret alone: not with John, at Bromholm, nor with her son Edmund in St. Peter, Hungate, Norwich, nor in the cathedral itself (where her father-in-law had been interred). Her last will was her turf.[130] To reinforce her assertion of a proprietary interest, Margaret also bequeathed twelve pence to every household in Mautby, "as hastily as it may be conuenyently doo."

The bequests to Mautby parish church and Mautby village were the lead items in what was an articulated pattern of giving and remembering (and of being remembered): church and community, and other churches and communities, all untouched by other Pastons. In four instances she singled out such parish churches and the village or manor in which they stood. For Fretton, Bassingham, Matelask, and Gresham, there was a bequest for church repair ("to the emendyng of the cherch") *and* something for the people thereabouts. The ecclesiastical bequests were chasubles and albs, and then came six pence per household for her tenants at Fretton, eight pence at Bassingham, six pence for "euery pore" household of her tenants at Matelask, and six pence for every household at Gresham. She expressed more interest in the church at Redham, "there as I was borne," but left nothing for the people of the parish, whereas at Sparham there would be six pence for each poor household but nothing for the church.[131]

When she turned her thoughts to Norwich, she balanced established Paston traditions against what would be expected of any rich widow of the day. In the cathedral city, she left bequests to St. Michael Coslany as well as the more conventional recipients: the cathedral, St. Peter Hungate (rebuilt by Margaret and John I and burial site of Edmund), and houses in that parish. In addition to support for Norwich's established institutions, such as the four friaries, she was generous with alms to individual recipients, including the "anker" at the White Friars and anchoresses ("ankeres") at the Dominican house and at Conesford (giving about 3s. 4d. each). Nor was this the end of her individualized bequests: each leper at the five "yates" of Norwich, three pence; each whole and half-sister at Norman, eight pence; the four poor men and either of the sisters at St. Giles Hospital, two pence; and to each "forgoer" at the gates of Norwich, two pence.[132]

But family, in the most basic of ways, was what it was all about. If not, why had the Pastons been writing all those letters, scheming and plotting, and litigating and toadying over the decades? This too was Margaret to the core, and her swathe of Paston bequests is wide, reaching to some of the near and dear who make few appearances in her letters. It is almost as though she were making the Pastons wait—baiting them, if we will—before she got down to her bequests for the family. To give Margaret credit, once the time for chiding, reforming, or cutting folks dead was over, she more than did her duty as the *grande dame* of the lineage. She named and enriched her four living children: Edmund, Anne (and her husband, William Yelverton), William, and John III (and his children, William and Elizabeth). John II's bastard daughter was remembered, as were three children of the ill-married Margery (presumed dead, though Richard Calle lived until 1503 or 1504). Godchildren (Marie Tendall, by name, and otherwise just "ich of myn other godchildren") were mentioned. So were servants, where she proved to be surprisingly generous. Apart from individual bequests, the household was to be kept together "by haff a yer" and then one-quarter's wages were also to be paid.

Very last of all, her executors. There were four men, with John III (finally) being taken at full value and included among them. In earlier years he may have been slow to accept responsibility, and he had been slow in doing his duty by way of marriage and fatherhood, but he came through in the end and he was now worthy of her trust, along with the other executors.[133] Blood was thicker than almost anything. It is fitting that our final record of Margaret Paston is her recognition of this basic social reality.

CONCLUSION: SOME FINAL REFLECTIONS

In winding up this journey through some late medieval sources that have enabled us to eavesdrop on various aggregations of discourse, testimony, and memory, I offer a few general observations that have patiently awaited their turn. Much of what I have to say here, by way of closing reflections, has already been suggested, though an overview at the very end permits some comparative and retrospective observations that are perhaps more germane now that all the rest has been explored at considerable length. Rather than summarize the material discussed above, I offer some general comments about society, discourse, and social interaction. These remarks have been fueled by the analysis of the different types of documents—the "events" the sources recapture and the way in which that recollection is articulated.

One aspect of the speech and interaction reflected in the sources we have been reading is the high level or degree of partisanship that they incorporate. Though this assertion will be qualified and even countered below when we look at other aspects of the tale, we can begin by remarking on the extent to which an oppositional mode of presentation has been such an essential part of what we have covered. A striking characteristic of the sources—of all the various forms of discourse and testimony we have considered—is that virtually all our speakers, in the vast cast list of the three types of dramatic presentation, were inclined to approach the issue at hand in terms of "our" side and "their" side. Underlying this aspect of exposition is the natural tendency to believe and to side with the others who spoke on behalf of "our" side, to accept what they said as correct, true, reliable, and useful grist for "our" mill.

Against this in-group or team approach to social relations would be the colder and less accepting approach to information offered by "the others." A very real alterity in the presentation of memory and testimony might not always be particularly hostile, in the sense that the teams might be engaged in ritualized play rather than in a war game. The Proofs of Age are an example of this sort of controlled or limited manifestation of ritualized opposition. But in the Scrope and Grosvenor depositions—matters whose importance we must accept as an article of faith, given the gravity of the contemporary convictions about their import—the aspect of ritualized opposition is preeminent. Despite the occasional chivalric lip-service by some of Scrope's partisans about the presumed worthiness of Sir Robert Grosvenor and his clan, the general tone was one of hostility, spurious indignation, and the collective bravado of macho memories.

When we turn to the Pastons, we are indisputably in a world where real enemies really were near at hand and usually plotting the next episode in the family's many woes and trials. Whether the level of enmity was elevated, or even caused in good part, by the aggressive style that was part and parcel of the Pastons' own social climbing and scheming is beside the point—or rather, it was but an inherent element of the world Margaret Paston entered at the moment of her marriage. Though she clearly indicated an uneasiness, if not outright disagreement, with her husband's most intractable schemes in the last year or two of his life, her letters are mostly square pegs cut from the start to fit square holes. They are well shaped for the long-term purpose of learning and then writing about "them" to advance "us" on the socioeconomic and political game board of East Anglian chess and checkers. Letters in which she took her sons to task—either as written to their father or directly to them—express her worry that the boys (and daughter Margery, on her marriage to Richard Calle) would fail to be of full value to the team. But we should note that it was never a question of deserting the home team and joining another one, or even of siding with Uncle William. Rather, she worried whether they would carry their full weight when their turn came to shoulder the family enterprise. It was all so partisan, so focused on the unbridgeable bifurcations of their world and their worldview. In fairness to these choleric folk, a milder stance would have meant being trampled by those with whom they did their business.

As I said above, this is one way to extricate or reconstruct social relations from these sources. At the same time, the thesis I offer about the polarization of relationships and the tailoring of speech and memory to fit this world of alterity has an antithesis—an alternate reading of the sources, an alternate construction of the world they recall. Against the "us versus them" view of the world we can pose, by way of contrast, a scenario—as illustrated by much we find in the Proofs of Age—that looks more to harmony and consensus. I tried to indicate how the Proofs, beneath their seemingly simple veneer, were crafted to touch deeper aspects of life than are hinted at by their jejune literary form and shallow discursive style. They can be read as strong statements on behalf of the good health of the structural-functional community: working, playing, doing serious business to satisfy the king's men, and more of the same. They were intentionally crafted to deflect those who read and used them, to turn us away from a world of conflict and of adversarial elements. They give a softer view of society, woven though it might have been from the rough fibers that bound the unfriendly men (and women) with whom we dealt in the unfriendly confines of the Scrope and Grosvenor depositions and the Paston letters.

CONCLUSION

Through their weave of narration, remembrance, and assertion, the Proofs guide us to a promised land, an imagined community of agreement, concord, and a harmonious common past. It is not always clear, reading them today in an effort to re-create their hazy reality, whether we should rejoice or despair at the way in which so many jurors strove to blend their voices into a chorale directed by the "haves" of their world. The gulf between the jurors themselves and those whose interests they were serving and helping to perpetuate, at least into the next generation, was often remarked upon in the testimonies, but rarely so as to cast aspersions on that mythical symbiosis of upstairs and downstairs. Of course, the Proofs as a document or form of record had been designed to cover over the social chasm between village and lord, and the reduction of memories to one-line assertions helped ensure that everything would remain in sharp but short focus.

There is an element of irony in the fact that, of our various collections of sources, that which most closely reflects everyday life at its middling and lower ranges bespeaks a romanticized world of consensus, while the sources that focus on upper-middling and upper-class life take us closer to—if not over the edge of—the social precipice. This distinction says something about the difference between the sources as much as (or more than) it does about the niceties and nastiness of social life at any and all levels. But we come to the brink of crisis and confrontation, though hardly total breakdown or dysfunction, when we comb through the quarrels of "their betters"—the Pastons, the Scropes, and the Grosvenors. At least, we might offer, the Pastons were fighting for something tangible: land, a knighthood for the eldest son, election to Commons, power to dominate local offices such as those of the sheriff, the escheators, the local bench, and so on. These are things we can still get our figurative hands on. A reading of the Scrope and Grosvenor depositions, however, shows that in the eyes of all of those hundreds of men involved in any way in the great fight over a coat of arms, the prize at stake was just as real. And in such a game, there had to be a winner and a loser. By the same token, there were winners and losers in most of the Paston issues. Whatever symbolism underlay the quarrels, flesh and blood and the accounts were never far away. These people lived in a world of honor, umbrage, and the ready quarrel.

In many ways the Scropes of Bolton, as a family and a collective enterprise, have a good deal in common with the Pastons. Both families were on the make, typical and mostly successful case studies in pushy mobility. And in both instances the path upward was not only rocky but also marked with numerous dips and downturns during the long march. The Scropes had had to overcome the stigma of rising by way of service: lawyers and judges first, and only later men of tourneys, battlefields, and writs of summons to the House of Lords. The Pastons were likewise plagued by the fact that William I's father had pretty surely been of a villein family. Judging by their sensitivity about such matters, it is not much of a stretch to suggest that both families suffered from "status anxiety." The reference in a deposition—offered on behalf of Scrope's case—to a time when he almost assaulted a French prisoner of war because the unfortunate man's arms looked like the much-coveted Azure, a bend Or, shows what we would consider an almost pathological sensitivity. Nor were the Pastons much less low-key about their claims and pretensions.

The story of the Pastons' rise—ultimately to the peerage, though not until well after our tale has closed—is a tortuous if familiar one. Their cyclical patterns of gains and losses have now been thoroughly chronicled by Colin Richmond, with his running comments on their moral and psychological standing; they need no rehearsal here. But for an assessment of their fortunes during the years in which Margaret helped hold the fort, we can fall back on Lenin's idea of one step forward and two steps back, or however we distribute the numbers. Their progress was often halted, and even reversed, but by dint of good fortune (such as the death of the young duke of Norfolk), reasonable family solidarity within the inner ranks, and more extra-familial support than they were wont to admit to, they got "there," wherever that happened to be.

If we apply this same paradigm of family fortune to the Scropes and pick up their tale with their triumph in the Court of Chivalry in 1390, we have a comparable pattern before us. Not far into the future beyond 1390 would be some dramatic moments as they too walked out their destiny of a step or two forward and then (at least) one backward. Richard, our hero of the controversy, was soon to fall from favor at Richard II's court. But his son and heir would rise to the earldom of Wiltshire, the son's elevation more than balancing, for a few years, the relative demotion of his father. But then came Wiltshire's execution in 1399 *and* his father's need to eat humble pie in atonement for his misdirected fatherhood. Abject humility did recapture the favor of the new dynasty, though family fortunes continued to alternate from sunshine to cloud, and we can end our summary with a need to seek a pardon, in 1485, after the current Lord Scrope had chosen the wrong side at the Battle of Bosworth. The peerage was preserved, and modest noble status and wealth were retained into modern times, but quite often it was a damned near-run thing, as Wellington summed up Waterloo.

The historian usually does well to reflect on Marx's comments about the extent to which we make our own history and the extent to which we are actors caught up in currents larger and more powerful than we can perceive or control. Our conscious exercise of agency must be set into a context of impersonal forces like those of class, social structure, and gender. If we cannot ask much of these men and women we have been looking at in terms of articulating pithy summations about the structure of their world—beyond an occasional nod to the pieties of the three orders and the like—we do find that they had a reasonable self-consciousness about their roles, at least in a localized and provincial setting. Testimony of a solemn sort and letters written to enhance a long-term family agenda reveal countless instances of people speaking with due deliberation regarding the legacy of the past and its effect on the present. Most of them had little doubt that their own memories were building blocks—albeit small and ephemeral ones—in the wall of social construction. History as process—the flight of time's arrow and its irreversible direction and consequences—seems to have figured into how they shaped their memories and how they chose the words through which those memories took form.

But before we award too many honors at this convocation called to focus on self-consciousness and articulation in late medieval English society, I want to end with a comment on the extent of male-identified and male-oriented memories. Were it not for the happy chance of many letters from Margaret Paston, we would have even less idea than we do of the balance between the sexes in the world of action, speech, and mnemonic recollection. That lost world of women has recently been labeled "the imaginary society" by Sylvia Federico, who looked at their role in the rebellion of 1381. While the Proofs of Age carried many memories that centered on women or on male-female relations and activities, the world of the Scrope and Grosvenor depositions was about as sexless as an early *chanson de geste* (and about as humorless).

The sources I have chosen to analyze certainly leave Margaret Paston "alone of all her sex," as the phrase goes. Perhaps the message should be, in a sanguine vein, that this appearance of social exclusion was not social reality. We know so much more about this world than we once did, and we like to think in terms of a more equitable distribution between the sexes of its rewards as well as its burdens. As an empiricist and a relativist, I argue for the right to judge the *bona fide* voice of any given source, to determine how far we should follow its lead and how much we should take it on trust as a representative sample of a larger whole that remains hidden. The Scrope and Grosvenor depositions transport us to a world so remote from family and gender that even the realities of procreation and lineage seem immaculate, male-bonded, male-generated matters. There is no reference in the depositions to the rather interesting fact that Sir Richard himself had married the daughter of the earl of Suffolk—a noteworthy "two steps forward" accomplishment for a parvenu peer. And while the Proofs of Age talk much of women's roles and of knowledge (and thus memories) imparted to jurors by the women of the village or neighborhood, there is not even the smallest hint that women's exclusion from the process of government or the subsequent reconstruction of memory was seen in any way as restrictive and exclusionary.

So, appropriately, it comes down to assessing the tension or dissonance between the realities of social structure, about which the men rarely spoke, and their

CONCLUSION

comforting reminiscences of male bonding. These patterns and forms of behavior did not seem to differ whether we look at a situation of harmony and accord or deal with documents that reflect occasions of opposition and alterity. Gender is more noteworthy for its absence, with all apologies to Margaret Paston, and any cynicism about our ability to see the whole society may be compounded by a consideration of the identity of those whom we have heard and of the proceedings whence their words came.

In the acknowledgments at the beginning of this book, I paid a personal tribute to my own support group: friends, colleagues, editors. At the very end, I wish to acknowledge that without a lot of fair folk of the fourteenth and fifteenth centuries—and one particular woman of solid and rather haughty East Anglian stock—it would all have been impossible. In its own way, the past can be coaxed to yield some of its secrets. The rest, however much that amounts to, is up to us.

NOTES

INTRODUCTION

1. The Proofs of Age that supply the principal data for analysis are the five volumes of *Calendars of Inquisitions Post Mortem* that cover the reigns of Richard II and Henry IV. They are all published in London by His/Her Majesty's Stationery Office (HMSO). In chronological order: *Calendar of Inquisitions Post Mortem, XV: 1–7 Richard II* (1970); *Calendar of Inquisitions Post Mortem, XVI: 7–15 Richard II* (1974); *Calendar of Inquisitions Post Mortem, XVII: 15–23 Richard II* (1988); *Calendar of Inquisitions Post Mortem, XVIII: 1–6 Henry IV*, ed. J. L. Kirby (1987); *Calendar of Inquisitions Post Mortem, XIX: 7–14 Henry IV*, ed. J. L. Kirby (1992)—referred to below simply as XV, XVI, XVII, XVIII, and XIX. References to other volumes in the series include *CIPM*, with details in each citation. The convention of the (mostly unnamed) editors has been, from the start of this series in 1904, to present the material in English calendared form, though the gist of each entry is largely a translation of its Latin substance. Such calendaring saved space by omitting the standardized phraseology and the mimetic recitation of juror after juror. The convention of calendaring has also been adopted by editors of local record societies and of the List and Index Society. The HMSO editors—like medieval scribes—sometimes give a direct quote in contemporary English for a particularly pithy turn. I quote below from the English calendars. No editor has ever deemed the Latin to be of sufficient interest to merit verbatim publication.

For the Scrope and Grosvenor controversy, see Nicholas Harris Nicolas, *The Controversy Between Sir Richard Scrope and Sir Robert Grosvenor*, 2 vols. (London, 1832), cited below simply as *S&G*. I only focus on the case presented on behalf of Sir Richard Scrope and on his family's history. Though a comparable case concerning Grosvenor could be presented, we have more information about the Scrope side of the controversy—about him, his family, and his deponents—and the exposition of one set of partisans suffices for an exercise in the re-creation of social memory. Nicolas did not complete the background work on the second (and lesser) family in the controversy when he published the proceedings, and I have chosen to rest my analysis on the fuller record and the deeper documentation of the Scrope family.

For Margaret Paston's letters, see Norman Davis, ed., *The Paston Letters and Papers of the Fifteenth Century*, 2 vols. (Oxford, 1970–76).

2. Diana Greenway, ed. and trans., *Henry, Archdeacon of Huntington: Historia Anglorum: History of the English People* (Oxford, 1996). In fairness, by looking at Henry, I have chosen a chronicler whose work exists in a large number of manuscripts and therefore may have been preserved in a more piecemeal fashion than is often the case. At the other extreme, and arguing against the case I am building here, are chronicles we know from a single manuscript. See, for example, Chris Given-Wilson, ed. and trans., *The Chronicle of Adam Usk, 1377–1421* (Oxford, 1997), and Wendy R. Childs and John Taylor, eds., *The Anonimalle Chronicle, 1307 to 1334: From Brotherton Ms. 29*, Yorkshire Archaeological Society Record Series, vol. 147 ([Leeds], 1991). But even the single manuscript chronicle of Adam of Usk had leaves that became detached (now restored and reunited as British Library Additional Manuscript 10104). Yorkshire Archaeological Society will be cited hereafter as YAS.

3. G. A. Lester, *Sir John Paston's 'Grete Boke': A Descriptive Catalogue with an Introduction of B.L. Ms. Lansdowne 285* (Cambridge, 1984). Though this particular codex is more slanted toward

chivalric, military, and heraldic texts than historical ones, it offers what is probably a fair guide to lay reading tastes and interests. For a comparable collection but with an emphasis on epistolary material, see M. Dominica Legge, ed., *Anglo-Norman Letters and Petitions from All Souls Ms. 182*, Anglo-Norman Texts, no. 3 (Oxford, 1941). The manuscript miscellany was a common item, probably in demand from the booksellers: see Peter Murray Jones, "British Museum Ms. Sloane 76: A Translator's Holograph," in *Medieval Book Production: Assessing the Evidence*, ed. Linda L. Brownrigg (Los Altos Hills, Calif., 1990), 21–39, for a discussion of how a translator was apt to work in preparing items for his market.

4. Sue Sheridan Walker, "Proof of Age of Feudal Heirs in Medieval England," *Mediaeval Studies* 35 (1973): 306–23. For the evolution of the Proofs of Age as a specific document and/or procedure, see Henry Maxwell-Lyte's introduction to *CIPM, I: Henry III* (London, 1904), vii–xiii, on the recognition of the need for a special writ and the emergence of escheators as distinct officials, with two per county, circa 16–18 Henry III (more on escheators in Chapter 1, below). According to William A. Morris, *The Medieval English Sheriff to 1300* (Manchester, 1927), escheators were generally to be found by 1274, and they took their oath of office in the county court under the gaze of the sheriff (193, 238). See M. S. Giuseppi, *A Guide to the Manuscripts in the Public Record Office*, 2 vols. (London, 1923), on the many types of writs.

5. R. F. Hunnisett, "The Reliability of Inquisitions as Historical Evidence," in *The Study of Medieval Records: Essays in Honour of Kathleen Major*, ed. D. A. Bullough and R. L. Storey (Oxford, 1971), 206–35. Pages 206–7 are most relevant for the Proofs of Age, and the comments are rather caustic.

6. R. C. Fowler, "Legal Proofs of Age," *English Historical Review* 22 (1907): 101–3. A comparison of some suspect reminiscences found in Proofs from 2 Henry IV led Fowler to suggest that "these witnesses, 'sworn and separately examined,' were all speaking the truth can hardly be admitted" (103). Subsequent references to *English Historical Review* will use the abbreviation *EHR*.

7. M. T. Martin, "Legal Proofs of Age," *EHR* 22 (1907): 526–27. On striking similarities in different Proofs, see Crawford Hodgson, "Proof of Age of Heirs of Estates in Northumberland," *Archaeologia Aeliana* 3, no. 3 (1907): 297–309. T. A. M. Bishop, reviewing *CIPM, IX: 21–25 Edward III* in *EHR* 52 (1937): 437–40, discusses discrepancies in jurors' ages in Proofs from the same county within a short span of time.

8. A. E. Stamp, "Legal Proofs of Age," *EHR* 29 (1914): 323–24.

9. John Horace Round, reviewing *CIPM, IX* in *EHR* 32 (1917): 453–54. He said the element of duplication "throws even graver doubt than has been felt hitherto on the trustworthiness of these documents." Charles Ross also remarked on a "striking correspondence" in statements from different hearings, reviewing *CIPM, XIII: 44–47 Edward III* and *CIPM, XIV: 48–51 Edward III* in *EHR* 72 (1957): 109–11. But Ross acknowledged their value for social history, and he mentioned early references to villagers as church wardens (111). Bertram P. Wolffe, reviewing *Calendar of Inquisitions Miscellaneous, VI (1392–99)* in *EHR* 83 (1968), reflected on "how reliable was this process of extent . . . on the verbal testimony of jurors" (385). An early word, and usually a reliable last word, comes from Pollock and Maitland: jurors were asked "how they come to remember the time of his birth, and they answer with talk of coincidences." Frederick Pollock and Frederic William Maitland, *The History of English Law Before the Time of Edward I*, intro. S. F. C. Milsom (Cambridge, 1905; 2d ed., rev., Cambridge, 1968), 2:640.

10. T. A. M. Bishop, reviewing *CIPM, XII: 39–43 Edward III* in *EHR* 55 (1940): 329. He distinguishes between "pre-fabricated" memories and malicious falsehoods, where an underage heir's claim was offered in a serious attempt to appropriate what was not yet his. For a likely suggestion regarding the escheator's *modus operandi*, see C. J. Crump, "A Note on the Criticism of Records," *Bulletin of the John Rylands Library* 8 (1924), where Crump suggests that records were "deliberately drawn up in such a fashion as to conceal the character, the opinion, and the mental equipment of the writer . . . and even of the man who caused them to be written" (140) and where he speculates that, in preparing for a Proof, the heir's steward made a statement about age that the escheator would verify, and when these parties were in agreement, the formal questions were put to the jury, at which time it was all explained "in the vulgar tongue" (142).

11. Josiah Cox Russell, *British Medieval Population* (Albuquerque, 1948), 102–4, and 365, where Russell points out that it was "upon the basis of a couple of forgeries . . . [that] the Proofs had acquired a very bad reputation. The value of the Proofs, however, was proved without much difficulty." Also see 17–33 on medieval numbers and 208–14 on mortality calculations based on IPMs.

12. Lawrence R. Poos, *A Rural Society After the Black Death: Essex, 1350–1525* (Cambridge, 1991), makes extensive use of the Proofs. See his discussion of their data as applicable to questions about migration and servanthood (164–79); a general vindication of their testimony (190–91); and his explanation of how the preamble to depositions could be shaped to intersect with questions about length of acquaintance, familiarity between parties, and so on (164). For Proofs as a basis of "soft" demographic analysis, see my *Old Age in Medieval England* (Philadelphia, 1996), 33–43.

13. Her "Proof of Age" offers a concise exposition of the development of the procedure. The writ *de aetate probando* was in use by 1259, and Walker traces the development of the proceedings into the fourteenth century. She calls attention to the "judicious presentations of gifts" (316) by parents or godparents to fix a given day in memories, a practice we will encounter and discuss below. Walker also notes that some Proofs can be checked against references to external events, such as a memory of the Battle of Strivelyn, the coronation of Edward II, and the like.

14. Rodney H. Hilton, reviewing *CIPM, XV: 1–7 Richard II* in *EHR* 88 (1973): 170–71, argues that Proofs "throw interesting light" on the mentality of those questioned. Their answers reveal what events stuck in their minds to remind them of the birth, though many remain "laconic and uninformative." An older reading came to much the same conclusion: see L. B. L. [sic], "Probatio Aetatis of William Septvans," *Archaeologia Cantiana* I (1858): 124–36. In tracing a false claim to legal age, L. B. L. points out that "the evidences adduced in Proofs of Age are among the most interesting of those preserved among national records," offering a "very graphic picture of domestic life . . . [and] valuable notions of historical facts and local incidents."

15. For Proofs making a serious effort to falsify the heir's age, see *CIPM, XI: 35–38 Edward III*, 611, and *CIPM, XII*, 96. The original case (July, 38 Edward III) had produced a false return, and in 40 Edward III (writ of 13 April) the sheriff was directed, by writ of *venire facias*, to provide a panel of twenty-one knights and others, twelve of whom would constitute a jury and rectify the earlier error. Also see *CIPM, XIV*, 63: "this proof [was] insufficient" because the husband of one of the coheiresses had not been warned of the proceeding. This was easily remedied: "so another writ was issued to warn him." Sue Walker, in "Proof of Age," gives a case (*tempore* Henry III) where the principal was "accused of having maliciously, by suborned testimony, established a false age" (321). The case ends without conclusion, perhaps because Roger Sunbray made his peace with the king (or so Walker speculates, and she is usually fairly cautious). She points out that there are virtually no references, even in disputed cases, to any form of cross-examination. For a less sanguine view of this whole business, see Scott Waugh, *The Lordship of England: Royal Wardships and Marriage in English Society and Politics, 1217–1327* (Princeton, 1988), on petitions presented to halt or slow down a proceeding (114) and on fraudulent claims of age (136).

16. The scholarship on the controversy is cited in Chapter 2. For a pithy summation—more tongue-in-cheek than one would expect from an editor of *Burke's Peerage*—see L. G. Pine, *Heraldry and Genealogy* (London, 1957), 51–55. Pine recounts the eventual fall of the Scropes and the mighty rise of the Grosvenors to the dukedom of Westminster. He quotes Bartholus: "arms were like names, and could be assumed as a person pleased" (54), though this view was clearly no longer accepted in England by the later fourteenth century. Pine notes that the duke of Westminster's winning horse in the Derby of 1880 was named Bend Or (a long Grosvenor memory to avenge the adverse judgment of 1390). Also on the Grosvenors' long memories and subsequent efforts to claim a victory, see Richard Cust, ed., *The Papers of Sir Richard Grosvenor, First Baronet (1585–1645)*, Record Society of Lancashire and Cheshire, vol. 134 ([Chester], 1996).

17. Thirteen hearings were held on Scrope's behalf between 16 June and 19 October 1386 (9 Richard II). They were held at Gaunt's palace by the Plymouth Carmelites, at Tiverton (the earl of Devon's manor), in the refectory of Abbotsbury Abbey in Dorset, at St. John Without the Walls, Chester, at various places in and around York, at Aton, Pickering, and Scarborough, and in the refectory of Westminster Abbey.

18. Maurice Keen, "The Jurisdiction and Origins of the Constable's Court," in *War and Government in the Middle Ages: Essays in Honour of J. O. Prestwich,* ed. John G. Gillingham and J. C. Holt, 159–69 (Woodbridge, 1984), where he differs from and expands on the views of G. D. Squibb, *The High Court of Chivalry: A Study in the Civil Law of England* (Oxford, 1959). For other cases before the court, see Ian Jack, "Entail and Descent: The Hastings Inheritance, 1370 to 1436," *Bulletin of the Institute of Historical Research* 38 (1965): 1–19, and Maurice Keen and Mark Warner, eds., "Morley vs. Montagu (1399): A Case in the Court of Chivalry," *Camden Miscellany* 34, Camden Society, 5th ser., vol. 10 (Cambridge, 1997), 141–95. For a challenge that led to a duel to the death, see John Bellamy, "Sir John de Annelsey and the Chandos Inheritance," *Nottingham Mediaeval Studies* 10 (1960): 94–105. Charles Boutrell, *Heraldry, Historical and Popular* (London, 1964), discusses Richard II's intervention in the Scrope and Grosvenor dispute. The king declared that "a bordure" did not suffice to differentiate between strangers' arms in the same kingdom, though it would for cousins by blood (216–17). In *Calendar of the Patent Rolls, 1391–96* (London, 1905), there are numerous commissions appointed to hear appeals of decisions from the court of the constable and marshal; ironically, Sir Richard Scrope was named to four of them. They were to hear cases touching on ransoms, military service, quarrels that arose at sea, and disputes over coats of arms.

19. Consult Nigel Saul, *Richard II* (New Haven, 1997), on Derby vs. Norfolk (400–401) and on Richard's weakness for theatrical moments (461). Michael J. Bennett, *Richard II and the Revolution of 1399* (Stroud, 1999), also describes this side of the king's behavior (132–35).

20. James L. Gillespie, "Richard II: Chivalry and Kingship," in *The Age of Richard II,* ed. James L. Gillespie (Stroud, 1997), 115–38.

21. Rosenthal, *Old Age,* compares the ages of the Scrope deponents and the Grosvenor ones (46). The seniority and higher status of the Scrope "team" indicated that they would be the winners, though G. D. Squibb has commented that there is "no reasoned judgement stating why the Court found in favor of the plaintiff." See his "Law of Arms in England," *Coat of Arms* 2 (1953): 245.

22. There is an entry for Sir Robert Grosvenor and an account of the controversy in the old *DNB* (C. L. Kingsford), as well as biographical material in S&G. A decade after these hearings, Richard II's ties to Cheshire might have led to a different conclusion. See James L. Gillespie, "Richard II's Chester Archers," *Transactions of the Historic Society of Lancashire and Cheshire* 125 (1975): 1–33.

23. Giles Constable, *Letters and Letter Collections,* Typologie des Sciences du Moyen Age Occidental, fasc. 17 (Turnhout, 1976); Malcolm Richardson, "Medieval English Vernacular Correspondence: Notes Toward an Alternative Rhetoric," *Allegorica* (1989): 95–118; Janet G. Altman, *Epistolarity: Approaches to a Form* (Columbus, 1982); Roger Chartier, Alain Boureau, and Cécile Dauphin, *Correspondence: Models of Letter Writing,* trans. E. Woodell (Philadelphia, 1997).

24. On the "how to do it" literature, see D. J. Polak, "Dictamen," and James J. Murphy, "Rhetoric: Western Europe," both in *Dictionary of the Middle Ages,* ed. Joseph R. Strayer (New York, 1984), 4:173–77 and 10:351–64, respectively.

25. Richard W. Southern, "Toward an Edition of Peter of Blois's Letter Collection," *EHR* 110 (1995): 925–37; Elizabeth Ravell, ed., *The Later Letters of Peter of Blois* (Oxford, 1993). This process of subsequent editing to control publication is discussed by many editors of medieval letters. Alain Boureau offers a general caveat on such letters: "As is well known, the letter, in the central middle ages, is an ambivalent genre, addressed to one person but often intended for a wider audience. In a twelfth-century correspondence, we pass from humdrum matters to what amounts to little treatises on spirituality or theology." See Boureau, "Richard Southern: A Landscape for a Portrait," *Past and Present* 165 (November 1999): 226.

26. Edith Rickert, "A Leaf from a Fourteenth-Century Letter Book," *Modern Philology* 25 (1927–28): 249–55, mainly from the letter book of Lady Alice de Bryene (c. 1393–96); Rickert, "Some English Personal Letters of 1402," *Review of English Studies* 8 (1932): 257–63; Paddy Payne and Caroline M. Barron, "The Letters and Life of Elizabeth Despenser, Lady Zouche (d. 1408)," *Nottingham Medieval Studies* 41 (1997): 126–56.

27. One wonders how many other family letters may once have existed. Beyond the Paston letters, see Alison Hanham, ed., *The Cely Letters, 1472–1488,* Early English Text Society, no. 273 (Oxford,

1975); Joan Kirby, ed., *The Plumpton Letters and Papers,* Camden Society, 5th ser., vol. 8 (Cambridge, 1996); and Christine Carpenter, ed. and intro., *Kingsford's Stonor Letters and Papers, 1250–1483* (Cambridge, 1996). Alison Truelove is preparing a new edition of the Stonor letters; see her "Commanding Communications: The Fifteenth-Century Letters of the Stonor Women," in *Early Modern Women's Letter Writing, 1450–1700,* ed. James Daybell (Basingstoke, 2001), 42–58.

28. Christine Carpenter, ed. and intro., *The Armburgh Papers: The Brokholes Inheritance in Warwickshire, Hertfordshire, and Essex, c. 1417–c. 1453: Chetham's Manuscript Mun. E.6. 10 (4)* (Woodbridge, 1998).

29. Karen Cherewatuk and Ulrike Wiethaus, eds., *Dear Sister: Medieval Women and the Epistolary Genre* (Philadelphia, 1993). As well as the editors' valuable introduction to the volume, see the contributions by Gillian T. W. Ahlgren, "Visions and Rhetorical Strategy in the Letters of Hildegard of Bingen," 46–63 (56 and 58–59 on the number of her letters), and Karen Scott, "'Io Catarina': Ecclesiastical Politics and Oral Culture in the Letters of Catherine of Siena," 87–121. Additionally, see Joseph L. Baird and Radd K. Ehrman, eds. and trans., *The Letters of Hildegard of Bingen,* 2 vols. (New York, 1994–98).

30. See Chapter 3 for more quantitative comparisons of Margaret as a letter writer. For women and the letter collections, see Diane Watt, "'No Writing for Writing's Sake': The Language of Service and Household Rhetoric in the Letters of the Paston Women," in *Dear Sister,* ed. Cherewatuk and Wiethaus, 122–38; Joan Kirby, "Women in the Plumpton Correspondence: Fiction and Reality," in *Church and Crown in the Middle Ages: Essays Presented to John Taylor,* ed. Ian Wood and G. A. Loud, 219–32 (London, 1991); and Jennifer C. Ward, "Letter Writing by English Noblewomen in the Early Fifteenth Century," in *Early Modern Women's Letter Writing,* ed. Daybell, 29–41.

31. For a full account of the history and publication of the Paston material, see David A. Stoker, "'Innumerable Letters of Good Consequence in History': The Discovery and First Publication of the Paston Letters," *The Library,* 6th ser., 17 (1995): 107–55; M. F. Serpell, "Sir John Fenn, His Friends, and the Paston Letters," *Antiquaries Journal* 63 (1983): 95–121. Also see Davis, ed., *Paston Letters and Papers,* 1:xxiv–xxxix, for a short account of discovery and publication, loss, and vindication, as well as James Gairdner, ed., *The Paston Letters, 1422–1509 A.D.,* New Complete Library Edition, 6 vols. (London, 1904; reprint, New York, 1965), I:1–23. On Blomefield's role: S. W. Rix, "Cursory Notes on the Reverend Francis Blomefield, the Norfolk Topographer," *Norfolk Archaeology* 2 (1849): 201–24, and David A. Stoker, ed., *The Correspondence of the Reverend Francis Blomefield (1708–52),* Norfolk Record Society, vol. 55 ([Norwich], 1992).

32. The first edition was that of John Fenn, *Original Letters, Written During the Reigns of Henry VI, Edward IV, and Richard III,* 5 vols. (London, 1787–1823), with the first two volumes issued in 1787 but the fifth not until long after Fenn's death in 1794. In 1840, A. Ramsay brought out a two-volume edition based on Fenn's but with "the less important letters . . . abridged" and with his own additions to the notes. James Gairdner's first edition (*The Paston Letters: A New Edition Containing Upward of 400 Letters, etc., Hitherto Unpublished*) appeared in three volumes between 1872 and 1875. He followed with an edition of 1896, the 1900 edition (with "more letters in supplement" after the introduction) in four volumes, and then the six-volume New Complete Library edition. The catalogue of the British Library steers us to various editions and editors between 1909 and 1958, when Norman Davis entered the picture, with a selection for the Clarendon Medieval and Tudor Series. He next published a set of selections ("in modern spelling") for the World's Classics series in 1963. Since Davis's major two-volume edition of 1970–76, Richard Barber has published a selection in modernized English: see Richard Barber, ed., *The Pastons: A Family in the Wars of the Roses* (London, 1981).

33. Fenn says, "She appears to have been an active wife, and attentive to the interest of her family after she became a widow" (*Original Letters,* 1:xxviii–xxix). Given his dim view of the grasping Pastons and the selfish nobles who led the realm to civil war, this was fairly heady stuff. There are mixed readings, though. While one reader says that Margaret "would hardly be anyone's candidate for mother of the year," another reminds us that she looks pretty good when set next to Agnes: see, respectively, Laurie Finke, *Women's Writings in English: Medieval England* (London, 1999), 194, and H. S. Bennett, *The Pastons and Their England* (Cambridge, 1922), 77, 79. Frances and Joseph Gies

offer strong praise in *A Medieval Family: The Pastons of Fifteenth-Century England* (New York, 1998): "the central figure of the Paston story, the indomitable lady who was carried bodily out of Gresham . . . who worked tirelessly for her husband's interests against his enemies . . . one of the most attractive and sympathetic personalities, as well as one of the most prolific and vigorous writers" (329). Roger Virgoe thought that "she was no heroine but she was an admirable woman . . . the central character of the Paston story." See his *Private Life in the Fifteenth Century: Illustrated Letters of the Paston Family* (London, 1989), 282.

34. The enabling documents—calling the court to order, charging it to do its duty, and so on—are all in Latin.

35. On the multilingualism of late medieval English society, see Helen Sugget, "The Use of French in England in the Later Middle Ages," *Transactions of the Royal Historical Society*, 4th ser., 28 (1946): 61–83; Basil Cottle, *The Triumph of English, 1350–1400* (London, 1965); Linda E. Voigts, "What's the Word: Bilingualism in Late Medieval England," *Speculum* 71 (1996): 813–26; W. Rothwell, "The Trilingual England of Geoffrey Chaucer," *Studies in the Age of Chaucer* 16 (1994): 45–67; and Mildred K. Pope and Eleanor C. Lodge, eds., *The Life of the Black Prince by the Herald of Sir John Chandos* (Oxford, 1910; reprint, New York, 1974), xii–xxix. Saul's *Richard II* suggests that French may have been Richard's first language (14). In addition, consult the following studies by Norman Davis: "The Language of the Pastons," *Proceedings of the British Academy* 40 (1955): 120–44; "Styles in English Prose in the Late Medieval and Early Modern Period," *Langue et littérature: Actes de VIIIème congrès de la Fédération Internationale des Langues et Littératures Modernes* 21 (1961): 165–84; "Style and Stereotype in Early English Letters," *Leeds Studies in English*, n.s., 1 (1967): 7–17; and "Language and Letters from Sir John Fastolf's Household," in *Medieval Studies for J. A. W. Bennett*, ed. P. L. Heyworth (Oxford, 1981), 329–46. Finally, see John H. Fisher's "Chancery and the Emergence of Standard Written English in the Fifteenth Century," *Speculum* 52 (1977): 870–99, and his "Language Policy for Lancastrian England," *Publications of the Modern Language Association* 107 (1992): 1168–80, as well as C. Paul Christianson, "Chancery Standard and the Records of Old London Bridge," in *Standardization of English: Essays in the History of Language Change in Honor of John Hurt Fisher*, ed. Joseph B. Trahern Jr., Tennessee Studies in Literature, no. 31 (Knoxville, 1989), 82–112.

36. The literature is too large to cite in more than a cursory fashion. Consult A. J. Pollard, *North-Eastern England During the Wars of the Roses: Lay Society, War, and Politics, 1450–1500* (Oxford, 1990); Simon Payling, *Political Society in Lancastrian England: The Greater Gentry of Nottinghamshire* (Oxford, 1991); Michael J. Bennett, *Community, Class, and Careerism: Cheshire and Lancashire Society in the Age of "Sir Gawain and the Green Knight"* (Cambridge, 1983); and Susan M. Wright, *The Derbyshire Gentry in the Fifteenth Century*, Derbyshire Record Society, vol. 8 (Chesterfield, 1983). *Journal of British Studies* 33, no. 4 (1994), is devoted to the topic of "Vill, Guild, and Gentry: Forces of Community in Late Medieval England," with a pertinent introduction by Maryanne Kowaleski and articles by Christine Carpenter, Elaine Clark, Christopher Dyer, and Gervase Rosser. For an attempt at revisionism, see Christine Carpenter, *Locality and Polity: A Study of Warwickshire Landed Society, 1401–1499* (Cambridge, 1992). Nigel Saul's *Knights and Esquires: The Gloucestershire Gentry in the Fourteenth Century* (Oxford, 1981) and his *Scenes from Provincial Life: Knightly Families in Sussex, 1280–1400* (Oxford, 1986) offer a more mainstream approach. Much of Roger Virgoe's relevant work is now in his *East Anglian Society and the Political Community of Late Medieval England*, ed. Caroline M. Barron, Carole Rawcliffe, and Joel T. Rosenthal (Norwich, 1997). From a student of the peasantry, see Anne R. DeWindt, "Defining the Peasant Community in Medieval England," *Journal of British Studies* 26 (1987): 163–207; for the "county" approach, Eric Acheson, *A Gentry Community: Leicestershire in the Fifteenth Century, c. 1422–c. 1485* (Cambridge, 1992).

37. See Michael Bennett, *Community, Class, and Careerism*, for an insightful re-creation of the gathering of the gentry at Macclesfield on 24 April 1412 (22–40). Ironically, it was to help settle a quarrel between the Grosvenors and the Legh family. Also see Simon Payling, "County Parliamentary Elections in Fifteenth-Century England," *Parliamentary History* 18, no. 3 (1999): 137–59, and several papers by Virgoe in his *East Anglian Society*.

38. Philippa Maddern, "'Best Trusted Friends': Concepts and Practices of Friendship Among Fifteenth-Century Norfolk Gentry," in *England in the Fifteenth Century: Proceedings of the 1992 Harlaxton Symposium,* ed. Nicholas Rogers (Stamford, 1994), 100–117; Patricia Crawford, "Friendship and Love Between Women in Early Modern England," in *Venus and Mars: Engendering Love and War in Medieval and Early Modern England,* ed. Andrew Lynchy and Philippa Maddern (Nedlands, 1995), 47–61. A little further afield is Ulrike Wiethaus, "In Search of Medieval Women's Friendship: Hildegard of Bingen's Letters to Her Friends and Contemporaries," in *Maps of Flesh and Light,* ed. Ulrike Wiethaus (Syracuse, 1993), 93–111.

39. For material that explicates the Grosvenor side of the issue, see Philip Morgan, *War and Society in Medieval Cheshire, 1277–1403,* Chetham Society, 3d ser., vol. 34 (Manchester, 1987). Morgan notes that for Grosvenor's supporters, the dispute became "a spontaneous demonstration of a class unity in Cheshire which suggests the operation of a community" (129). He speaks of "the formation of a collective memory of already distant campaigns" and includes statistics on how many of Grosvenor's deponents had been on Edward III's last French expedition (in 1359) and how many had been with the Black Prince in Gascony in 1369.

40. On social memory, see Maurice Halbwachs, *La Memoire collective,* 2d ed., rev. (Paris, 1968); James Fentress and Chris Wickham, *Social Memory* (Oxford, 1992); and Simon Kemp, *Cognitive Psychology in the Middle Ages* (Westport, Conn., 1996). Kemp deals with William of Ockham's rejection of "species" in the attempt to explain how and why memories are linked. One remembered (1) the event and (2) one's participation in the event (78–79).

41. Though I may be doing an injustice to a perceptive study by asserting that the author shares my view, see Elisabeth Van Houts, *Memory and Gender in Medieval Europe, 900–1200* (London, 1999). For case studies that expand on the theme of "Oral History, Memory, and Written Tradition," see *Transactions of the Royal Historical Society,* 6th ser., 9 (1999), especially the papers by Patrick J. Geary, Sarah Foot, Elisabeth Van Houts, Christine Shaw, Adam Fox, and Andy Wood. For other approaches, see the invaluable work of Jan Vansina, *Oral Tradition in History* (Madison, 1985); David R. Olson, *The World on Paper: The Conceptual and Cognitive Implications of Writing and Reading* (Cambridge, 1994); and Joyce Coleman, *Public Reading and the Reading Public in Late Medieval England and France* (Cambridge, 1996).

42. Mary Carruthers, *The Book of Memory: A Study of Memory in Medieval Culture* (Cambridge, 1990); Francis Yates, *The Art of Memory* (Chicago, 1966); Mary Warnock, *Memory* (London, 1987); Patrick H. Hutton, *History as the Art of Memory* (Hanover, 1993); Douglas J. Herrmann and Roger Chaffin, eds., *Memory in Historical Perspective: The Literature Before Ebbinghaus* (New York, 1988); Paul Connerton, *How Societies Remember* (Cambridge, 1989); and Jonathan Spence, *The Memory Palace of Mateo Ricci* (New York, 1984).

In *The Cheese and the Worms* (London, 1980), Carlo Ginzburg sagely writes: "In societies founded on oral tradition, the memory of the community involuntarily tends to mask and reabsorb changes. To the relative flexibility of material life there corresponds an accentuated immobility of the image of the past. Things have always been like this; the world is what it is" (77).

CHAPTER 1

1. This chapter had been substantially completed when John Bedell's "Memory and Proof of Age in England, 1272–1327" appeared in *Past and Present* 162 (February 1999): 3–27. I am in agreement with virtually all of Bedell's observations about Proofs as a window onto society and a fixed record of memory. I have not tried to enter our many points of accord (or the very few of discord), however; confirmation of my material can be found in the earlier Proofs that Bedell uses and in most others available, whether in print or in manuscript. I do offer an occasional reference to a parallel set of Proofs, but the picture remains much the same.

2. See the William Salt Archaeological Society, "Inquisitions Post Mortem, Ad Quod Damnum, etc.," in *Staffordshire, Henry III, Edward I, and Edward II (1223–1327)* (London, 1911), for a Proof that says, "the king therefore wishes the said Edmund . . . to prove his age before the said

Malculine [the escheator], who is thereupon desired to inquire, by the oath of knights and other liege men of that county, into the proof of the age" (232). According to David Roffe's "Hundred Rolls of 1255," *Historical Research* 69 (1996), to contemporaries, the inquisition was seen as a "dialectic of investigation, legislation, and enforcement" (203).

3. Intervals were usually short, as borne out by some random examinations. XV, 158: escheator told to take the Proof on 5 February, 2 Richard II, and Proof taken on 12 February; XV, 159: escheator instructed on 8 January, 2 Richard II, and Proof taken Wednesday after St. Peter in Cathedra (22 February); XV, 160: instructions of 26 November, 2 Richard II, and Proof taken Wednesday after feast of St. Nicholas (6 December); XV, 449, instructions of 20 February, 4 Richard II, and Proof taken Saturday after St. Gregory (12 March); instructions of 17 November, 4 Richard II, and Proof taken 19 November. Because my concern is for the process and not the recovery of the estates, it suffices to note that most guardians surrendered control with little demur. They were to be warned of the hearing and given a chance to present their side of the story in person or through an attorney. The report from an escheator on the March of Wales was typical: "I caused the said earl to be warned . . . to be present at Shrewsbury . . . and he signified by William Herdewyk, his attorney, by letters directed to me and remaining in my possession, that the said heir was 22 years of age . . . and that he [the earl] had nothing to say against the lands of his inheritance being delivered to him" (XV, 659). Heiresses, as women of property, tended to marry (or be married) young, and it was often the husband who petitioned for the Proof: "Writ to the escheator to take proof of the age of the said Margaret daughter of Henry de Saxlyngham and kinswoman of the said Thomas his brother; on the petition of Robert de Plumleye, her husband" (XVI, 1053). On the interval between petition and hearing, see James F. Willard, "The Dating and Delivery of Letters Patent and Writs in the Fourteenth Century," *Bulletin of the Institute of Historical Research* 10 (1932–33): 1–11, especially 9–11.

4. In a few Proofs, usually for nobles, we find some men of considerable status (e.g., the Proof for John Mowbray, earl marshal [XIX, 336]). Sometimes other barriers were raised regarding the suitability of men for this kind of jury service. See Angelo Raine, ed., *York Civic Records, I*, YAS Record Series, vol. 98 (Wakefield, 1939): the debate was whether the subject was "a Skotte and no Ynglysman" (17); it was "wrongfully noysed, slaundered and defamed that he shold be a Scotisheman, and born in Scotland" (24).

5. Though the escheator was hardly a lofty royal official, the office was often held, as part of their *cursus honorum*, by men of some local stature. See E. R. Stevenson, "The Escheator," in *The English Government at Work, Volume II: Fiscal Administration*, ed. William A. Morris and Joseph R. Strayer (Cambridge, Mass., 1947), 109–67, for the basic treatment. A. L. Brown, *The Governance of Late Medieval England, 1272–1461* (Stanford, 1989), notes that "in practice they [escheators] were likely to be knights or esquires of the county, but men not quite the same substance as the sheriffs" (145). Eleanor C. Lodge and Gladys A. Thornton give the escheator's oath of office in their edition of *English Constitutional Documents, 1307–1485* (Cambridge, 1935), 356–58. On a dishonest escheator, see Carpenter, ed., *The Armburgh Papers*, 7–8. In Richard II's time there were usually about twenty escheators. Also on the escheator, see note 4 to the introduction of this volume.

6. For other ways of presenting and assessing evidence, see Charles Donahue Jr., "Proof by Witnesses in the Church Courts of Medieval England: An Imperfect Reception of the Learned Law," and Donald W. Sutherland, "Legal Reasoning in the Fourteenth Century: The Invention of 'Color' in Pleading," both in *On the Laws and Customs of England: Essays in Honor of Samuel E. Thorne*, ed. Morris S. Arnold, Thomas A. Green, Sally A. Scully, and Stephen S. White (Chapel Hill, 1981), 127–58 and 182–94, respectively. For "factual deviation," see XIX, 476 and 477: the editor of the *CIPM* says, "findings [for 477] exactly as last except that the ages of Stephen Petley and Roger Loundres are given as 56 and 51, and that the mayor and sheriff are named as Nicholas Brembre and John Organ [mayor and sheriff in the previous year]." In XIX, 476, Petley was aged 47, Loundres 45, and witnesses said they had been in church with Nicholas Exton, "then mayor." XVIII, 666: "writ for proof . . . because he claims to be of full age, although found to be under age by the inquisitions taken after the death of his father [XVIII, 66–68: three inquisitions of which two said five years and more, and one (evidently correct) twelve years and more, October and November, 1391, June 1392]." Sherri Olson discusses the jurors' roles as village leaders in "Jurors of the Village Court: Local Lead-

NOTES TO PAGES 3–6

ership Before and After the Plague in Ellington, Huntingdonshire," *Journal of British Studies* 30 (1991): 252.

7. Few ages were actually questioned. Sue Walker, in "Proof of Age," asserts that "no one ever seems to have cross-examined the jurors" (321), though she cites cases with internal contradictions. Against the view in XVIII, 666, of underage heirs pushing ahead, there are numerous instances of heirs already well beyond age 21 when the Proof was held, including XIX, 102 (heir is 25 at the Proof); XIX, 141 (heir of 24 and more); XIX, 158 (heir of 21 and more); XIX, 336 (heir born 3 August 1390, Proof of 1 December 1412); XIX, 339 (heir born 6 January 1384, Proof taken 28 January 1407); and XIX, 341 (heir born 25 April 1384, Proof taken 14 May 1407).

8. Supposedly, men were quick to resort to the use of round numbers. To some extent this can be tested. An analysis of jurors' ages in XV shows 355 men who stated their age. By respective decades of age, 6 claimed to be in their 30s, 160 in their 40s (45 percent of the total), 146 in their 50s (41 percent), and 43 in their 60s or 70s. In terms of stating age in decades or half-decades, 16 men claimed to be 40 (or 40 and more), 17 were 45, 75 were 50, 3 were 55, and 26 were 60. This gives 137 men at the three major decade breaks, or 39 percent of the total. But against this, at least one juror claimed each year of age between 38 and 64. In looking at the non-rounded ages we find at least 15 men with stated ages of 42, 43, 44, 46, 48, 52, and 62.

In the tables, I have only tallied ages and jurors for Proofs where at least eleven ages can be read. In the five volumes there are, respectively, two, eight, zero, two, and two mutilated or imperfectly preserved Proofs (ten being for male heirs, four for females).

9. Keith Thomas, "Age and Authority in Early Modern England," *Proceedings of the British Academy* 62 (1976): 205–48. Anthony Esler offers an approach that is more in keeping with cohort identification in *The Aspiring Mind of the Elizabethan Younger Generation* (Durham, N.C., 1966).

10. That the escheator might have randomly handed out ages, as he perhaps handed out memories of broken arms and burning roofs, cannot be disproved (reluctant as I am to accept it).

11. For men of the minimum possible age serving on juries, see Stephen H. Rigby, *English Society in the Later Middle Ages: Class, Status, and Gender* (London, 1995). Rigby discusses jurors from prosperous peasant families serving while in their 30s (47). Anne R. DeWindt, "Local Government in a Small Town: A Medieval Leet Jury and Its Constituents," *Albion* 23 (1991), also mentions some very young jurors, though of legal age (645).

12. See XVI, 375, for a man in his 80s. For a random sample of the very old, XIX has five Proofs with men of 70 or more on juries, covering ten men. XIX, 392, has a jury with a man in his 60s and one in his 70s; in XIX, 478, two jurors in their 70s, one in his 80s (and remembering because his son had been born in the critical year); XIX, 783, a jury with two men in their 60s, three in their 70s; XIX, 785, five in their 60s; XIX, 996, three in their 60s, one in his 70s, and two in their 80s. Among the handful of octogenarians, one person's memory rested on his having been made reeve twenty-one years before. Another simply recalled encountering the godfather on the way to church.

13. When we begin to examine for old age, we find it everywhere. It is assessed as a regular feature of the analysis of parliamentarians. See John S. Roskell et al., *The History of Parliament: The House of Commons, 1386–1421* (Stroud, 1992), vol. 1.

14. Using XIX as a data base, we have six jurors in three Proofs who are reported as now or still in their 30s: two in their 30s (and three in their 40s) in XIX, 340; one in his 30s and seven in their 40s in XIX, 344; and three in their 30s, eight in their 40s in XIX, 1001. This last Proof is the one that gives the ages "then" and the escheator, along with the reader, must add the requisite twenty-one years. We have young jurors with memories that sound reasonable. One was 38 and remembered the birth of his son (XV, 160); another, also 38, married Desoria within three weeks of the birth, "that is 22 years ago" (XV, 292). Still another, 31 years old, had been riding his bay and, "as a result of the horse's sudden leap, had broken his arm" (XV, 656). One man, now 30 and more, had been staying with the heiress's father (fourteen years before) at her birth (XVIII, 664). Yet another juror, 34 and more, was married on 7 August 1387, and "Alice was born before that and he saw her" (XVIII, 651). Again, this last was for an heiress just fourteen years before.

15. Joel T. Rosenthal, "Old Men's Lives—Elderly English Peers, 1350–1500," *Mediaevalia* 8 (1982): 211–37.

16. XV, 894. In this instance, each group of men of the same age also attested to a common memory. This kind of double bonding—by age and memory—was not infrequent. In a Proof from XV, 658, all the jurors are "aged 50 years and more" and their memories are hooked to those of their fellows in an interesting fashion. "Several" saw the baptism, and "all the other jurors believe it" (that is, they believe the tales of their fellows who had been firsthand witnesses).

17. Though her main focus is on heirs, not jurors, Sue Walker's comment is apt: "the detailed knowledge of everyone's personal business displayed by juries of neighbors may have kept wards from inventing abductions as defenses to forfeiture suits." See her "Feudal Family and the Common Law Courts: The Pleas Protecting Rights of Wardship and Marriage, c. 1225–1373," *Journal of Medieval History* 14 (1988): 24.

18. Joel Hurstfield was willing to trade off tighter reasoning and proof in return for lively tales: see Hurstfield, *The Queen's Wards: Wardship and Marriage Under Elizabeth I* (London, 1958), 158.

19. For a juror of limited modesty, see the William Salt Archaeological Society's "Inquisitions Post Mortem, Ad Quod Damnum, etc.," 323–25: Hugh, called the Carpenter, aged 50, "says the same, and knows it because in this same year he married Alice . . . and his memory is perfect." But against this breezy certainty we offer a fallible recollection. The sheriff says, "it was then said that the mother of the said Fulk was not there because she was pregnant but he [the juror] does not know whether it was this child or another": see Sidney J. Madge, ed., *Abstracts of Gloucestershire Inquisitiones Post Mortem . . . , Vol. 4: 20 Henry III–29 Edward I (1236–1300)*, British Record Society Index Library, no. 30 (London, 1903). On how information was collected and the data assembled, see Sandra Raban, "The Making of the 1278–80 Hundred Rolls," *Historical Research* 70 (June 1997), 123–45.

20. Edward A. Fry, ed., *Abstracts of Wiltshire Inquisitiones Post Mortem . . . Henry III, Edward I, and Edward II (A.D. 1242–1326)*, British Record Society Index Library, no. 37 (London, 1908): a juror says they "were asked to bear witness of the day and year of the birth of the said heir when he should come of full age" (352). Another explicit memory of this sort appears on 372.

21. In a similar vein, see XVI, 341: "Thomas . . . and Guy . . . know because the said Thomas had a son, who is still alive, on the same day, and he is now of the same age as the heir, because they met on the way to church to be baptized." Even Russell, a staunch defender of the Proofs, concedes their reliance on this sort of circular logic (*British Medieval Population*, 209). One juror remembered the twenty-one-year interval because he thought back in two stages: "questioned how he remembered about the lapse of time, says because the church of Sheffield was dedicated by Archbishop de Wikewan seventeen years ago, and then, as he says, the said Thomas was four years old" (see William Brown, ed., *Yorkshire Inquisitions*, IV, YAS Record Series, vol. 37 [Worksop, 1906], 16).

22. For instances of a warning to the guardian of the estates that sparked no interest, let alone an appearance, see XIX, 102 ("John Frank being warned but not attending") and XIX, 141 ("warned but he did not come"). For a warning to the guardian delivered by the escheator's servant, see XIX, 478; for four men bringing one such message, see XIX, 668.

23. One juror was married that day, and so the date "clearly comes to mind" (XIV, 68).

24. Michael Clanchy, "Hearing and Seeing," in *From Memory to Written Record: England, 1066–1307*, 2d ed. (Oxford, 1993), 253–93. See Ethel Stokes, ed., *Abstracts of Wiltshire Inquisitiones Post Mortem: Edward III (1327–1377)*, British Record Society Index Library, no. 48 (London, 1914): the heir's sister said she had been "told she had a brother then born, for which she thanked god" (311). One juror remembered that they had been beating a fox when someone said, "Sire, do you want to hear the news?" and someone else said, "Friend, what is the news?" and "then the said William told all the company that on the preceding evening a son was born to the said Richard." The antiphonal style of the dialogue, as reported, is of interest in its own right. For a father who said, upon learning of a daughter's birth, that he would have preferred a son, see *CIPM, XIII*, 66.

25. This is one of those Proofs where either in the testimony or the transcription there was confusion over factual matters. The "John" who held the candle is called "Henry" in the Proof. The editor of the *CIPM* had queried this ["(? *recte* John)"] and I have accepted the change of the name. Perhaps it is just a case of so many Henrys and Johns in the village that not even the men themselves could impose clarity.

26. XVII, 1321. There are a number of accounts that touch this theme of rustic humor; some will resurface when we look at the relations between masters and their former servants.

27. This memory was a common one, offered by four jurors as a joint statement. For another common memory that worked in this way, see XV, 890: the Proof is composed of a common recollection from "the first six jurors," and then one from "the other jurors" about events of the following week. For the transmission of common information, see Chris J. Wickham, "Gossip and Resistance Among the Medieval Peasantry," given as an inaugural lecture in 1995 at the University of Birmingham and then published in *Past and Present* 160 (1998): 3–24. My thanks to Daniel L. Smail, who brought this lecture to my attention. Also see Melanie Tebbutt, *Women's Talk? A Social History of "Gossip" in Working-Class Neighbourhoods, 1880–1960* (Aldershot, 1995), and Jörg Bergmann, *Discreet Indiscretions: The Social Organization of Gossip,* trans. John Bednarz Jr. (New York, 1993).

28. In XV, 447 and 957, two jurors offer a common memory—that the first juror's wife had been buried then, and the rector told them of the heir's birth.

29. Fry, ed., *Abstracts of Wiltshire:* "the said William immediately caused to be written on the wall of his hall the day and year of the birth . . . and by this he knows how much time has elapsed" (352).

30. For a date remembered because it had been written in English "and read out while they were there," see *CIPM, XX: 1–5 Henry V,* ed. J. L. Kirby (London, 1995), 131; for one written into a "porthous" in English, "so he has often read it," see *CIPM, XIII,* 62.

31. XVIII, 309 and 311, respectively. There are many references of this sort: he "has seen the abbot [of Selby, the godfather] shew a book in which this date of the birth was entered" (XVIII, 854); he remembers because he took land by indenture, "and by the date of the indenture he knows and proves the age" (XVIII, 665); the "parson wrote the release of all personal actions" (XIX, 777); "the birth was noted in the roll of the said court" (XVII, 954).

32. An earlier juror remembered that the "date of birth is written in the missal . . . and he has seen it there" (*CIPM, XIV,* 63).

33. This proof combines the "seen" and "heard" themes. The appeal to the knowledge of friends reveals an accepted hierarchy of likely information—from family to friends to "mere" villagers. One juror heard "everything from neighbours" touching the birth (*CIPM, XIV,* 159); another said he had heard from "good and lawful men" (*CIPM, XIV,* 162).

34. XVIII, 1179; XV, 348. In a case of two separate Proofs for the heir, the second says that the jurors "agree with the date of birth and age of the said John, son of John, given in the previous inquisition" (XV, 659).

35. XVI, 336, offers a Proof where jurors affirm the first story and then add theirs with a "moreover" to separate what was commonly agreed upon from that which was individualized. For uniform agreement, see XVI, 106. Also see W. Brown, ed., *Yorkshire Inquisitions, IV:* "and many times [the juror] heard his friends and relations, whom he thoroughly believes, speak of the heir's birth, and the time and hour" (1–4).

36. Things seen could be a powerful common cord. In one case, eleven jurors "saw" the baptism, and the remaining juror had been present and so, presumably, had also been a firsthand witness (XIX, 998). In another, nine jurors "saw" what they remembered, though some memories strayed so far from the baptismal font as to include a hanging on that day (XIX, 347). One form of visual authentication found in some early Proofs but not in these later volumes rests on the appearance and physical maturity of the heir. W. Brown, ed., *Yorkshire Inquisitions, IV:* the "said heir has sufficiently proved his age before the Lord King, and it is also clear by the appearance of the body of the said Adam that he is of full age" (3), and "it is also clear by the appearance of his body" (5–8). Sue Walker notes that "throughout the period under consideration the judges used their eyes to determine age when, seemingly, it should have been apparent" ("Proof of Age," 312–13). Maitland says justices were encouraged in such proceedings to "trust their own eyes" (Pollock and Maitland, *History of English Law,* 2:638), and Stevenson, "The Escheator," argues along the same line: "probably no Proofs of age were required when the heir was obviously of age" (131, n. 1). Hurstfield came to the same conclusion (*The Queen's Wards,* 157). Walker notes that judges could decide, "et videtur justiciariis quod adhuc est infra etatem," though there is a reference to a case they put off until they could obtain better proof ("Proof of Age," 311–12).

37. Though a subject for a separate study, the Proofs could be discussed in terms of the performance and theatricality surrounding the proceeding. Did the escheator, perhaps in concert with the heir's agent, line up jurors and dish out memories? Where was the business actually conducted? Were there disinterested witnesses, or an audience? How much did the jurors "debrief" themselves in the village (over numerous jugs of ale) when the escheator had moved on?

38. On marriage, I have largely followed the exposition of M. M. Sheehan, whose work is most accessible in *Michael M. Sheehan: Marriage, Family, and Law in Medieval Europe: Collected Studies,* ed. James K. Farge (Toronto, 1996). Also invaluable are James Brundage, *Law, Sex, and Christian Society in Medieval Europe* (Chicago, 1987), and Richard H. Helmholz, *Marriage Litigation in Medieval England* (Cambridge, 1974). For our purposes, the most interesting of all the marriages we look at here was that of Margery Paston and Richard Calle: see H. S. Bennett, *The Pastons and Their England,* chapters 3 and 4, and Colin F. Richmond, "The Pastons Revisited: Marriage and the Family in Fifteenth-Century England," *Bulletin of the Institute of Historical Research* 58 (1985): 25–36.

39. For the European marriage pattern, see J. Hajnal, "European Marriage Patterns in Perspective," in *Population in History,* ed. D. V. Glass and D. E. C. Eversley (London, 1965), 101–43; R. M. Smith, "Geographical Diversity in the Resort to Marriage in Late Medieval Europe," in *Woman Is a Worthy Wight: Women in English Society, c. 1200–1500,* ed. P. J. P. Goldberg (Stroud, 1992), 16–59; L. R. Poos, Zvi Razi, and R. M. Smith, "The Population History of Medieval English Villages: A Debate on the Use of Manorial Court Records," in *Medieval Society and the Manorial Court,* ed. Zvi Razi and Richard Smith (Oxford, 1996), 298–368. Assumptions about age at marriage are risky here except when the juror gives us reason to think that his reference is to his *first* marriage.

40. A busy year for Robert, as another of the jurors had also contracted with him the Sunday before for marriage with another daughter (Alice). For a juror who remembered paying forty marks to arrange his own marriage, see XV, 159. For another of the "married his present wife" references, see XV, 293. (A second wife, or a minor flourish on a bald statement?)

41. In XV, 891, the juror, now aged 60, had married on 31 March in the year of the heir's birth.

42. For a juror of 45 and a memory of a daughter's marriage, see XIX, 791; see XIX, 1002, for a juror aged 44 and a daughter's wedding. XVI, 947: the juror is *now* aged 43.

43. Here, too, the straightforward memories are most common, even when they beg for further elucidation: William, age 45, "gave his daughter Agnes . . . in marriage that day" twenty-one years before (XIX, 791). A juror of 40 also told of his daughter's marriage (XIX, 1001).

44. In XVI, 336, the date was "written in the missal of the church of Glossop."

45. The age of the father is of interest. In XIX, 349, a man of "60 and more" referred back to a daughter's baptism.

46. On twins, Shulamith Shahar, *Childhood in the Middle Ages* (London, 1990), 34; on raising upper-class boys but with little on their identity as twins, David Crouch, *The Beaumont Twins: The Roots and Branches of Power in the Twelfth Century* (Cambridge, 1986), 3–10.

47. The juror says that the heir was 27, a statement in agreement with the escheator's response to the writ of *precipimus* of 12 April, 8 Richard II (XVI, 106). The writ concerned the death of Richard Barry, who died on Monday on the Eve of the Close of Easter, 7 Richard II. The Proof was only taken on the Monday after the Exaltation of the Holy Cross, 9 Richard II. An over-age heir also had to await the outcome of an unusually protracted proceeding.

48. The bishop in September 1390 was Richard le Scrope (1386–98); as the baptism was at Alderbury, he was well within his appointed rounds. Though I have not made a tally to determine naming patterns of the jurors or of those to whom they make reference, this may be the only Diggory in our entire universe of several thousand men and women. I offer a limited analysis of jurors' names in my introduction to *Names and Naming Patterns in Medieval England* (co-edited with David Postles), forthcoming from Medieval Institute Publications, Western Michigan University.

49. Paul Binski, *Medieval Death: Ritual and Representation* (London, 1996); Christopher Daniell, *Death and Burial in Medieval England, 1066–1550* (London, 1997); Philippe Ariès, *The Hour of Our Death,* trans. Helen Weaver (New York, 1981); and Margaret Aston, "Death," in *Fifteenth-Century Attitudes: Perceptions of Society in Late Medieval England,* ed. Rosemary Horrox (Cambridge, 1994), 202–28.

50. Though there probably were more widows than widowers among the middle-aged and elderly, the demographic balance is not likely to be the reason for the husbands' relative silence. On widows and widowhood, see Sue Sheridan Walker, ed., *Wife and Widow in Medieval England* (Ann Arbor, 1993); Caroline M. Barron and Anne F. Sutton, eds., *Medieval London Widows, 1300–1500* (London, 1994); Louise Mirrer, ed., *Upon My Husband's Death: Widows in the Literature and History of Medieval Europe* (Ann Arbor, 1994). For a juror who explicitly stated that his memory was attached to his (re)marriage with a widow, see Stokes, ed., *Abstracts of Wiltshire IPMs*, 235. The man recalled that in "the week following he married his wife, Margery, the relict of John le Eyre of Rusteshale [Rusthall]."

51. Though it offers but limited insight, we can track jurors' ages and their reliance on deaths for mnemonic references. For men who told of a child's death, eleven were in their 40s, nine in their 50s, and five in their 60s. For the death of a wife, the numbers are two, four, and three jurors (moving with their respective ages, in decades); for a parent, it is eight (for men in their 40s) and then four and four. A total of twenty-one men in their 40s told of a death, seventeen in their 50s, and twelve in their 60s. If we subtract twenty years (or fewer, for heiresses' Proofs), we are pretty close to when the death had occurred.

52. W. Pailey Baildon and J. W. Clay, eds., *Inquisitions Post Mortem Relating to Yorkshire, of the Reigns of Henry IV and Henry V*, YAS Record Series, vol. 59 (n.p., 1918), 181–82: "his son Robert, who had been languishing for some time, died."

53. This was the statement of the first juror, the quasi-foreman, and it came after he filled in the details regarding dates and godparents' names.

54. This is also the case with XVIII, 1180, where the memory is that "his eldest son died within a week of the day of the birth" of the heir.

55. Another drowning death: "in the week of Robert's birth Richard his brother was drowned in the water flowing under the bridge of Turveye [Turvey]" (XV, 297). This is a 47-year-old juror, looking back twenty-two years.

56. The juror was 43, some twenty-two years on in this case, and as the sister was using her maiden name, we infer that she was younger and still in the parental household. On the death of siblings, see also XVIII, 856, for the juror who "came to church to bury Margaret his sister."

57. The juror was 64 at the time of the Proof. He had been in his early 40s at the time of the memory.

58. Thomas M. Blagg, ed., *Abstracts of the Inquisitiones Post Mortem Relating to Nottinghamshire*, III, 1321–1350, Thoroton Society, no. 6 (n.p., 1939), 54–56: a juror's father had fallen from a cart, "whereof he died within 15 days."

59. Peter McClure, "Patterns of Migration in the Later Middle Ages: The Evidence of Place-Name Surnames," *Economic History Review*, 2d ser., 32 (1979): 167–82; J. A. F. Thomson, "Piety and Charity in Late Medieval London," *Journal of Ecclesiastical History* 16 (1965): 178–98.

60. K. S. Train, ed., *Abstracts of Inquisitions Post Mortem Relating to Nottinghamshire, 1350–1436*, Thoroton Society, no. 12 (n.p., 1949–52), 14–15: his grandfather died "within a quindene" of the heir's birth.

61. Edith Rickert, *Chaucer's World* (New York, 1948), 414: a horse was taken as mortuary.

62. Jurors seemed at home recalling the rituals of the Church. On baptism: John Bossy, "Blood and Baptism: Kinship, Community, and Christianity in Western Europe from the Fourteenth to the Seventeenth Century," *Studies in Church History* 10 (1973): 129–43; Robert Dinn, "Baptism, Spiritual Kinship, and Popular Religion in Late Medieval Bury St. Edmunds," *Bulletin of the John Rylands University Library* 72 (1990): 93–106. On baptism being closely connected to exorcism, see Eamon Duffy, *The Stripping of the Altars: Traditional Religion in England, c. 1400–c. 1580* (New Haven, 1992), 280–81.

63. On banqueting and ritualized public eating: Roy Wood, *The Sociology of the Meal* (Edinburgh, 1995); William E. Mead, *The English Medieval Feast* (New York, 1967); Stephen Mennell, *All Manners of Food: Eating and Taste in England and France from the Middle Ages to the Present*, 2d ed. (Urbana, 1996); Peter Hammond, *Food and Feast in Medieval England* (Stroud, 1993); Patricia D. LaBahn, *Feasting in the Fourteenth and Fifteenth Centuries: A Comparison of Manuscript Illuminations to*

Contemporary Written Sources (St. Louis, 1975). On drinking, see Peter Clark, *The English Alehouse: A Social History, 1200–1830* (London, 1983). In *Food and Eating in Medieval Europe,* ed. Martha Carlin and Joel T. Rosenthal (London, 1998), see relevant papers by Elizabeth Biebel, ffiona Swabey, and Susan F. Weiss.

64. The ceremony was on the appropriate scale: one juror told of having seen "four honourable men, knights and esquires, carrying a golden awning above John from the church." Another told of being given 10s. for his "good services to the godfathers and the godmother," and the gift-giver seems to have been just a friend of the family. *CIPM, XIII,* 66: when asked how he knew "after so long an interval," the rejoinder was that the heir's father had given him an arrow "to remember and bear witness." Sue Walker, "Proof of Age," mentions memories that were "stimulated by the parents" through strategic gift-giving (314). Stokes, ed., *Abstracts of Wiltshire IPMs,* 268–69: a great-grandmother held a lavish feast and gave out doeskin gloves, "that they might remember the age of the heir."

65. We wonder at the literal significance of "saw Robert born." Another statement in this Proof says that "he knows because he saw him born." The father had not been at home but had been "immediately" summoned. *CIPM, XIV,* 62: the messengers who brought news of the birth to the grandfather were given "husbandland in Staunton for life" as their reward—which was unusual in scope and in kind. *CIPM, XX,* 131: a servant of the abbot of Newenham who was involved in the day's festivities received 40d., but "never before or after that day did he [the abbot] give him 1d."

66. Another juror had met William Chamberlane while he was carrying the news, and this juror was *told* of the birth. *CIPM,* 138, and 130: when the father heard the news, "rejoicing, he raised his hands in thanks to God and immediately mounted his horse and rode home."

67. Joseph H. Lynch, *Godparents and Kinship in Early Medieval Europe* (Princeton, 1986), 172–209. Michael J. Bennett, "Spiritual Kinship and the Baptismal Name in Traditional European Society," in *Principalities, Powers, and Estates,* ed. L. O. Frappell (Adelaide, 1979), notes that "even if the testimonies regarding baptismal ceremonies can be shown to have been fabricated, it is fair to assume that the fabrication would actually reflect the customs of the time. Indeed, since the evidence would have to appear credible to contemporaries, it would perhaps be of even greater value to the historian of the mores of late medieval England" (5). Hurstfield, in *The Queen's Wards,* addresses the mix and match of "logic [that] does not seem watertight" and the resort to "colourful details" (158).

68. The editor of the IPMs notes that Thomas was duke, not earl, at the time reported. Thomas (b. 7 January 1355, d. 9 September 1399) was created earl of Buckingham on 16 July 1377 (at Richard II's coronation), earl of Essex on 26 October 1380, and duke of Gloucester on 6 August 1385. One man told of seeing Thomas give the infant a "golden reliquary with precious stones and a picture of the Trinity." On the social network of the baptism at which Thomas of Woodstock (as "earl of Buckingham") had appeared, Keen and Warner, eds., "Morley vs. Montagu," 163–64. Stokes, ed., *Abstracts of Wiltshire IPMs,* 71: at a Proof taken in 1331, jurors talked of seeing Queen Isabella as a godmother. One, as under-sheriff, had conducted the queen and the king's aunt to the christening, and a groom recalled that Edward III had also been there, though in the king's case it was to attend a wedding.

69. Six jurors shared the memory of seeing Henry Despenser, bishop of Norwich, and Edward le Despenser, the godfathers of Edward Carent, "lift him from the sacred font" (XVII, 148).

70. Also see XVIII, 1140: "Robert Skipton . . . was present in the church. John de Rukewyk, abbot of Jervaulx, was godfather, and he was surprised that Thomas was not given his godfather's name." See M. Bennett, "Spiritual Kinship," 208, on who picked the name, as well as Philip Niles, "Baptism and the Naming of Children," *Medieval Prosopography* 3, no. 1 (1982): 95–107, and Jacques Gelis, *The History of Childbirth: Fertility, Pregnancy, and Birth in Early Modern Europe* (Boston, 1991), 205. *CIPM, XX,* 272: the jurors told of comments made to the effect that perhaps the babe would be the man his grandfather had been. Hodgson, "Proof of Age of Heirs," 123: the juror's memory of the priest's words ran in this fashion: "asked whose son he was, to whom he answered that he [the infant] was the son of William, and the said priest said to him, 'thanks be to God for now William has his own heir of his own name.'" For a pithy view of a godparent's role, *CIPM, XX,* 131: the godfather was sent for "to make the boy a Christian." And *CIPM, XX,* 130, offers an elaborate

tale. A would-be godmother was told, while on her way to the church, that she was too late: "Kate, Kate, ther to by myn pate comyst ow to late." She took umbrage, rode home, and did not see the child's mother again for six months. The original insult seemingly was compounded because the officious servant was "grinning" when he told her of her error.

71. XVII, 186: three jurors offer a brief narrative that covers meeting the godfather, learning from him of the birth and the mother's health, and then meeting the father and having a drink with him. Their sociable odyssey culminated in a fall on the highway whereby one of the jurors broke "three of his right ribs."

72. Another juror remembered because he accompanied the godmother to the church. In *CIPM, II,* 81, a juror had been in church to serve as godfather for another infant, baptized on the same day. Requests to serve as a godparent were an awkward honor to refuse: see Lynch, *Godparents and Kinship,* 173. See Sue Walker, "Proof of Age," 317, for a juror who refused to be a godparent because he had his eye on a possible wife who would have become related to him by spiritual affinity had he accepted the honor at the christening (*CIPM, XIII,* 141).

73. In XVIII, 315, "after the baptism [the juror] washed the hands of the godfather and godmothers."

74. *CIPM, XIII,* 66: here a godmother seems to have been chosen because she bore the name the parents wished the child to have—the onomastic cart before the horse! This is also one of those cases where the expressed family preference had been for a son, the daughter being but a second choice. For more on the performative aspects of the baptism, see Duffy, *The Stripping of the Altars,* 280–81: the priest was to see that no one but the babe touched the holy water, and the godparents were to wash their hands at the end "in case any of the holy oils remained from contact with the child."

75. This was a double Proof of Age for two sisters. The same juror said, regarding his memory of the older sister, that he "was building a house . . . when William de Netylworth, the grandfather, gave him a beam and told him of the birth." Did he transmit the news while extending a plank of wood, or did he bestow the beam as a present to mark the occasion?

76. Several jurors got the news from members of the official party as they dispersed and returned home.

77. In this Proof is a memorable tale offered jointly by two others: they, "each 53, were sitting on chairs in the church, fell asleep and were left sleeping; the clerk of the church, not noticing, shut the door. They were left there until the third hour after noon." *CIPM, xiv,* 346: jurors recalled that for the christening of the daughter of the earl of Athol they had "carried a red carpet over her on four lances."

78. Hodgson, "Proof of Age of Heirs," 123: the juror had seen the infant's grandfather meet a woman in "the churchyard, carrying John to the church for baptism; he said to the woman, 'I ask thee, show me the child's face,' and she showed him, and he kissed him and said to him, 'my son, God bless thee and give thee good strength on earth' *(bonam vigenciam in terram)*." And, from the same Proof, a memory runs: "saw a chaplain . . . baptising John in the font when he fell from the chaplain's hands into the font, and John Wedryngton, knight, his god-father, said to the chaplain, 'Prest, prest, fond be thi heued.'"

79. Holding the book for the priest was reported by numerous jurors; presumably the priest needed both hands for the baby (XVIII, 1182), as the previous note suggests.

80. Another juror carried water for washing the godfathers' hands; no mention, this time, of the godmother.

81. These jurors mentioned seeing the godmother, seeing the abbot of Evesham with the bishop (Richard Wakefield, bishop of Worcester), seeing Alice, wife of Sir Richard Stury, seeing the bishop holding the baby, seeing a man carrying the sword given as a baby present by the earl of Stafford, seeing the abbot of Pershore attending the baptism, and finally seeing Sir John Beauchamp of Holt, carrying a cloth of gold with the arms of King Richard (perhaps a present sent by the king). This being the baptism of Richard, son and heir of Thomas, earl of Warwick, the status of those attending and the impression they left on local memory are credible details.

82. Another juror had been a torch bearer, and a third man remembered seeing the unlit torches on their way to church. Also, XVIII, 1140, for four men carrying unlit torches and then

returning with them "alighte"; XVIII, 666, seeing the godparents on their way home. *CIPM, XX,* 130: in the church, for the ceremony, were three burning torches, two silver lamps, and two silver jugs of water.

83. This had been a very festive occasion, as other jurors referred to a gold noble as a present for the babe and also to the purchase of a barrel of red wine for the feast.

84. *CIPM, XX,* 263: four jurors, in a common memory, recalled that they had "drunk wine, which was brought to the church, and such was its effect that they could hardly walk out of church."

85. The juror, a knight, had come from Roxburgh to Witherington, Northumberland, for the baptism, and some socializing was to be expected before he undertook his return journey.

86. This was the baptism of the earl of Warwick's heir; the earl of Stafford gave a sword to the infant.

87. The John Hachard with whom Spencer is in agreement had been a servant to the chaplain and had assisted at the baptism. Hachard makes no reference to the act of writing or to written evidence; his recollection was based on a memory of his personal role.

88. Only the one juror (John Belasis, aged 54) mentions this, though several others saw the baby being carried to or from church and some met and talked with the godparents.

89. He carried a lantern with a candle, though we do not know if this was for the service or to light his way to Clervaux's house.

90. Another juror reported that his own wife, at that time the mother's servant, had carried the baby to church. W. Brown, ed., *Yorkshire Inquisitions, IV,* 130–32: a juror had missed the purification of the mother because of his own father's funeral.

91. See Gelis, *History of Childbirth,* 104–9, on the midwife's ambiguous social standing; the evidence of the Proofs is also that she is usually set firmly among the non-elite. For her technical expertise, Beryl Rowland, *Medieval Woman's Guide to Health* (Kent, Ohio, 1981), 123–39. See also Barbara A. Hanawalt, ed., *Women and Work in Preindustrial Europe* (Bloomington, 1986): the relevant papers are by Leah H. Otis, "Municipal Wet Nurses in Fifteenth-Century Montpellier," 83–93, and Merry E. Wiesner, "An Early Modern Midwife: A Case Study," 94–113. Most recently, Doreen Evenden, *The Midwives of Seventeenth-Century London* (London, 2000), has taken up the topic.

92. XVIII, 315, for a juror whose wife had been the midwife. Sue Walker, "Proof of Age," 318, mentions men who remembered hearing the mother cry out in childbirth.

93. Though midwives depended heavily on such tips, this is the only reference to the economic aspect of their services, and this sounds like an extra bonus thrown in by a great layman when he was in an expansive mood, rather than her usual fee.

94. Shahar, *Childhood in the Middle Ages,* 55–76 on wet nurses; 77–83 on milk, weaning, and infants' food. On wet nursing, see also Barbara A. Hanawalt, *Growing Up in Medieval London: The Experience of Childhood in History* (New York, 1993), 56–59.

95. The first statement names the nurse and her husband; the second simply says that the baby "was put to nurse at Aveley." The second juror had been sent by the baby's aunt "to see how Maurice was kept and nursed." The aunt was an active figure, sending various messengers to carry the news and to summon godparents and guests (and then to reward the messengers).

96. *CIPM, XIV,* 300: a juror said that the mother had complained to him "that she had no milk to nourish her child" and that she asked the juror to provide a nurse. This sounds like a transgression of normal sexual-behavioral boundaries. Might the juror have been condensing a complex chain of dialogue and the roles of various intermediate parties (such as his wife)?

97. The same attestation recounts how the chaplain had put the baby's name and birth date "in a missal in the church, and this writing proves his age."

98. This is another Proof where the literal statement is less than lucid. We note that Ouseby chose to stake his claim—or to use his minute on stage—to tell of this decision making. One juror told of a journey with the child's nurse, "within a fortnight after the baptism," in order to have the baptism confirmed by the bishop of Norwich (XVI, 1053). There was some sort of strategy of rhetoric, as well as of memory; what would one choose to say to support his testimony?

99. A comparable domestic touch, reminiscent of "just dropping in on friends to see the new baby," is provided by a juror who recalled (XV, 656) having seen "the said Mary at her mother's

breast immediately after birth." In xv, 891, the editor of the *Inquisitions* has included the Latin: *lactantem matricem suam.*

100. David Cressy, "Purification, Thanksgiving, and the Churching of Women in Post-Reformation England," *Past and Present* 141 (1993): 106–46, for a thorough discussion. Poos, *Rural Society*, 121–27, with special interest in what Lollards in Essex thought about the ritual of churching. Poos points out (125, n. 35) that a mother had to be churched even if the infant died. There are several suggestive papers in *Women as Mothers in Pre-Industrial England: Essays in Memory of Dorothy McLaren*, ed. Valerie Fildes (London, 1990): Patricia Crawford, "The Construction and Experience of Maternity in Seventeenth-Century England" (3–38); Linda A. Pollock, "Embarking on a Rough Passage: The Experience of Pregnancy in Early Modern Society" (39–67); Adrian Wilson, "The Ceremony of Childbirth and Its Interpretation" (68–107; references to churching on 78–93). On marriage and mothering in the context of young women's lives, see Kim M. Phillips, "Maidenhood as the Perfect Age of a Woman's Life," and Katherine J. Lewis, "Model Girls? Virgin Martyrs and the Training of Young Women in Late Medieval England," both in *Young Medieval Women*, ed. Katherine J. Lewis, Noël J. Menuge, and Kim M. Phillips (New York, 1999), 1–24 and 25–46, respectively.

101. *CIPM*, XIV, 343: the jurors said they had paid a visit to the mother "and each of them gave gifts according to the estate to the heir and his nurse." *CIPM*, XIV, 346: the lord's purveyor of victuals "bespoke 5 lambs of his against the churching of the countess her mother," and he also paid 13s. 4d. for ale to be drunk at the churching. See Gelis on visiting the new mother (*History of Childbirth*, 188–89).

102. Merely having observed the service could be offered as a foundation for one's recollection, as the disinterested gaze is resurrected as memory (XVI, 1053).

103. Hazel Hudson and Frances Neal, "A Busy Day in Wedmore Church," *Notes and Queries for Somerset and Dorset* 33 (1992 "Wedmore church seems to have been particularly busy on the Sunday 21 years earlier, with a baptism, a wedding, a manorial court, and a property transaction" (171–73). See also Beat A. Kümin, *The Shaping of a Community: The Rise and Reformation of the English Parish, c. 1400–1560* (Aldershot, 1996), 125–47; J. A. F. Thomson, *The Early Tudor Church and Society, 1485–1529* (London, 1983), chapter 9; Alexandra F. Johnson, "Parish Entertainments in Berkshire," in *Pathways to Medieval Peasants,* ed. J. Ambrose Raftis (Toronto, 1981), 335–38; and Miri Rubin, "What Did the Eucharist Mean to Thirteenth-Century Villagers?" in *Thirteenth-Century England, IV,* ed. P. R. Coss and S. D. Lloyd (Woodbridge, 1992), 51–52.

104. See XVI, 76, for a recollection of work on a stone cross in the churchyard.

105. The query is that of the editor of the IPMs volume.

106. For an example of benefaction: a juror "had a wooden cross made and raised in the church on that day in honour of the Trinity and for the health of his soul" (XVIII, 667).

107. In one Proof we have statements from jurors who referred to their accounts as church wardens, as well as to fellows in comparable positions in urban guilds and fraternities (XV, 449). See also Thomson, *Early Tudor Church,* 274–88; Julia Carnwath, "The Church Wardens' Accounts of Thame, Oxfordshire, c. 1443–1524," in *Trade, Devotion, and Governance: Papers in Later Medieval History,* ed. Dorothy J. Clayton, Richard G. Davies, and Peter McNiven (Stroud, 1994), 177–97; Katherine L. French, Gary G. Gibbs, and Beat A. Kümin, eds., *The Parish in English Life, 1400–1600* (Manchester, 1997); and Katherine L. French, *The People of the Parish: Community Life in a Late Medieval English Diocese* (Philadelphia, 2001).

108. *CIPM*, XIV, 158: four jurors, jointly "wardens of the works and fabric," remembered making a "covenant by indenture" to repair the wall. This was dated 7 June (26 Edward III), and they know the heir's age "by inspection of the indenture."

109. Josephine W. Bennett, "The Mediaeval Loveday," *Speculum* 33 (1958): 351–70; Thomas J. Heffernan, "A Medieval Poem on Lovedays," *Chaucer Review* 10 (1975–76): 172–85; R. H. Bowers, "A Middle-English Poem on Lovedays," *Modern Language Review* 47 (1952): 374–75; J. W. Spargo, "Chaucer's Lovedays," *Speculum* 15 (1940): 36–56; J. B. Post, "Equitable Resorts Before 1450," in *Law, Litigants, and the Legal Profession,* ed. E. W. Ives and A. H. Manchester (London, 1983), 68–79, on the use of counsel by the parties in a loveday; Michael Clanchy, "Law and Love in the Middle Ages," in *Disputes and Settlements: Law and Human Relations in the West,* ed. John Bossy (Cam-

bridge, 1983), 47–67; Ben R. McRee, "Peacemaking and Its Limits in Late Medieval Norwich," *EHR* 109 (1994): 831–66; and Gerd Althoff, "Satisfaction: Peculiarities of the Amicable Settlement of Conflicts in the Middle Ages," in *Ordering Medieval Society: Perspectives on Intellectual and Practical Modes of Shaping Social Relations*, ed. Bernhard Jussen and trans. Pamela Selwyn (Philadelphia, 2001), 270–84. Virtually every episcopal register offers instances of pollution and purification: see G. R. Dunstan, ed., *The Register of Edmund Lacy, Bishop of Exeter, 1420–1455*, Devon and Cornwall Record Society, vols. 7, 10, 13, 16, and 18 ([Torquay], 1963–72). Madge, ed., *Abstracts of Gloucestershire IPMs*, 75–76: the church "was interdicted on account of the shedding of blood there, and all services there suspended except for baptisms of children." It has just been "reformed and reconciled" by the bishop of Worcester before the birth of the heir.

110. The suffragan bishop of Winchester had done the honors at Southwick, Hampshire.

111. None of the other three statements (in a Proof with four sets of three-apiece memories) referred to the homicide. Ironically, the heir's uncle had married, in the year of his birth, a certain Elizabeth, daughter of John Loveday.

112. For another quarrel between two rectors, "touching tithes of wool," see xv, 158. It was resolved by a loveday, concluded on the crucial day, but "before the rector baptized." In Reginald Brocklesby, ed., *The Register of William Melton, Archbishop of York, 1317–1340*, Canterbury and York Society, vol. 85 (Woodbridge, 1997), nos. 324 and 643 touch upon tithe disputes and violence involving clerics.

113. On the other hand, we can assume that everyone in the community knew that a juror's brother had "received priest's orders from the bishop of Chichester" (XVI, 77). For a brother who was not a rector, see xv, 656.

114. xv, 888, for a recollection of a son who became a subdeacon at the critical moment; *CIPM*, I, 450, for a brother's entry into Wenlock priory.

115. This first juror also names the three godparents. For a memory that involved an exchange of benefices, see XIX, 341.

116. They also point out that it was the rector who received the infant at the church door for the baptism.

117. John Eade and Michael J. Sallnow, eds., *Contesting the Sacred: The Anthropology of Christian Pilgrimage* (London, 1991), and Jonathan Sumption, *Pilgrimage: An Image of Medieval Religion* (London, 1975). For the problems a pilgrim might encounter, see Antonia Gransden, "Letters of Recommendation from John Whethamstede for a Poor Pilgrim, 1453–54," *EHR* 106 (1991): 932–39. For licenses permitting clerics to go on pilgrimage, *Melton's Register*, nos. 750, 807, and 640 (when the respective absences could run up to nine months, one year, and two years).

118. 10 June 1381 was about the time when men were moving toward rebellion and beginning to make their presence felt in Bedfordshire. See R. Barrie Dobson, ed., *The Peasants' Revolt of 1381* (London, 1970), 43, where Dobson indicates that on 15 June tenants demanded charters of privileges from the prior of Dunstable. Also on Bedfordshire men, consult Charles Oman, *The Great Revolt of 1381* (Oxford, 1906; reprint, New York, 1969), 140–41, though Oman mostly picks them up as they merge with the London crowd.

119. Another juror here recalled the birth because he had set off for Compostela on 2 February, following a baptism of 28 October. This memory seems to fall in the "in the same year" bracket, despite the presence of exact dates.

120. *CIPM*, XX, 844: the juror's father had set out that day for "the Promised Land."

121. As exemplified by such useful volumes as Matthew Browne, *Chaucer's England* (London, 1869), or G. T. Salusbury-Jones, *Street Life in Medieval England* (London, 1939).

122. Two jurors used John de Eppyng's death as their memory point, including one juror who had been his brother. They, however, simply referred to his death as occurring on the day of the baptism.

123. *CIPM*, XIV, 299: a juror remembered because he had been "summoned by a letter of the Archbishop of York to appear . . . (to) make answer touching diverse articles concerning the salvation of his soul."

124. Blagg, ed., *Abstracts of Nottinghamshire IPMs*, 113–14: a juror knew the date "because Thomas de Bingham, his kinsman, was found in the bed of Laurence's nurse . . . and he himself was

helping to capture the said Thomas, and since then 21 years have passed." XIX, 783: "Margaret Morys of Loddan was then pregnant by Thomas Holm, chaplain, and for shame took her goods on the following morning and left the town." For Ms. Morys's not unlikely fate, see Ruth Mazo Karras, *Common Women: Prostitution and Sexuality in Medieval England* (Philadelphia, 1996), 48–64, on "becoming a prostitute."

125. Thomson, *Early Tudor Church*, 169.

126. On peasants and the land market, C. N. L. Brooke and M. M. Postan, eds., *Carte Nativorum: A Peterborough Cartulary of the Fourteenth Century*, Northampton Record Society, vol. 20 (Oxford, 1960); Edwin B. DeWindt, *Land and People in Holywell-cum-Needingworth: Structures of Tenure and Patterns of Social Organization in an East Midland Village, 1252–1457* (Toronto, 1972); Eleanor Searle, *Lordship and Community: Battle Abbey and Its Banlieu, 1066–1538* (Toronto, 1974); Sherri Olson, *A Chronicle of All That Happens: Voices from the Village Court in Medieval England* (Toronto, 1996); Rosamund Faith, *The English Peasantry and the Growth of Lordship* (Leicester, 1997); Christopher Dyer, "Were There Any Capitalists in Fifteenth-Century England?" in *Enterprise and Individuals in Fifteenth-Century England*, ed. Jennifer Kermode (Stroud, 1991), 1–24; Jane Whittle, "Individualism and the Family Land Bond: A Reassessment of Land Transfer Patterns Among the English Peasantry, c. 1270–1580," *Past and Present* 160 (1998): 25–63. For a general view of village life, see Rodney H. Hilton, *A Medieval Society: The West Midlands at the End of the Thirteenth Century* (Oxford, 1965), especially 149–66, and S. Olson, *Chronicle*.

127. These are, respectively, XVIII, 997, 663, 665, 996, and 1178; XIX, 139; XV, 166; XIX, 782; XVI, 336; XV, 3; and XIX, 342, 343. On mortgages and bonds among the peasants, see Elaine Clark, "Debt Litigation in a Late Medieval Village," in *Pathways to Medieval Peasants*, ed. Raftis, 247–79. J. Ambrose Raftis addresses peasant mobility in *Tenure and Mobility: Studies in the Social History of the Mediaeval English Village* (Toronto, 1964), especially 129–82.

128. XVIII, 315. Baildon and Clay, eds., *IPMs Relating to Yorkshire*, note that a juror remembered that the mother's churching coincided with his wife's death, an event still memorable because he took possession of lands "in right of his wife" (62–64).

129. Two jurors offered the common memory of having been appointed as co-executors, and a fellow juror fell back on defensive (or passive-aggressive) wording: "his father died the same day and his lands descended to him by hereditary right" (XVI, 77).

130. Peasant wills were still unusual in the late fourteenth century, and it is interesting to see that some jurors chose to use them as their mnemonic. They presumably knew the procedures that surrounded a will's creation as well as its legal weight. In the William Salt Archaeological Society's "Inquisitions Post Mortem, Ad Quod Damnum, etc.," the juror had fallen ill while on a pilgrimage, "on account of which he made his will which he still has in his possession" (52).

131. XIX, 577: "Returning [from church] he fell from his horse in a stony lane and broke his right shin, whence he has often suffered pain." According to Sue Walker, "Proof of Age witnesses appear to have been accident prone, the victims of mishaps that harmed the body but sharpened the memory" ("Proof of Age," 320).

132. Another memory here covers a thief who broke his shin while slipping the stocks and making his escape. High winds and sloping roofs were a bad combination: see XVII, 957, for a carpenter and a "tyler" who were blown off, leaving lasting memories for four men and broken arms for the two craftsmen.

133. XIX, 139: The juror remembered that he "broke his leg at York that week and was laid up for 20 weeks and more."

134. My debt to Barbara A. Hanawalt's *Ties That Bound: Peasant Families in Medieval England* (Oxford, 1986) is particularly pronounced in this area.

135. One juror had cut himself, "for which cause he carried his hand in a linen cloth for a year afterwards around his neck" (Hodgson, "Proof of Age of Heirs," 117).

136. The person who fell from the ladder "broke his right arm and was badly crushed" (XIX, 341); in the case of the house builder, "the wind blew suddenly from the north [and he] fell to the pavement and broke his arm" (XVII, 957). The same source also tells of the injury sustained while tiling a house. John Colton, the injured juror, was a "tyler."

137. Though I have not tallied these tales, we seem to have more broken right arms than left. Another member of this same urban jury had been "kicked on the right leg" while at the church door for the baptism. He too, poor fellow, was then "laid up for 20 weeks and more." See Rickert, *Chaucer's World,* for an account of a "hit and run driver" (13). For a case that still elicits pity and fear, at least among some readers, see *CIPM, XIV,* 65: "in that year he made such an effort in lifting a tree in the park of Kyrkeby Ravenswath that he ruptured his testicles."

138. Four jurors pooled a recollection of "when the cross of the belfrey was blown down by the wind" (XVI, 55). In another Proof the domino chain was "a storm of wind," which resulted in (as four jurors recalled) a toppled tree "called 'Notebemtre' growing on the highway," and finally, "a cottage of the said William Matthewe, so that the whole house was destroyed." Four others in the same jury said that the west part of the church "was thrown down by the said storm." These marvels had taken place "on the morrow of the birth" (XVI, 186).

139. XV, 652: three jurors recalled that "on the same day they and others began to make and fill in the foundations of the belfry" for the parish church. XIX, 341, offers a memory that entailed receiving £13. 6s. 8d. for building a hall and chamber as additions to an already standing house.

140. See Rickert, *Chaucer's World,* for indentures for construction projects (7–9).

141. There is no gloss in the text to shed light on his social status. Many of the knights and esquires who served on juries for aristocratic heirs were so designated.

142. See XVI, 1056, for a reference to reaping in the fields; the juror so engaged met people who told him of their journey to the baptism. *CIPM, XIV,* 342: the juror had then been "the thresher of the corn in the barn of William, the heir's father." Hodgson includes a juror of higher status: he, on the day of moment, had been at Whittingham "to hire Patrick Gaire to serve him for a year as ploughman" ("Proof of Age of Heirs," 128). For a wide context in which to "read" the harvest, see Llana Vardi, "Imagining the Harvest in Early Modern Europe," *American Historical Review* 101 (1996): 1357–97.

143. Compare this to *CIPM, XIV,* 64: a juror had an interesting account of being with the heir's father when the latter's three greyhounds, which they were leading, slipped free and strangled three swans of the abbess of Ramsey. She then "purchased the king's writ of trespass and recovered 100s." from the father.

144. Everyone has his (or her) own memories; another juror dated the same baptism by having seen a thief hanged at Bury. Still other jurors told of a thief who was arrested with ten stolen sheep and of how upsetting a cart killed the "white horse attached to it" (XIX, 783).

145. The proceedings illuminate a bucolic jury and a busy day, as others talked of building a dovecote and mowing a meadow. Bad bargains at the market also left a lasting impression, as a juror told of buying six oxen for six marks but having one die that afternoon, buying one hundred sheep for 10s. and having two die, selling twelve cows for 100s. and having one prove worthless, and buying twelve pigs for 33s. and having two die immediately (*CIPM, XX,* 267). This is another of those themed Proofs, where numerous memories cluster around one type of activity.

146. The smith's surname was Awre and some jurors were named Cardemaker, Plowright, Outlawe, and Skynnere. *A Midsummer Night's Dream,* or Monty Python?

147. The concept of the just price must have been in abeyance. A juror who had been robbed of a black horse said it was equal in value to five mares (Blagg, *Abstracts of Nottinghamshire IPMs,* 65–67). This sounds like an early version of a fraudulent insurance claim.

148. Markets and fairs clearly played a large role in both life and memory: see Ellen Wedemeyer Moore, *The Fairs of Medieval England: An Introductory Study* (Toronto, 1985); Maryanne Kowaleski, *Local Markets and Regional Trade: Medieval Exeter* (Cambridge, 1995), with an emphasis on hinterland and transaction costs; Richard H. Britnell, "The Proliferation of Markets in England, 1200–1349," *Economic History Review,* 2d ser., 34 (1981): 209–31; Bradley A. McLain, "Factors in Market Establishment in Medieval England: The Evidence from Kent, 1086–1356," *Archaeologia Cantiana* 117 (1997): 83–103; Bryan E. Coates, "The Origin and Distribution of Markets and Fairs in Medieval Derbyshire," *Derbyshire Archaeological Journal* 85 (1965): 92–111 (with maps on 98, 103, and 106). In thirty-three grants for Derbyshire markets, where the market day of the week is stipulated, the breakdown is Monday, seven; Tuesday, five; Wednesday, nine; Thursday, six; Friday, two; Saturday,

three; Sunday, one. Hilton, *A Medieval Society*, 161–77, provides a map of West Midland markets on 172. For a summary that looks beyond England, see Steven Epstein, "Regional Fairs: Institutional Innovation and Economic Growth in Late Medieval Europe," *Economic History Review*, 2d ser., 47 (1994): 458–82.

149. In XIX, 102, five men offered a single recollection (though we are told that the jurors' tales had been "separately stated") to the effect that they had been together at the fair at Beaminster near Netherbury on the critical day. And in XIX, 478, we find two separate statements about having been at the market at Grantham.

150. The Proof was taken at Ludlow, where such business was a matter of course.

151. For more references to economic activity, though hardly exhausting this line of recollection, see a Proof that mentions various jurors buying fish, corn, and two oxen (XVIII, 677). In another Proof, two jurors bought horses—one paying 100s.—and another was involved in buying pease for the heiress's father (XVIII, 664).

152. On the same jury were men who remembered a brother's pilgrimage to Rome ([he] "has not yet returned") and one whose brother "returned from the parts of France."

153. For the new world that might open up when one got to town, Miri Rubin, "Religious Culture in Town and Country: Reflections on a Great Divide," in *Church and City, 600–1500: Essays in Honour of Christopher Brooke*, ed. David Abulafia, Michael Franklin, and Miri Rubin (Cambridge, 1992), 3–22; Virginia R. Bainbridge, *Gilds in the Medieval Countryside: Social and Religious Change in Cambridgeshire, c. 1350–1558* (Woodbridge, 1996). *CIPM*, XX, 842: a juror spoke of how that year (in the 1390s) in London in the month of May there had been "two free ridings of fishmongers and goldsmiths, all parading and celebrating on horseback as was never before seen."

154. These men had been in Gloucester with a more exalted colleague, one John de Awre, whose bakehouse—according to other jurors—burned that same day.

155. XVIII, 316, 996, and 529, where four jurors say that they had been "before the king's justices" at Warwick but give no hint as to the reasons or scope of their presence.

156. Not a unique recollection, though one that certainly seems to lend itself to exaggeration (and retelling) as the years pass.

157. XVI, 77: a juror who had been distrained by the bailiff for arrears of service on a manor. *CIPM*, XI, 550: a juror said that his father had been a collector of fifteenths. When he asked the heir's father for his assessment, "the latter threatened him in life and limb so that he dared not approach the house for a fortnight, and by the date of the rolls of assessment of that 1/15 he knows [that] Robert is 21."

158. XVIII, 1180, where the juror had been with the coroner because "a stranger was killed by accident at Haddenham on 25 November." Because the heir had been born there on 28 October, this must just be a mnemonic link, though one of unusual precision.

159. The juror now claimed to be 60, so—assuming some accuracy in the self-stated age—his mother would probably have been about 60 at the time and presumably living as a remarried widow in Hurstmonceaux.

160. This is one of those interesting recollections that touches nothing at all in the saw-heard-involved loop. How did John Grenegrass, 48 and more, know what he knew? At least we are told that John Lysle, 65, saw a robber "hanged there at that time" (XIX, 347). On the speed of the legal machine, John Bellamy, *Crime and Public Order in England in the Late Middle Ages* (London, 1973), 162–98, plus index entries to "execution, summary."

161. Here we learn the felons' fates, while in another memory we just leave the poacher "imprisoned for that cause at Beverly" (XVII, 1320). On "quick justice," see R. B. Pugh, "The Duration of Criminal Trials in Medieval England," in *Law, Litigants, and the Legal Profession*, ed. Ives and Manchester, 104–15.

162. In XIX, 677, violence and chance were side by side: one juror witnessed a loveday, another went to look at a corpse and a wreck. An odd social mix in XIX, 347: two jurors talked of the earl of Northumberland being at the baptism, and several of their fellows remembered Lady Greystoke and the abbot of Alnwick. But one other juror, living in the same community, was more impressed by having seen a robber hanged that day. For an attempt to gauge the likelihood of a personal encounter

with violence, see A. J. Finch, "The Nature of Violence in the Middle Ages: An Alternative Perspective," *Historical Research* 70 (1997): 249–68.

163. In XVII, 741, jury members "know this *because* John Pyel was mayor at that time and Nicholas Brembre, the said Brian's godfather, and John Phelipot were sheriffs," while Richard Ouchawe "knows this because he was made a freeman of the city that year."

164. F. J. Furnivall, ed., *Political, Religious, and Love Poems,* Early English Text Society, o.s., 15 (1866; reprint, London, 1966), 56: a bit of doggerel headed "Put thieving millers and bakers in the pillory." For bad food as a health hazard, Carole Rawcliffe, *The Hospitals of Medieval Norwich* (Norwich, 1995), 21.

165. XIX, 791. The Proof was taken at Aspatria; the heir had been born at Dovenby and baptized at Bridekirk, Cumberland. Northern Proofs are rich in such memories. XVII, 275: the juror had been taken captive to Scotland, "where he stayed for the next six weeks"; in XIX, 897, there is another capture by the Scots. The village of Altonburn had been "burnt by the Scots, the king's enemies," in 1413–14, according to a Proof of 13 Henry VI, and another juror affirmed that "a day of truce between England and Scotland was kept at Hawdenstark, 3 November next," referring, in 1436, back to events of 1415 (Hodgson, "Proof of Age of Heirs," 126). On this social environment, Cynthia J. Neville, "Keeping the Peace on the Northern Marches in the Later Middle Ages," *EHR* 109 (1994): 1–25. For an earlier reference to "an historical event," see Madge, ed., *Abstracts of Gloucestershire IPMs,* 75–77: the juror returned from the Holy Land, "now 22 years ago," and the year before "Louis, King of the French, was taken by the enemies of the Cross of Christ at Damieta."

166. This is the expedition at which Sir Richard Scrope challenged Sir Robert Grosvenor's use of a coat of arms, as we will see below.

167. The Proof of an important heir (Roger Deyncourt) accounts for the involvement of these jurors. *CIPM, XX,* 184: "on that day Owyn Glendordy came with his large army to the gates of Cardiff"; 842: two old men "remember because at that time [1377] all persons of both sexes, aged 14 and more, had to pay the king 4d." For the "rumors" of 1388, Bertie Wilkinson, *The Constitutional History of Medieval England, II: Politics and the Constitution, 1307–1399* (London, 1952), 252–83, on the Merciless Parliament and the political world of that year.

168. XIX, 791: while one juror remembered having been captured by the Scots, another said the moment was when the earl of Northumberland "rode with a large force to Scotland." XIX, 341: the juror had been retained by Henry Percy to serve Richard II on the Scottish expedition, 25 April 1384. The juror was Robert Vavasour of Rudeston.

169. This is the only explicit reference in the Proofs to the Peasants' Rebellion, though we did have one oblique reference to a barn found by the jurors to have been burned to the ground when they returned home.

170. Several men dated a birth or baptism by its coincidence with their sons' leaving for France: XVII, 1319, 1320 (perhaps another instance of formulaic memory, as the first Proof was taken at Stafford and the second at York, within one day of each other). For other specific historical references, *CIPM, XX,* 184 ("Owyn Glendordy" at Cardiff), 842 ("all persons . . . had to pay the king 4d."), and 846 ("a pestilence in the summer before"). In this vein, *CIPM, XIV,* 344: "about the time of the middle pestilence, now 16 years ago, the said heir was 8 years old and more." This Proof was taken in 51 Edward III, so we are going back to 1353 or thereabouts.

171. Also, XIX, 778; the wording is much the same in this case, except that X wrote to release Y and Y did the same for X. The two cases provide an example of similar problems resolved in similar ways and of the Proof referring to the action in what had become its standard idiom.

172. Another memory here rests on settling a dispute between the juror and the heir's father; "hearing of the birth he came to the chapel and asked all the neighbours to intercede with John [the father] to pardon him . . . he knows by the date of the release."

173. The juror was now 70, so he had been a man of mature years when he had played arbitrator. Though we are not told the cause of the quarrel, it had been "a notable discord."

174. XVIII, 315: the juror had witnessed the resolution of a dispute and so he now remembers. XVIII, 890: the two jurors, now giving a common memory, had been the disputants. They made up on the day of the baptism and they know the date because an indenture, written and precisely dated,

served to remind them of their common past. XVIII, 673: the infant's father had prevailed on the two jurors to resolve their quarrel. Perhaps the festive air of birth and baptism generated an irenic spirit and gave the father some moral suasiveness.

175. The Proof was held at Gloucester, some thirteen or fourteen miles from Tetburg.

176. This Proof offers unusual topographic detail. The godmother carried the baby "from the church to Itchen to cross the river Itchen in a boat called 'le Passeger' to the manor of Woolston."

177. See Rickert, *Chaucer's World*, 201–2, for more instances of gambling. For a general discussion of leisure time and leisure activities, see A. Compton Reeves, *Pleasures and Pastimes in Medieval England* (Stroud, 1995).

178. Though we have remarked that the church was the center of village life, this is more than we might expect to encounter.

179. In this account the winner is now listed as aged 48, he of the broken shin 64; they should have known better, even twenty-one years before, especially as the birth and baptism had occurred in mid-January.

180. The juror who had given a silk purse must have felt that he missed the bus. XVIII, 999: the Proof held for Margaret, wife of Thomas Segrave, and for Isabel, wife of William Ulkerthorp, was also rich in hunting memories. Most of the Proofs that rested heavily on hunting memories were Proofs held for aristocratic heirs and heiresses.

181. A juror remembered the birthday in question because "with his greyhounds he killed a doe in the park at Whichemore on the same day" (XVII, 1319). For another memory that hinged on the juror's greyhounds taking a doe that day, see XVIII, 1148. See also Nicholas Orme, "Medieval Hunting: Fact and Fancy," in *Chaucer's England: Literature in Historical Context*, ed. Barbara A. Hanawalt (Minneapolis, 1992), 133–53, and Richard Almond, "Medieval Hunting: Ruling Classes and Commonalty," *Headstart: Medieval History* 3 (1991–93): 147–55.

182. See Hodgson, "Proof of Age of Heirs," 125, for a juror who said that he had been run down by a stag and had come away with a broken arm.

183. Geoffrey H. Martin, ed. and trans., *Knighton's Chronicle, 1337–1396* (Oxford, 1995), 47, for the earthquake of 15 February 1344 "felt in all parts of the kingdom." There is a detailed description of the quake of 21 May 1382 occurring during the Blackfriars council being held to condemn Wyclif. H. B. Workman, *John Wyclif: A Study of the English Medieval Church* (London, 1926), 2:267: Archbishop Courtenay said that the quake portended a purging of the realm, whereas Wyclif countered that the "earth din" was "an outcry of the world against the heretic prelates." *Calendar of the Patent Rolls, 1381–85* (London, 1897), 164 (25 July 1382): masons were sent to repair damage to Christ Church Canterbury, reported as "greatly injured." See Jeremy Catto and Linne R. Mooney, eds., "The Chronicle of John Somer, O.F.M.," *Camden Miscellany* 34, Camden Society, 5th ser., vol. 10 (Cambridge, 1997), 239–80; for references to earthquakes, 241 and 266; to high winds, 275. There are also references to comets, eclipses, dry spells, and the like.

184. In the same Proof, two jurors had a common memory of losing the hay from six mown acres, "washed away by the flood following the rain that fell that day." In another Proof, the reference was simply to "thunder, lightening and heavy rain, destroying much corn" (XIX, 782). Floods were a good point for recollection: "on the same day the head of the mill-pond of Maleswykemull was broken by floods" (XVI, 75). Hodgson, "Proof of Age of Heirs," 128: the juror said the Tyne had risen so high "through the abundance of rain and overflow of the sea" that water had come into his house.

185. A juror also told of when "it rained so heavily and the waters rose so much that they scarcely avoided being drowned" (XVIII, 886).

186. One unexplored topic is leisure time. If people were free to go on pilgrimages (to nearby Walsingham or as far as Jerusalem), they were at least this free when it came time for jury calls and the like. On intra-village dynamics, S. Olson, "Jurors of the Village Court," 237–56. *CIPM, XIV*, 166, offers an account by a juror who had been at the baptism of the heir because he asked someone (the grandmother in this case) on the way to the church about her destination and then decided to tag along for the fun: "he went with her and saw the baptism." Helen M. Jewell, *English Local Administration in the Middle Ages* (Newton Abbot, 1972), 150: a jury was composed of men "who knew the

facts and came to court to attest them." Also, P. D. A. Harvey, *A Medieval Oxfordshire Village: Cuxham, 1240 to 1400* (Oxford, 1965), 112.

187. Sue Walker, in her "Proof of Age," and E. R. Stevenson, in "The Escheator," encounter men of higher status among their jurors than most of those we have encountered. Either there was a social decline by the late fourteenth century (and Walker is more interested in the late thirteenth and early-to-mid-fourteenth century), or their focus on controversial and important cases gives an appearance of an upward social tilt not found in the common business of the village. Though we, too, can move in a world of some rank: W. Brown, ed., *Yorkshire Inquisitions*, IV, 72–75, takes us to the other extreme. The godfathers for the heir in question had been "Nicholas a scullery boy" and "the son of a glover who called himself Ank."

188. The Proof was held at Calais, where the baptism had been in the church of St. Mary on 9 August 1390. In keeping with the aristocratic nature of this affair, the queen had held the heir's wardship during his minority. *CIPM*, XIV, 298: the status is honorable but far below the case just cited. Two jurors had just (at the time of the baptism) made covenant with the heir's father to "serve him in the offices of pantry and butler." Well above this was the juror who claimed (*CIPM*, XX, 265) to have been "retained that day by Thomas Sakevyl, knight, for life, to serve him in war and peace by a fee of 10 marks."

189. At the time of her Proof, Anne, daughter of Lord Bardolf, was already married to Sir William Clifford. Despite these aristocratic links, no juror stated his rank in the Proof (XIX, 665).

190. The Proof for Robert Roos had three jurors identified as esquires (XIX, 1000). Every juror, however, gave a place of origin or of residence along with his name; this was unusual and seems a mark of some distinction. The Proof for Isabel Fychet, married to Robert Hull, opened with the mayor of Launceston as first juror, but after that we have eleven men of no social distinction (XVII, 953).

191. In XV, 889, the juror, a sacristan, remembered that he had brought the water for the baptism. Another juror was "reeve of Holbeach church that year" (XIX, 998).

192. On the size of large households, see Jennifer C. Ward, *English Noblewomen in the Later Middle Ages* (London, 1992), 56–69, for some numbers; Kate Mertes, *The English Noble Household, 1250–1600* (Oxford, 1988), 52–74, and a table showing "average household size" for gentle, monastic, and aristocratic households (238); ffiona Swabey, *Medieval Gentlewoman: Life in a Widow's Household in the Later Middle Ages* (Stroud, 1999), 9–29.

193. XIV, 336; XVIII, 1148; XVII, 576. This last, in what we might call a pregnant moment in English history, was the Proof for Thomas Swynford, son and heir of Hugh de Swynford (and son of Katherine, his wife, though she is not named in the Proof). The baptism had been on the day after the feast of St. Matthias, 47 Edward III. For another Proof that sets out the hierarchy of service, see XVII, 955, where the juror had been chamberlain to the heir's grandfather (who had also been a godfather).

194. Given the importance of servant labor for the peasantry and the workforce, the topic has been long ignored; see Poos, *Rural Society*, and P. J. P. Goldberg, *Women, Work, and the Life Cycle in a Medieval Economy: Women in York and Yorkshire, c. 1300–1520* (Oxford, 1992). Rodney H. Hilton recognized servanthood as important in his *English Peasantry in the Later Middle Ages* (Oxford, 1975), passim.

195. XV, 450; XVIII, 1148, 855. Two jurors had been servants of the prior of Kenilworth (XVIII, 313) and others had served in a similar capacity for John, prior of Kirkham (XVII, 954), the abbot of Spalding (who had been the godfather [XVII, 955]), and the abbot of Missenden (the abbot was the godfather, and the servant had been his esquire [V, 339]). On servants: P. J. P. Goldberg, "What Was a Servant?" in *Concepts and Patterns of Service in the Late Middle Ages,* ed. Anne Curry and Elizabeth Matthew (Woodbridge, 2000), 1–20. For the ideology of service, mostly at the higher social levels, see Rosemary Horrox, "Service," in *Fifteenth-Century Attitudes: Perceptions of Society in Late Medieval England,* ed. Rosemary Horrox (Cambridge, 1994), pp. 61–78.

196. The servant of Robert Braibrook, "then bishop of London," delivered the white palfrey that Braibrook had sent as a birthday present. He only received 6s. 8d. for his efforts (XIX, 343).

197. XIX, 663: a servant sent to the vicar of Brampton "to warn him for the baptism." XV, 291, mentions unspecified help if needed while accompanying William de Wauton, knight. The juror

himself, "at the time of the birth, was servant of John de Coggeshalle, knight, grandfather of the said William."

198. We might like to think that the servant remembered this beating because it was so unusual that it fixed his memory. For a near miss, XVII, 955: the juror had been a servant of Master Peter de Dalton, parson of Surfleet. He "brought wine, bread and lights and broke the lights and was greatly reproved for that cause by his master." W. Brown, ed., *Yorkshire Inquisitions*, IV, 92–93: the juror had been at school, where he "was so badly beaten . . . that he left school from that time, whereby he well knows that 21 years have elapsed." Rickert, *Chaucer's World*, 108: the beating and ill treatment of a girl apprentice and a complaint brought by her father. Also, two Canterbury men said their master's wife had "beaten them maliciously and had struck William on the left eye so violently that he lost the sight of that eye" (107–8). For an extreme case—that is, for a beating given so as to establish a memory—Elisabeth van Houts, "Gender and Authority of Oral Witnesses in Europe (800–1300)," *Transactions of the Royal Historical Society*, 6th ser., 9 (1999): 206–7.

199. XV, 652. Three jurors, in a common statement, said that on "the same day" they decided to buy a missal for the church, though it was only "a month later [they] bought the book." Also, XIX, 783: ten jurors offered "same day" memories, one resorted to "the following morning" for his scenario, and one recalled events of "the following night."

200. The heiress is now known to be "14 1/2 years of age and more," now married to John Mowthe, who petitioned for her Proof.

201. In this case, only two of the jurors' memories were related to the heiress's baptism.

202. None of them is more precise. We have no inkling of whether the reported activities were months before, around the time of, or months after the birth.

203. Other recollections in this Proof had secular dating: 20 July and 8 October, 32 Edward III.

204. A few memories go back to a time shortly before the heir's birth, though it is just a matter of a week or two.

205. Unfortunately, this intriguing Proof is damaged and we can read no further insights into the hours of the day.

206. Also see XVIII, 667, for a baptism that took place "before 9 o'clock." W. Brown, ed., *Yorkshire Inquisitions*, IV, 5: the juror said that the heir had been born "about the hour of cock crowing [*circa horam gallicantur*]."

207. On the precision (or imprecision) of time keeping, Linne R. Mooney, "The Cock and the Clock: Telling Time in Chaucer's Day," *Studies in the Age of Chaucer* 15 (1993): 91–109.

208. The jurors offered two individual statements, then one from four men ("examined separately"), and then statements from three groups of two. In another instance of all twelve saying that they had been in church, the groupings were of six separate statements, then four together (again, they "said separately"), and then two in a common memory (XIX, 899).

209. XVIII, 999: one juror sold the grandfather a horse; another met him in the fields on the birthday; a third was in church with him and saw the birth noted in the missal; a fourth, with two recollections, received a beam from him while doing construction, and then later gave him a hare; the fifth had seen him receive some land and on the second occasion had heard of the birth from a servant of the grandfather.

210. The dating is for a birth on 5 April 1381 (that is, 4 Richard II), and the editor of the *Inquisitions* suggests that 6 Richard II (1383) should have been given.

211. See Russell, *British Medieval Population*, on fictions in the testimony. Russell pretty much says what Poos and Hurstfield, among others, were quoted as saying above, and he gives marks for creative writing to the chancery scribes: "if these are fictions then the most original and brilliant story tellers of the Middle Ages were clerks dealing with royal business" (103).

CHAPTER 2

1. My presentation of the controversy is wholly partisan; it only looks at the depositions that support Scrope's claim. This is mainly for clarity of focus, as we know more about the world of the

Scropes than of the Grosvenors in the fourteenth century. For a summary of the hearings and decisions, see J. G. Nichols, "The Scrope and Grosvenor Controversy," *Herald and Genealogist* (1863): 385–400. R. Stewart-Brown takes a similar approach, but from the Grosvenors' perspective, in "The Scrope and Grosvenor Controversy," *Transactions of the Historic Society of Lancashire and Cheshire* 89 (1938): 1–22. A few of Grosvenor's partisans somehow got summoned to depose on Scrope's behalf in the hearing at the church of St. John Without the Walls of Chester, 4 September, 10 Richard II, before Sir Nicholas Haryngton, Scrope's proctor. They were generally uncooperative (in terms of supporting Scrope), were adjudged contumacious, and were fined £20 (see the testimony of Sir William Brereton, *S&G*, 2:268). Some took the position that they had not seen Scrope bear the arms prior to the recent Scottish campaign, though they had seen him over the years. Some admitted to being Grosvenor's relatives; one was of his affinity; others were friends and neighbors. On the persuasive power of "the constant refrain," see Jonathan J. G. Alexander and Paul Binski, eds., *Age of Chivalry: Art in Plantagenet England, 1200–1400* (London, 1987), 59, and, in the same volume, M. Camille's discussion of the power of "the urge to witness, as well as to read writing" in the world of chivalric behavior (35). Robin Frame addresses "witnesses whose memories served as authentication" in *The Political Development of the British Isles, 1100–1400* (Oxford, 1995), 76.

2. Though I speak about the ritualized nature of the testimony in detail, I make little of its confrontational aspects. The depositions can be interpreted as a series of challenges and counter-challenges, with the scenario of a tournament as the context for interpretation. See Charles V. Phythian-Adams, "Rituals of Personal Confrontation in Late Medieval England," *Bulletin of the John Rylands University Library* 73 (1991): 65–90, for a stimulating example of how this approach can be pursued; for the traditional chivalric approach, see Patricia J. Eberle, "Richard II and the Literary Arts," in *Richard II: The Art of Kingship*, ed. Anthony Goodman and James L. Gillespie (Oxford, 1999), especially 237–38, on a French treatise addressing "rules and procedures for conducting judicial combat in the High Court of Chivalry," supposedly written by the duke of Gloucester to present to the king.

3. Squibb, *High Court of Chivalry*, discusses the need for an open display of one's arms (189).

4. A few Scrope partisans did speak well of Sir Robert Grosvenor, though they rejected his claim to the arms. One affirmed that Sir Robert was "a gentleman of high degree ("est grant gentile home"), though little could be said in support of his claim (see *S&G*, 2:167 and 212, as well as 465, on an honorable marriage made by the Grosvenors). Previous challenges to Scrope arms are treated below. It is possible that in a world where rolls of arms had localized circulation and the arms were simple, in heraldic terms, coincidence and converging taste did lead to inadvertent duplication. On the other hand, trained memories were powerful tools. One Scrope deponent talked of "the noble King Edward the Third, who had good knowledge of all manner of right to arms," in recalling how the king summoned Sir Geoffrey Scrope to raise his banner and lead his men (*S&G*, 2:385). See Noel Denholm-Young, *The Country Gentry in the Fourteenth Century* (Oxford, 1969), on the likelihood that witnesses had been coached (134–35).

5. Though these depositions strike me as a source of great riches, they have been characterized by a learned student of fourteenth-century life and politics as "often tedious": see Michael Prestwich, *Armies and Warfare in the Middle Ages: The English Experience* (New Haven, 1996), 113.

6. See Nichols, "The Scrope and Grosvenor Controversy," 389: "In order to avoid battle in this case, according to the law and custom of the Court, they [the judges] appointed him to prove his said arms by good, noble, and sufficient witnesses deriving information from their ancestors, and by ancient charters and other authentic Proofs." For comparable material on a bourgeois level, see Deborah March, "'I See by the Sizt of Evidence': Information Gathering in Late Medieval Cheshire," in *Courts, Counties, and the Capital in the Later Middle Ages,* ed. Diana E. S. Dunn (Stroud, 1996), 71–92.

7. Most deponents began by stating their age and years of bearing arms, though the ages may be problematic. The self-stated age situates each deponent on a continuum, however, and it accords with my general treatment of testimony and social memory to argue for the relative accuracy of the statements. The given ages of the deponents are considered in Rosenthal, *Old Age,* 44–53; they are dismissed by Donald R. Howard, *Chaucer, His Life, His Works, His World* (New York, 1987): "the age is a formalized guess made by the royal clerk, who gave the deponents' ages in round numbers and got most of them wrong" (4).

8. *S&G*, 2:166 (the deposition of Henry Bolingbroke, earl of Derby). For one of the most comprehensive or inclusive statements, see that of Sir Maurice de Bruyn, who knew of "the said Sir Richard and his ancestors, such as his father, his uncle, his cousins, and elder brother" (367).

9. See Jean Dunbabin, "Discovering a Past for the French Aristocracy," in *The Perception of the Past in Twelfth-Century Europe,* ed. Paul Magdalino, 1–14 (London, 1992), especially 2: "genealogies provided the skeleton of all family histories and through their form deeply influenced the attitudes of those who exploited them."

10. *S&G*, 2:273. The abbot also referred to (and perhaps brought along) muniments or charters and a release without date but with the Scrope seal. He quotes from the latter; that is, he had its opening lines entered into the record as part of his deposition. The release said that Geoffrey le Scrope had conceded to the house at "Joreval" (Jervaulx) the "eight marks of silver of a mine of coals" that the house had owed him, "and my [that is, the Scrope] heirs" were bound to continue to honor the gift.

11. S&G, 2:279. The chaplain of Marigg, John de Brereton, told of "two glass windows, the one in front of the high altar, and the other in the porch of St. Thomas, in which were the arms of one of the Scropes . . . [and also] in a glass window in the dormitory of the nuns in the south part" (333). Some lay depositions also refer to Scrope arms in the glass of various ecclesiastical sites. Lord Dacre referred to glass at Lanercost priory (413); Richard de Beaulieu made reference to Henry's arms in the window at Wetherall (441); and Richard de Hamptone had seen the arms on banners and "in churches on windows, and they were always called the arms of Scrope" (453).

12. S&G, 2:279. The parson of Wensley parish church added that "there is graven thereon *hey gist William le Scrope,* without date, for the bad weather, wind, snow, and rain, had so defaced it, that no man could make out the remainder of the writing, so old and defaced was it" (329).

13. *S&G*, 2:276. Stewart-Brown, "The Scrope and Grosvenor Controversy," offers a comparable survey of churches and the like with Grosvenor arms and blazons (17–19).

14. *S&G*, 2:331: "a frontore worked in silk before an altar, on which frontore were the said arms of Scrope, the making of which was beyond human memory." For later Scrope memorabilia and family history preserved in cloth, see Hugh Murray, "The Scrope Tapestries," *Yorkshire Archaeological Journal* 64 (1992): 145–56.

15. *S&G*, 2:279, documents a deposition about "banners which were used at the funeral of great lords, embroidered with their arms, amongst which were those of Scrope entire."

16. This was the prior of Marton, in a deposition unusually rich for its heraldic knowledge. He told of the arms of old admirers of the Scropes, the Quenbys of Cornburgh, who had had Scrope arms set into a window immediately beside their own arms (Argent, a saltire Sable).

17. Maurice Keen, *Chivalry* (New Haven, 1984), 134. On the narrow gap between the culture and worldview of knights and that of esquires and gentlemen, see Keen, "Heraldry and Hierarchy: Esquires and Gentlemen," in *Orders and Hierarchies in Late Medieval and Renaissance Europe,* ed. Jeffrey Denton, 94–108 (Basingstoke, 1999); Anthony Richard Wagner, *Heralds and Heraldry in the Middle Ages,* 2d ed. (Oxford, 1956), 50.

18. Rolls of arms might well figure into this topic, though only Laton's deposition talks of them. See Anthony Richard Wagner, *Catalogue of English Mediaeval Rolls of Arms* (London, 1950); Robert W. Mitchell, ed., *English Mediaeval Rolls of Arms, 1: 1244–1334* (Edinburgh, 1983); Wagner, *Heralds and Heraldry,* especially 12–24; Noel Denholm-Young, *History and Heraldry, 1254–1310: A Study of the Historic Value of the Roll of Arms* (London, 1965), remarking on the absence of either Scrope or Grosvenor arms from the earlier rolls that have been preserved (113); Peter Coss, *The Knight in Medieval England* (Stroud, 1993), especially 72–99; and John A. Godall, "A Fifteenth-Century Anglo-French-Burgundian Heraldic Collection," *Antiquaries Journal* 70 (1990): 435.

19. *S&G*, 2:273 (the abbot of Jervaulx). One would imagine that the physical existence of the seal would more than cover the absence of a date. On heraldic seals and shields in regular and mendicant houses, see Wagner, *Heralds and Heraldry,* 51, who quotes Langland railing against the mendicant practice: "Wyde wydowes y-wrought y-writen full thikke, / Schynen with schapen scheldes to schewen about / With merkes of marchauntes y-medled bytwene, / Mor than twenty and two twyes y-noumbred / There is now heraud that hath half swich a rolle."

20. *S&G*, 2:281; in the "solemn seals" we find "the seals effigies of knights on horseback." Some of the charters were the earl of Lincoln's, and they supported Scrope's claim by way of what the prior had been told about the arms by old friars, "then deceased."

21. At St. Agatha, the abbot distinguished between the most eminent, "under raised stones" and "sculpted on a high tomb," and their sons and brothers, more apt to be "interred under flat stones." On the Scropes and the church of St. Agatha, consult *Victoria County History: Yorkshire*, vol. 3, ed. William Page (London, 1913; reprint, Folkestone, 1974), 245–46, which refers to "the famous stained glass shield which he [the abbot] mentioned as existing in his abbey . . . and which played such a prominent part in the settlement [and] has recently been identified. It is in a curiously confused condition" (246). See *S&G*, 2:331, for a reference by Master William de Irby, identified as an "official of Richmond," to Scrope arms in forty northern churches.

22. *S&G*, 2:329–30. See H. B. McColl, *Richmondshire Churches* (London, 1900), 163–74, for Holy Trinity, Worsley. The fifteenth-century buttresses have niches that display shields of Scrope of Bolton, de la Pole, Fitzhugh, Scrope of Masham, Neville, Ros, Neville of Raby, and Montague. A Scrope chantry, c. 1398, had been endowed to the sum of 106s. 8d. *per annum*. A brass in the church covers the grave of our deponent priest who presided there from 1361 until 1394.

23. *S&G*, 2:278–79. The church was St. Martin, Mickelgate, York; the living was held by Warter priory, and it was the prior who told this tale.

24. *S&G*, 2:281, with numerous references to the mysterious Gants (Robert and Walter). See *S&G*, 2:344, for the reference to "Edward the King."

25. For another deposition with a mix of modes of cognition, see *S&G*, 2:213: "he had seen and known . . . and never saw nor heard that any other person was armed in these arms; but he had heard from old knights. . . . As for Sir Robert Grosvenor, he never saw him armed, nor had any knowledge of him." The put-down of the Grosvenors is a fairly standard closing remark.

26. *S&G*, 2:164: John of Gaunt, the first deponent. But others, both of high and of relatively low status, said much the same: "he often saw also Sir Henry and Sir Richard armed in the king's expedition in France . . . and saw Sir Richard Scrope armed . . . [and] he had heard from his ancestors that the Scropes had always borne the said arms" (441). The hearsay accounts are usually presented as the final or key link in a chain of transmitted lore. In an unusual instance, Sir Edward Dalyngrigge named the intermediary informant who had filled him in—the earl of Arundel (372).

27. *S&G*, 2:281. The case against Grosvenor was concisely put by an esquire from Kent, James Pecham: "If any other man had a right to the arms of Scrope, it must have been well known, either by hearsay from old persons or by branches of the said arms, or by collaterals, in so long a time" (436).

28. Why had no one of the Grosvenors' world ever objected to Scrope's arms? As one Scrope partisan, Sir Thomas Roos of Kendal, noted, "the late king and the great lords of the whole realm were present [at a tournament]; and if there had been anyone there who had borne those arms for the name of Grosvenor, the King and the lords and knights present, must have known the name of the said Grosvenor and his arms, or of some of his ancestors, for it is through tournaments or service that a knowledge is acquired of chivalry" (*S&G*, 2:335). It is possible that assuming a coat of arms had once been a more casual affair than the seriousness of this great controversy would make us think. "Arms were assumed as and when nobles and knights required them," asserted L. G. Pine in a letter in *Coat of Arms* 2 (1953): 155.

29. This was the myth of the "Norman yoke" turned inside out for upper-class purposes. For the Pastons and their Norman roots, see Coss, *The Knight*, 1–3, and see Colin F. Richmond, *The Paston Family in the Fifteenth Century: The First Phase* (Cambridge, 1990), 5–6: Edward IV said that the Pastons were "'gentlemen descended lineally of worshipfull blood sithen the Conquest,'" though Richmond adds, "whether he believed it is another matter." Anthony Richard Wagner, *English Genealogy*, 2d ed. (Oxford, 1972), discusses the construction of extended kin networks (178–79) and compilations of pedigrees (305–10).

30. In *Life of the Black Prince*, Pope and Lodge offer a eulogistic account of the prince in action. For a formulation of this ideology a century or two before the Scropes and the Grosvenors, see Richard W. Kaeuper, *Chivalry and Violence in Medieval Europe* (Oxford, 1999).

31. Richard Poynings, about 28 at the time, referred to "during the time he was armed, which was from his youth" (S&G, 2:166–67). Heir to the Poynings estates and peerage since 1375, his military role and his political maturity would have begun early.

32. See also the testimony of William Heselrigge, an esquire now perhaps in his 70s (S&G, 2:327). He had "heard from his ancestors in his youth that the Scropes were as ancient as the Conquest." Adam Fox, *Oral and Literate Culture in England, 1500–1700* (Oxford, 2000), follows this line of historiographical analysis into early modern times; see especially 214–27. On the transition from folklore to historical record, Fox writes, "Many of these fireside stories remained unwritten because they were too narrow in interest or too local in scope to make the recording of them either necessary or desirable. They had meaning for particular communities and it was this parochial relevance which both kept them alive and ensured their confinement" (215).

33. S&G, 2:166; also see 449, where Sir Richard le Zouche, now aged 67, speaks of what he heard from his grandfather, Lord Zouche. His grandfather had come by his knowledge of the Scropes before he himself had been born.

34. This was Sir Hugh Hastings, who cut his own memorable swathe in this world. Binski, *Medieval Death*, notes that the canopy of Hastings's tomb had "a number of male 'weepers' constituting Sir Hugh's brotherhood of arms" (104). See Coss, *The Knight*, for a depiction of the brass (98), and Anthony Richard Wagner, with notes on the armor by James G. Mann, "A Fifteenth-Century Description of the Brass of Sir Hugh Hastings at Elsing, Norfolk," *Antiquaries Journal* 19 (1939): 421–28. In testimony from the Grey vs. Hastings dispute in 1403, a reference appears; at a hearing in Norwich Priory, the court was told of relevant material at Elsing, whence they adjourned to examine the brass of Edward Hastings's great-grandfather, the Sir Hugh of the Scrope and Grosvenor depositions. The description of 1408 mentions coats of arms no longer extant on the brass. In addition, a Scrope deponent (Sir Thomas Erpingham—see S&G, 2:196) was also, years later, a deponent in the Grey and Hastings controversy.

35. S&G, 2:307, 314. Variations on this ran to "he had heard from old knights and esquires in the north parts, and especially from his ancestors," and "he had heard from his father and valiant knights and esquires now deceased." It was also expressed as "He [Sir John Mauleverer] had heard from his father, and valiant knights and esquires now no more, and *never to the contrary*" (S&G, 2:299; emphasis added).

36. The most disputatious and querulous assertions in favor of the Scropes were reported at second hand by the sons and descendants of old men who had supposedly passed them along. The old men's honor and veracity were clearly at stake, along with the honor and veracity of the Scropes.

37. S&G, 2:172, and 198: the Scropes were "descended by right line from a race entitled to the said arms from time beyond memory." Though the power of "legal memory" rested in part on its independence from normal chronological boundaries (at least back to 1189), some depositions give specific numbers of "years ago" and add precision to assertions about "time out of mind." Muniments in Marrick nunnery went back 68 years (331); a charter at Appleby went back 160 years (342); Scrope arms in Marton church dated from 200 years before (345); the chamber in "Hynendale manor house" was 160 years old, and Scrope arms had been set into its wall from the beginning (313); the relevant burial was 183 years before (305). On legal memory, see Pollock and Maitland, *History of English Law:* "Possibly this date [1189] was chosen because it was just possible that a living man should have been told by his father of what that father had seen in the year 1189" (1:168). Howard, *Chaucer,* discusses the distinction between "before human memory" and "time out of mind" (390–91). Howard holds that the former indicates the earliest time that could be remembered by someone alive, while the latter simply rests on the accession of Richard I. See also Paul Brand, "Time Out of Mind: Knowledge and Use of the Eleventh- and Twelfth-Century Past in Thirteenth-Century Litigation," *Anglo-Norman Studies* 16 (1993): 37–54. It has been suggested that in this case, at least, the court may have accepted the Norman Conquest rather than 1189 as the beginning of legal memory, thereby distinguishing the tighter boundaries of common law and the more flexible ones of traditional lore. See Squibb, "Law of Arms," 245.

38. North-country identity, of course, was a strong feature of the sense of community. For the Scropes of Bolton and a family agenda, see Joel T. Rosenthal, *Patriarchy and Families of Privilege in*

Late Medieval England (Philadelphia, 1991), 77–91. On the northern community, consult James C. Holt, *The Northerners: A Study in the Reign of King John* (Oxford, 1961); Pollard, *North-Eastern England;* and Helen M. Jewell, *The North-South Divide: The Origins of Northern Consciousness in England* (Manchester, 1994).

39. *S&G,* 2:351, Sir Richard Roucliffe of Roucliffe. He was one of those who affected a weariness over the controversy, saying that "it would be too tedious to mention all the places" in which Scropes had displayed their arms. This sounds like calculated exasperation, designed to put the other side on the defensive.

40. Also see *S&G,* 2:319, "according to common report through his country," and 243, "public report testified." One deposition included an unusual urban touch: the deponent spoke of "a similar escocheon which he knew by common parlance contained the arms of Scrope, and that such was known throughout the city of York" (279).

41. It is clear that many of the Scrope family's supporters knew that Sir Richard's father and uncle had begun as lawyers who worked their way up to king's justices and finally wound up as knights, eventually becoming peers of the realm.

42. The abbot had also learned some of his lore from "old lords of the country, knights, and esquires, and others."

43. *S&G,* 2:280; the abbot of Coverham had learned of the Scrope claims from the "most ancient men of the country."

44. They "came into England at the Conquest" (*S&G,* 2:445), or, variously, "in right line from the time of the Conquest" (281), or as Sir Richard Waldegrave expressed it, "he had heard that his [Scrope's] ancestors came direct from the Conquest" (377).

45. See *S&G,* 2:281; another reference may be to the same charter (293). Simon le Scrope is now the family's patriarch.

46. H. J. Hewitt, *The Organization of War Under Edward III, 1338–62* (Manchester, 1966), treats the brutality and cruelty behind the chivalric facade, the destruction wrought by the marches of 1345–55 (from 111 on), and the antisocial behavior of returning veterans ("a companionship of violence for personal advantage") (from 173 on).

47. *S&G,* 2:426–27. Not often do we find a man of 54 (young Thirwalle) falling back on a presentation of himself as still wrapped in dewy inexperience to bolster the validity of an older chain, based on oral transmission. In another deposition, William Scrope captured a French knight with an identical coat of arms, and the knight's life was only spared because John Charnels (the deponent) "made him take off the coat of arms" before Scrope killed him (223).

48. *S&G,* 2:272, 278. Also see *S&G,* 2:281–82: the two men representing Bridlington displayed six charters. Similarly, the parson of Wensley church showed the commissioners an "albe with flaps upon which were embroidered the arms of the Scropes entire" (330).

49. For a document reflecting the sort of material a herald had at his fingertips, see Viscount Dillon, "On a Manuscript Collection of Ordinances of Chivalry of the Fifteenth Century Belonging to Lord Hastings," *Archaeologia* 57 (1900): 29–70. We noted a deponent who spoke of how well versed Edward III had been in matters of heraldry; along this line, Jack R. Lander, *English Justices of the Peace* (Gloucester, 1989), describes Edward IV's equally impressive memory concerning the knightly families of the realm (41).

50. Biographical material on the Scropes is readily available, with the fullest collection being in *S&G,* vol. 1. *The Dictionary of National Biography* has entries for Henry (d. 1336), Geoffrey (d. 1340), Henry, I Lord Scrope of Masham (d. 1391), "our" Richard, and his son William (x. 1399); in addition, there is a useful entry for Sir Robert Grosvenor (d. 1396). *The Complete Peerage* covers both branches of the Scrope family and offers information on the family prior to the fourteenth century. See George E. Cokayne et al., eds., *The Complete Peerage* (London, 1910–59), for the Scropes of Bolton in these years (11:539–46) and for those of Masham (11:561–69); George P. Scrope, *The History of Castle Combe* (London, 1852); E. L. G. Stones, "Sir Geoffrey le Scrope (c. 1285–1340), Chief Justice of the King's Bench," *EHR* 69 (1954): 1–17; Brigette Vale, "The Profits of the Law and the 'Rise' of the Scropes: Henry Scrope (d. 1330) and Geoffrey Scrope (d. 1340), Chief Justices to

Edward II and Edward III," in *Profit, Piety, and the Professions in Later Medieval England*, ed. Michael Hicks (Gloucester, 1990), 91–102.

51. The Chandos Herald speaks with pride of the diverse composition of the troops, drawing in men of England, France, Brittany, Normandy, Picardy, and Gascony. See Pope and Lodge, eds., *Life of the Black Prince*, 149.

52. *S&G*, 2:381: Sir Robert was aged 60, armed for thirty-nine years. Also see *S&G*, 2:261.

53. For an extreme articulation of a personal sense of honor, see William Askins, "The Brothers Orléans and Their Keepers," in *Charles d'Orléans in England (1415–1440)*, ed. Mary-Jo Arn, 27–46 (Cambridge, 2000).

54. For references to rolls of arms, see note 18 above.

55. Maurice Keen, "Brotherhood in Arms," *History* 47 (1963): 1–17, and Jonathan Sumption, *The Hundred Years War: Trial by Battle* (Philadelphia, 1991), 181–82, provide a sanguine view of military brotherhood. Colin F. Richmond is less enchanted, describing "a predatory governing elite, with care for the honour of the Crown, the French war, birth and title, royal finance and government only because these nourished and enhanced itself," in his review essay, "An English Mafia?" *Nottingham Medieval Studies* 36 (1992): 235–43. Nor is there much idealization in Hewitt, *The Organization of War*.

56. Respectively, *S&G*, 2:203, 284–85, and 292–93. Also in this vein, *S&G*, 2:298, gives an account of how Scrope accompanied the king when Edward learned of the loss of Berwick and had to rush from a French chevauchée back to England and then to the Scottish border.

57. *S&G*, 2:317: he displayed his arms "on banner, pennon, and coat of arms."

58. William died in the Vale of Zorie when he was with the Prince in Spain (*S&G*, 2:440).

59. *S&G*, 2:385, 357, and 261. Other depositions provide a recollection of Sir Richard and Sir Henry together on service in Spain, France, Gascony, and Scotland (218) and memories of differencing arms: the "label argent" (212); "armed with a white label" (297); and "armed Azure, a bend or, with a white label" (299). On differencing arms, see Gerald Brault, *Eight Thirteenth-Century Rolls of Arms in French and Anglo-Norman Blazon* (University Park, Pa., 1973), 94, and Coss, *The Knight*, plate opposite 79. For the Scrope of Masham arms, see *S&G*, 2:104–32, 154–58.

60. *S&G*, 2:296 (for Henry); 321, 353, and 444 (for Geoffrey); and 170, 327, and 352 (for William).

61. Thomas Frederick Tout, *Chapters in the Administrative History of Mediaeval England* (Manchester, 1920–33), notes that Geoffrey, when well into middle age, gave up the life of chief justice coram rege for one of diplomacy and warfare (3:88).

62. Sumption, *Hundred Years War*, 127: "a rich Yorkshire parvenu, a lawyer of strong martial tastes." W. Mark Ormrod, *The Reign of Edward III: Crown and Political Society in England, 1327–1377* (New Haven, 1990), argues that "this was the age of the trimmer. Sir Geoffrey Scrope . . . is the classic example of the civil servant who preferred to reach an accommodation with each successive regime rather than lose income, perquisites and social standing" (81).

63. *S&G*, 2:291: Sir Robert Roos of Ingmanthorpe, who at 76 remembered back to "when he was of young and tender years." Scrope had been prominent in the expedition to Burenfoos and was reported as having had "40 lances under his banner" (366). This was presumably intended to lay to rest the stubborn ghost of his dubious social origins.

64. Also see *S&G*, 2:254–55, on Geoffrey's experience and prowess in tournaments. Geoffrey had been knighted at a tournament at Northampton in 1323. See Richard Barber and Juliet Barker, *Tournaments* (New York, 1989), 31.

65. *S&G*, 2:334; see also the discussion of William, "the ablest tourneyer of all their country" (335), one who "always tourneyed in the arms Azure, a bend Or" (350). On William in Italy in the 1370s, where he commanded Hungarian troops against Venice, see L. W. Vernon-Harcourt, *His Grace the Steward and the Trial of Peers* (London, 1907), 347–48. Various deponents waxed eloquent about tournaments as the school in which chivalry was shaped: see *S&G*, 2:366 ("schools for knowledge of arms").

66. S&G, 2:385. The same point is made by Sir William Aton, now aged 87, sixty-six years in arms (366, 349). That Geoffrey commanded forty lances was well attested, though whether this was a comfortable round number or a strong memory is another matter.

67. *S&G*, 2:313 (Sir John Warde, aged 46); for more of this, see 390 and 320.

68. *S&G*, 2:340. Also see 467, where the deponent said that Stephen had been in Lancaster's company and John in that of the duke of Gloucester.

69. The only references to the young Richard II are in the context of the Scottish expedition during which Scrope challenged Grosvenor's arms. On Richard's irenic foreign policy—probably at odds with that of most of Scrope's deponents—see Anthony Tuck, "Richard II and the Hundred Years War," in *Politics and Crisis in Fourteenth-Century England*, ed. John Taylor and Wendy R. Childs (Gloucester, 1990), 117–31; J. J. N. Palmer, *England, France, and Christendom* (London, 1972); and Hewitt, *The Organization of War*, 173–78, on the difficult adjustment from war to peace for old soldiers. That Richard's expedition to Scotland had been one of the largest of the century did little to win these old soldiers to his policy: see Saul, *Richard II*, 143–45.

70. Evocative references to the "old wars" and to a distinction between the old wars and the new wars (presumably a divide marked by the deaths of Edward III and the Black Prince) are a common theme. See, for example, *S&G*, 2:204, 285, 465, and 305.

71. Maurice Keen, *Nobles, Knights, and Men-at-Arms in the Middle Ages* (London, 1996), 177–81, contrasts the big battles that had involved the Scrope and Grosvenor deponents with the experiences of the men involved in the Grey-Hastings controversy ("small beer").

72. *S&G*, 2:147, 326. In the first of these depositions, the deponent was 66, armed for forty-six years; in the second, aged 70, and fifty years in arms.

73. *S&G*, 2:255, 320, 261 (Richmond, in his company at the king's chevauchée, "made last" in France). Also see 398, the expedition "in Caux with the lord of Lancaster."

74. Simon Walker, *The Lancastrian Affinity, 1361–1399* (Oxford, 1990), and Anthony Goodman, *John of Gaunt: The Exercise of Princely Power in Fourteenth-Century Europe* (New York, 1992), proffer detailed examinations of the man and his network, with references to the published volumes of Gaunt's registers. Comparing the names of Scrope's deponents against the men indexed by Walker shows the extent to which the whole Scrope team was an in-house crowd. Lancastrian old boys banded together on behalf of one of their own against the challenge of an outsider (the defendant).

75. *S&G*, 2:228, 377. Though Bolingbroke's adventures as a crusader and knight errant really peaked a few years later, they offer a well-documented look at Englishmen abroad: F. R. H. Du Boulay, "Henry of Derby's Expeditions to Prussia, 1390–91 and 1392," in *The Reign of Richard II: Essays in Honour of May McKisack*, ed. F. R. H. Du Boulay and Caroline M. Barron (London, 1971), 153–72; John L. Kirby, *Henry IV of England* (London, 1970), 28–40. For burial far from home, see Siegrid Düll, Anthony Luttrell, and Maurice Keen, "Faithful Unto Death: The Tomb Slab of Sir William Neville and Sir John Clanvowe, Constantinople, 1391," *Antiquaries Journal* 71 (1991): 147–90, especially 182, on the Scrope arms to be seen at Messembria on the Black Sea, and 183, on Sir Hugh Hastings, who left his escutcheon of arms "in all the important places where he stayed, and in particular in the *maison d'honneur* of the Hospitallers at Rhodes." Binski, *Medieval Death*, argues that Hastings's tomb at Elsing, Norfolk, "expresses a form of corporate identity, embedded in shared military honour and badges of allegiance" (104).

76. See *S&G*, 2:206, for the challenge of Carminow of Cornwall, which had been issued before the earl of Northampton (also see note 91, below). *S&G*, 2:449, offers a memory going back to "the battle of the Spaniards on the sea" (and with the "earl of Richmond, then duke of Lancaster"). On the career of Bohun (identified in one deposition as "cousin germain to the king") in the 1340s and 1350s, consult Michael Jones, "Edward III's Captains in Brittany," in *England in the Fourteenth Century: Proceedings of the 1985 Harlaxton Symposium*, ed. W. M. Ormrod (Woodbridge, 1986), 99–118.

77. At this time, the Suffolk title was held by the de la Poles and the family link was through Sir Richard's marriage to the earl's daughter.

78. *S&G*, 2:210, for the late Sir Ralph Neville; 336, for Sir Richard at Durham in company with Sir Henry Percy, grandfather of the earl of Northumberland; 285, for the company of the earl of Warwick at Espagnols-sur-Mer. The earl is further identified as "then [i.e., now] deceased."

79. To us, if not to warriors of the fourteenth century, the shadow of William the Marshal looms over the topic of upward mobility through military prowess (in tournaments even more than on battlefields). See Sidney Painter, *William Marshal: Knight-Errant, Baron, and Regent of England*

(Baltimore, 1933), and Georges Duby, *William the Marshal: The Flower of Chivalry,* trans. Richard Howard (New York, 1985).

80. On the war's contribution to xenophobia, see Richmond's "An English Mafia?" review essay in *Nottingham Mediaeval Studies.* John Barnie, *War in Medieval English Society: Social Values in the Hundred Years War, 1337–39* (Ithaca, 1974), argues that the political and popular poetry of the day displays a "virulent hatred of the French" (48).

81. On William the Marshal's deathbed reflections, see F. M. Powicke, *The Thirteenth Century* (Oxford, 1953), 16–17, and Hewitt, *The Organization of War,* 154–55.

82. Barnie, *War in Medieval English Society,* 25: most of the old captains were dead by the time Edward III left the scene. This would make the memories of the deponents even more pious about the old days and the great leaders. See Frame, *Political Development,* for a view of the court of Richard II as composed of men ranging from those "whose hopes of distinguishing themselves, and making a profit, as commanders, had been disappointed, to senior knights who recalled the glories of twenty or thirty years before" (177).

83. Keen, "Jurisdiction and Origins," 168, on the "sharpening sensitivities about such matters as the right to particular bearings." For the sustained life of these ideas, see Sidney Anglo, ed., *Chivalry in the Renaissance* (Woodbridge, 1990), especially the papers by K. Lippincott (49–76) and N. Llewellyn (145–60). For a duel to the death, see Bellamy, "Sir John de Annelsey," 94–105.

84. See Alexander and Binski, eds., *The Age of Chivalry,* on the power of "the constant refrain" that Scrope had borne these arms, in combat, in the king's wars (59).

85. *S&G,* 2:300–301. The father had only been 70—a realistic age for such activity. See Keen, *Chivalry,* 134, on a "retired" knight's compilation of what was in effect a book or roll of arms.

86. The theme of knights and archers of Cheshire, "who neither at that time nor afterward gainsaid the said arms of Sir William or Sir Henry Scrope," was played by a number of Scrope's partisans: "as to Sir Robert Grosvenor, the said Sir Ralph had no knowledge of him excepting once when he saw him at Chester" (*S&G,* 2:261). One deponent had never heard of Grosvenor, "notwithstanding that he [the deponent] held lands in the county of Chester and Lancaster" (303). Another held that the arms in the glass at Marrygg priory were always held to be those of Scrope, not of Grosvenor (353). But at least Grosvenor was known to be a gentleman (212, 228, 465).

87. See *S&G,* 2:423, for a deponent who spoke of "having been in those expeditions for 40 years."

88. Sir John Chydioke claimed to be 100 and upwards, first armed at Stanmow, "soon after the coronation of Edward the third" (*S&G,* 2:256). The chances are that the latter memory is a real one. This would take us back about fifty-five or sixty years, an appropriate span for a man who was perhaps 75 or 80 in the late 1380s.

89. *S&G,* 2:335: he asserted that "though he was an old man he was not so old as to be able to recollect who was the first ancestor of Sir Richard."

90. *S&G,* 2:343: this is John de Neulande, esquire. He stands as the only "enlisted man" in this whole entourage.

91. This is no less a personage than John of Gaunt, the greatest of the deponents and first to be called. But if his memories gave an inauspicious opening to the Scrope innings, they were either ignored or forgotten. On John's personal friendship with Sir Richard, see Goodman, *John of Gaunt,* 289–90. Robert Somerville, *History of the Duchy of Lancaster, 1: 1265–1603* (London, 1953), mentions Scrope as an executor of John's earlier will (67). Sidney Armitage Smith, *John of Gaunt* (London, 1904), notes that John of Gaunt "held the laws of chivalry more sacred than those of parliament"—which tells us about a number of these themes (411). The other knowledgeable reference to the Carminow challenge comes in the testimony of John Rither, a Yorkshire esquire (see *S&G,* 2:354, and see 206 and 324 for references to other challenges). Rither's deposition is the longest and most detailed of all (352–54). He either knew a great deal about the Scropes, or he was allowed to talk at some length, or the recording process of the court was inclined to capture a great deal of his testimony. Consult Arthur C. Fox-Davies, *A Complete Guide to Heraldry* (London, n.d.), on a man's right to *his own* arms (22) and on the Carminow decision (110). G. R. Gayre, "Scrope and Carminow," *Coat of Arms* 2 (1953): 177–78, mentions that the Carminow family eventually added a wrinkle

to their arms, choosing a label of three points Gules over the original Azure, a bend Or. Their motto ("Cala rak ger dha") supposedly meant "a straw for thy judgement."

92. *S&G*, 2:426–27. When old Thirwalle died (at "seven score and five"), he was "the oldest esquire of all the North," as we might well imagine. Further dates are given: he had been armed for sixty-nine years, dead now for forty-four. He had heard "from old knights and esquires" that Scrope was descended "from ancient gentry" (359). The deponent had heard his father say that he had heard from his father and other old knights—a string that runs pretty far back as oral memory usually is recounted (338). For Scrope partisans, upward mobility from the bench was a possible source of embarrassment, though all worked hard to cover it up. One deponent went so far as to say that Edward III had taken his chief justice with him on military expeditions "in places where the king challenged prerogative" (366).

93. Howard, *Chaucer*, 4: the concern is for Chaucer's age, and I think Howard is too judgmental or dismissive when he says, as noted above, that "the age is a formalized guess made by the royal clerk, who gave the deponents' ages in round numbers and got most of them wrong." He adds, "It is the one sample we have of Chaucer's native gift as a storyteller when reporting viva voce something that happened, or that he claimed happened" (392). Also see Derek Pearsall, *The Life of Geoffrey Chaucer* (Oxford, 1992), 202–4. Paul Strohm, *Theory and the Pre-Modern Text* (Minneapolis, 2001), 5–7, offers insights into the topographical and symbolic values of Chaucer's London stroll.

94. Martin M. Crow and Clair C. Olson, eds., *Chaucer Life Records* (Austin, 1966), 370–71. Crow and Olson edit the text directly from chancery documents, not from Nichols's edition (370–74); like Howard (93), they are mainly interested in the reliability of Chaucer's statement about his age. Their notes and discussion offer a useful guide to the controversy itself.

95. On the beginnings of the Grosvenor rise, see Cust, ed., *Papers of Sir Richard Grosvenor*, which includes the baronet's commission, an illuminated manuscript of the proceedings "to demonstrate the family's standing in the shire and support the claim to their ancient coat of arms" (xii).

CHAPTER 3

1. Michael K. Jones and Malcolm Underwood, *The King's Mother: Lady Margaret Beaufort, Countess of Richmond and Derby* (Cambridge, 1992); Christine Weightman, *Margaret of York, Duchess of Burgundy, 1446–1503* (Stroud, 1989). Though there are older studies, such as E. M. G. Routh, *Lady Margaret: A Memoir* (Cambridge, 1924), it is hard to go much beyond these recent treatments of outstanding women in the quest for biography.

2. Of John's eleven letters to Margaret, eight are to her alone; two are to Margaret, John Daubeney, and Richard Calle together; one is addressed to the threesome of Margaret, James Gresham, and Richard Calle.

3. For a caveat, see Helen M. Jewell, *Women in Medieval England* (Manchester, 1996): women like Margaret and Isabella de Fortibus "have become perhaps too prominently known, being credited with more typicality than can be proven" (129; also see 132). Peter Coss argues for Margaret's typicality in *The Lady in Medieval England, 1000–1500* (Stroud, 1998), 1–3.

4. Agnes's letter to William (Davis, ed., *Paston Letters and Papers*, *1*, 13) tells him that the couple have met and that a match looks likely and promises well. The letter is probably dated 20 April 1440, and Agnes speaks of her future daughter-in-law as a valuable commodity: "þe brynggyn hoom of þe gentylwomman þat ye wetyn of from Redham." (References to the Paston Letters hereafter will appear as *PL*, followed by the volume and letter number.) Colin Richmond says the old folks must have heaved a sigh of relief when this advantageous marriage was safely in the bag: see his *Paston Family, First Phase*, 120–24. Margaret will refer to Redham in her will, almost forty years later, as her fondly remembered birthplace. On the family, in addition to the work of Richmond, see Francis Worship, "The Genealogy of the Paston Family," *Norfolk Archaeology* 4 (1855): 1–55; Edgar C. Robbins, *William Paston, Justice, Founder of the Paston Family (1378–1444)* (Norwich, 1932).

5. Davis's decision to aggregate each family member's letters, rather than to run them in an overarching chronological arrangement, helps frame each writer and highlights patterns in his or her

epistolary practice and style. The trade-off is that Davis's method makes it difficult to follow the intertwining of family business (of less interest, anyway, for my purposes).

6. See Cherewatuk and Wiethaus, eds., *Dear Sister,* editors' introduction and 1–19; also see Finke, *Women's Writings,* 111–17, for a summary of medieval women's letter writing.

7. Watt, "'No Writing for Writing's Sake.'" Watt's title comes from Virginia Woolf's essay "The Pastons and Chaucer" in *The Common Reader* (London, 1979), 37.

8. On Margaret's disagreement with the hard line John I was taking regarding the Fastolf lands and his legal assaults on his opponents in the last year or so of his life, see Virgoe, *Private Life,* 140–47.

9. *Cely Letters,* ed. Hanham, 55, letter 59. I assume the "Joyce" of letters 120, 126, and 142 to be a man. Of ninety-three Cely family letters and documents, letters to women appear on 67, 75, 114, and 184. In the Armburgh papers, three letters are by women (and two more are from "Robert or Joan"). Letter 92 is both by and to a woman.

10. This is out of 349 letters. The problem of these tallies is highlighted by letter 192, endorsed, "to his right reuerent & worshipful master Sir Robt Plumpton knight or my lady his wyfe or ayre William or my mystress or Sir Richard his chaplain or any of you." For more on Agnes Plumpton, see Joan Kirby, "Women in the Plumpton Correspondence," 221–22.

11. See Kingsford's *Stonor Letters,* ed. and intro. Carpenter, for more examples of mixed authorship or attribution. Letter 75 is a joint letter from Thomas Hampden and his wife. Letter 157 is an arbitration between William Stonor and his mother.

12. In the first half of the sixteenth century, Isabel Plumpton received nine letters, but over a long span—from June 1519 (letter 217) to February 1552 (letter 251).

13. Document 227 actually is a bill for wax and tapers running from February 1477 to September 1478 and totaling xxj s. vj d.

14. Margaret's early letters are harder to date than many of the later ones. Of *PL,* I, 124 (her first letter), Davis says "this letter cannot be exactly dated." There are many editorial phrases like "the date is not quite clear" (*PL,* I, 143) or "the approximate date may be deduced" (*PL,* I, 130), or "the date is very doubtful" (*PL,* I, 145). Davis is at pains to indicate where he agrees with Gairdner's dating (*PL,* I, 146, 187, 197, and so on) or with Fenn's (*PL,* I, 156, 158)—perhaps contrary to Gairdner—or where he goes against both his predecessors (*PL,* I, 148, 176). To spot a misattribution or misdating earns editorial kudos (e.g., *PL,* I, 153). Also see *PL,* I, 338, where he sides with Fenn against Gairdner in a letter of John III. For a recent study that argues for some redating, see Marjorie A. Rowling, "New Evidence on the Disseisin of the Pastons from the Norfolk Manor of Gresham, 1448–1451," *Norfolk Archaeology* 40, no. 3 (1989): 302–8.

15. On Margaret's changing voice, see H. S. Bennett, *The Pastons and Their England.* (In the index, under "Paston, Margaret," Bennett has an entry for "treatment of children.")

16. Norman Davis, in his World's Classics version of the letters, speaks of her reliance on scribes, "from which it seems likely that she could not write, or at any rate, did not like it" (xxv). The idea that the women actually penned their letters is effectively laid to rest in V. M. O'Mara, "Female Scribal Ability and Scribal Activity in Late Medieval England: The Evidence," *Leeds Studies in English,* n.s., 27 (1996): 87–130; the case for women as the writers can be found in Josephine Koster Tarvers, "In a Woman's Hand? The Question of Medieval Women's Holograph Letters," *Postscript: Publications of the Philological Association of the Carolinas* 13 (1998): 89–100 (thanks to one of my readers, who pointed me toward this article). On some of Margaret's individual usages, see Davis, "The Language of the Pastons," especially 120–21, and "Margaret Paston's Uses of 'Do,'" *Neuphilologische Mitteilungen* 73 (1972): 55–62. We generally accept the direction of John II to John III (*PL,* I, 248) as evidence that Margaret could read: "I praye yow schewe ore rede to my moodre suche thyngez as ye thynke is fore here to knowe." On fifteenth-century scribal practices in a more general context, see A. I. Doyle, "The Work of a Late-Fifteenth-Century English Scribe, William Ebesham," *Bulletin of the John Rylands Library* 39 (1956–57): 298–325.

17. See *PL,* I:lxxv–lxxix, for biographical snippets on the men whose hands can be identified, with some specific ascriptions.

18. *PL,* I, 58 (a letter of 12 July 1461). Margaret answered on 15 July, and the letter was in Daubeney's hand (*PL,* I, 161).

19. For letters in the hand of both John I and Gloys, see *PL,* 1, 51, 74, and 80; for John I and an unknown hand, *PL,* 1, 58; by John III, writing for his father and then with corrections entered by John himself, *PL,* 1, 57 (from 1460); by Pampyng and then completed by John I himself, *PL,* 1, 59; by Pampyng with John I adding the address, *PL,* 1, 76; and by William of Worcester with John I's additions, *PL,* 1, 53.

20. For the letter in five different hands, see *PL,* 1, 63: we have John III, Gresham, Pampyng, John I, and an unidentified clerk, all on a draft of a petition to the sheriff. For John I's autograph, *PL,* 1, 37, 44; *PL,* 1, 73, is an autograph letter to Margaret, Daubeney, and Calle from June 1465.

21. Some of the petitions and legal papers were written by familiar figures rather than by unknown or hired scribal hands. Gloys wrote a petition to chancery (*PL,* 1, 41); Pampyng drafted a petition (*PL,* 1, 60).

22. *PL,* 1, 265, an inventory of papers; *PL,* 1, 314, a memorandum; *PL,* 1, 316, a book inventory.

23. *PL,* 1, 376, a memorandum stating terms of a marriage negotiation; *PL,* 1, 377, a memorandum; *PL,* 1, 382, some accounts; *PL,* 1, 385, "a memoir of complaints against William Paston II." About this last document, Davis says that the paper bore "marks of folding but not soiled by carrying."

24. See *PL,* 1, 152, from around September 1459 (and Davis says of *PL,* 1, 255, "the writing, though irregular and awkward, is reasonably competent and gives some evidence of practice"). *PL,* 1, 154 is dated 21 October 1460, and John III both wrote and addressed the letter.

25. *PL,* 1, 164. Later the sons would take over the running quarrel with (uncle) William II (as in *PL,* 1, 385). Colin F. Richmond, *The Paston Family in the Fifteenth Century: Endings* (Manchester, 2000), offers a more sympathetic view of William's position in this quarrel than we get when we approach it from the John I–Margaret–John II and John III perspective.

26. John I had failed to come home for Christmas.

27. For Edmund as a scribe for Margaret, see the following letters. *PL,* 1, 203, to John II, was dated September 1469. It was a long letter of 81 lines (as printed by Davis, as are all lengths given below) with a note in an unidentified hand. *PL,* 1, 205, also to John II, and also from September 1469, was 63 lines, with the address in a more formal hand, though perhaps Edmund's as well. *PL,* 1, 211, to John II in November 1471, was 26 lines, and the hand like that of Edmund's own letters (see *PL,* 1, 394, written to John III in that same month). *PL,* 1, 212, also from November 1471, was addressed to John III and was 55 lines long. Edmund wrote the letter and the address (as he did for *PL,* 1, 216, to John II in June 1472, running to 41 lines). According to O'Mara, the scribe was "regarded as an almost invisible presence—a sort of human typewriter" ("Female Scribal Ability," 117).

28. Respectively, *PL,* 1, 203: Calle writes (lines 39–40), "Thes leud worddys gereue me and here grandam as myche as alle þe remnauwnte." In *PL,* 1, 205, amid lots of general advice, see lines 46ff.: "to gader there-of þat may be had in haste, and also of Ser John Fastolffys lyuelod þt may be gadyrd in pesybyle wyse," whereas Calle "wulle no more gadyre yt but yf ye comaund hym" (as she wrote in September, 1469). *PL,* 1, 211, to John III, expresses her distress at John II in November 1471: "At þe reuerens of God, avyse hym yet to be ware of hys expencys and gydyng, þat yt be no schame to vus alle." This letter had also carried Margaret's semi-formulaic greeting: "I merevel þat ye send me no answere ageyn of þe letter þat I send yow."

29. On Calle as a scribe, see *PL,* 1:lxxv; he wrote six letters in whole or in part for Margaret and one for Margery.

30. See Norman Davis, "The Text of Margaret Paston's Letters," *Medium Aevum* 18 (1949): 12–28, and his "Scribal Problem in the Paston Letters," *English and Germanic Studies* 4 (1951–52): 31–64.

31. See Swabey, *Medieval Gentlewoman,* especially 97–114, on the likelihood that dinner and household guests of status could well have written letters for their hostess.

32. *PL,* 1, 124, 125, 126, and 127, written between 1441 and July 1444.

33. *PL,* 1, 226, 227, and 228 (between June 1477 and May 1475), and the draft of the will (*PL,* 1, 230, from February 1482).

34. Unknown (or unidentified) scribal hands who wrote for others besides Margaret are given by Davis in *PL,* 1:lxxviii–lxxix. Five of twelve such men wrote for Margaret and another Paston.

35. The whole letter, with a one-line postscript ("Yf it plese yow to send aney thyng by the berer herof, he is trusty jnough") is only eighteen or nineteen lines, one of the shortest of all. *PL,* 1, 195, is

an inventory of stolen goods: the first leaf was penned by Wykes, the second by Calle, and then it was finished by "an unidentified unskilled hand." *PL*, I, 201: Gloys and Edmund to John III; *PL*, I, 169: John III, with a postscript by Daubeney and Playter; *PL*, I, 153: a mix of Daubeney and an unidentified hand.

36. *PL*, I, 209 (draft version B), Margaret to John III, 5 November 1471: "I warn yw kepe þis letter close and lese yt not, rather brenyt."

37. I discuss variations on the formula below.

38. These are random examples; messengers are dealt with below.

39. H. S. Bennett, *The Pastons and Their England*. (The heading at the top of 115 is "The Labour of Letter Writing.")

40. The physical size of the paper, probably as trimmed after the letter had been written, varies a great deal—as do the lengths of the letters. Some examples, again just chosen at random: *PL*, I, 125: 31 lines, 7 1/2 inches x 7 inches; I, 128: 88 lines, 11 5/8 x 11; I, 129: 71 lines, 11 3/8 x 11; I, 131: 118 lines, 11 1/2 x 16 1/2; I, 143: 25 lines, 8 1/2 x 7 1/2; I, 158: 20 lines, 11 3/4 x 5 1/4; I, 207 (to John II): 22 lines, 11 5/8 x 4. Margaret's will is 228 lines (in print) and the roll measures 12 inches by 66 inches. Few of the letters have much by way of margin or unused space, at least as they were trimmed for their final destination.

41. See Davis, "The Language of the Pastons," for some of Margaret's East Anglianisms: "for the most part, the language (of Agnes and Margaret) is manifestly the speech of the time, plain and direct, only organized and sometimes heightened a little for the written page" (137; see also 134). Also see Davis, "Styles in English Prose," on "the fundamental importance of the spoken word in the creation and development of clear, serviceable prose" (181).

42. Though the news might be incorrect, as when John Rouse misinformed John I in September or October 1462 about French raiders and a battle at sea (*PL*, II, 676).

43. The Paston valentine, in reality, is a letter from Margery Brews to John III, dated February 1477: "Vn-to my ryght welbelouyd Voluntyn . . . be þis bill delyuered, etc." In *The Armburgh Papers* there is a long love poem, or series of poems, appearing without explanation or context in the manuscript and published by Carpenter (155–68).

44. H. S. Bennett, *The Pastons and Their England*, 72–82. When Bennett wrote this, there was virtually no social or family history for the fifteenth century. The Pastons had to stand without the protective coloring of familiarity, context, or comparison.

45. As well as material cited above for family letters, see Chartier, Boureau, and Dauphin, *Correspondence*.

46. Norman Davis, "The Litera Troili and English Letters," *Review of English Studies* n.s., 16 (1964): 233–44.

47. Ibid., 240–41.

48. That five of John I's letters are to multiple recipients indicates that many of them are perhaps better read as memoranda of instruction than as personal communications. *PL*, I, 66 is to Pampyng, Calle, and Wykes; *PL*, I, 67 is a petition to Robert Welles et al.; *PL*, I, 72 and 73 are to Margaret, Calle, and Daubeney; *PL*, I, 75 is to Margaret, Gresham, and Calle.

49. This estimate is based on a tally of several dozen of the letters in manuscript. The wayward styles of composition—across, at a slant, into odd corners, and so on—reinforce the idea that composition, even for a practiced hand, had an element of improvisation.

50. The next-best letters from a woman are from Elizabeth Stonor, and she too ran to good length when she wrote. For her eight letters between 18 August 1476 and 7 March 1477 (168, 169, 170, 172, 173, 175, 176, and 180, respectively, as published): 13 lines and a postscript of 5 lines, 40 lines, 21 lines and 2 more in a postscript, 63 lines, 27 lines, 28 lines, 37 lines, and 26 lines. These compare well with the men's letters in the Stonor collection.

51. In the first case, the external address is exactly the same as the internal salutation. In a letter of May 1465—when the boys were presumably away from home and about their business—Margaret addressed a letter to John I as "my ryght wyrshypfull mayster John Paston the oldest be þis delyvered in haste" (*PL*, I, 181).

52. A letter to John II from January 1475 carried the conventional address but closed with "Ao xiiijo" for the fourteenth year of Edward IV, which was an unusual style for Margaret.

53. Letters without the customary "in hast" tag include *PL*, I, 171, to John I; *PL*, I, 186, 218, and 219, to John III; and *PL*, I, 201, to John II.

54. Was this helpful address an indication that she still worried about the details of sending a letter, as we would assume that it was easier to run John to ground at Peterhouse than in London?

55. This was a letter of 29 October 1460, written in John III's young hand. Margaret says that she is sending a canvas bag with as many of Christopher Hanson's accounts as she and John II have been able to find.

56. John II and John III sometimes used (or needed) more complex addresses. *PL*, I, 290, John II to John III, is addressed "to hys brother John Paston, ore to hys oncle William Paston in Werwykk Lane, ore to Edmond Paston at þe George at Powlys Wharffe: to delyuer to any of these." *PL*, I, 312: "to John Paston, esquyere, bc thys lettre delyueryd, ore to my mestresse hys wyffe, at Norwych to delyuer to hym." *PL*, I, 375 (John III to John II): "Thy bylle be delyuerd to Thomasgrene, good-man of þe George by Powlys Wharffe, or to hys wyff, to send to Syr John Paston wherso evere he be, at Caleys, London, or other placys." The brothers also used a touch of French. *PL*, I, 267: "a Jehan Paston, esquiere, soit doné." *PL*, I, 273: "A soun treschere et ben amé freere, John de Paston, esquiere." *PL*, I, 355: "a monser John Paston, cheualler." I suspect that the use of French was a private joke between the children of difficult parents.

57. *PL*, I, 139, from 1451; the more expansive salutation is from her first, and earliest, letter to John (*PL*, I, 124, addressed to "my worshepfull husbond").

58. *PL*, I, 198; the second is when she was taking him to task for having left John III on his own during the siege at Caister.

59. Also, *PL*, I, 224, where it is "Cristes blissyng." This seems more theologically charged than the general "godes blissyng and myn" (*PL*, I, 225), but this may be too much liberty for a curt and standard phrase.

60. Also see *PL*, I, 274, where "Weell belovyd brother" gives way to "best belovyd brother."

61. *PL*, I, 375: "Ryght worchepfull syr and my most good and kynde brodyr, in as humbyll wyse as I can I recomand me to yow."

62. Also, *PL*, I, 347: "Most worchefull and my ryght specyall good modyr, as humbylly as I can I recomand me on-to yow, besechyng yow of youyr blyssyng."

63. The *Oxford English Dictionary* gives 1603 as the earliest usage of "motherhood," while the *Shorter OED* goes back to 1473—presumably a Paston usage (but not specified). "Mothership," however, is a mystery, or a novel contribution.

64. As in *The Armburgh Papers*, ed. Carpenter, 119–20. The salutation is "My dere frendis, I gret you wele," but Richard Armburgh goes on, some lines later, to warn the recipients that "I hope to God with short tyme I shal, that yt shal lye in my power to undo you at the utmust or fore hyndre you."

65. *Romeo and Juliet* offers insight into the identification of servants, even those of low status, with *their* house—its liveries and its feuds.

66. Swabey, *Medieval Gentlewoman;* Ward, *English Noblewomen;* Mertes, *English Noble Household;* Margaret Wade Labarge, *A Baronial Household of the Thirteenth Century* (New York, 1965).

67. *PL*, I, 131, a long letter, with numerous phrases like "I conseyvd wele be hem þat þey were wery of þat" and "I seyd to him" and "I rehersyd to hem" and "I here seyn þat."

68. Margaret goes on to a revealing, "As wee spede owr materys we chall sende yow answerys of them as hastely as we may."

69. There is a gap in the manuscript after "alle her kyn were," and Davis estimates that about a dozen characters are lost. On Margaret's prose in this vivid letter, Janel M. Mueller, *The Native Tongue and the Word: Developments in English Prose Style, 1380–1580* (Chicago, 1984), 90–94, notes that such news would "prompt a long distance call" today—an apt observation and one that reminds us of the rate of change in communications since Mueller wrote this in 1984, before e-mail had become our stock-in-trade.

70. Margaret goes on to tell John that there was "meche grete langage þat xall ben told yw qhen ye kom hom." Loneliness seems to come through here, perhaps with a touch of Scheherazade's narrative technique.

71. See Davis, "The Language of the Pastons," on pronunciation as we are guided by orthographic variations.

72. Also see *PL,* I, 131, especially lines 64–85; *PL,* I, 135, lines 11–23; and *PL,* I, 136, lines 11–22.

73. Though before this closing, at the end of the text, she had said, "I prey you þat ye be not strange of wryting of lettyrs to me betwix þis and þat ye come hom; if I myght I wold haue euery day on from yow."

74. *PL,* I, 160: "God for hys merci send vs a good world, and send yow helthe in body and sowle and good speed in all your maters."

75. She also reminds him to keep in touch with Agnes: "Your grandam wold fayne her sum tydyngs from yow. It were welle do þat ye sent a letter to hyr howe ye do as astely as ye may." On these relationships, see my "Looking for Grandmother: The Pastons and Their Counterparts in Late Medieval England," in *Medieval Mothering,* ed. John Carmi Parsons and Bonnie Wheeler, 259–77 (New York, 1996).

76. I treat the issue of dating on the assumption that Margaret herself was responsible for this detail and that the style of dating reflected her choice or preference. Needless to say, this is conjecture. Both the date's place in the letter (i.e., as part of the text, though toward the end, in contrast to the extra-textual address or the postscript) and the evidence of a sustained personal style that sets Margaret apart from many other letter writers argue for her agency in this matter.

77. There are also references in dating clauses to St. Thomas the Apostle.

78. In a number of cases there is an internal reference, somewhere in Margaret's letter, to the hours of the day: "and on the sam day at evynsong tyme" (*PL,* I, 182); the villains came to do their damage "erly in the mornyng an oure by-fore the sonne rose" (*PL,* I, 184); men came by night and were not recognized "tylle the Thevsday at x of þe cloke" (*PL,* I, 192); and, regarding the siege of Hellesdon, "the Duke came to Norwich on Tuesday at x of clok" (*PL,* I, 194).

79. After the date/time clause, she adds thanks to Pampyng for help with fresh horses: "I schall aquyt them a-nothyr day and I maye."

80. Davis's headnotes for each letter indicate the presence of seals, though they mostly exist in fragments. Interesting fragments can be found. *PL,* I, 132, for instance, has stitch holes and wax traces; *PL,* I, 137 has wax, string, and a paper seal.

81. See *PL,* I, 153 and 193, as examples of unsigned letters.

82. Frances and Joseph Gies suggested that the "gronyng" wife was an affectionate and pregnant one (A Medieval Family, 71). Neither Gairdner nor Davis (let alone Fenn) refers to such intimate matters as the likely reason for Margaret's odd comment.

83. The postscript of *PL,* I, 141 is "I pray yow trost nott to þe sheryve for no fayre langage."

84. *PL,* I, 180: "I thynk ryght long to hyre tydyngs tyll I haue tydyngys from you."

85. The whole postscript is on the dorse; either the paper had been trimmed in advance or upon completion of the main text of the letter. The latter practice was the one Davis thought the norm. The surviving manuscript is 11 3/8 x 11 inches, for fifty lines on recto and twenty-one more on the dorse. The hand in this case is rather sprawling.

86. Also of interest is *PL,* I, 187, a letter to John II, with a postscript of only five printed lines, but consisting of two separate and unrelated items. The whole affair is in an unidentified hand. The first postscript, two lines squeezed onto the recto, tells of young Heydon, while that on the dorse (of three lines) carries instructions for John II's dealings with Calle.

87. *PL,* I, 155; there is more in this vein, amid the tangle of affairs around the time of Fastolf's death, and this letter was accompanied by a canvas bag full of accounts.

88. Also see *PL,* I, 137: to be doubly sure, "Gloys telleth me þat he hath sent yow word of Heydonys hors, and of oþer thyngys more, of whiche I was purposid to a sent yow word of."

89. Davis refers to the second letter as, in effect, a separate postscript to the first.

90. P. C. Pearsons, "The Paston Letters: Carriage of Mail in the Fifteenth Century," *London Philatelist* (July–August 1990): 178–83; (September 1990): 192–95; (October–November 1990): 232–37; (December 1990): 276–79. I owe this reference to a Colin Richmond footnote and then to the diligence of the InterLibrary Loan services and librarians of SUNY at Stony Brook.

91. The reference in the postscript indicates that the courier had been lined up before the letter had been sealed, but probably only just before.

92. This letter (*PL*, I, 201) was to John II—probably not Margaret's idea of the most trustworthy recipient for the diamond nowche, but that was a larger question than simply one of safe delivery.

93. She was pushing John II to move with dispatch and she naturally wanted to know if he was following her counsel, so we must assume that "þe next man" was the best she could ask for.

94. As well as the articles by Pearsons cited earlier, see Colin F. Richmond, "Hand and Mouth: Information Gathering and Use in England in the Later Middle Ages," *Journal of Historical Sociology* I (1988): 233–52; Willard, "Dating and Delivery," 1–11; Mary C. Hill, *The King's Messengers, 1199–1377* (London, 1961), especially 104–9; C. A. J. Armstrong, "Some Examples of the Distribution and Speed of News at the Time of the Wars of the Roses," in *Studies in Medieval History Presented to F. M. Powicke*, ed. R. W. Hunt, W. A. Pantin, and R. W. Southern (Oxford, 1948), 429–54.

95. H. S. Bennett, *The Pastons and Their England*, 55–58, has a reference to the Cely letters.

96. The tally has an element of flexibility, as many of John's letters were petitions to men in office or to his social/political betters, and some of the letters—in both directions—were to multiple recipients. But for our comparative purposes, seventy-nine is a tolerable working number.

97. When the women of the Stonors or Plumptons did write, they too operated within a circumscribed circle of correspondents.

98. Davis says, regarding how one qualified for inclusion in his index, "most names of persons and places which occur more than once" (*PL*, II:619). Gairdner was more inclusive in his multivolume editions, though he too seems to have either ignored or missed some of those mentioned but once.

99. He first appears in Margaret's letters in *PL*, I, 154 (21 October 1460), and he lasted until a final mention in *PL*, I, 224 (23 May 1475). He wrote fourteen letters to John I, from *PL*, I, 519 (May 1455) to *PL*, I, 690 (July 1465); three to Margaret between July 1461 and 1473 (*PL*, I, 717, 728, 279); six to John II between October 1461 and July 1469, and one to Margery in 1469.

100. John (of) Damme, recorder of Norwich: John I wrote to him in 1444 but not afterward.

101. His death at the siege of Caister ended his letter-writing activities. He wrote one letter to John I in May 1455 (*PL*, II, 519), one to Margaret from September 1465 (*PL*, II, 722), and one to John II in August 1467 (*PL*, II, 748).

102. The mysteries abound. We have Sym, who carried "xxty li" to London and who must have been a trusted figure (*PL*, I, 224); "old Tauerham," who may have been Roger Taverham, a chaplain (*PL*, I, 165), and—in the same letter—"Jane Gaynys mater" and "the gold-smyth" who would serve as the drop-off contact for a letter to John I.

103. She even had to put up with teasing from her father-in-law about her condition and her interest in a change of costume. William I—a man whose sense of humor comes through hardly at all—must have been elated at the prospect of his first grandchild (John II-to-be).

104. Early in the marriage, when John was recovering from the illness that caused his mother and his wife such uneasiness, Margaret had stuck to her guns: "wochesaffe to remember my gyrdyl" (*PL*, I, 126).

105. In a follow-up letter, Margaret seconded her request and added that "she hath nede þer-of."

106. See Davis, ed., *PL*, I:lxii–lxiii. Anne did not marry Yelverton until 1477, and there seems to have been some earlier tie to John Pampyng—an alliance to send chills down the collective family back after the marriage of Margery and Calle.

107. *PL*, I, 135, 156. John I wanted murrey or "blwe" or "good russettys vndernethe iij s. the yerde" for his "leveryes."

108. *PL*, I, 130; *PL*, I, 149: "I send yow an excample" as a guide regarding color. This request is uncharacteristically near the top of a short letter of 14 November 1453.

109. See, among numerous studies, Ward, *English Noblewomen*, 50–69.

110. Other than *PL*, I, 149, the requests are almost always in the letter's tail.

111. Also in *PL*, I, 151: if they have another son, Margaret urges that he be named Harry, "in remembranc of your brother Harry." She recovers from this touch of intimacy or sentimentality and goes on to place her order for "datys and synamum."

112. On the London suburbs and consumerism (shopping), consult Martha Carlin, *Medieval Southwark* (London, 1996), and Gervase Rosser, *Medieval Westminster, 1200–1540* (Oxford, 1989), though Rosser shows less interest than Carlin in economic life. Also see various papers in *The Medieval Town: A Reader in English Urban History, 1200–1540*, ed. Richard Holt and Gervase Rosser (London, 1990).

113. *PL*, I, 215: she sent 5s. by the bearer for a sugar loaf, dates, and almonds, and she assured John II "if ye be ware of any more money whan ye come home I shal pait you ageyn." In *PL*, I, 212, Margaret asked for a "rowndlet of wyne" but was afraid to send money, "there be so many theves stereng." In justification of her nervousness, she points out that John Loveday's man had recently been robbed "in-to hys schyrte."

114. They were reestablishing housekeeping after the loss of Caister, and she did not want to lay in more than was needed, "till we be suerrere þer-of" about where they would be staying.

115. He was also to look for a book with "chardeqweyns," which she needed in the morning, because "the eyeres be not holsom." This letter was written in 1452, and morning sickness, rather than the plague or evil vapors, might have been the issue.

116. This letter was from 13 November 1463; it was best to be prepared, as winter could arrive early across the bleak East Anglian landscape.

117. See *PL*, I, 56 (28 July 1460) for an exception: John told Margaret of a death ("your vnkyll John Berney is deed, whoos soule God haue mercy").

118. If he was interested, he was to contact "my cosyn William, here son"—and to do so ASAP.

119. *PL*, I, 177, 190. In *PL*, I, 177, it was probably news that she had just learned, as it was contained in a four-line postscript.

120. The midwife, Elysabet Pevral, "hath leye seke xv or xvj wekys of þe seyetyke."

121. *PL*, I, 200 (to Gloys) and 221 (to John II). In the first letter, Margaret wonders if Berney has made his will: "yeue it be not doo, and to doo well to my cosyn his wiff, and else it were peté." This lay injunction supports ecclesiastical counsels about the need to make a will, though one may speculate on the Paston motives.

122. It is part of the closing, where we would expect to encounter it.

123. There are but few references to age in the letters. In *PL*, I, 174, a potential suitor thought their daughter "a goodly yong woman." The potential bridegroom was "Ser John Cley son that is chamberleyn wyth my lady of York; and he ys of age of xviij yer old."

124. Is this ironic? Paston humor might be worth a separate, if very short, paper.

125. Of interest is this letter's biblical allusion (known, presumably, from the drama, or from sermons, or perhaps from personal reading, though this last alternative may be the least likely).

126. In the same letter, when giving Gloys advice about a young man considering the priesthood while in his early 20s, she told Gloys to convey her warning against an intemperate career choice: "I will loue hym bettere to be a good seculare man þan to be a lewit prest."

127. It is hard to imagine what she had not spoken of!

128. See Gies and Gies, *A Medieval Family*, 325–27, for Margaret's will; also see H. S. Bennett, *The Pastons and Their England*, 202–4. In Davis (*PL*, 1:382–89, letter 230), the will is printed from British Library Additional Charter 17253, with marginal notes in the hand of John III.

129. All four sets of "scochens" carried Mautby arms in some fashion, while the epitaph on the tomb identified Margaret as wife of John Paston and "daughter *and heire* of John Mawteby" (emphasis added).

130. The books she left the church ("a compleet legende in oon book and an antiphoner in an other book") are about the only ones whose ownership she ever claimed, though the Paston household clearly contained a number of books. See *PL*, I, 316, for John II's inventory, which is our main source of information about family books (though whether they were "his" books, or family ones, is unclear). The books are presented in categories in H. S. Bennett, *The Pastons and Their England*, 261–62.

131. Some of these churches were in southern and eastern Norfolk, in the Mautby countryside whence she had come, while those to the north and west were Paston holdings. The map in Davis's edition (*PL*, 1:671) is helpful in tracking the bequests.

132. There were lesser but comparable gifts for Yarmouth (as with the four orders of friars): three pence per Yarmouth leper at the North gate, and two pence for the "forgoer" there. It is almost as though there were a formula that guided the Norfolk gentry around the region, in more general terms, and then let them zero in on their own favorites. It makes sense to think that wealthy widows discussed the disposition of their estates with their chaplains and friends, as well as with the family and its lawyers.

133. The other men were Thomas Drentall, clerk, Simon Gerard, and Walter Wymyngton. Of these, only Gerard is mentioned elsewhere in the letters. I take this as another indication of how, late in life, Margaret was separating *her* concerns from those she had covered in the letters for almost forty years.

BIBLIOGRAPHY

Acheson, Eric. *A Gentry Community: Leicestershire in the Fifteenth Century, c. 1422–c. 1485.* Cambridge, 1992.

Ahlgren, Gillian T. W. "Visions and Rhetorical Strategy in the Letters of Hildegard of Bingen." In *Dear Sister: Medieval Women and the Epistolary Genre,* edited by Karen Cherewatuk and Ulrike Wiethaus, 46–63. Philadelphia, 1993.

Alexander, Jonathan J. G., and Paul Binski, eds. *Age of Chivalry: Art in Plantagenet England, 1200–1400.* London, 1987.

Almond, Richard. "Medieval Hunting: Ruling Classes and Commonalty." *Headstart: Medieval History* 3 (1991–93): 147–55.

Althoff, Gerd. "Satisfaction: Peculiarities of the Amicable Settlement of Conflicts in the Middle Ages." In *Ordering Medieval Society: Perspectives on Intellectual and Practical Modes of Shaping Social Relations,* edited by Bernhard Jussen and translated by Pamela Selwyn, 270–84. Philadelphia, 2001.

Altman, Janet G. *Epistolarity: Approaches to a Form.* Columbus, 1982.

Anglo, Sidney, ed. *Chivalry in the Renaissance.* Woodbridge, 1990.

Ariès, Philippe. *The Hour of Our Death.* Translated by Helen Weaver. New York, 1981.

Armstrong, C. A. J. "Some Examples of the Distribution and Speed of News at the Time of the Wars of the Roses." In *Studies in Medieval History Presented to F. M. Powicke,* edited by R. W. Hunt, W. A. Pantin, and R. W. Southern, 429–54. Oxford, 1948.

Askins, William. "The Brothers Orléans and Their Keepers." In *Charles d'Orléans in England (1415–1440),* edited by Mary-Jo Arn, 27–46. Cambridge, 2000.

Aston, Margaret. "Death." In *Fifteenth-Century Attitudes: Perceptions of Society in Late Medieval England,* edited by Rosemary Horrox, 202–28. Cambridge, 1994.

Baildon, W. Paley, and J. W. Clay, eds. *Inquisitions Post Mortem Relating to Yorkshire, of the Reigns of Henry IV and Henry V.* Yorkshire Archaeological Society Record Series, vol. 59. N.p., 1918.

Bainbridge, Virginia R. *Gilds in the Medieval Countryside: Social and Religious Change in Cambridgeshire, c. 1350–1558.* Woodbridge, 1996.

Baird, Joseph L., and Radd K. Ehrman, eds. and trans. *The Letters of Hildegard of Bingen.* 2 vols. New York, 1994–98.

Barber, Richard, ed. *The Pastons: A Family in the Wars of the Roses.* London, 1981.

Barber, Richard, and Juliet Barker. *Tournaments.* New York, 1989.

Barlow, Frank, ed. *The Letters of Arnulf of Lisieux.* Camden Society, 3d ser., vol. 61. London, 1939.

Barnie, John. *War in Medieval English Society: Social Values in the Hundred Years War, 1337–99.* Ithaca, 1974.

Barron, Caroline M., and Anne F. Sutton, eds. *Medieval London Widows, 1300–1500.* London, 1994.

Bedell, John. "Memory and Proof of Age in England, 1272–1327." *Past and Present* 162 (February 1999): 3–27.
Bellamy, John. "Sir John de Annelsey and the Chandos Inheritance." *Nottingham Mediaeval Studies* 10 (1960): 94–105.
———. *Crime and Public Order in England in the Late Middle Ages*. London, 1973.
Bennett, H. S. *The Pastons and Their England*. Cambridge, 1922.
Bennett, Josephine W. "The Mediaeval Loveday." *Speculum* 33 (1958): 351–70.
Bennett, Michael J. "Spiritual Kinship and the Baptismal Name in Traditional European Society." In *Principalities, Powers, and Estates,* edited by L. O. Frappell, 1–13. Adelaide, 1979.
———. *Community, Class, and Careerism: Cheshire and Lancashire Society in the Age of "Sir Gawain and the Green Knight."* Cambridge, 1983.
———. *Richard II and the Revolution of 1399*. Stroud, 1999.
Bergmann, Jörg. *Discreet Indiscretions: The Social Organization of Gossip*. Translated by John Bednarz Jr. New York, 1993.
Binski, Paul. *Medieval Death: Ritual and Representation*. London, 1996.
Bishop, T. A. M. Review of *CIPM, IX: 21–25 Edward III*. *English Historical Review* 52 (1937): 437–40.
———. Review of *CIPM, XII: 39–43 Edward III*. *English Historical Review* 55 (1940): 329.
Blagg, Thomas M., ed. *Abstracts of the Inquisitiones Post Mortem Relating to Nottinghamshire, III, 1321–1350*. Thoroton Society, no. 6. N.p., 1939.
Blumenfeld-Kosinski, Renate. *Not of Woman Born: Representations of Caesarian Birth in Medieval and Renaissance Culture*. Ithaca, 1990.
Bossy, John. "Blood and Baptism: Kinship, Community, and Christianity in Western Europe from the Fourteenth to the Seventeenth Century." *Studies in Church History* 10 (1973): 129–43.
Boureau, Alain. "Richard Southern: A Landscape for a Portrait." *Past and Present* 165 (November 1999): 218–29.
Boutrell, Charles. *Heraldry, Historical and Popular*. London, 1964.
Bowers, R. H. "A Middle-English Poem on Lovedays." *Modern Language Review* 47 (1952): 374–75.
Brand, Paul. "Time Out of Mind: Knowledge and Use of the Eleventh- and Twelfth-Century Past in Thirteenth-Century Litigation." *Anglo-Norman Studies* 16 (1993): 37–54.
Brault, Gerald. *Eight Thirteenth-Century Rolls of Arms in French and Anglo-Norman Blazon*. University Park, Pa., 1973.
British Library Additional Mss. 27444, 24775, 34888, 34889: Additional Charter 17253.
Britnell, Richard H. "The Proliferation of Markets in England, 1200–1349." *Economic History Review*, 2d ser., 34 (1981): 209–31.
Brocklesby, Reginald, ed. *The Register of William Melton, Archbishop of York, 1317–1340*. Canterbury and York Society, vol. 85. Woodbridge, 1997.
Brooke, C. N. L., and M. M. Postan, eds. *Carte Nativorum: A Peterborough Cartulary of the Fourteenth Century*. Northampton Record Society, vol. 20. Oxford, 1960.
Brown, A. L. *The Governance of Late Medieval England, 1272–1461*. Stanford, 1989.
Brown, William, ed. *Yorkshire Inquisitions, IV*. Yorkshire Archaeological Society Record Series, no. 37. Worksop, 1906.
Browne, Matthew. *Chaucer's England*. London, 1869.
Brundage, James. *Law, Sex, and Christian Society in Medieval Europe*. Chicago, 1987.

Calendar of Inquistions Miscellaneous (Chancery), VII, *1399–1422*. London, 1969.
Calendar of Inquisitions Post Mortem, I: Henry III. Edited by Henry C. Maxwell-Lyte. London, 1904.
Calendar of Inquisitions Post Mortem, XI: 35–38 Edward III. London, 1935.
Calendar of Inquisitions Post Mortem, XII: 39–43 Edward III. London, 1938.
Calendar of Inquisitions Post Mortem, XIII: 44–47 Edward III. London, 1954.
Calendar of Inquisitions Post Mortem, XIV: 48–51 Edward III. London, 1952.
Calendar of Inquisitions Post Mortem, XV: 1–7 Richard II. London, 1970.
Calendar of Inquisitions Post Mortem, XVI: 7–15 Richard II. London, 1974.
Calendar of Inquisitions Post Mortem, XVII: 15–23 Richard II. London, 1988.
Calendar of Inquisitions Post Mortem, XVIII: 1–6 Henry IV. Edited by J. L. Kirby. London, 1987.
Calendar of Inquisitions Post Mortem, XIX: 7–14 Henry IV. Edited by J. L. Kirby. London, 1992.
Calendar of Inquisitions Post Mortem, XX: 1–5 Henry V. Edited by J. L. Kirby. London, 1995.
Calendar of the Patent Rolls, 1381–85. London, 1897.
Calendar of the Patent Rolls, 1391–96. London, 1905.
Carlin, Martha. *Medieval Southwark*. London, 1996.
Carlin, Martha, and Joel T. Rosenthal, eds. *Food and Eating in Medieval Europe*. London, 1998.
Carnwath, Julia. "The Church Wardens' Accounts of Thame, Oxfordshire, c. 1443–1524." In *Trade, Devotion, and Governance: Papers in Later Medieval History*, edited by Dorothy J. Clayton, Richard G. Davies, and Peter McNiven, 177–97. Stroud, 1994.
Carpenter, Christine. *Locality and Polity: A Study of Warwickshire Landed Society, 1401–1499*. Cambridge, 1992.
———, ed. and intro. *Kingsford's Stonor Letters and Papers, 1250–1483*. Cambridge, 1996.
———. *The Armburgh Papers: The Brokholes Inheritance in Warwickshire, Hertfordshire, and Essex, c. 1417–c. 1453: Chetham's Manuscript Mun. E.6. 10 (4)*. Woodbridge, 1998.
Carruthers, Mary. *The Book of Memory: A Study of Memory in Medieval Culture*. Cambridge, 1990.
Catto, Jeremy, and Linne R. Mooney, eds. "The Chronicle of John Somer, O.F.M." *Camden Miscellany* 34. Camden Society, 5th ser., vol. 10. Cambridge, 1997.
Chartier, Roger, Alain Boureau, and Cécile Dauphin. *Correspondence: Models of Letter Writing*. Translated by E. Woodell. Philadelphia, 1997.
Cherewatuk, Karen, and Ulrike Wiethaus, eds. *Dear Sister: Medieval Women and the Epistolary Genre*. Philadelphia, 1993.
Childs, Wendy R., and John Taylor, eds. *The Anonimalle Chronicle, 1307 to 1334: From Brotherton Ms. 29*. Yorkshire Archaeological Society Record Series, vol. 147. [Leeds], 1991.
Christianson, C. Paul. "Chancery Standard and the Records of Old London Bridge." In *Standardization of English: Essays in the History of Language Change in Honor of John Hurt Fisher*, edited by Joseph B. Trahern Jr., 82–112. Tennessee Studies in Literature, no. 31. Knoxville, 1989.
Clanchy, Michael. "Law and Love in the Middle Ages." In *Disputes and Settlements: Law and Human Relations in the West*, edited by John Bossy, 47–67. Cambridge, 1983.
———. *From Memory to Written Record: England, 1066–1307*. 2d ed. Oxford, 1993.

Clark, Elaine. "Debt Litigation in a Late Medieval Village." In *Pathways to Medieval Peasants,* edited by J. Ambrose Raftis, 247–79. Toronto, 1981.
Clark, Peter. *The English Alehouse: A Social History, 1200–1830.* London, 1983.
Clover, Helen, and Mary Gibson, eds. *The Letters of Lanfranc, Archbishop of Canterbury.* Oxford, 1979.
Coates, Bryan E. "The Origin and Distribution of Markets and Fairs in Medieval Derbyshire." *Derbyshire Archaeological Journal* 85 (1965): 92–111.
Cokayne, George E., et al., eds. *The Complete Peerage.* 12 vols. in 13. London, 1910–59.
Coleman, Joyce. *Public Reading and the Reading Public in Late Medieval England and France.* Cambridge, 1996.
Connerton, Paul. *How Societies Remember.* Cambridge, 1989.
Constable, Giles. *Letters and Letter Collections.* Typologie des Sciences du Moyen Age Occidental, fasc. 17. Turnhout, 1976.
Coss, Peter. *The Knight in Medieval England.* Stroud, 1993.
———. *The Lady in Medieval England, 1000–1500.* Stroud, 1998.
Cottle, Basil. *The Triumph of English, 1350–1400.* London, 1965.
Crawford, Ann, ed. *Letters of the Queens of England, 1100–1547.* Stroud, 1994.
Crawford, Patricia. "The Construction and Experience of Maternity in Seventeenth-Century England." In *Women as Mothers in Pre-Industrial England: Essays in Memory of Dorothy McLaren,* edited by Valerie Fildes, 3–38. London, 1990.
———. "Friendship and Love Between Women in Early Modern England." In *Venus and Mars: Engendering Love and War in Medieval and Early Modern England,* edited by Andrew Lynchy and Philippa Maddern, 47–61. Nedlands, 1995.
Cressy, David. "Purification, Thanksgiving, and the Churching of Women in Post-Reformation England." *Past and Present* 141 (1993): 106–46.
Crouch, David. *The Beaumont Twins: The Roots and Branches of Power in the Twelfth Century.* Cambridge, 1986.
Crow, Martin M., and Clair C. Olson, eds. *Chaucer Life Records.* Austin, 1966.
Crump, C. J. "A Note on the Criticism of Records." *Bulletin of the John Rylands Library* 8 (1924): 140–49.
Cust, Richard, ed. *The Papers of Sir Richard Grosvenor, First Baronet (1585–1645).* Record Society of Lancashire and Cheshire, vol. 134. [Chester], 1996.
Daniell, Christopher. *Death and Burial in Medieval England, 1066–1550.* London, 1997.
Davis, Norman. "The Text of Margaret Paston's Letters." *Medium Aevum* 18 (1949): 12–28.
———. "A Scribal Problem in the Paston Letters." *English and Germanic Studies* 4 (1951–52): 31–64.
———. "The Language of the Pastons." *Proceedings of the British Academy* 40 (1955): 120–44.
———. "Styles in English Prose in the Late Medieval and Early Modern Period." *Langue et littérature: Actes de viiième congrès de la Féderation Internationale des Langues et Littératures Modernes* 21 (1961): 165–84.
———. "The Litera Troili and English Letters." *Review of English Studies,* n.s., 16 (1964): 233–44.
———. "Style and Stereotype in Early English Letters." *Leeds Studies in English,* n.s., 1 (1967): 7–17.
———. "Margaret Paston's Uses of 'Do.'" *Neuphilologische Mitteilungen* 73 (1972): 55–62.
———. "Language and Letters from Sir John Fastolf's Household." In *Medieval Studies for J. A. W. Bennett,* edited by P. L. Heyworth, 329–46. Oxford, 1981.

―――, ed. *The Paston Letters and Papers of the Fifteenth Century*. 2 vols. Oxford, 1970–76.
―――. *The Paston Letters*. World's Classics. Oxford, 1983.
Denholm-Young, Noel. *History and Heraldry, 1254–1310: A Study of the Historic Value of the Roll of Arms*. London, 1965.
―――. *The Country Gentry in the Fourteenth Century*. Oxford, 1969.
DeWindt, Anne R. "Defining the Peasant Community in Medieval England." *Journal of British Studies* 26 (1987): 163–207.
―――. "Local Government in a Small Town: A Medieval Leet Jury and Its Constituents." *Albion* 23 (1991): 627–54.
DeWindt, Edwin B. *Land and People in Holywell-cum-Needingworth: Structures of Tenure and Patterns of Social Organization in an East Midland Village, 1252–1457*. Toronto, 1972.
Dillon, Viscount. "On a Manuscript Collection of Ordinances of Chivalry of the Fifteenth Century Belonging to Lord Hastings." *Archaeologia* 57 (1900): 29–70.
Dinn, Robert. "Baptism, Spiritual Kinship, and Popular Religion in Late Medieval Bury St. Edmunds." *Bulletin of the John Rylands University Library* 72 (1990): 93–106.
Dobson, R. Barrie, ed. *The Peasants' Revolt of 1381*. London, 1970.
Donahue, Charles, Jr. "Proof by Witnesses in the Church Courts of Medieval England: An Imperfect Reception of the Learned Law." In *On the Laws and Customs of England: Essays in Honor of Samuel E. Thorne*, edited by Morris S. Arnold, Thomas A. Green, Sally A. Scully, and Stephen S. White, 127–58. Chapel Hill, 1981.
Doyle, A. I. "The Work of a Late-Fifteenth-Century English Scribe, William Ebesham." *Bulletin of the John Rylands Library* 39 (1956–57): 298–325.
Du Boulay, F. R. H. "Henry of Derby's Expeditions to Prussia, 1390–91 and 1392." In *The Reign of Richard II: Essays in Honour of May McKisack*, edited by F. R. H. Du Boulay and Caroline M. Barron, 153–72. London, 1971.
Duby, Georges. *William the Marshal: The Flower of Chivalry*. Translated by Richard Howard. New York, 1985.
Duffy, Eamon. *The Stripping of the Altars: Traditional Religion in England, c. 1400–c. 1580*. New Haven, 1992.
Düll, Siegrid, Anthony Luttrell, and Maurice Keen. "Faithful Unto Death: The Tomb Slab of Sir William Neville and Sir John Clanvowe, Constantinople, 1391." *Antiquaries Journal* 71 (1991): 147–90.
Dunbabin, Jean. "Discovering a Past for the French Aristocracy." In *The Perception of the Past in Twelfth-Century Europe*, edited by Paul Magdalino, 1–14. London, 1992.
Dunstan, G. R., ed. *The Register of Edmund Lacy, Bishop of Exeter, 1420–1455*. Devon and Cornwall Record Society, vols. 7, 10, 13, 16, and 18. [Torquay], 1963–72.
Dyer, Christopher. "Were There Any Capitalists in Fifteenth-Century England?" In *Enterprise and Individuals in Fifteenth-Century England*, edited by Jennifer Kermode, 1–24. Stroud, 1991.
Eade, John, and Michael J. Sallnow, eds. *Contesting the Sacred: The Anthropology of Christian Pilgrimage*. London, 1991.
Eberle, Patricia J. "Richard II and the Literary Arts." In *Richard II: The Art of Kingship*, edited by Anthony Goodman and James L. Gillespie, 231–53. Oxford, 1999.
Epstein, Steven. "Regional Fairs: Institutional Innovation and Economic Growth in Late Medieval Europe." *Economic History Review*, 2d ser., 47 (1994): 458–82.
Esler, Anthony. *The Aspiring Mind of the Elizabethan Younger Generation*. Durham, N.C., 1966.

Evenden, Doreen. *The Midwives of Seventeenth-Century London*. London, 2000.
Faith, Rosamund. *The English Peasantry and the Growth of Lordship*. Leicester, 1997.
Fenn, John. *Original Letters, Written During the Reigns of Henry VI, Edward IV, and Richard III*. 5 vols. London, 1787–1823.
Fentress, James, and Chris Wickham. *Social Memory*. Oxford, 1992.
Finch, A. J. "The Nature of Violence in the Middle Ages: An Alternative Perspective." *Historical Research* 70 (1997): 249–68.
Finke, Laurie. *Women's Writings in English: Medieval England*. London, 1999.
Fisher, John H. "Chancery and the Emergence of Standard Written English in the Fifteenth Century." *Speculum* 52 (1977): 870–99.
———. "A Language Policy for Lancastrian England." *Publications of the Modern Language Association* 107 (1992): 1168–80.
Fowler, R. C. "Legal Proofs of Age." *English Historical Review* 22 (1907): 101–3.
Fox, Adam. *Oral and Literate Culture in England, 1500–1700*. Oxford, 2000.
Fox-Davies, Arthur C. *A Complete Guide to Heraldry*. London, n.d.
Frame, Robin. *The Political Development of the British Isles, 1100–1400*. Oxford, 1995.
French, Katherine L. *The People of the Parish: Community Life in a Late Medieval English Diocese*. Philadelphia, 2001.
French, Katherine L., Gary G. Gibbs, and Beat A. Kümin, eds. *The Parish in English Life, 1400–1600*. Manchester, 1997.
Fry, Edward A., ed. *Abstracts of Wiltshire Inquisitiones Post Mortem . . . Henry III, Edward I, and Edward II (A.D. 1242–1326)*. British Record Society Index Library, no. 37. London, 1908.
Furnivall, F. J., ed. *Political, Religious, and Love Poems*. Early English Text Society, o.s., 15. 1866. Reprint, London, 1966.
Gairdner, James, ed. *The Paston Letters, 1422–1509 A.D.* Library Edition. 4 vols. London, 1900.
———. *The Paston Letters, 1422–1509 A.D.* New Complete Library Edition. 6 vols. London, 1904. Reprint, New York, 1965.
Gayre, G. R. "Scrope and Carminow." *Coat of Arms* 2 (1953): 177–78.
Gelis, Jacques. *The History of Childbirth: Fertility, Pregnancy, and Birth in Early Modern Europe*. Boston, 1991.
Gies, Frances, and Joseph Gies. *A Medieval Family: The Pastons of Fifteenth-Century England*. New York, 1998.
Gillespie, James L. "Richard II's Chester Archers." *Transactions of the Historic Society of Lancashire and Cheshire* 125 (1975): 1–33.
———. "Richard II: Chivalry and Kingship." In *The Age of Richard II*, edited by James L. Gillespie, 115–38. Stroud, 1997.
Ginzburg, Carlo. *The Cheese and the Worms*. London, 1980.
Giuseppi, M. S. *A Guide to the Manuscripts in the Public Record Office*. 2 vols. London, 1923.
Given-Wilson, Chris., ed. and trans. *The Chronicle of Adam Usk, 1377–1421*. Oxford, 1997.
Godall, John A. "A Fifteenth-Century Anglo-French-Burgundian Heraldic Collection." *Antiquaries Journal* 70 (1990): 424–38.
Goldberg, P. J. P. *Women, Work, and the Life Cycle in a Medieval Economy: Women in York and Yorkshire, c. 1300–1520*. Oxford, 1992.
———. "What Was a Servant?" In *Concepts and Patterns of Service in the Late Middle Ages*, edited by Anne Curry and Elizabeth Matthew, 1–20. Woodbridge, 2000.

Goodman, Anthony. *John of Gaunt: The Exercise of Princely Power in Fourteenth-Century Europe.* New York, 1992.
Gransden, Antonia. "Letters of Recommendation from John Whethamstede for a Poor Pilgrim, 1453–54." *English Historical Review* 106 (1991): 932–39.
Greenway, Diana, ed. and trans. *Henry, Archdeacon of Huntington: Historia Anglorum: History of the English People.* Oxford, 1996.
Hajnal, John. "European Marriage Patterns in Perspective." In *Population in History*, edited by D. V. Glass and D. E. C. Eversley, 101–43. London, 1965.
Halbwachs, Maurice. *La Memoire collective.* 2d ed., rev. Paris, 1968.
Hammond, Peter. *Food and Feast in Medieval England.* Stroud, 1993.
Hanawalt, Barbara A. *The Ties That Bound: Peasant Families in Medieval England.* Oxford, 1986.
———. *Growing Up in Medieval London: The Experience of Childhood in History.* New York, 1993.
Hanham, Alison, ed. *The Cely Letters, 1472–1488.* Early English Text Society, no. 273. Oxford, 1975.
Harvey, P. D. A. *A Medieval Oxfordshire Village: Cuxham, 1240 to 1400.* Oxford, 1965.
Heffernan, Thomas J. "A Medieval Poem on Lovedays." *Chaucer Review* 10 (1975–76): 172–85.
Helmholz, Richard H. *Marriage Litigation in Medieval England.* Cambridge, 1974.
Herrmann, Douglas J., and Roger Chaffin, eds. *Memory in Historical Perspective: The Literature Before Ebbinghaus.* New York, 1988.
Hewitt, H. J. *The Organization of War Under Edward III, 1338–62.* Manchester, 1966.
Hill, Mary C. *The King's Messengers, 1199–1377.* London, 1961.
Hilton, Rodney H. *A Medieval Society: The West Midlands at the End of the Thirteenth Century.* Oxford, 1965.
———. Review of *CIPM*, XV: *1–7 Richard II. English Historical Review* 88 (1973): 170–71.
———. *The English Peasantry in the Later Middle Ages.* Oxford, 1975.
Hodgson, Crawford. "Proof of Age of Heirs of Estates in Northumberland." *Archaeologia Aeliana* 3, no. 3 (1907): 297–309.
Holt, James C. *The Northerners: A Study in the Reign of King John.* Oxford, 1961.
———. Review essay. *Economic History Review*, 2d ser., 14 (1961): 328–29.
Holt, Richard, and Gervase Rosser, eds. *The Medieval Town: A Reader in English Urban History, 1200–1540.* London, 1990.
Horrox, Rosemary. "Service." In *Fifteenth-Century Attitudes: Perceptions of Society in Late Medieval England*, edited by Rosemary Horrox, 61–78. Cambridge, 1994.
Howard, Donald R. *Chaucer, His Life, His Works, His World.* New York, 1987.
Hudson, Hazel, and Frances Neal. "A Busy Day in Wedmore Church." *Notes and Queries for Somerset and Dorset* 33 (1992): 171–73.
Hunnisett, R. F. "The Reliability of Inquisitions as Historical Evidence." In *The Study of Medieval Records: Essays in Honour of Kathleen Major*, edited by D. A. Bullough and R. L. Storey, 206–35. Oxford, 1971.
Hurstfield, Joel. *The Queen's Wards: Wardship and Marriage Under Elizabeth I.* London, 1958.
Hutton, Patrick H. *History as the Art of Memory.* Hanover, 1993.
Jack, Ian. "Entail and Descent: The Hastings Inheritance, 1370 to 1436." *Bulletin of the Institute of Historical Research* 38 (1965): 1–19.
Jewell, Helen M. *English Local Administration in the Middle Ages.* Newton Abbot, 1972.

———. *The North-South Divide: The Origins of Northern Consciousness in England.* Manchester, 1994.
———. *Women in Medieval England.* Manchester, 1996.
Johnson, Alexandra F. "Parish Entertainments in Berkshire." In *Pathways to Medieval Peasants,* edited by J. Ambrose Raftis, 335–38. Toronto, 1981.
Jones, Michael. "Edward III's Captains in Brittany." In *England in the Fourteenth Century: Proceedings of the 1985 Harlaxton Symposium,* edited by W. M. Ormrod, 99–118. Woodbridge, 1986.
Jones, Michael K., and Malcolm Underwood. *The King's Mother: Lady Margaret Beaufort, Countess of Richmond and Derby.* Cambridge, 1992.
Jones, Peter Murray. "British Museum Ms. Sloane 76: A Translator's Holograph." In *Medieval Book Production: Assessing the Evidence,* edited by Linda L. Brownrigg, 21–39. Los Altos Hills, Calif., 1990.
Journal of British Studies 33, no. 4 (1994). [Special issue devoted to "Vill, Guild, and Gentry: Forces of Community in Late Medieval England." With papers by Maryanne Kowaleski, Christine Carpenter, Elaine Clark, Christopher Dyer, and Gervase Rosser.]
Kaeuper, Richard W. *Chivalry and Violence in Medieval Europe.* Oxford, 1999.
Karras, Ruth Mazo. *Common Women: Prostitution and Sexuality in Medieval England.* Philadelphia, 1996.
Keen, Maurice. "Brotherhood in Arms." *History* 47 (1963): 1–17.
———. "Chaucer's Knight, the English Aristocracy, and the Crusade." In *English Court Culture in the Later Middle Ages,* edited by V. J. Scattergood and J. W. Sherborne, 45–61. London, 1983.
———. *Chivalry.* New Haven, 1984.
———. "The Jurisdiction and Origins of the Constable's Court." In *War and Government in the Middle Ages: Essays in Honour of J. O. Prestwich,* edited by John G. Gillingham and J. C. Holt, 159–69. Woodbridge, 1984.
———. *Nobles, Knights, and Men-at-Arms in the Middle Ages.* London, 1996.
———. "Heraldry and Hierarchy: Esquires and Gentlemen." In *Orders and Hierarchies in Late Medieval and Renaissance Europe,* edited by Jeffrey Denton, 94–108. Basingstoke, 1999.
Keen, Maurice, and Mark Warner, eds. "Morley vs. Montagu (1399): A Case in the Court of Chivalry." *Camden Miscellany* 34. Camden Society, 5th ser., vol. 10. Cambridge, 1997.
Kemp, Simon. *Cognitive Psychology in the Middle Ages.* Westport, Conn., 1996.
Kingsford, Charles L. *Kingsford's Stonor Letters and Papers, 1250–1483.* Edited and introduced by Christine Carpenter. Cambridge, 1996.
Kirby, Joan. "Women in the Plumpton Correspondence: Fiction and Reality." In *Church and Crown in the Middle Ages: Essays Presented to John Taylor,* edited by Ian Wood and G. A. Loud, 219–32. London, 1991.
———, ed. *The Plumpton Letters and Papers.* Camden Society, 5th ser., vol. 8. Cambridge, 1996.
Kirby, John L. *Henry IV of England.* London, 1970.
Kowaleski, Maryanne. *Local Markets and Regional Trade: Medieval Exeter.* Cambridge, 1995.
Kümin, Beat A. *The Shaping of a Community: The Rise and Reformation of the English Parish, c. 1400–1560.* Aldershot, 1996.

L. B. L. "Probatio Aetatis of William Septvans." *Archaeologia Cantiana* 1 (1858): 124–36.
LaBahn, Patricia D. *Feasting in the Fourteenth and Fifteenth Centuries: A Comparison of Manuscript Illuminations to Contemporary Written Sources.* St. Louis, 1975.
Labarge, Margaret Wade. *A Baronial Household of the Thirteenth Century.* New York, 1965.
Lander, Jack R. *English Justices of the Peace.* Gloucester, 1989.
Legge, M. Dominica, ed. *Anglo-Norman Letters and Petitions from All Souls Ms. 182.* Anglo-Norman Texts, no. 3. Oxford, 1941.
Lester, G. A. *Sir John Paston's 'Grete Boke': A Descriptive Catalogue with an Introduction of B.L. Ms. Lansdowne 285.* Cambridge, 1984.
Lewis, Katherine J. "Model Girls? Virgin Martyrs and the Training of Young Women in Late Medieval England." In *Young Medieval Women*, edited by Katherine J. Lewis, Noël J. Menuge, and Kim M. Phillips, 25–46. New York, 1999.
Lodge, Eleanor C., and Gladys A. Thornton, eds. *English Constitutional Documents, 1307–1485.* Cambridge, 1935.
Lyell, Laetitia, ed. *A Medieval Post-Bag.* London, 1934.
Lynch, Joseph H. *Godparents and Kinship in Early Medieval Europe.* Princeton, 1986.
Maddern, Philippa. "'Best Trusted Friends': Concepts and Practices of Friendship Among Fifteenth-Century Norfolk Gentry." In *England in the Fifteenth Century: Proceedings of the 1992 Harlaxton Symposium*, edited by Nicholas Rogers, 100–117. Stamford, 1994.
Madge, Sidney J., ed. *Abstracts of Gloucestershire Inquisitiones Post Mortem . . . , Vol. 4: 20 Henry III–29 Edward I (1236–1300).* British Record Society Index Library, no. 30. London, 1903.
March, Deborah. "'I See by the Sizt of Evidence': Information Gathering in Late Medieval Cheshire." In *Courts, Counties, and the Capital in the Later Middle Ages*, edited by Diana E. S. Dunn, 71–92. Stroud, 1996.
Martin, Geoffrey H., ed. and trans. *Knighton's Chronicle, 1337–1396.* Oxford, 1995.
Martin, M. T. "Legal Proofs of Age." *English Historical Review* 22 (1907): 526–27.
McClure, Peter. "Patterns of Migration in the Later Middle Ages: The Evidence of Place-Name Surnames." *Economic History Review*, 2d ser., 32 (1979): 167–82.
McColl, H. B. *Richmondshire Churches.* London, 1900.
McLain, Bradley A. "Factors in Market Establishment in Medieval England: The Evidence from Kent, 1086–1356." *Archaeologia Cantiana* 117 (1997): 82–103.
McRee, Ben R. "Peacemaking and Its Limits in Late Medieval Norwich." *English Historical Review* 109 (1994): 831–66.
Mead, William E. *The English Medieval Feast.* New York, 1967.
Mennell, Stephen. *All Manners of Food: Eating and Taste in England and France from the Middle Ages to the Present.* 2d ed. Urbana, 1996.
Mertes, Kate. *The English Noble Household, 1250–1600.* Oxford, 1988.
Millor, W. J., and C. N. L. Brooke, eds. *The Letters of John of Salisbury: II: The Later Letters (1163–1180).* Oxford, 1978.
Millor, W. J., and H. E. Butler, eds. *The Letters of John of Salisbury: I: The Early Letters (1153–1161).* Revised by C. N. L. Brooke. Edinburgh, 1955.
Mirrer, Louise, ed. *Upon My Husband's Death: Widows in the Literature and History of Medieval Europe.* Ann Arbor, 1994.
Mitchell, Robert W., ed. *English Mediaeval Rolls of Arms, 1: 1244–1334.* Edinburgh, 1983.
Mooney, Linne R. "The Cock and the Clock: Telling Time in Chaucer's Day." *Studies in the Age of Chaucer* 15 (1993): 91–109.

Moore, Ellen Wedemeyer. *The Fairs of Medieval England: An Introductory Study.* Toronto, 1985.
Morgan, Philip. *War and Society in Medieval Cheshire, 1277–1403.* Chetham Society, 3d ser., vol. 34. Manchester, 1987.
Morris, William A. *The Medieval English Sheriff to 1300.* Manchester, 1927.
Mueller, Janel M. *The Native Tongue and the Word: Developments in English Prose Style, 1380–1580.* Chicago, 1984.
Murphy, James J. "Rhetoric: Western Europe." In *Dictionary of the Middle Ages,* edited by Joseph R. Strayer, 10:351–64. New York, 1984.
Murray, Hugh. "The Scrope Tapestries." *Yorkshire Archaeological Journal* 64 (1992): 145–56.
Neville, Cynthia J. "Keeping the Peace on the Northern Marches in the Later Middle Ages." *English Historical Review* 109 (1994): 1–25.
Nichols, J. G. "The Scrope and Grosvenor Controversy." *Herald and Genealogist* (1863): 385–400.
Nicolas, Nicholas Harris. *The Controversy Between Sir Richard Scrope and Sir Robert Grosvenor.* 2 vols. London, 1832.
———, ed. *Proceedings and Ordinances of the Privy Council (1386–1542).* 7 vols. London, 1834–37.
Niles, Philip. "Baptism and the Naming of Children." *Medieval Prosopography* 3, no. 1 (1982): 95–107.
Olson, David R. *The World on Paper: The Conceptual and Cognitive Implications of Writing and Reading.* Cambridge, 1994.
Olson, Sherri. "Jurors of the Village Court: Local Leadership Before and After the Plague in Ellington, Huntingdonshire." *Journal of British Studies* 30 (1991): 237–56.
———. *A Chronicle of All That Happens: Voices from the Village Court in Medieval England.* Toronto, 1996.
Oman, Charles. *The Great Revolt of 1381.* Oxford, 1906. Reprint, New York, 1969.
O'Mara, V. M. "Female Scribal Ability and Scribal Activity in Late Medieval England: The Evidence." *Leeds Studies in English,* n.s., 27 (1996): 87–130.
Orme, Nicholas. "Medieval Hunting: Fact and Fancy." In *Chaucer's England: Literature in Historical Context,* edited by Barbara A. Hanawalt, 133–53. Minneapolis, 1992.
Ormrod, W. Mark. *The Reign of Edward III: Crown and Political Society in England, 1327–1377.* New Haven, 1990.
Otis, Leah H. "Municipal Wet Nurses in Fifteenth-Century Montpellier." In *Women and Work in Preindustrial Europe,* edited by Barbara A. Hanawalt, 83–93. Bloomington, 1986.
Painter, Sidney. *William Marshal: Knight-Errant, Baron, and Regent of England.* Baltimore, 1933.
Palmer, J. J. N. *England, France, and Christendom.* London, 1972.
Payling, Simon. *Political Society in Lancastrian England: The Greater Gentry of Nottinghamshire.* Oxford, 1991.
———. "County Parliamentary Elections in Fifteenth-Century England." *Parliamentary History* 18, no. 3 (1999): 137–59.
Payne, Paddy, and Caroline M. Barron. "The Letters and Life of Elizabeth Despenser, Lady Zouche (d. 1408)." *Nottingham Medieval Studies* 41 (1997): 126–56.
Pearsall, Derek. *The Life of Geoffrey Chaucer.* Oxford, 1992.

Pearsons, P. C. "The Paston Letters: Carriage of Mail in the Fifteenth Century." *London Philatelist* (July–August 1990): 178–83; (September 1990): 192–95; (October–November 1990): 232–37; (December 1990): 276–79.

Phillips, Kim M. "Maidenhood as the Perfect Age of a Woman's Life." In *Young Medieval Women*, edited by Katherine J. Lewis, Noël J. Menuge, and Kim M. Phillips, 1–24. New York, 1999.

Phythian-Adams, Charles V. "Rituals of Personal Confrontation in Late Medieval England." *Bulletin of the John Rylands University Library* 73 (1991): 65–90.

Pine, L. G. Letter. *Coat of Arms* 2 (1953): 155.

———. *Heraldry and Genealogy*. London, 1957.

Polak, D. J. "Dictamen." In *Dictionary of the Middle Ages*, edited by Joseph R. Strayer, 4:173–77. New York, 1984.

Pollard, A. J. *North-Eastern England During the Wars of the Roses: Lay Society, War, and Politics, 1450–1500*. Oxford, 1990.

Pollock, Frederick, and Frederic William Maitland. *The History of English Law Before the Time of Edward I*. With an introduction by S. F. C. Milsom. Cambridge, 1905. 2nd ed., rev. 2 vols. Cambridge, 1968.

Pollock, Linda A. "Embarking on a Rough Passage: The Experience of Pregnancy in Early Modern Society." In *Women as Mothers in Pre-Industrial England: Essays in Memory of Dorothy McLaren*, edited by Valerie Fildes, 39–67. London, 1990.

Poos, Lawrence R. *A Rural Society After the Black Death: Essex, 1350–1525*. Cambridge, 1991.

Poos, Lawrence R., Zvi Razi, and Richard M. Smith. "The Population History of Medieval English Villages: A Debate on the Use of Manorial Records." In *Medieval Society and the Manorial Court*, edited by Zvi Razi and Richard M. Smith, 298–368. Oxford, 1996.

Pope, Mildred K., and Eleanor C. Lodge, eds. *The Life of the Black Prince by the Herald of Sir John Chandos*. Oxford, 1910. Reprint, New York, 1974.

Post, J. B. "Equitable Resorts Before 1450." In *Law, Litigants, and the Legal Profession*, edited by E. W. Ives and A. H. Manchester, 68–79. London, 1983.

Powicke, F. M. *The Thirteenth Century*. Oxford, 1953.

Prestwich, Michael. *Armies and Warfare in the Middle Ages: The English Experience*. New Haven, 1996.

Pugh, R. B. "The Duration of Criminal Trials in Medieval England." In *Law, Litigants, and the Legal Profession*, edited by E. W. Ives and A. H. Manchester, 104–15. London, 1983.

Raban, Sandra. "The Making of the 1278–80 Hundred Rolls." *Historical Research* 70 (June 1997): 123–45.

Raftis, J. Ambrose. *Tenure and Mobility: Studies in the Social History of the Mediaeval English Village*. Toronto, 1964.

Raine, Angelo, ed. *York Civic Records*, 1. Yorkshire Archaeological Society Record Series, vol. 98. Wakefield, 1939.

Ravell, Elizabeth, ed. *The Later Letters of Peter of Blois*. Oxford, 1993.

Rawcliffe, Carole. *The Hospitals of Medieval Norwich*. Norwich, 1995.

Reeves, A. Compton. *Pleasures and Pastimes in Medieval England*. Stroud, 1995.

Richardson, Malcolm. "Medieval English Vernacular Correspondence: Notes Toward an Alternative Rhetoric." *Allegorica* (1989): 95–118.

Richmond, Colin F. "The Pastons Revisited: Marriage and Family in Fifteenth-Century England." *Bulletin of the Institute of Historical Research* 58 (1985): 25–36.

———. "Hand and Mouth: Information Gathering and Use in England in the Later Middle Ages." *Journal of Historical Sociology* 1 (1988): 233–52.
———. *The Paston Family in the Fifteenth Century: The First Phase*. Cambridge, 1990.
———. "An English Mafia?" *Nottingham Medieval Studies* 36 (1992): 235–43.
———. *The Paston Family in the Fifteenth Century: Fastolf's Will*. Cambridge, 1996.
———. *The Paston Family in the Fifteenth Century: Endings*. Manchester, 2000.
Rickert, Edith. "A Leaf from a Fourteenth-Century Letter Book." *Modern Philology* 25 (1927–28): 249–55.
———. "Some English Personal Letters of 1402." *Review of English Studies* 8 (1932): 257–63.
———. *Chaucer's World*. New York, 1948.
Rigby, Stephen H. *English Society in the Later Middle Ages: Class, Status, and Gender*. London, 1995.
Rix, S. W. "Cursory Notes on the Reverend Francis Blomefield, the Norfolk Topographer." *Norfolk Archaeology* 2 (1849): 201–24.
Robbins, Edgar C. *William Paston, Justice, Founder of the Paston Family (1378–1444)*. Norwich, 1932.
Roffe, David. "The Hundred Rolls of 1255." *Historical Research* 69 (1996): 201–10.
Rosenthal, Joel T. "Old Men's Lives—Elderly English Peers, 1350–1500." *Mediaevalia* 8 (1982): 211–37.
———. *Patriarchy and Families of Privilege in Late Medieval England*. Philadelphia, 1991.
———. "Looking for Grandmother: The Pastons and Their Counterparts in Late Medieval England." In *Medieval Mothering*, edited by John Carmi Parsons and Bonnie Wheeler, 259–77. New York, 1996.
———. *Old Age in Medieval England*. Philadelphia, 1996.
Roskell, John S., et al. *The History of Parliament: The House of Commons, 1386–1421*. 4 vols. Stroud, 1992.
Ross, Charles. Review of *CIPM, XIII: 44–47 Edward III* and *CIPM, XIV: 48–51 Edward III*. *English Historical Review* 72 (1957): 109–11.
Rosser, Gervase. *Medieval Westminster, 1200–1540*. Oxford, 1989.
Rothwell, W. "The Trilingual England of Geoffrey Chaucer." *Studies in the Age of Chaucer* 16 (1994): 45–67.
Round, John Horace. Review of *CIPM, IX: 21–25 Edward III*. *English Historical Review* 32 (1917): 453–54.
Routh, E. M. G. *Lady Margaret: A Memoir*. Cambridge, 1924.
Rowland, Beryl. *Medieval Woman's Guide to Health*. Kent, Ohio, 1981.
Rowling, Marjorie A. "New Evidence on the Disseisin of the Pastons from the Norfolk Manor of Gresham, 1448–1451." *Norfolk Archaeology* 40, no. 3 (1989): 302–8.
Rubin, Miri. "Religious Culture in Town and Country: Reflections on a Great Divide." In *Church and City, 600–1500: Essays in Honour of Christopher Brooke*, edited by David Abulafia, Michael Franklin, and Miri Rubin, 3–22. Cambridge, 1992.
———. "What Did the Eucharist Mean to Thirteenth-Century Villagers?" In *Thirteenth-Century England, IV*, edited by P. R. Coss and S. D. Lloyd, 47–55. Woodbridge, 1992.
Russell, Josiah Cox. *British Medieval Population*. Albuquerque, 1948.
Salusbury-Jones, G. T. *Street Life in Medieval England*. London, 1939.
Saul, Nigel. *Knights and Esquires: The Gloucestershire Gentry in the Fourteenth Century*. Oxford, 1981.

———. *Scenes from Provincial Life: Knightly Families in Sussex, 1280–1400.* Oxford, 1986.
———. *Richard II.* New Haven, 1997.
Scott, Karen. "'Io Catarina': Ecclesiastical Politics and Oral Culture in the Letters of Catherine of Siena." In *Dear Sister: Medieval Women and the Epistolary Genre,* edited by Karen Cherewatuk and Ulrike Wiethaus, 87–121. Philadelphia, 1993.
Scott-Giles, C. W. *Revisions of Boutrell.* London, 1950.
Scrope, George P. *The History of Castle Combe.* London, 1852.
Searle, Eleanor. *Lordship and Community: Battle Abbey and Its Banlieu, 1066–1538.* Toronto, 1974.
Serpell, M. F. "Sir John Fenn, His Friends, and the Paston Letters." *Antiquaries Journal* 63 (1983): 95–121.
Shahar, Shulamith. *Childhood in the Middle Ages.* London, 1990.
Sheehan, Michael M. *Marriage, Family, and Law in Medieval Europe: Collected Studies.* Edited by James K. Farge. Toronto, 1996.
Smith, Richard M. "Geographical Diversity in the Resort to Marriage in Late Medieval Europe." In *Woman Is a Worthy Wight: Women in English Society, c. 1200–1500,* edited by P. J. P. Goldberg, 16–59. Stroud, 1992.
Smith, Sidney Armitage. *John of Gaunt.* London, 1904.
Somerville, Robert. *History of the Duchy of Lancaster, 1: 1265–1603.* London, 1953.
Southern, Richard W. "Toward an Edition of Peter of Blois's Letter Collection." *English Historical Review* 110 (1995): 925–37.
Spargo, J. W. "Chaucer's Lovedays." *Speculum* 15 (1940): 36–56.
Spence, Jonathan. *The Memory Palace of Mateo Ricci.* New York, 1984.
Squibb, G. D. "The Law of Arms in England." *Coat of Arms* 2 (1953): 245.
———. *The High Court of Chivalry: A Study in the Civil Law of England.* Oxford, 1959.
Stamp, A. E. "Legal Proofs of Age." *English Historical Review* 29 (1914): 323–24.
Stevenson, E. R. "The Escheator." In *The English Government at Work, Volume II: Fiscal Administration,* edited by William A. Morris and Joseph R. Strayer, 109–67. Cambridge, Mass., 1947.
Stewart-Brown, R. "The Scrope and Grosvenor Controversy." *Transactions of the Historic Society of Lancashire and Cheshire* 89 (1938): 1–22.
Stoker, David A. "'Innumerable Letters of Good Consequence in History': The Discovery and First Publication of the Paston Letters." *The Library,* 6th ser., 17 (1995): 107–55.
———, ed. *The Correspondence of the Reverend Francis Blomefield (1708–52).* Norfolk Record Society, vol. 55. [Norwich], 1992.
Stokes, Ethel, ed. *Abstracts of Wiltshire Inquisitiones Post Mortem: Edward III (1327–1377).* British Record Society Index Library, no. 48. London, 1914.
Stones, E. L. G. "Sir Geoffrey le Scrope (c. 1285–1340): Chief Justice of the King's Bench." *English Historical Review* 69 (1954): 1–17.
Strohm, Paul. *Theory and the Pre-Modern Text.* Minneapolis, 2001.
Sugget, Helen. "The Use of French in England in the Later Middle Ages." *Transactions of the Royal Historical Society,* 4th ser., 28 (1946): 61–83.
Sumption, Jonathan. *Pilgrimage: An Image of Medieval Religion.* London, 1975.
———. *The Hundred Years War: Trial by Battle.* Philadelphia, 1991.
Sutherland, Donald W. "Legal Reasoning in the Fourteenth Century: The Invention of 'Color' in Pleading." In *On the Laws and Customs of England: Essays in Honor of Samuel E. Thorne,* edited by Morris S. Arnold, Thomas A. Green, Sally A. Scully, and Stephen S. White, 182–94. Chapel Hill, 1981.

Swabey, ffiona. *Medieval Gentlewoman: Life in a Widow's Household in the Later Middle Ages*. Stroud, 1999.
Tarvers, Josephine Koster. "In a Woman's Hand? The Question of Medieval Women's Holograph Letters." *Postscript: Publications of the Philological Association of the Carolinas* 13 (1998): 89–100.
Tebbutt, Melanie. *Women's Talk? A Social History of "Gossip" in Working-Class Neighbourhoods, 1880–1960*. Aldershot, 1995.
Thomas, Keith. "Age and Authority in Early Modern England." *Proceedings of the British Academy* 62 (1976): 205–48.
Thomson, J. A. F. "Piety and Charity in Late Medieval London." *Journal of Ecclesiastical History* 16 (1965): 178–98.
———. *The Early Tudor Church and Society, 1485–1529*. London, 1983.
Tout, Thomas Frederick. *Chapters in the Administrative History of Mediaeval England*. 6 vols. Manchester, 1920–33.
Train, K. S., ed. *Abstracts of Inquisitions Post Mortem Relating to Nottinghamshire, 1350–1436*. Thoroton Society, no. 12. N.p., 1949–52.
Transactions of the Royal Historical Society, 6th ser., 9 (1999). [Special issue devoted to "Oral History, Memory, and Written Tradition." With papers by Patrick J. Geary, Sarah Foot, Elisabeth Van Houts, Christine Shaw, Adam Fox, and Andy Wood.]
Truelove, Alison. "Commanding Communications: The Fifteenth-Century Letters of the Stonor Women." In *Early Modern Women's Letter Writing, 1450–1700*, edited by James Daybell, 42–58. Basingstoke, 2001.
Tuck, Anthony. "Richard II and the Hundred Years War." In *Politics and Crisis in Fourteenth-Century England*, edited by John Taylor and Wendy R. Childs, 117–31. Gloucester, 1990.
Vale, Brigette. "The Profits of the Law and the 'Rise' of the Scropes: Henry Scrope (d. 1330) and Geoffrey Scrope (d. 1340), Chief Justices to Edward II and Edward III." In *Profit, Piety, and the Professions in Later Medieval England*, edited by Michael Hicks, 91–102. Gloucester, 1990.
Vale, Juliet. *Edward III and Chivalry: Chivalric Society and Its Context, 1270–1380*. Woodbridge, 1982.
Van Houts, Elisabeth. "Gender and Authority of Oral Witnesses in Europe (800–1300)." *Transactions of the Royal Historical Society*, 6th ser., 9 (1999): 201–20.
———. *Memory and Gender in Medieval Europe, 900–1200*. London, 1999.
Vansina, Jan. *Oral Tradition in History*. Madison, 1985.
Vardi, Llana. "Imagining the Harvest in Early Modern Europe." *American Historical Review* 101 (1996): 1357–97.
Vernon-Harcourt, L. W. *His Grace the Steward and the Trial of Peers*. London, 1907.
Victoria County History: Yorkshire. Vol. 3. Edited by William Page. London, 1913. Reprint, Folkestone, 1974.
Virgoe, Roger. *Private Life in the Fifteenth Century: Illustrated Letters of the Paston Family*. London, 1989.
———. *East Anglian Society and the Political Community of Late Medieval England*. Edited by Caroline M. Barron, Carole Rawcliffe, and Joel T. Rosenthal. Norwich, 1997.
Voigts, Linda E. "What's the Word: Bilingualism in Late Medieval England." *Speculum* 71 (1996): 813–26.

Wagner, Anthony Richard. "A Fifteenth-Century Description of the Brass of Sir Hugh Hastings at Elsing, Norfolk." With notes on the armor by James G. Mann. *Antiquaries Journal* 19 (1939): 421–28.
———. *Catalogue of English Mediaeval Rolls of Arms*. London, 1950.
———. *Heralds and Heraldry in the Middle Ages*. 2d ed. Oxford, 1956.
———. *English Genealogy*. 2d ed. Oxford, 1972.
Walker, Simon. *The Lancastrian Affinity, 1361–1399*. Oxford, 1990.
Walker, Sue Sheridan. "Proof of Age of Feudal Heirs in Medieval England." *Mediaeval Studies* 35 (1973): 306–23.
———. "The Feudal Family and the Common Law Courts: The Pleas Protecting Rights of Wardship and Marriage, c. 1225–1373." *Journal of Medieval History* 14 (1988): 13–31.
———, ed. *Wife and Widow in Medieval England*. Ann Arbor, 1993.
Ward, Jennifer C. *English Noblewomen in the Later Middle Ages*. London, 1992.
———. "Letter Writing by English Noblewomen in the Early Fifteenth Century." In *Early Modern Women's Letter Writing, 1450–1700*, edited by James Daybell, 29–41. Basingstoke, 2001.
Warnock, Mary. *Memory*. London, 1987.
Watt, Diane. "'No Writing for Writing's Sake': The Language of Service and Household Rhetoric in the Letters of the Paston Women." In *Dear Sister: Medieval Women and the Epistolary Genre*, edited by Karen Cherewatuk and Ulrike Wiethaus, 122–38. Philadelphia, 1993.
Waugh, Scott. *The Lordship of England: Royal Wardships and Marriage in English Society and Politics, 1217–1327*. Princeton, 1988.
Weightman, Christine. *Margaret of York, Duchess of Burgundy, 1446–1503*. Stroud, 1989.
Weiss, Roberto. *Humanism in England During the Fifteenth Century*. Oxford, 1941.
Whittle, Jane. "Individualism and the Family Land Bond: A Reassessment of Land Transfer Patterns Among the English Peasantry, c. 1270–1580." *Past and Present* 160 (1998): 25–63.
Wickham, Chris J. "Gossip and Resistance Among the Medieval Peasantry." *Past and Present* 160 (1998): 3–24.
Wiesner, Merry E. "An Early Modern Midwife: A Case Study." In *Women and Work in Preindustrial Europe*, edited by Barbara A. Hanawalt, 94–113. Bloomington, 1986.
Wiethaus, Ulrike. "In Search of Medieval Women's Friendship: Hildegard of Bingen's Letters to Her Friends and Contemporaries." In *Maps of Flesh and Light*, edited by Ulrike Wiethaus, 93–111. Syracuse, 1993.
Wilkinson, Bertie. *The Constitutional History of Medieval England, II: Politics and the Constitution, 1307–1399*. London, 1952.
Willard, James F. "The Dating and Delivery of Letters Patent and Writs in the Fourteenth Century." *Bulletin of the Institute of Historical Research* 10 (1932–33): 1–11.
William Salt Archaeological Society. "Inquisitions Post Mortem, Ad Quod Damnum, etc." *Staffordshire, Henry III, Edward I, and Edward II (1223–1327)*. London, 1911.
Williams, George, ed. *Memorial of the Reign of King Henry VI*. Rolls Series 52. London, 1872.
Wilson, Adrian. "The Ceremony of Childbirth and Its Interpretation." In *Women as Mothers in Pre-Industrial England: Essays in Memory of Dorothy McLaren*, edited by Valerie Fildes, 68–107. London, 1990.
Wolffe, Bertram P. Review of *Calendar of Inquisitions Miscellaneous*, VI (1392–99). *English Historical Review* 83 (1968): 385.

Wood, Roy. *The Sociology of the Meal*. Edinburgh, 1995.
Woolf, Virginia. "The Pastons and Chaucer." In *The Common Reader*. London, 1979.
Workman, H. B. *John Wyclif: A Study of the English Medieval Church*. 2 vols. London, 1926.
Worship, Francis. "The Genealogy of the Paston Family." *Norfolk Archaeology* 4 (1855): 1–55.
Wright, Susan M. *The Derbyshire Gentry in the Fifteenth Century*. Derbyshire Record Society, vol. 8. Chesterfield, 1983.
Yates, Francis. *The Art of Memory*. Chicago, 1966.

INDEX

accidents and injuries, 23, 40–41
age, xv–xviii, 4–6, 24–25, 58, 143
  of church monuments, 71
  dubious ages, 24–25
  of jurors, 4–8, 11, 17, 19
  of Scrope and Grosvenor deponents, 76–77, 80, 87
agricultural labor, 42–44
Alcuin, xix
Alice de Bryene, 122
ancestors, memories of, 74
Anglo-Saxon Chronicle, xv
animals and stock, 43–44
apprenticeships, 43
archery, 51
Armburgh letters, xix–xx, 120
arms: coats of arms and rolls of arms, xvii–xix, 64, 66–70, 94, 86, 88, 91–92, 151
  arms, differenced, 84, 87–88
Arnold, Davy, "your cook," 137
arrests, 45–46
Ars dictaminis, xix, 115
Arthur, king of Britain, 93
Augustine of Hippo, xxiv

baptism and birth, 17–18, 26, 26–31
Beaufort, Margaret, 95
Beowulf, 73
Berney family, 119, 130, 136–37, 142
Bede, xiv
Bennett, Henry Stanley, 134
Bernard of Clairvaux, xix
Birgitta, Saint, of Sweden, 100
birth, xv–xvi, 19–20. *See also* baptism
Bishop, T. A. M., xvi
blind man, 41
Bohun, William, earl of Northampton, 86, 90
books, 13–14, 30–31
Bosworth, battle of, 152
Brews, Elizabeth and Margery, 117, 119, 128

Bryon (Brienne), Guy, 92
Byland abbey, 70

Caesar's *Gallic War*, 90
Caister, siege of, 116
calendar, 58, 126–27. *See also* saints' days, and time
Calle, Richard, 107, 110–11, 116, 121, 129, 131, 136, 146, 150
Canterbury, archbishop of, 137
Carminow of Cornwall, 93
Catherine of Siena, xx, 100
Cely Letters, xix–xx, 101–2
Chandos Herald's *Life of the Black Prince*, 90
charters, indentures, and muniments, 39, 69–72, 78
Chaucer, Geoffrey, 93–94
Cheshire knights and Cheshire society, 72, 91–92
children: births, baptisms, marriages, 9, 19–20
  deaths of, 22–23
chivalry and heraldry, 77, 84, 91–92
Christine de Pizan, 100
Christmas, 130, 141
chronicles as a historical sources, xiv–xv
church wardens, 34
churching of mothers, 33. *See also* mother's role and matriarchy
Cicero, xix
Clavering, Sir Robert, 84
Clere family, 122, 131, 136
cloth and clothing, 32–33, 70–71, 138–40
coals from Newcastle, 45
cock fighting, 51
cohorts, 4, 17
community, xxii–xxiii, 2, 7, 53–54. *See also* social bonding
Complete Peerage, 79
coroner, 46–47
couriers, 129–33. *See also* messengers

INDEX

Court of Chivalry, xv, xvii–xviii, xxiii, 64, 152
Coverham abbey, 69

Damme, John, 136
Daniel, Thomas, steward of the duchy of Lancaster, 137
Daubney, John, 108, 110, 113, 116, 121, 129, 136
Davis, Norman, 104–5, 108, 110, 112–13, 129, 132–33, 135–37, 143
death, as a mnemotic memory, 22–23, 50, 141–42
  by murder or execution, 35, 46–47, 50, 140
demography, xvi–xvii, 5–7. *See also* life cycle, and vital statistics
Denholm-Young, Noel, 84
deponents and depositions, 65–66
Devon, earl of, 91
Dictionary of National Biography, 79
doctors, physicians, and leeches, 41, 142–43
Duras, duke of, 88

earthquake, 9, 52, 60
East Anglian and Norfolk society, 122, 126, 134–37, 141
Edward I, xxi, 72, 77, 89
Edward II, xxii, 89
Edward III, xviii, 48, 84, 89
  knowledge of heraldry, 88
Edward IV, 136
Edward, the Black Prince, xxiv, 48–49, 85, 89
elections, 47, 50
Eloise, 100
England, royal arms of, 69
English as a language, xxi
Erpingham, Sir Thomas, 107
Escheator, xvii, 2, 10
European marriage pattern, 17, 19
Everingham, Thomas, 102

family lore and tradition, 73–74, 79–80, 86
Fastolf, Sir John, 107, 136
Federico, Sylvia, 153
Fen, Hugh of, 122, 143
Fenn, John, xx, 133
fighting and wounding, 46
fire, 41–42
flooding, 52. *See also* storms
food and shopping for food, drink, and spices, 33, 139–41
France, royal arms of, 69
freemen of a town, 47
French invaders, 48
French as a language, xxi

funeral monuments, 69, 71, 110, 145
Fylby (Filby), parson of, 129, 132

Gairdner, James, 133
Gant, ancestor of the Scropes, 76
gender bias in the sources, xx, 60–61
  male focused, 153–54
Gerald of Wales, xv
gifts, to infants and to messengers, 27, 31–32
glass, stained and in windows, 69, 71
Gildas, xv
Gloys, James, 107–8, 110–11, 113, 119, 121, 123, 129, 136, 144
godparents, 3, 26–29, 49, 55, 146
gossip, 13
grandparents, 24, 29, 74
Great Sea, 87–88, 90
Greenway, Diana, xv
Gresham, James, 106–8, 110, 129, 142
Grosvenor, Sir Robert, and the Grosvenor family and family arms, xvii–xviii, 63–64, 66, 72, 79, 91, 94, 150
Guisborough, abbot of, 69, 71

Hastings family arms, 70
hearsay evidence, 12–13, 27, 64, 66, 68, 72–73, 86, 122–23. *See also* memory
heir coming of age, xv, 3, 5, 11. *See also* age
Henry IV (as earl of Derby), 73–74, 90
Henry Grosmont, duke of Lancaster, 90
Henry of Huntington's *Historia Anglorum*, xv, xxi
heraldry, 68–70, 78, 84. *See also* arms
Heydon, John (and wife and son), 136, 143
Hildegard of Bingen, xx, 100
houses: burnt, built, or blown down, 32, 41–42
Howes, Thomas, parson of Blofield, 136
Hroswitha of Gandersheim, 100
Hundred Years War, 80, 82–83
  battles of, Burenfos, 88
  Calais, siege of, 84, 87, 90
  Crecy, 89
  Espagnols-sur-Mer, 85, 89
  Morlaix, 86–87
  Najara, 85, 89
  Poitiers, 89
  Sluys, 89
  Spain, 84, 90
  Tournay, 88
  chivauchees, 88, 90
hue and cry, 46
hunting and game, 31, 51–52, 59

214

INDEX

The Iliad, 73
illness and plague, 28, 32, 139, 142
imprisonment and kidnapping, 48–49
Inglose, Henry, 140, 142
inheritance, 2–3, 36, 40
in-laws, 24, 101–2
Inquisitions Post Mortem, xvi–xvii

Jervaulx, abbot of, 69–70
John of Gaunt, lord of Lancaster, 85, 88–90
John Paston's *Great Book* ("*Grete Book*"), xv
Julian of Norwich, 95
jury and jurors, xv–xvi, xxiii, 2–8, 12–13, 54–55
   social class and status, 15, 27–28, 28–49, 47–48, 54–57, 150
   statistical analysis of juries, 5–8

Kempe, Margery, 95

Lancastian affinity, 90, 93
Lanercost abbey, 69, 71, 76
Latin as a language, xxi
last rites, 37
Laton, Robert, 70, 91
Lenin, V. I., 152
letters as a genre and as family letters, xix–xxi, 95–96, 105–14
   component sections of, 112–13, 117–19, 125, 128–30
   dating of, 104–5, 130–31
   length of, 115
   scribes of, 104–14
life cycle, 15–16, 20–21. *See also* vital statistics
literacy: lay, of women, and of messengers, 31, 67, 105, 117–18
London, 44, 47, 94, 118, 130, 133, 137–40
lovedays and arbitration, 34–35, 49–50

"Main unknown hand" of Paston letters, 108–10
male bonding, 88. *See also* social bonding
markets and fairs, 44
Marmyn (Marmion) family arms, 70
marriage, 16–19, 110, 150
Marx, Karl, 152
Matthew Paris, xiv
Mautby, Norfolk, 95, 141, 145
memory and modes of cognition, xiii–xiv, xvi–xvii, xxii, xxiv–xxv, 3, 8–12, 14–16, 20, 23, 27, 57–60, 65–69, 73–74
   visual memory and memory based on tangible objects, 11–13, 30–31, 66–69, 72, 78, 85

memory and "common knowledge," 14–15, 58–59, 71, 78
   See also hearsay
messengers and couriers, 26–27, 29–30, 113, 117, 130–33
midwives, 21, 32–33, 142. *See also* nurses
missal and prayer books preserving a written record, 31, 34, 36
Moleyns, lord and lady, 123–24, 137
monasticism, 35
mother's role and matriarchy, 31–32, 96, 119, 128, 140–41, 150. *See also* churching
Mowthe, John, prior of Holy Trinity, Norwich, 110
Mowbray (Moubray), arms of, 69

names and naming, 28
narration and narrative, xiii–xv, xxi–xxii, 1, 65. 73, 79, 104, 124–24, 143–44, 149
Near East, Englishmen fighting in, 84
Neville, family arms, 70, 90
Newburgh, prior of, 69, 75
Norfolk, duke and duchess of, 123, 137, 143, 152
Norwich and its ecclesiastical institutions, 121, 128, 133, 138, 140–41, 145–46
nurse and wet-nurse, 32–33. *See also* midwife

orality and memory, xiii, xxi, xxiii–xxiv, 1, 13–14
Order of the Garter, xviii
ordination and entry into regular life, 21, 35

Pampyng, John, 106–7, 110, 131, 136
parents, 22–24, 27
Paris, 84–85
parish church and parish priest, 33–35
Parliament, 5
partisan testimony, 149
Paston family, xx–xxi, 95–99, 101, 103, 146
   Agnes, 96, 100–102, 109–11, 114, 129, 136, 144–45
   Anne, 138, 146
   bastard daughter of John II, 146
   Clement, 118
   Edmund, 103, 108–10, 113, 119, 145–46
   Elizabeth, 101, 136
   household, servants, and accounts, 105, 110, 121–22, 134, 137–38, 140–41
   John I, xix, 95–96, 100, 102–4, 106–9, 111–18, 122–24, 126, 128–41
   John II, xix, 95–96, 103–4, 107–10, 116–19, 121, 123, 126, 135–36, 138, 140, 144, 146
   John III, xix, 95, 103–4, 107–9, 113, 116–17, 119, 126, 128–29, 135, 138, 146–47

INDEX

Paston family (cont'd)
  John III's children, William and Elizabeth, 146
  letters and letters' scribes, xiii, xix, 100–106
  Margaret, xv, xviii–xix, xx–xxi, xxiii–xxiv, 95, 100–147; pregnant, 112, 138, 142–43; her letters, xiii, 100–102, 115–16, 119–21, 133–354, 139, 153; Will, 95, 143–47
  Margery, Margaret's daughter, 110, 138, 146
  Margery, Margaret's daughter-in-law, 101
  Walter, 103, 119
  William I, 96, 114, 143, 151
  William II, xxii, 100, 103, 110, 129, 134–36, 145, 150
  William III, 146
Peasants' Rebellion of 1381, 36, 49, 60
Percy, family and family arms, 48, 69, 90
Peter of Blois, xix
Peter the Venerable, xix
pilgrimages, 5, 36
pillory as punishment, 47
Playtor, Thomas, 129, 132, 136
Plumpton family and letters, xix–xx, 102
de la Pole family (duke and duchess of Suffolk), 90, 137, 144, 153
Pontius Pilate, 143
Poos, Lawrence R., xvii
popular religion, 25
priest and his role in baptism, 29–30, 35–37
prison and prisoners, 48
Proof of Age, as a source, xiii, xv, xviii, xxi, xxiii, 53–54, 57, 59, 63, 75, 79, 104, 149–50, 153
  circular reasoning found in, xxiv, 9–11, 13–14
  problematic or false, xiii, xvi–xvii, 1–2, 19, 25, 40
  thematic focus of some proofs, 59–60
Prussia and Lithuania, where Englishmen fought, 84, 87–88
Pycard the Vicar of Tombland, 142

real property, buying and selling, xvii, 38–39, 142
Redham, Norfolk, 146
Richard I, 74
Richard II, xviii, 9, 48, 88, 94, 152
Richard, duke of York, 109
Richmond, Colin F., 152
Richmond and Richmondshire, Yorkshire, 70–71, 75
Rievaulx abbey, 75, 78
robbery and robbers, 10, 34, 46–47
Roos, Thomas of Kendal, 87
Round, John Horace, xvi
Rouse of Suffolk, 142
Russell, Josiah Cox, xvi

St. Quintyn, family arms, 70
Saints' days, 58, 125–27
Salatt, Master John, 123–24
Satalia, Turkey, 90
Scotland, royal arms of, 69
  expedition to, battles in, and raids from, 72, 84, 86, 89
  battles at: Balyngham Hill, 86; Berwick, 86, 89; burning of Dumfries, 91; Hallidon Hill, 89; Longhaven, 90; Neville's Cross (Battle of Durham), 85, 89, 92; Stanmow, 92; Stirling, 85
Scrope and Grosvenor depositions as a source, xiii, xvii–xviii, xxi–xxii, 1, 9, 63–65, 122, 149–51, 153
Scrope family, 65, 67, 70, 73, 76, 85–86, 91–93, 151–53
  Geoffrey (Richard's uncle) and his sons, 69, 71, 74, 86–88
  Henry (Richard's father), 70–71, 78, 80, 86–87
  other Scropes, 71, 47, 76, 80, 87–88, 152
  questionable origins, 87, 91–93, 151–52
  Richard, I lord Scrope of Bolton, xvii, 64–75
  Roger, II lord of Bolton, 88
  Stephen of Castle Combe, 88
Seals, 71, 112, 128
Selby, abbey of, 69, 70, 75
servants, 10, 30–31, 43, 48, 56, 121, 146
sexual scandal, 37, 143
Shakespeare, 3
Sheriff, 45, 47, 49, 129
shopping in London (and elsewhere), 44, 137–39
silk, 34, 70. See also cloth
siblings of jurors, memories and deaths of, 18, 22–23
social bonding, xxiii, 3–4, 8, 17, 36, 54, 59–60, 65–66, 73, 78–79, 88, 91, 151
sources, nature of, xiii–xv
Sparham, John of, 143
Sparham, Norfolk, 146
status anxiety, 151–52
Stephen, king of England, 72
Stonor family and letters, xix–xx, 102
storms, rain, wind, and flooding, 40–42, 45, 49, 52

tenants in chief and recovery of estates, 2–3, 11
Tendall, Marie, Margaret Paston's goddaughter, 146

216

INDEX

Thirwalle, John, 77, 87, 89, 93
Thomas Aquinas, xxiv
Thomas of Woodstock, duke of Gloucester, xviii, 90
time of day, 50, 58–59, 128
  of memories, 9, 11, 57–58
  time out of mind, 74, 76
tournaments, 80, 87, 89
travel, 44–45
Trivet, Nicholas, xv
twins, 21

Venice, 88
village headman, 2, 54–55, 57
vital statistics, 13, 141, 143. *See also* demography

Walker, Sue Sheridan, xvii
Warter, priory of, 78
Warwick, earl of, 85, 90, 109
Watton, priory of, 76
Wensley, parish church of, 71
Wetheral, parish church of, 71
William I and the Norman Conquest, 73–74, 76, 79, 92–93

William of Jumiege, xv
William the Marshal, *History of,* 90
William of Worcester, 107, 129
wills, 40, 142, 144–47
wind, 40–42, 52. *See also* storms
wives, 24
women as letter writers, xx–xxi, 101–2, 113, 134–35, 153
wrestling, 51
writ *de eatate probando,* xv, 2
written records, xiv–xv, xxv, 1–2, 13–14, 31, 39, 67, 70–71, 79. *See also* charters
Wykes, John, 110, 136
Wymondham, John, 123, 129, 143

Yelverton family, 130, 146
York, 39, 46, 78
Yorkshire, baronage of, 75. *See also* Richmondshire

Zouche, Richard la, 80

www.ingramcontent.com/pod-product-compliance
Lightning Source LLC
Chambersburg PA
CBHW021402290426
44108CB00010B/344